Happiness is not a station one comes to,
but rather a manner of travel.
- origin unknown.

Lykken er ikke en stasjon man ankommer til,
men en måte å reise på.
- av ukjent opprinnelse.

Das Glück ist nicht ein Ort, zu dem man kommt,
sondern eine Art zu reisen.
- Herkunft unbekannt.

The Norway
Bed & Breakfast Book

8th edition

Editor & illustrator:
Anne Marit Bjørgen

PELICAN PUBLISHING COMPANY
GRETNA 2011

The word "Pelican" and the depiction of a pelican are trademarks
of Pelican Publishing Company, Inc., and are registered in the
U.S. Patent and Trademark Office.

Maps: Source STATENS KARTVERK   712064-561   fra Ugland IT Group AS

Editor & illustrator: Anne Marit Bjørgen
Co-editor: Melanie Tulke

If you want to be listed in future editions of this guide, please write to:
Hvis du ønsker å bli presentert i neste utgave av denne boken, vennligst skriv til:
Bed & Breakfast Norway, Anne Marit Bjørgen, Dalsegg, 6653 Øvre Surnadal, Norway.
Phone: (+47) 99 23 77 99   Fax: (+47) 94 76 38 33

  B&B Guide Series "Registered U.S. Patent and Trademark Office"

ISBN 9781589809734
E-book ISBN 9781589809819

Printed in the United States of America
Published by Pelican Publishing Company, Inc.
1000 Burmaster Street, Gretna, Louisiana 70053

Preface

Forord

Vorwort

Welcome to the 8th edition of "The Norway Bed & Breakfast Book". Our aim is to make it easy for you to locate friendly and hospitable hosts in cities and in the countryside. Our host families look forward to having you, your family and friends visit them in Norway.

Here you will find a diverse selection to choose from. Breakfast is included with most overnight accommodations. However, we also feature rental units with "self-catering" since Norway does not have as long a B&B tradition as some other countries. Breakfast is not served at such places, but guests may prepare meals in well-equipped kitchens.
You choose the type of atmosphere you prefer: houses, cabins, manor homes or old-fashioned storage huts (stabbur), etc.
Prices tend to vary. If you and your family are economizing, you will find some excellent offerings in the Self-catering category and among some of the B&B's. If you are less concerned about price and perhaps more interested in experiences to be enjoyed, you will also find accommodations that are more traditional, cozier, exotic and unique.
Accommodations are sorted geographically by county (fylke). On page 12 there is a

Velkommen til den 8te utgaven av "The Norway Bed & Breakfast Book". Her finner du vennlige og gjestfrie menneskene i by og på land. Våre vertsfamilier ser fram til å ta imot deg og ditt følge på din neste ferie i Norge.
Tilbudet er variert. Ved de fleste overnattingsstedene er frokost inkludert i prisen. Men siden vi ikke har den samme lange rom-og-frokost-tradisjon som i enkelte andre land, har vi også inkludert utleie-enheter med 'selvhushold'. Her serveres ikke frokost, men gjestene kan stelle sine egne måltider på et dertil egnet og utstyrt kjøkken.
Ut fra boken vil du kunne velge mellom ulike typer hus, hytter, stabbur, villaer etc. Prisene varierer også. Hvis du er ute etter de rimeligste alternativene kan du i selvhusholds-kategorien og enkelte B&B finne gode løsninger. Bryr du deg mindre om pris, men mer om opplevelse, kan du finne atmosfære blandt de mest tradisjonsrike, koselige, eksotiske og orginale overnattingstilbudene som er samlet her.
Tilbudene er sortert geografisk, fylkesvis. På side 12 ser du en oversikt over fylkene og i hvilken rekkefølge de kommer.
Redaksjonen har stolt på utleiernes ærlighet og redelighet.
Opplysningene i boken er basert på informasjon som er innsendt til oss.

Willkommen zur 8. Ausgabe von "The Norway Bed & Breakfast Book". Hier finden Sie nette und gastfreundliche Menschen in Stadt und Land. Unsere Gastgeberfamilien freuen sich, Sie und Ihre Lieben bei Ihrem nächsten Norwegenurlaub zu empfangen.

Dieses Buch hält ein vielseitiges Angebot für Sie bereit. Bei den meisten Gastgebern ist Frühstück im Preis enthalten. Da wir jedoch in Norwegen keine so lange "Bed & Breakfast"-Tradition wie in einigen anderen Ländern haben, sind auch Angebote für Selbstversorger aufgeführt. Diese bieten kein Frühstück, dafür aber eine gut ausgestattete Küche für die Zubereitung von Mahlzeiten.
Sie können unter verschiedenen Häusertypen, "Stabbur" (trad. Speicher), Villen usw. wählen. Auch die Preise sind unterschiedlich. Preisgünstige Alternativen findet man bei Häusern für "Selbsthaushalt". Ist der Preis nicht so wichtig, sondern das Erlebnis, so finden Sie in diesem Buch viele traditionsreiche, gemütliche, exotische und originelle Übernachtungsmöglichkeiten. Die Angebote sind geografisch und nach Provinzen geordnet. Übersicht der Provinzen und deren Reihenfolge auf Seite 12. Die Redaktion hat sich auf Ehrlichkeit und Redlichkeit der

handy overview of the counties in the same order of presentation as in the book.

The editors have relied upon the honesty and integrity of the hosts, who have provided the information presented.

Great effort has been made to ensure accuracy, but the editors and publisher take no responsibility for errors. Likewise, if quality or standard does not fulfill your expectations the editors have no responsibility regarding any agreements or reservations between guests and hosts based on information from this book.

This book undergoes continual change, and we rely on you to help us improve it. We hope you will turn to page 223 and write down and share with us your impressions and experiences as a B&B-guest and as a user of this book.

We wish you happy travels and bid you welcome on behalf of our B&B hosts – all across Norway – the land of majestic mountains and fjords.

Hvis standardnivå eller øvrig kvalitet ikke står i forhold til forventningene kan ikke redaksjonen ta ansvar for det, heller ikke ved eventuelle feil. Ethvert leieforhold som baseres på denne boken er en avtale mellom vert og gjest. Vi har kun en informasjonsoppgave.

Denne boken ønsker vi å videreutvikle, og bare du kan fortelle oss hvordan den kan bli bedre. Vi ønsker derfor å høre fra deg. På side 223 kan du skrive noen ord om dine inntrykk og erfaringer. Send det så til vår redaksjon.

Vi håper at du vil få en rik ferieopplevelse ved å treffe nordmenn i sine hjemlige omgivelser. God ferietur og velkommen til våre B&B-verter i det vakre fjell- og fjordlandet Norge.

Vermieter verlassen. Alle Angaben in diesem Buch basieren auf Information, die uns zugesendet wurde.

Sollten Standard oder übrige Qualität nicht den Erwartungen entsprechen, kann unsere Redaktion dafür keine Verantwortung übernehmen. Jedes Mietverhältnis aufgrund dieses Buches ist eine Vereinbarung zwischen Gastgebern und Gästen. Wir erbringen nur die Information.

Wir möchten dieses Buch gerne weiterentwickeln und nur Sie können uns berichten, wie wir es verbessern können. Auf Seite 223 können Sie Ihre Erfahrungen als B&B-Gast und Benutzer dieses Buches aufschreiben und an uns schicken.

Wir wünschen Ihnen wertvolle Urlaubserlebnisse bei der Begegnung mit Norwegern in ihrer heimischen Umgebung. Willkommen zu unseren "Bed & Breakfast"-Gastgebern in Norwegen, dem herrlichen Land der Fjorde und Berge!

Many B&Bs in the countryside offer close contact with farm animals.

Contents   Innhold   Inhalts- verzeichnis

Symbol reference	Symbolforklaring	Symbolerklärung

 Bed & Breakfast open year round — Bed & Breakfast åpent hele året — Bed & Breakfast ganzjahrig geöffnet

 Bed & Breakfast open in summer — Bed & Breakfast åpent om sommeren — Bed & Breakfast im Sommer geöffnet

 Selfcatering open year round — Selvhushold åpent hele året — Selbsthaushalt ganzjahrig geöffnet

 Selfcatering open in summer — Selvhushold åpent om sommeren — Selbsthaushalt im Sommer geöffnet

The number refers to page number. — Tallet refererer til sidetallet i boken. — Die Zahl bezieht sich auf die Seitenzahl des Buches.

The departments / Fylkene / Die Provinzen

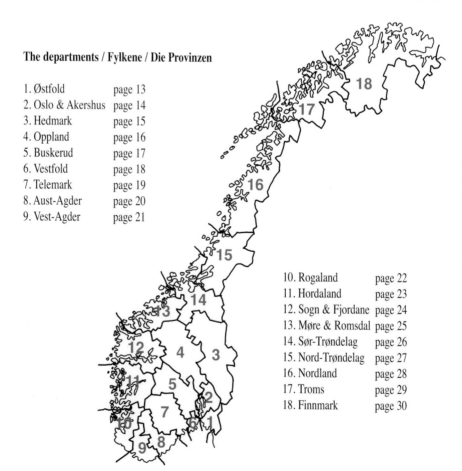

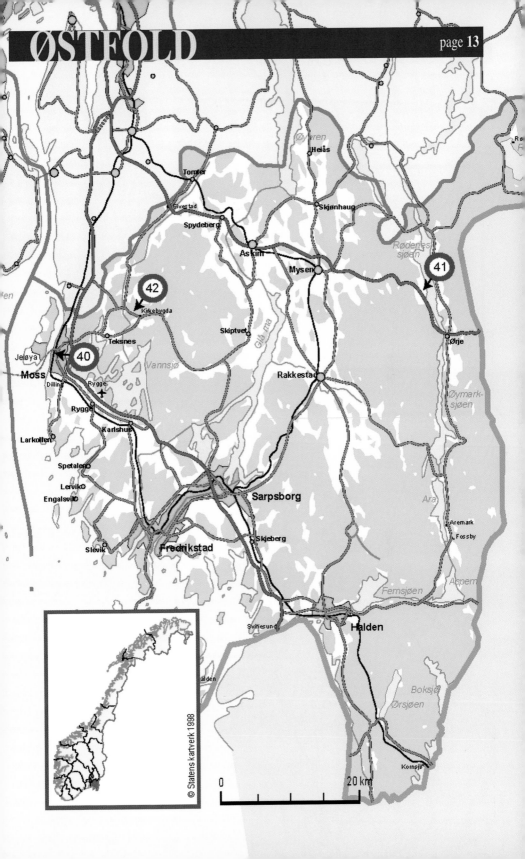

Øyeren

Heiås

Rødenes-sjøen

Tomter

Elvestad

Spydeberg

Skjønhaug

Askim

Mysen

41

42

Kirkebygda

Skiptvet

Teksnes

Ørje

Jeløya

40

Moss

Dilling

Rygge

Rakkestad

Øymark-sjøen

Rygge

Karlshus

Larkollen

Spetalen

Lervik

Engalsvik

Sarpsborg

Ara

Slevik

Fredrikstad

Skjeberg

Aremark

Fossby

Femsjøen

Aspern

Svinesund

Halden

alden

Boksjø

Ørsjøen

© Statens kartverk 1998

0

20 km

Kornsjø

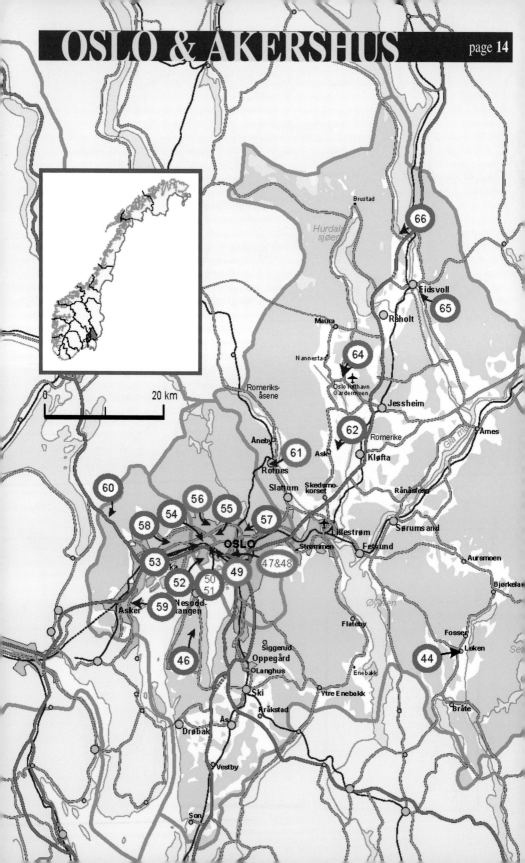

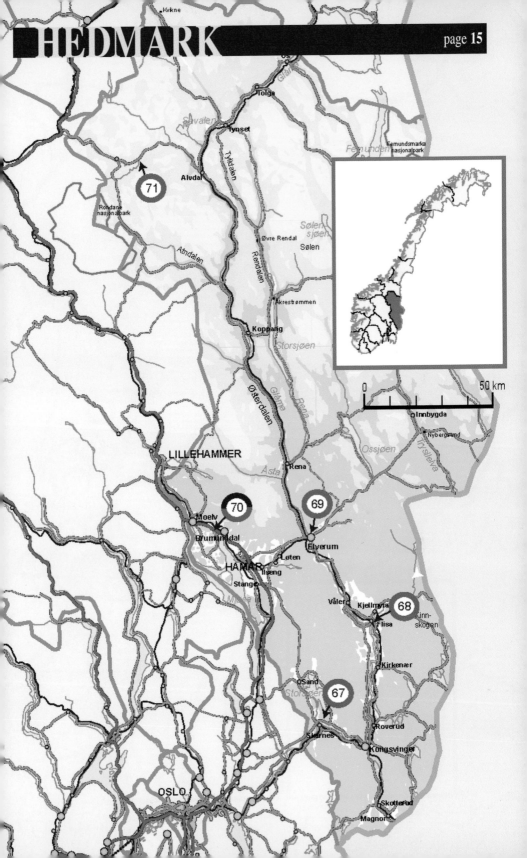

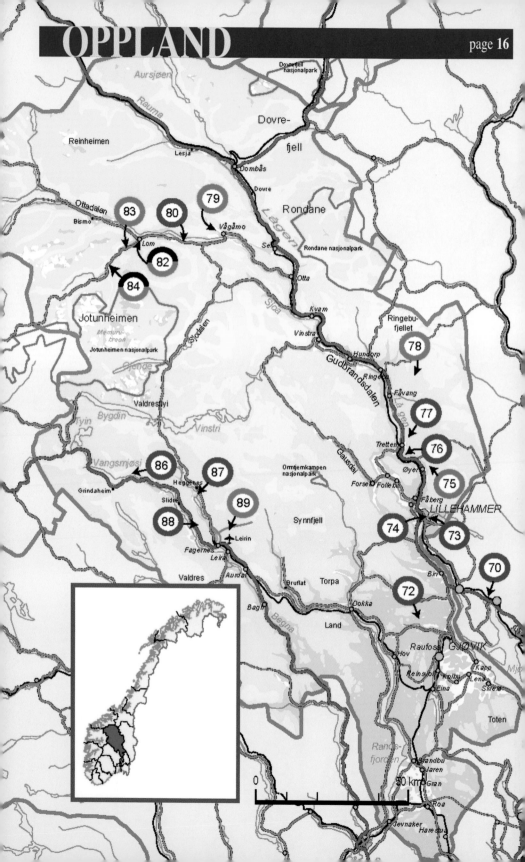

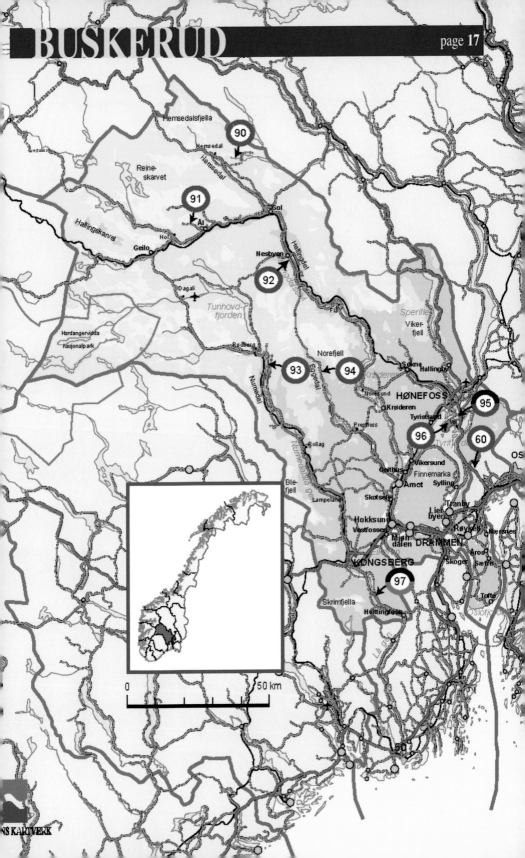

BUSKERUD

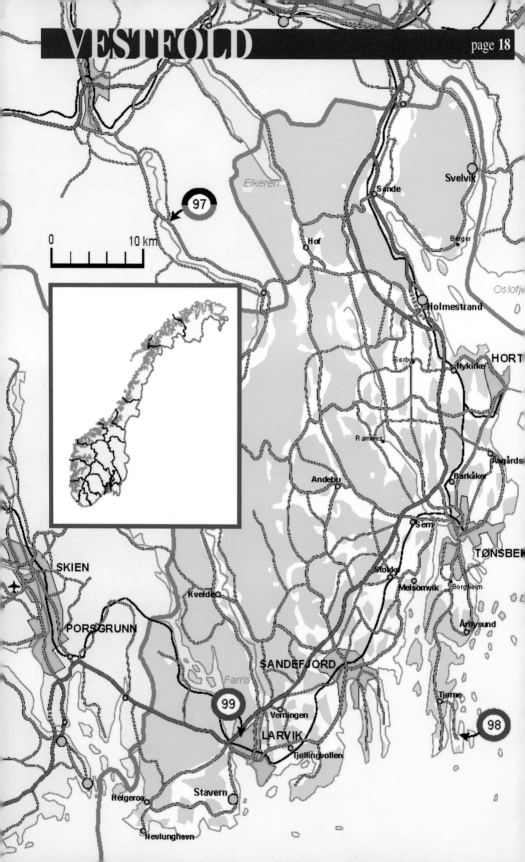

Eikeren

97

0   10 km

Svelvik

Sande

Berger

Hof

Oslofj

Holmestrand

Sørbyw

Nykirke

HORT

Ramnes

Åsgårds

Barkåker

Andebu

Sem

TØNSBE

SKIEN

Stokke

Melsomvik

Borgheim

Kvelde

PORSGRUNN

Årøysund

SANDEFJORD

Farris

99

Tjøme

98

Vemingen

LARVIK

Tjøllingvollen

Helgeroa

Stavern

Nevlunghavn

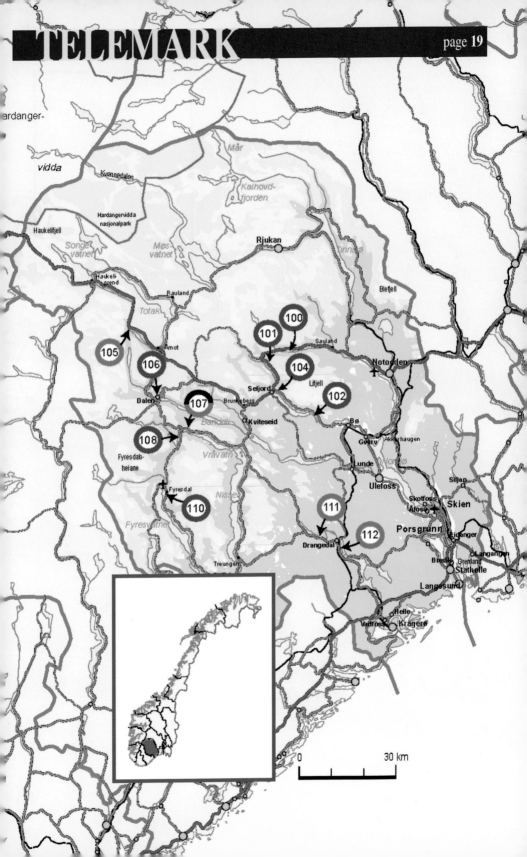

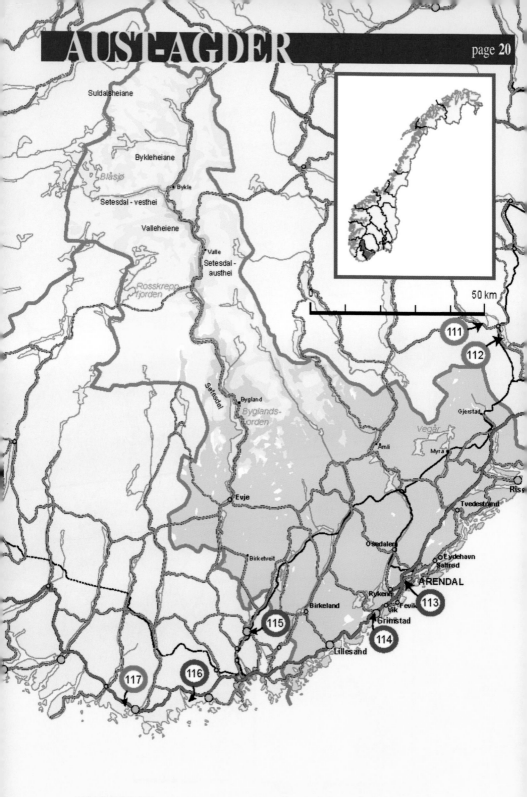

Suldalsheiane

Bykleheiane

Blåsjø

Bykle

Setesdal - vesthei

Valleheiene

Valle

Setesdal - austhei

Rosskrepp fjorden

50 km

Setesdal

Bygland

Byglands-fjorden

Vegår

Gjerstad

Åmli

Myra

Ris

Evje

Tvedestrand

Osedalen

Birketveit

Eydehavn

Saltrød

ARENDAL

Rykene

111

112

113

Vik

Fevik

Birkeland

Grimstad

114

115

Lillesand

117

116

SKAGERRAK

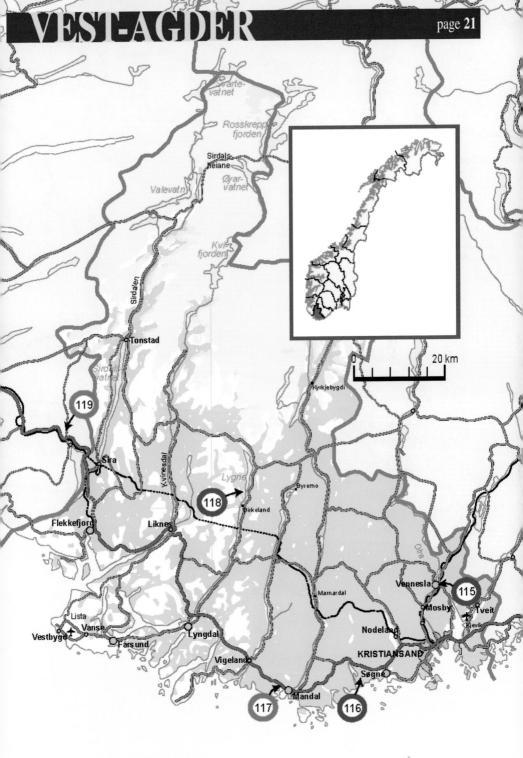

SKAGERRAK

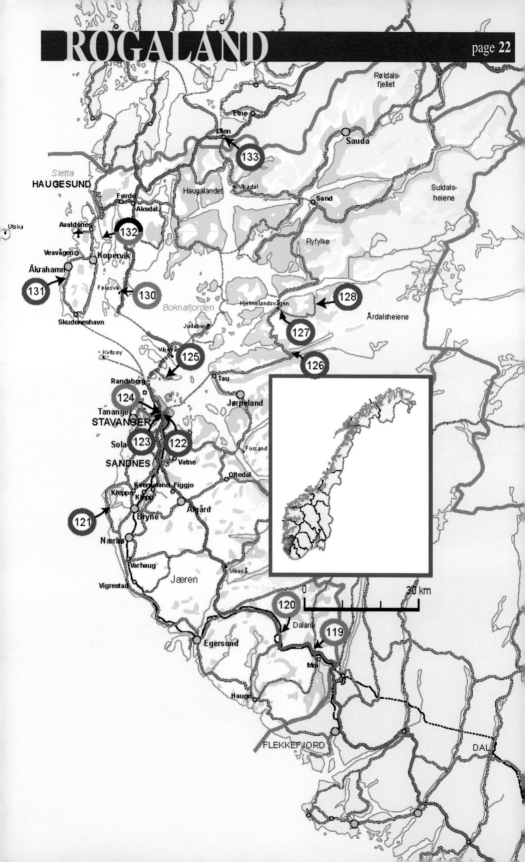

Røldals-fjellet

Etne

Ølen

133

Sauda

Sletta
HAUGESUND

Førde

Aksdal

Haugalandet

Vkadal

Sand

Suldals-heiene

Utsira

Avaldsnes

132

Veavågen

Kopervik

Ryfylke

Åkrahamn

131

Følesvik

130

Boknafjorden

Hjelmelandsvågen

128

Årdalsheiene

Skudeneshavn

Judaberg

127

Kvitssy

Vikevåg

125

126

Randaberg

Tau

124

Jørpeland

Tananger
STAVANGER

Sola

123

122

Forsand

SANDNES

Vatne

Kvernaland Figgjo

Oltedal

Kleppe

Klepp

121

Bryne

Ålgård

Nærbø

Varhaug

Vikeså

Jæren

Vigrestad

120

Dalane

119

Egersund

Moi

Hauge

FLEKKEFJORD

DAL

0   30 km

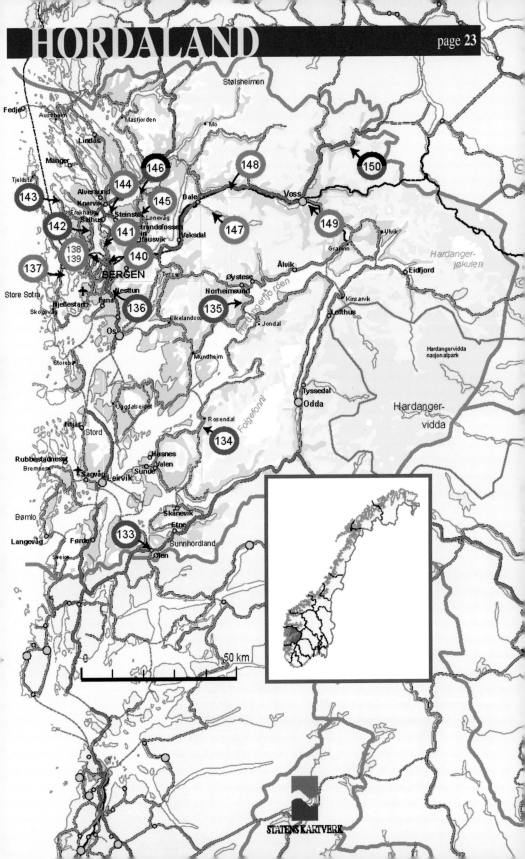

Stølsheimen

Fedje

Austrheim

Masfjorden

Mo

Lindås

Manger

Tjeldstø

146

148

150

143

Alversund

144

Knarvik

145

Dale

Voss

Frekhaug

Steinstø

Lonevåg

149

142

Salhus

141

Brandsfosse

147

Ulvik

138
139

Hausvik

Vaksdal

Granvin

*Hardanger-
jøkulen*

140

137

BERGEN

Tysse

Ålvik

Eidfjord

Store Sotra

Øystese

Hjellestad

Fana

Norheimsund

Kinsarvik

Skogsvåg

136

135

Lofthus

Eikelandso

Hardangerfjorden

Jondal

Os

Storeb

Mundheim

Hardangervidda
nasjonalpark

Uggdalseidet

Tyssedal

*Hardanger-
vidda*

Fitjar

Stord

Rosendal

Odda

Folgefonni

Rubbestadnes

Husnes

134

Bremnes

Valen

Sagvåg

Sunde

Leirvik

Bømlo

Skånevik

Langevåg

Etne

Førde

133

Sunnhordland

Sveio

Ølen

50 km

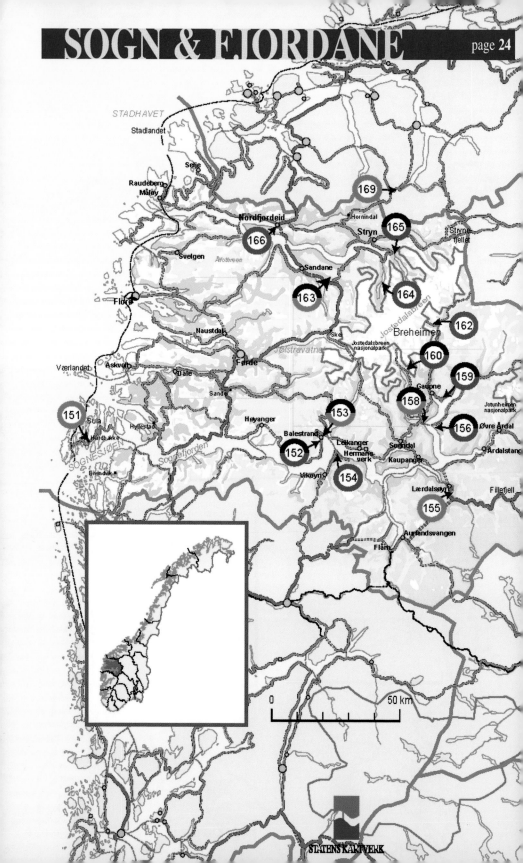

STADHAVET

Stadlandet

Selje

Raudeberg
Måløy

Nordfjordeid

Svelgen

Florø

Naustdal

Værlandet

Askvoll

Dale

Sande

Førde

Høyanger

Sula

Hyllestad

Hardbakke

SOGNESJØEN

Eivindvik

Sognefjorden

Balestrand

Vikøyri

Leikanger
Hermans-
verk

Sogndal

Kaupanger

Aurlandsvangen

Flåm

Ålfotbreen

Jølstravatnet

Sandane

Skei

Hornindal

Stryn

Strynefjellet

Jostedalsbreen

Breheimen

Jostedalsbreen
nasjonalpark

Gaupne

Jotunheimen
nasjonalpark

Øvre Årdal

Årdalstangen

Lærdalsøyri

Fillefjell

169

166

165

164

163

162

160

159

158

156

153

152

154

155

151

0   50 km

STATENS KARTVERK

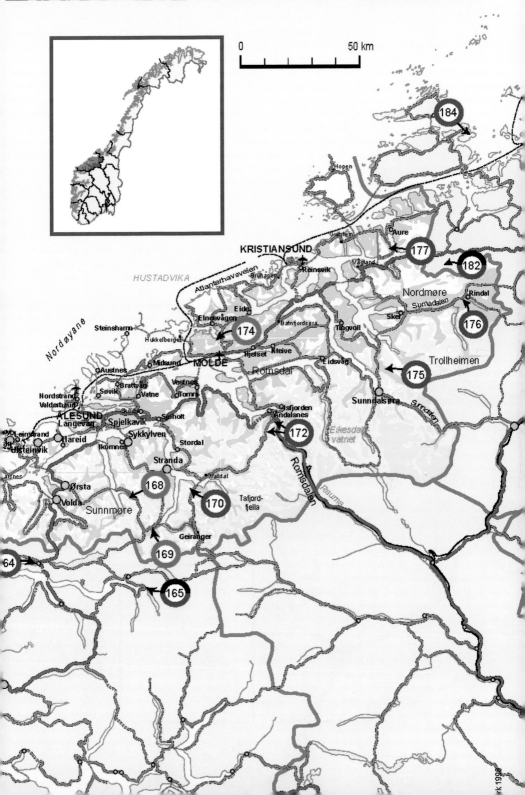

NORSKEHAVET

Leknes

Rørvik

Kolvereid

FOLDA

Selersta

Høylandet

Lauvsnes

Namsos

Ranemsletta

Grong

Sandnes

Bangsund

Namsan

Namdalseid

Snåsa

Snåsa

Gressåmoen
nasjonalpark

Malm

Follafoss

Steinkjer

Innherad

Sparbu

Straumen

Mosvik

Verdalsøra

190

Fosen

Levanger

Leksvik

Skogn

Trondheimsfjorden

Vanvikan

Frosta

184

189

Stjørdal

0   50 km

Bergsdal
nasjonalpark

Store
Namsskret

Namsskogan

Røyrvik

Linnangen

Namsvatnet

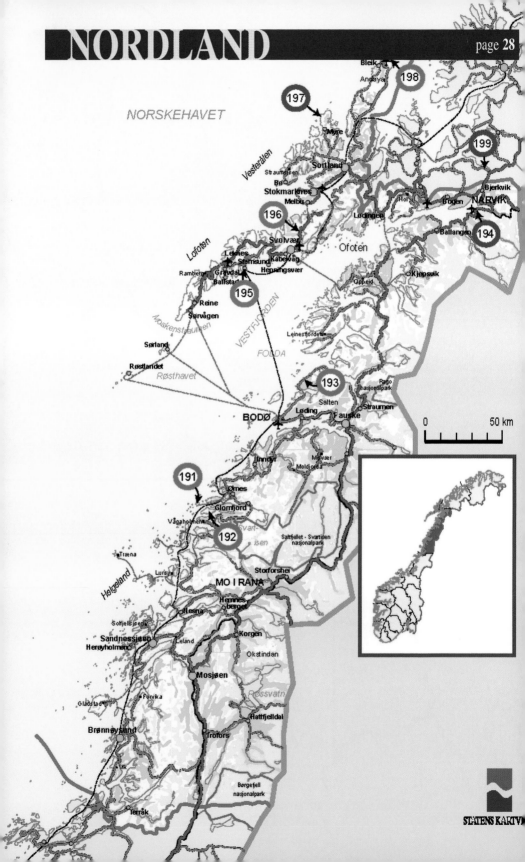

NORSKEHAVET

Vesterålen

Bleik
Andøya
198

197
Myre

Straumsjøen
Bø
Stokmarknes
Melbu
Sortland

199

Hol
Brogen
Bjerkvik
NARVIK

196
Ledingen
194
Ballangen

Lødes
Svolvær
Stamsund Kabelvåg
Henningsvær
Ofoten

Lofoten
Ramberg Gravdal
Ballstad
195

Reine

Sørvågen

Kjøpsvik
Oppeid

Moskenstraumen

VESTFJORDEN

Sørland

Røstlandet

Røsthavet

FOLDA

Leinesfjorden

193
Rago
nasjonalpark

Salten
Løding
Fauske
Straumen

BODØ

0   50 km

191

Innøyr
Mørsver
Moldjorda

Ørnes

Glomfjord

Vågaholmen

192
Svart-
isen
Saltfjellet - Svartisen
nasjonalpark

Træna

Lurøy

Storforshei

Helgeland

MO I RANA

Solfjellsjøen
Hemnes
berget
Nesna

Sandnessjøen
Herøyholmen
Leland
Korgen

Okstindan

Mosjøen

Forvika
Røssvatn

Gladstad

Hattfjelldal

Brønnøysund

Trofors

Vik

Børgefjell
nasjonalpark

Terråk

STATENS KARTV

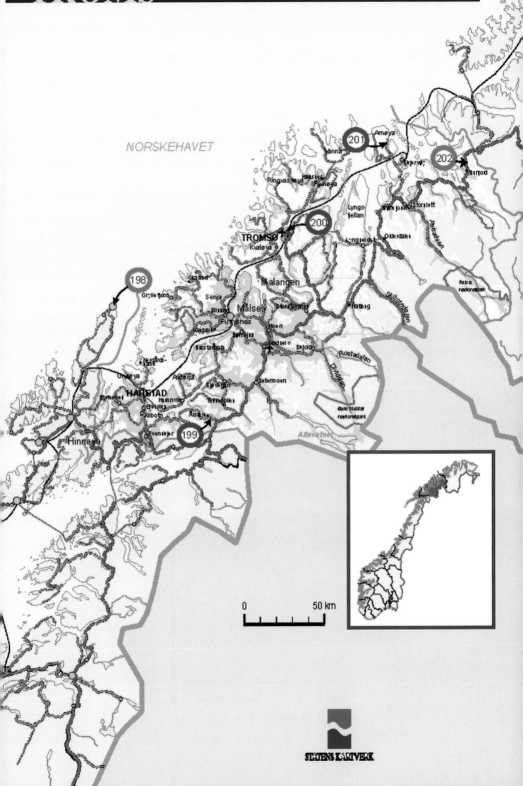

NORSKEHAVET

201

Amøya

Vanna

202

Skjervøy

Birtord

Ringvassøya

Reinøya

Lyngs-
fjellan

Storslett

200

TROMSØ

Kvaløya

Lyngseidet

Olderdalen

Reisa
nasjonalpark

Stakkvik

Malangen

198

Grylle fjord

Senja

Storfjorden

Ratteng

Skibotndalen

Silsand

Målselv

Finnsnes

Moen

Valgaltta

Sørreisa

Andfjorden

Brøstadbotn

Andselv

Skjoldo

Rostadalen

Øvre Dividal
nasjonalpark

Kvernmoen

Setermoen

HARSTAD

Hamnvik

Andørja

Sjøvegan

Brøstad

Tennevollen

Øverbygd

Kilbotn

Årstein

Hinnøya

Evenskjer

199

Altevatnet

0   50 km

STATENS KARTVERK

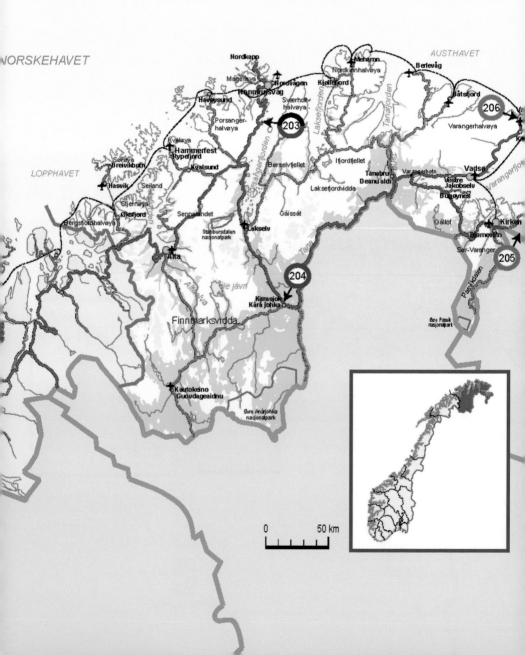

How to use this book

All hosts are presented in this book by name, address and telephone/fax number and e-mail address. You are welcome to contact them directly. Most hosts prefer reservations in advance; they are then prepared to welcome you, and you are assured of lodging.
Not all hosts are available by telephone at all times. The "time to call" is given for each host. When you reserve a room, remember to give your expected time of arrival. B&B hosts do not have a 24-hr reception service: they are private individuals who are occasionally very busy.

"Calling Norway"
Remember that when phoning abroad you must use the prefix to access international phones, then the prefix for Norway (47) before dialing the accommodation's phone number.
From Europe: 00 47 + tel. no.
From USA: 011 47 + tel. no. (also from Canada). All of Norway is within a single phone area with no area code.

Reserving a room
When you send your reservation via mail, fax, or e-mail, please provide the following information:

Hvordan bruke boken

Alle vertsfolk som er presentert i boken står oppført med navn, adresse, telefon-/faxnummer og e-postadresse. Du er velkommen til å ta direkte kontakt med den enkelte utleier. De fleste foretrekker å motta forhåndsbestillinger. Vertsfolket liker å være forberedt slik at rommene står klar til deg.
Ikke alle verter er tilgjengelig på telefon til enhver tid. "Best tid å ringe" er indikert for hvert sted. Når du bestiller rom, husk alltid å nevne hvilken tid på dagen du forventer å ankomme. B&B-verter har ingen 24-timers resepsjonsbetjening, de er privatpersoner som til tider kan ha mye å gjøre.

Når du ringer
Ringer du fra et annet land må du bruke prefix ut av ditt eget land og inn i Norge (+47) foran telefonnummeret, f.eks.:
Fra Europa: 00 47 + tlf.nr.
Fra USA: 011 47 + tlf.nr.
Hele Norge er bare ett telefondistrikt, her er ingen lokale retningsnummer.

Bestilling av rom
Når du sender din bestilling pr. brev, fax eller e-post, oppgi følgende opplysninger:
*Navn og adresse samt telfon-/faxnummer og e-post adresse

Gebrauch des Buches

Alle Gastgeber in diesem Buch sind mit Name, Straße, PLZ o. Ort, Telefon-/Faxnummer und E-Mail-Adresse aufgeführt. Sie können somit direkt mit dem einzelnen Vermieter Kontakt aufnehmen. Die meisten bevorzugen Voranmeldungen, damit sie sich auf den Empfang der Gäste vorbereiten können. Und für Sie ist dann die Unterkunft gesichert. Nicht alle Vermieter sind zu jeder Zeit telefonisch erreichbar.
"Zeit für Anrufe" ist für jeden Vermieter angeführt. Geben Sie, bitte, bei einer Bestellung immer Ihre voraussichtliche Ankunftszeit an. Die B&B-Gastgeber haben keinen 24-Stunden-Empfangsdienst, sondern sind Privatpersonen, die oft viel zu tun haben.

Wie Sie anrufen
Rufen Sie aus dem Ausland an, wählen Sie bitte zuerst die Vorwahl für Norwegen (+47). Dann folgt die Tlf.-Nr., z.B.:
Aus Europa: 00 47 + Tlf.-Nr.
Aus USA: 011 47 + Tlf.-Nr.
Ganz Norwegen ist nur ein Telefongebiet, es gibt keine lokalen Vorwahlnummern.

Zimmerbuchung
Bitte geben Sie bei Bestellung per Brief, Fax oder E-Mail

*Name of guest along with the address, fax-/phone number and e-mail address *Arrival date and time of day *Date of departure *Number in party *Number of rooms/beds needed *Age of children *Special requirements.

Prices

All prices are given in Norwegian currency, on a per day basis. The value of the Norwegian 'kroner' (NOK) can vary:
1 EUR = 7,7 - 9,1 NOK
1 USD = 5,1 - 6,6 NOK
(exchange rate through 2010)
This book is valid for several years. "Prices valid for..." inducates the durations of the prices. After the given years prices might change.

GPS-coordinates

The named geographical coordinates are based on the WGS 84. They are displayed in degrees (°), minutes (') and seconds ("). Newer navigation systems allow the entry of coordinates in different formats. Help tools to convert between the different formats are to be found on the web.

Smoking restriction

We have a general smoking restriction in Norway at all public accommodations: hotels, cafes, restaurants, bars, etc. It is not allowed to smoke inside at any of the B&Bs or rental places,

*Ankomstdato og tidspunkt for ankomst *Avreisedato *Antall personer i reisefølget *Antall rom/senger *Barns alder *Spesielle behov.

Priser

Alle priser er oppgitt pr. døgn, i norske kroner (NOK). Verdien av norske kroner kan variere:
1 EUR = 7,7 - 9,1 NOK
1 USD = 5,1 - 6,6 NOK
(kurs gjennom året 2010)
Denne boken er aktuell i flere år. 'Priser gyldig for...' indikerer prisenes varighet. Etter de angitte år kan prisene bli justert.

GPS-koordinater

De geografiske koordinatene er basert på WGS 84. De er angitt i grader (°), minutter (') og sekunder ("). På nyere GPS er det mulig å legge inn koordinater i ulike formater. Hjelpeverktøy for omregning finnes på Internett.

Røykeforbud

Vi har et generelt røykeforbud i Norge på alle offentlige steder: hoteller, caféer, restauranter, barer etc. Det er heller ikke tillatt å røyke innendørs ved noen av våre B&B/utleiesteder, med mindre det er spesifisert at de har eget røykerom.

Bed & Breakfast

For B&B-kategorien inkluder prisen: oppredde senger og frokost for det antall personer som

Folgendes an:
*Name, Adresse, Telefon-/Faxnummer und E-Mailadresse *Datum und Uhrzeit Ihrer Ankunft *Abreisedatum *Anzahl Zimmer/Betten *Alter der Kinder *Besondere Anforderungen.

Preise

Alle Preise sind pro Nacht in norwegischen Kronen angegeben. Der Wert der norwegischen Krone kann variieren:
1 EUR = 7,7 - 9,1 NOK
1 USD = 5,1 - 6,6 NOK
(Kurs binnen 2010)
Dieses Buch ist mehrere Jahre gültig. „Preise gültig für..." gibt die Gültigkeitsdauer der Preise an. Nach den angegebenen Jahren können die Preise variieren.

GPS-Koordinaten

Grundlage der angegebenen geografischen Koordinaten ist das WGS 84. Sie werden in Grad (°), Minuten (') und Sekunden (") dargestellt. Die neueren Navigationsgeräte ermöglichen es, Koordinaten in verschiedenen Darstellungsvarianten einzugeben. Hilfewerkzeuge zur Umrechnung finden sich im Internet.

Rauchverbot

In Norwegen gilt ein generelles Rauchverbot in allen öffentlichen Gebäuden: Hotels, Cafés, Restaurants, Bars, etc. Es ist unless specified as a smoking room.

Bed & Breakfast

For the B&B category, the price includes beds made with linen and breakfast for the number of people the room is designed for. It is often possible to have an extra bed put in the room for an additional fee. Some B&B's also offer family rooms or rooms with several beds. Ask the host about prices.

Self catering

For the self-catering category, prices are given either for the whole unit or per person. Wherever a charge for bed linen is specified as an additional cost item, the charge pertains to each complete set per person for the first night's stay. You may subsequently use your own bed linen. When breakfast prices are listed, they represent a per person charge.

The book's organization

The included establishments are organized by county. Individual homes are marked on the maps by a number that refers to the page number where you will find their presentation. More detailed directions is given in the back of the book.

rommet er beregnet for. Det er i mange tilfeller mulig å få inn en ekstraseng på rommet for et tillegg i prisen. Noen B&B tilbyr også familierom eller flersengsrom. Spør vertskapet om pris.

Selvhushold

For utleie-enheter med selvhushold er prisene gitt enten for hele enheten eller pr. person. Der hvor sengetøy er spesifisert som tilleggspris, gjelder prisen pr. oppredning, altså pr. person, den første natten. Man kan eventuelt benytte medbrakt sengetøy.

Der hvor frokost er spesifisert gjelder prisen pr. person.

Bokens organisering

Tilbudene er sortert fylkesvis. På kartsidene finner du tall som refererer til de sidetallene hvor tilbyderne er presentert. Helt bakerst i boken finnes en liste med veibeskrivelser for de av tilbyderne hvor det ikke ble plass nok på presentasjonssiden.

auch grundsätzlich nicht erlaubt innerhalb unserer B&B-Wohnstätten zu rauchen, es sei denn, ein eigenes Raucherzimmer ist besonders ausgewiesen.

Bed & Breakfast

Für die B&B-Kategorie schließt der Preis bezogene Betten und Frühstück für die Zahl der Personen, für die das Zimmer berechnet ist, ein. Gegen Preiszuschlag kann oft ein Extrabett erstellt werden. Bei einigen B&B gibt es auch Familienzimmer oder Mehrbettzimmer. Fragen Sie die Vermieter nach dem Preis.

Selbsthaushalt

Für Objekte mit Selbsthaushalt gelten die Preise für die ganze Einheit oder pro Person. Wenn für Bettwäsche ein zusätzlicher Preis angegeben ist, gilt der Preis pro Person und Bettwäscheset. Eventuell kann mitgebrachte Bettwäsche benutzt werden. Wenn Frühstück aufgeführt ist, gilt der Preis pro Person.

Aufbau des Buches

Die Angebote sind nach Provinzen geordnet. Auf den Karten sind sie mit einer Zahl angegeben, die sich auf die Seitenzahl der jeweiligen Beschreibung bezieht. Liste mit Zufahrtsbeschreibungen ganz hinten im Buch.

B&B or Self-catering

B&B eller Selvhushold

B&B oder Selbsthaushalt

There are two main categories of lodgings:

1) Bed & Breakfast

2) Self-contained rental units consisting of either rooms, apartments, cabins or houses, all with kitchen access where guests can prepare their own meals. Breakfast is generally not served, but may be available upon request.

For both categories, the hosts live on the premises.

Uppermost on each page is a symbol indicating what is offered:

Det er to hovedkategorier blandt overnattingstilbudene:

1) Rom & Frokost (Bed & Breakfast)

2) Boenheter med selvhushold; det kan være rom, leiligheter, hytter eller hus, alle med kjøkken tilgjengelig hvor gjestene kan stelle sine egne måltider. Her serveres det normalt ikke frokost, men likevel vil du finne at noen kan tilby morgenmat.

Felles for alle tilbudene er at vertsfolket bor på stedet.

Symboler øverst på hver side indikerer hva som tilbys:

Das Angebot ist in zwei Hauptkategorien aufgeteilt:

1) Zimmer und Frühstück (Bed & Breakfast)

2) Wohneinheiten für Selbsthaushalt, d.h. Zimmer, Ferienwohnungen, Hütten oder Ferienhäuser, alle mit Kochmöglichkeit, damit sich die Gäste eigene Mahlzeiten zubereiten können. Von wenigen Ausnahmen abgesehen, wird hier von den Gastgebern kein Frühstück zubereitet.

Bei beiden Kategorien wohnen die Gastgeber an der selben Stelle.

Symbole zuoberst auf jeder Seite geben die Art des Angebotes an:

 Bed & Breakfast

 Self-catering

 Rom og Frokost

Selvhushold

 Zimmer und Frühstück

 Selbsthaushalt

Standard and quality

In order to provide the readers of our book with a more accurate idea of what each rental location has to offer, we have implemented a grading system for the B&B category. The criteria we use pertain only to the physical facilities being offered such as which items are in the room, how many share a bathroom, etc. The grading system gives no indication as to *quality*, such as the amount of service, cleanliness, decorations, quality of the furniture and equipment, etc. The most important indicator in the grading system for standards is that for *bathroom facilities*. The levels are as follows:

♣ Shared bathroom, where more than 4 people share.

♣ ♣ Shared bathroom with a max. of 4 people, or there is a sink in each of the rooms.

♣ ♣ ♣ Private bath comes with each room.

On the next pages you will find the full designation of requirements for each level of standard.

Standard og kvalitet

For at du som bruker av boken lettere skal få et riktig bilde av hva hvert enkelt utleiested har å tilby har vi innført et graderingssystem for B&B-kategorien. Inndelingen gjelder kun de fysiske faciliteter som tilbys; hva som finnes på rommet, hvor mange som deler bad etc. Graderingssystemet sier ingenting om *kvaliteten* av tilbudet, slik som servicegrad, renhold, dekorering, kvaliteten på møbler og utstyr etc.

Den viktigste indikatoren i graderingssystemet for standard er *baderomsfacilitetene*. Her er en tommelfingerregel for inndelingen:

♣ Delt bad hvor mer enn 4 personer deler bad når det er fullt belegg.

♣ ♣ Delt bad hvor max. 4 personer deler bad, eller det er vaskeservant på hvert av rommene.

♣ ♣ ♣ Hvert rom har eget bad.

På de neste sidene finner du den fulle fortegnelsen av hva som inngår i hvert av standardnivåene.

Standard und Qualität

Um allen Benutzern des Buches einen besseren Überblick über die Qualität des jeweiligen Übernachtungsbetriebs zu verschaffen, haben wir eine Klassifizierung der Angebote vorgenommen. Diese Einstufung bezieht sich allerdings nur auf die Ausstattung der Zimmer; wie z.B. was es im Zimmer gibt, wieviele das Bad teilen usw. Das System berücksichtigt nicht *Qualitäten* wie Dienstbereitschaft, Sauberkeit, Dekoration oder Qualität von Möbeln, Ausstattung usw. Das wichtigste Kennzeichen im Einstufungssystem für Standard sind die *Badverhältnisse*. Hier gilt als Grundregel:

♣ Gemeinsames Bad, das bei voller Belegung von mehr als 4 Personen geteilt wird.

♣ ♣ Gemeins. Bad, von höchstens 4 Pers. geteilt, oder Handwaschbecken in jedem der Räume.

♣ ♣ ♣ Jedes Zimmer hat ein eigenes Bad.

Auf der nächsten Seite finden Sie ein vollständiges Verzeichnis darüber, was jede der Standardstufen erfordert.

Standards for all Bed and Breakfasts

General:
*All guest rooms are clean and tidy. *Local tourist information and transport schedules available. *Regulation fire extinguishing equipment. *Key to the front door and/or room.

In the room:
*Good beds with proper mattresses. *Beds made with clean bed linen. *Extra pillow available. *Good lighting in the room - a night lamp by each bed. *Waste paper basket. *All electrical outlets must be secure and functioning. *Water glass available. *Curtains with functioning / drawing mechanism. *Chest of drawers / cupboards. *Chair(s). *Books and/or periodicals available. *Writing pad and pencil available.

In the bathroom:
*Toilet, hand basin and bath/shower, hot and cold water. *Mirror. *Soap and two hand towels per guest. *Waste paper basket. *Toilet paper. *Bathroom doors that can be locked. *Electrical outlets for shaver and hairdryer.

The Breakfast:
*Tea/coffee, milk and juice. *Bread with 4-6 different sandwich fillings. *Breakfast cereal. *Boiled egg upon request.

In addition to the above:
*Hand basin in the bedroom or max. 4 persons share a bathroom. *Mirror in the room. *Alarm clock in the room. *Iron and ironing board available. *Access to telephone.

In addition to the above:
*Ensuite bathroom. *Shampoo and hair conditioner available. *Coffee and tea making facilities. *Radio in the room. *Minimum one room with a writing desk.

In addition to the above:
*TV in the room. *Own guests' lounge. *Access to laundry. *Accept major credit cards.

Standardinndeling for Rom og Frokost

Generelt:
*Rent og ryddig i alle rom som gjestene benytter. *Lokal turistinformasjon og /eller rutetabeller. *Forskriftsmessig brannvern. *Nøkkel til ytterdør og/eller rom.

Rommet:
*Gode senger med gode madrasser. *Oppredde senger med rent sengetøy. *Ekstra pute med putetrekk tilgjengelig. *Godt lys på rommet - nattbordslampe til hver seng. *Avfallskurv. *Alle stikkontakter er i orden og fungerer. *Vannglass tilgjengelig (på rommet eller på badet). *Gardiner med fortrekksmekanisme som fungerer. *Skuffer og/eller skap som er tomme og rene. *Stol(er). *Bøker og/eller tidsskrift tilgjengelig. *Skriveblokk og blyant tilgjengelig.

Bad og toalett:
*Toalett, håndvask og badekar eller dusj, varmt og kaldt vann. *Speil. *Såpe og håndklær - to til hver gjest. *Avfallskurv. *Toalettpapir og ekstrarull, boks el. rull m/tørkepapir. *Låsbar dør til baderom og toalett. *Stikkontakt til barbermaskin el. hårtørrer.

Frokosten:
*Te/kaffe, melk og juice. *Brødmat med 4-6 påleggstyper. *Cornflakes eller kornblandinger el.l. *Kokt egg ved ønske.

I tillegg til ovenstående oppfylles følgende:
*Håndvask på soverom el. maks 4 pers. deler bad. *Speil på rommet. *Vekkerklokke på rommet. *Strykemuligheter. *Mulighet for bruk av telefon.

I tillegg til ovenstående oppfylles følgende:
*Eget bad til hvert rom. *Tilgang på shampo og hårbalsam. *Kaffe og te-selvbetjening. *Radio på rommet. *Minst ett rom med skrivebord.

I tillegg til ovenstående oppfylles følgende:
*TV på rommet. *Egen stue/oppholdsrom til gjestene. *Mulighet for klesvask. *Kan ta kreditt-kort.

Standardeinteilung für Zimmer und Frühstück

Allgemein:
*Sauber und aufgeräumt in allen Räumen. *Örtliche Touristeninformation und Fahrpläne. *Vorschrifts-
mässiger Brandschutz. *Schlüssel für Haus- oder Zimmertür.

Das Zimmer:
*Gute Betten mit guten Matratzen. *Bezogene Better mit sauberer Bettwäsche. *Zusätzliches Kopfkis-
sen mit Bezug zugänglich. *Ausreichendes Licht im Zimmer, Bettlampe über jedem Bett. *Abfalleimer.
*Alle Steckdosen müssen in Ordnung sein. *Wasserglas zugänglich. *Gardinen, die sich vorziehen lass-
en. *Schublade und/oder Schrank müssen leer und sauber sein. *Stuhl/Stühle. *Bücher und/oder ander-
es Lesematerial zugänglich. *Schreibmaterial zugänglich.

Toilette und Bad:
*Toilette, Handwaschbecken und Badewanne oder Dusche, W & K Wasser. *Spiegel. *Seife und Hand-
tuch - 2 Handtücher für jeden Gast. *Abfalleimer. *Toilettenpapier und Extrarolle, Behälter oder Rolle
mit Papierhandtüchern. *Abschliessbare Tür zu Bad und Toilette. *Stecker für Rasierapparat und Haar-
fön.

Das Frühstück:
*Tee/Kaffee, Milch und Saft. *Brot mit 4-6 verschiedenen Belägen. *Cornflakes, Müsli usw. *Gekoch-
tes Ei oder Spiegelei nach Wunsch.

Zusätzlich wird folgendes geboten:
*Handwaschbecken aut dem Zimmer, oder max. 4 Personen teilen ein Bad. *Spiegel im Zimmer.
*Wecker im Zimmer. *Möglichkeit zum Bügeln. *Telefonbenutzung.

Zusätzlich wird folgendes geboten:
*Eigenes Bad auf dem Zimmer. *Shampoo und Haarbalsam zugänglich. *Kaffee und Tee - Selbstbedie-
nung. *Radio auf dem Zimmer. *Mindestens ein Zimmer mit Schreibtisch.

Zusätzlich wird folgendes geboten:
*Fernsehapparat auf dem Zimmer. *Aufenthaltsraum für die Gäste. *Möglichkeit zur Kleiderwäsche.
*Kreditkarten werden angenommen.

Seal of approval ## Olav's Rose www.olavsrosa.no	Kvalitetsmerket ## Olavsrosa www.olavsrosa.no	Das Qualitätszeichen ## Die Olavsrose www.olavsrosa.no

Norwegian Heritage's seal of approval, the Olav's Rose, points the way to special products whose roots are planted in Norwegian heritage. It is only awarded to sites and products that have undergone the strictest of quality controls. Olav's Rose holders are committed to being good ambassadors for a thriving cultural heritage and to provide the guest with the history of the site.

Norsk Kulturarvs kvalitetsmerke Olavsrosa viser vei til unike opplevelser med røtter i vår kulturarv. Før kvalitetsmerket blir tildelt, blir stedet og den opplevelsen du som gjest blir tilbudt, underlagt en streng kvalitetskontroll. Innehaverne av Olavsrosa har forpliktet seg til å være gode ambassadører for en levende kulturarv og til å formidle stedets historie til deg som gjest.

Die Olavsrose der Stiftung Norwegisches Kulturerbe weist auf Wurzeln in unserem Kulturerbe. Die Olavsrose wird erst nach einer strengen Qualitätskontrolle des Angebots verliehen. Die Träger der Olavsrose verpflichten sich, gute Botschafter eines lebendigen Kulturerbes zu sein und Ihnen als Gästen die besondere Geschichte der jeweiligen Stätte zu vermitteln.

Hanen

Hanen

Hanen

Hanen is a trade- and marketing organization for establishments working in the field of rural tourism, farm food products and freshwater fishing. All members are marked with:

Hanen er en bransje- og markedsorganisasjon for virksomheter innen bygdeturisme, gardsmat og innlandsfiske. Alle medlemmer er merket med:

Hanen ist eine Branchenorganisation für Betriebe, die im Landtourismus, der Binnenfischerei tätig sind, und Hofprodukte vertreiben. Alle Mitglieder sind gekennzeichnet mit:

This is also a road sign symbol which is found along the country roads in Norway.

Norwegian main streets. Dette er også et veiskiltsymbol som du finner langs norske hovedveier.

Dies ist auch das Symbol, das Sie entlang der norwegischen Hauptstraßen finden.

Hanen
Phone: (+47) 22 05 46 40
Fax: (+47) 22 17 17 87
E-mail: post@hanen.no
Web: www.hanen.no

Kallum Søndre

Your host:
**Ann Elizabeth &
Karl Otto Molvig**

Address:
**Rabekkgata 38
N - 1526 Moss**
Phone: **69 25 63 50**
Mobile: **90 94 98 65**
E-mail: **molvig@online.no**
Web: **www.kallumsondre.com**

Best time to call:
**08.00 - 22.00
GPS: 59°24'55"N 10°40'01"E**

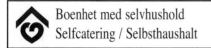

Double room:	**500,-/600,-**	Dobbeltrom:	**500,-/600,-**	Doppelzimmer:	**500,-/600,-**
No. of rooms: 2		Antall rom: 2		Anzahl Zimmer: 2	
Shared bath		Delt bad		Gemeins.Bad	
1 room w/kitchen		1 rom med kjøkken		1 Zimmer mit küche	
1 room w/kitchenette		1 rom med minikjøkken		1 Zimmer mit kleine Küche	
Prices valid for 2011/12		Priser gyldig for 2011/12		Preise gültig für 2011/12	
TV in one of the rooms		TV på et av rommene		TV in einem der Zimmer	
Patio/yard		Uteplass/hage		Außenbereich/Garten	
Open year round		Åpent hele året		Ganzjährig geöffnet	
English spoken				Sprechen Deutsch	

Kallum Søndre is an old farm house situated in the outskirt of Moss, only 200 m from shopping street and 900 m from the beach. It is 9 km to Rygge Airport. The rental rooms is in a separate apartment with own entrance.

Kallum Søndre er et gårdshus som ligger i utkanten av Moss, bare 200 m til handlegate og 900 m til stranden. Det er 9 km til Rygge flyplass. Utleierommene ligger i en egen leilighet med egen inngang.

Kallum Søndre ist ein Bauernhaus, das am Stadtrand von Moss liegt, nur 200 m bis zur Einkaufsstraße und 900 m zum Strand. Zum Flughafen Rygge sind es 9 km. Die zu vermietenden Zimmer befinden sich in einer eigenen Wohnung mit separatem Eingang.

Too often travel, instead of broadening the mind,
merely lengthens the conversation.
~Elizabeth Drew~

The World is a book, and those who do not travel read only a page.
~St. Augustine~

Don't be fooled by the calendar.
There are only as many days in the year as you make use of.
~Charles Richards~

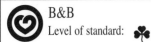
Lund Gård

Your host:
Beate Nicolaissen

Address:
Lund Gård
N - 1870 Ørje
Mobile: 90 83 33 84
E-mail: beanico@online.no
Web: www.lund-gaard.no

Best time to call:
08.00 - 22.00
GPS: 59°32'03"N 11°35'25"E

| Double room: | 800,- | Dobbeltrom: | 800,- | Doppelzimmer: | 800,- |
| Single room: | 500,- | Enkeltrom: | 500,- | Einzelzimmer: | 500,- |

No. of rooms: 4	Antall rom: 4	Anzahl Zimmer: 4
Discount for children	Rabatt for barn	Ermäßigung für Kinder
Breakfast buffet	Frokostbuffét	Frühstücksbüfett
Selfcatering possible	Selvhushold er mulig	Selbstverpflegung möglich
Other meals available	Andre måltider	Auch andere Mahlzeiten
Fully licensed	Skjenkebevilling	Schankerlaubnis
Prices valid for 2011/12	Priser gyldig for 2011/12	Preise gültig für 2011/12
TV available	TV tilgjengelig	TV vorhanden
Terrace/deck/yard	Terrasse/uteplass/hage	Terrasse/Außenbereich/Garten
Canoe and boat for rent	Kano- og båtutleie	Kanu u. Boot zu mieten
Open year round	Åpent hele året	Ganzjährig geöffnet
English spoken		Sprechen Deutsch

Lund Gård was the farm of the bailiff in the 1600's. It is protected as a historical landmark, and is idyllically situated near a lake. Excellent terrain for walking tours in both the forest and along the lakeshore. Swimming areas and canoe/boat rentals. Possibilities for a fishing trip in the surrounding area or steamboat trip through the system of locks along the beautiful Halden waterway. The farm is home to ponnies, goats, sheep, dogs, cats and rabbits. Horseback-riding facilities for children. In summers: art exhibition in the store house.

Lund Gård er en gammel lens-mannsgård fra 1600-tallet. Den er fredet og ligger idyllisk til ved et vann. Fine turmuligheter i skog og ved sjø, badeplasser og utleie av kano og båt gir varierte aktiviteter. Du kan dra på fisketur eller reise med dampbåt gjennom slusene i vakre Haldenvassdraget. På gården er det ponnier, geiter, sauer, hund-er, katter og kaniner. Ridning mu-lig for barn.
Kunstutstilling på stabburet i peri-oder om sommeren.

Der denkmalgeschützte Lund Gård ist eine alte Polizeiwache aus dem 17. Jh. und liegt idyllisch an einem See. Schöne Wandermöglichkeiten im Wald und am Wasser (Badestel-len, Kanu-/Bootsvermietung). Man kann Angeltouren unternehmen, oder per Dampfschiff durch die Schleusen des Haldenkanals schip-pern. Auf dem Hof findet man Ponys, Ziegen, Schafe, Hunde, Katzen und Kaninchen. Reitmöglichkeiten für Kinder. Im Sommer Kunstausstellung im alten Lebensmittelspeicher.

Østre Tveter Gård

Your host:
Liv Scott Anstensrud

Address:
N - 1592 Våler
Phone: **69 28 98 23**
Mobile: **99 44 44 66**
E-mail: **liv@anstensrud.no**
Web: **www.anstensrud.no**

Best time to call:
17.00 - 22.00
GPS: 59°31'14"N 10°57'5"E

Double room:	**1000,-**	Dobbeltrom:	**1000,-**	Doppelzimmer:	**1000,-**
1 pers. in double room:	**600,-**	En pers. i dobbeltrom:	**600,-**	1 Pers. im DZ.:	**600,-**
No. of rooms: 3		Antall rom: 3		Anzahl Zimmer: 3	
Laid breakfast table		Dekket frokostbord		Gedeckter Frühstückstisch	
Prices valid for 2011		Priser gyldig for 2011		Preise gültig für 2011	
Terrace/deck/yard		Terrasse/uteplass/hage		Terrasse/Außenbereich/Garten	
Open year round		Åpent hele året		Ganzjährig geöffnet	
English spoken				Sprechen etwas Deutsch	

Cloaked by beautiful landscape and forest you'll find this traditional farm with horses, chickens, cats and the world's finest Norwegian elkhound. There is also signmaker and gallery and tourist-friendly forest. 7 km to Vansjø, a protected lake- and river. area.

At Østre Tveter Gård you'll discover art, culture and silence. The host serves traditional Norwegian breakfast in a former brewhouse or you can use the guest kitchen. Welcome!

Omkranset av vakkert kulturlandskap og skog finner du denne tradisjonsrike bondegården med hester, høner og katter og verdens snilleste elghund. Her er skiltverksted og galleri og flott turterreng i skogen. 7 km til Vansjø, et vernet vassdrag. På Østre Tveter Gård kan du få oppleve kunst, kultur og stillhet. I trivelig bryggerhus serverer vertinna god norsk frokost eller du kan benytte deg av selvhushold på stabburet. Velkommen til gards!

Umgeben von schöner Kulturlandschaft und Wald finden Sie diesen traditionsreichen Bauernhof mit Pferden, Hühnern, Katzen und dem liebsten Elchhund der Welt. Der Hof beherbergt eine kleine Werkstatt, wo Holzschilder enstehen, und eine Gallerie. Tolles Wandergebiet im Wald ringsherum. 7 km zum See Vansjø. Auf dem Østre Tveter Hof kann man Kunst & Kultur erleben, aber auch die Stille genießen. Im gemütlichen Bryggerhus, dem alten Koch-, Back- und Brauhaus, serviert die Wirtin gutes norwegisches Frühstück. Willkommen auf dem Hof!

Wandering re-establishes the original harmony
which once existed between man and the universe.
~Anatole France~

'Store-house' for 2-4 persons
1 bedroom, kichen,
  Bath/toilet in adjacent building
Price for 2 pers.:   **800,-**
Price for 4 pers.:   **1000,-**
Bed linen included
Breakfast service available: **100,-**
Prices valid for 2011
Yard/terrace/dekk access
Open year round
English spoken

Stabbur for 2-4 personer
1 soverom, kjøkken,
  bad/toalett i sidebygning
Pris for 2 pers.:   **800,-**
Pris for 4 pers.:   **1000,-**
Sengetøy er inkludert
Frokost kan serveres: **100,-**
Priser gyldig for 2011
Hage/terrasse/uteplass
Åpent hele året

'Das Voratshaus' für 2-4 Personen
1 Schlafzimmer, Küche,
  Bad/Toilette im Seitengebäude
Preis für 2 Pers.:   **800,-**
Preis für 4 Pers.:   **1000,-**
Inkl. Bettwäsche
Frühstück auf Bestellung: **100,-**
Preise gültig für 2011
Garten/Terrasse/Außenbereich
Ganzjährig geöffnet
Sprechen etwas Deutsch

Directions:
From Moss: Follow RV 120 to-wards Våler. Get on RV 115 at the Rødsund Bru and continue straight ahead, while RV 120 veers in an-other direction. Keep driving until you see a sign for Våler kirke, and turn left towards the church. Note: Just before the church, turn right towards Mørk and drive 6.5 km until you see a sign for Østre Tveter Gård.

Veibeskrivelse:
Fra Moss ta RV 120 mot Våler. Ved Rødsund Bru, hvor RV 120 svinger av, skal du fortsette rett fram på RV 115. Kjør til du ser skilt med Våler kirke, ta til venstre mot kirken, men like før kirken tar du til høyre, mot Mørk, og kjører 6,5 km til du ser skilt til Østre Tveter Gård.

Wegbeschreibung:
Von Moss: Folgen Sie der Str. 120 Richtung Våler. Bei der Rødsund Brücke, wo die Str. 120 abbiegt, fahren Sie weiter geradeaus auf die Str. 115. Fahren Sie bis Sie ein Schild 'Våler Kirke' sehen. Hier biegen Sie links Rcihtung Kirche ab; genau vor der Kirche fahren Sie aber nach rechts Richtung 'Mørk'. Nach 6,5 km sehen Sie das Schild Østre Tveter Gård.

Høland Gardsmotell

Your host:
Torunn & Tom Rolfson

Address:
Elverhøy
N - 1960 Løken
Phone: 63 85 05 55
Mobile: 90 06 31 71
E-mail: tom.rolfson@re-to.as
Web: www.gaardsmotell.no
Best time to call: 08.00 - 22.30
GPS: 59°48'6"N 11°26'44"E

Double room:	**594,-**	Dobbeltrom:	**594,-**	Doppelzimmer:	**594,-**
Luxurious room w/kitch.,terr.	**750,-**	Luksusrom m/kjk. og terrasse	**750,-**	Luxuszi. mit Küche, Terrasse	**750,-**
Single room:	**500,-**	Enkeltrom:	**500,-**	Einzelzimmer:	**500,-**
Extra bed:	**200,-**	Ekstraseng:	**200,-**	Extrabett:	**200,-**
No. of rooms: 10		Antall rom: 10		Anzahl Zimmer: 10	
Kitchen available		Kjøkken tilgjengelig		Küche kann genutzt werden	
Breakfast tray	**100,-**	Frokostbrett:	**100,-**	Frühstückstablett	**100,-**
Other meals served on request		Andre måltider etter avtale		Andere Mahlzeiten nach Vereinb.	
Prices valid for 2011/12/13		Priser gyldig for 2011/12/13		Preise gültig für 2011/12/13	
TV/Internet available		TV/Internett tilgjengelig		TV/Internet vorhanden	
Terrace/patio/yard		Terrasse/uteplass/hage		Terrasse/Außenbereich/Garten	
Bike available		Sykkel kan lånes		Fahrrad zu leihen	
Suitable for handicapped		Handikaptilgjengelig		Behindertengerecht	
Pets welcome		Kjæledyr velkommen		Haustiere willkommen	
VISA, MC, DC, AmEx accepted		Vi tar VISA, MC, DC, AmEx		VISA, MC, DC, AmEx	
Open year round		Åpent hele året		Ganzjährig geöffnet	
English spoken				Sprechen etwas Deutsch	

Directions:
From Oslo; Follow E-6 towards Trondheim, then take RV159 towards Strømmen/Lillestrøm. Continue to Fetsund on RV 170 (signs are marked Bjørkelangen). Over a bridge. Exit RV 22 towards Mysen. Exit onto RV 169 towards Løken and look for the sign to Bransrud after about 20 km. Turn left at the sign and drive 50 m. The farm is on the right-hand side, see sign; 'Høland Gardsmotell'.

Veibeskrivelse:
Fra Oslo; Følg E-6 i retning Trondheim, ta RV 159 mot Strømmen/Lillestrøm. Kjør videre på RV 170 til Fetsund (skiltet mot Bjørkelangen). Bro over Glomma, ta RV 22 i retning Mysen. Ta av til RV 169 mot Løken, etter 20 km se etter skilt til Bransrud/ Gaardsmotell. Sving til venstre ved skilt, kjør 50 m. Gården ligger på høyre side. Se skilt; 'Høland Gaardsmotell'.

Wegbeschreibung:
Ab Oslo der E-6 in Ri. Trondheim folgen, dann auf die Str. 159 nach Strømmen/Lillestrøm abbiegen. Weiter auf der Str. 170 Ri. Bjørkelangen. In Fetsund über den Fluss Glomma; hinter der Brücke auf die Str. 22 nach Mysen abbiegen. Danach der Str. 169 Ri. Løken folgen; nach ca. 20 km sehen Sie ein Schild Bransrud/Gaardsmotell. Am Schild links abbiegen; dann liegt der Hof nach ca. 50 m auf der rechten Seite.

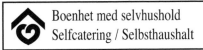
Guesthouse for 4-9 persons
No. of bedrooms: 3-5
2 baths, kitchen, DR, LR
Price for whole unit: **1500,-**
Bed linen included
No. of units: 4

'The Store-house':
The 'stabbur' is an exciting place for children who want to sleep in the hayloft.

Høland gård is 45 min. by car from Oslo. The barn at Høland farm has been expanded to serve as a 170 m^2. guesthouse. Six horses live next door. The guest rooms are modern and comfortable with heat, air conditioning and tiled floors. New spa opened in 2010. Høland features horseback-riding for children and touring for experienced riders. Here you will come across chickens, cats and dogs, along with a large garden area that includes a fish pond, outdoor grill area with gas grills, trampoline, trees to climb and sandbox. Activities include Moose Safaris, transportation to a wetlands area where you can go bird watching. Take walks in the woods, and pick berries and mushrooms. Nearby you'll find a forest with foot paths and lighted ski trails leading to a lake where you can fish or swim, and there are outdoor toilets. You may also drive to the lake. Also very handy are a bus stop and general store 150 m., football field 500 m. and the Løhren farm museum 1.5 km.

Gjestehus for 4-9 personer
Antall soverom: 3-5
2 bad, kjøkken, spisestue, stue
Pris for hele enheten: **1500,-**
Sengetøy inkludert
Antall enheter: 4

'Stabburet':
Stabburet er et spennende overnattingssted for barn som vil sove i høyet.

Høland gård ligger 45 min. med bil fra Oslo. Den gamle stallen er delvis ombygget og rommer nå et topp moderne gjestehus på 170 m^2. Vegg-i-vegg har fremdeles seks hester sitt hjem. Rommene er høyst komfortable med aircondition og flislagte gulv med varmekabler. Ny spa-avdeling åpnet i 2010. På gården tilbyr man barneridning på ridebane og turridning for erfarne ryttere. Her er også høner, katter og hund, samt en stor hage med fiskedam, grillplass med gassgriller, trampoline, klatretre og sandkasse. Tilbud om elgsafari, transport til fredet våtmarksområde med fugletitting og skogsturer med plukking av bær og sopp. I nærheten finnes det skogsveier og stier, lysløype og badevann med toaletter og fiskebrygge. Det er kjørevei til vannet. Fotballplass 500 m, Løhren gårdsmuseum 1,5 km, butikk/landhandel 130 m, bussholdeplass 150 m.

Gästehaus für 4-9 Personen
Anzahl Schlafzi.: 3-5
2 Bäder, Küche, Esszi., Stube
Ganze Einheit: **1500,-**
Inkl. Bettwäsche
Anzahl Einheiten: 4

'Das Vorratshaus':
Im Vorratshaus fühlen sich besonders Kinder, die gern im Heu schlafen möchten, sehr wohl.

Der Høland Hof liegt 45 Autominuten von Oslo entfernt. Der alte Stall wurde teilweise umgebaut und beherbergt nun ein topmodernes Gästehaus auf 170 m^2. Gleich nebenan sind noch immer 6 Pferde untergebracht. Die Zimmer sind äußerst komfortabel eingerichtet, mit Klimaanlage und Fussbodenheizung. 2010 öffnete die neue SPA-Abteilung. Kinder können auf dem Hof Reitstunden nehmen, für erfahrene Reiter sind sogar Ausritte möglich. Es gibt hier außerdem Hühner, Katzen und einen Hund und einen großen Garten mit Angelteich, Grillplatz, Trampolin, Kletterbaum und Sandkasten. Es werden Elchsafaris, Vogelexkursionen, Waldausflüge zum Beeren und Pilze sammeln angeboten. In der Nähe finden sich Wanderwege, eine beleuchtete Loipe, ein Badesee mit Toiletten u. Angelstelle. Straße zum See vorhanden. Fussballplatz 500 m, Løhren Hofmuseum 1,5 km, Geschäft/Laden 130 m und Bushaltestelle 150 m.

Not all those who wander are lost." ~J. R. R. Tolkien~

Porta Fortuna

Your host:
Anita Fagertun

Address:
Bjerkerudveien 63
N - 1450 Nesoddtangen
Mobile: 90 54 04 61
E-mail: anita.fagertun@gmail.com

Best time to call:
08.00 - 23.00
GPS: 59°48'8"N 10°40'48"E

Double room:	**800,-**	Dobbeltrom:	**800,-**	Doppelzimmer:	**800,-**
Single room:	**400,-**	Enkeltrom:	**400,-**	Einzelzimmer:	**400,-**
No. of rooms: 3		Antall rom: 3		Anzahl Zimmer: 3	
Breakfast buffet		Frokost buffét		Frühstücksbüfett	
Discount for children		Rabatt for barn		Ermäßigung für Kinder	
Prices valid for 2011		Priser gyldig for 2011		Preise gültig für 2011	
TV/Internet available		TV/Internett tilgjengelig		TV/Internet verfügbar	
Terrace/deck/yard		Terrasse/uteplass/hage		Terrasse/Außenbereich/Garten	
Open year round		Åpent hele året		Ganzjährig geöffnet	
English spoken				Sprechen etwas Deutsch	

At the end of a dead-end road atop a small hill you'll find Porta Fortuna. A house in the forest with a large, pretty terrace with a view of Bunnefjorden. Here lives Anita, 50, her 3 cats, a dog and from time to time her 3 children
Peaceful and natural beauty surround you. A horse-riding center is just down the hill. 10 min. walk to bus stop and store.

I enden av en blindvei, på en liten høyde finner du Porta Fortuna. Et hus i skogen med stor deilig terrasse og utsikt mot Bunnefjorden. Her bor Anita på 50 år med sine tre katter, en hund og tidvis sine tre barn. Rolige og naturskjønne omgivelser. Et ridesenter ligger like nedenfor eiendommen. 10 min. gange til bussholdeplass og butikk.

Porta Fortuna finden Sie am Ende einer Sackgasse auf einer kleinen Anhöhe. Das Haus liegt im Wald und die schöne große Terrasse bietet eine tolle Aussicht auf den Bunnefjord. Hier wohnt die 50-jährige Anita mit ihren drei Katzen, einem Hund und von Zeit zu Zeit mit ihren drei Kindern. Gleich unterhalb des Grundstücks befindet sich ein Reiterhof. 10 min zu Fuß zur Bushaltestelle und Geschäften.

> No one realizes how beautiful it is to travel until he comes home
> and rests his head on his old, familiar pillow.
> ~Lin Yutang~
>
> A good traveler has no fixed plans, and is not intent on arriving.
> ~Lao Tzu~

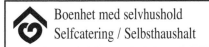
Den Blå Dør

Your host:
Anne Gutu

Address:
Skedsmogata 7
N - 0655 Oslo
Phone: 22 19 99 44

Best time to call:
09.00 - 21.00
GPS: 59°54'47"N 10°46'49"E

Room for 2 pers.:	**550,-**	Rom for 2 pers.:	**550,-**	Zimmer für 2 Pers.:	**550,-**
Room for 1 pers.:	**400,-**	Rom for 1 pers.:	**400,-**	Zimmer für 1 Pers.:	**400,-**
One night stay only; add:	**50,-**	Ettdøgnstillegg:	**50,-**	Zuschlag für nur 1 ÜN :	**50,-**
Shared bath and kitchen		Delt bad og kjøkken		Gemeins. Bad und Küche	
No. of rooms: 3		Antall rom: 3		Anzahl Zimmer: 3	
Bed linen included		Sengetøy er inkludert		Inkl. Bettwäsche	
Breakfast available:	**75,-**	Frokost kan serveres:	**75,-**	Frühstück auf Bestellung:	**75,-**
Prices valid for 2011		Priser gyldig for 2011		Preise gültig für 2011	
Terrace/patio/yard		Terrasse/uteplass/hage		Terrasse/Außenbereich/Garten	
Open year round		Åpent hele året		Ganzjährig geöffnet	
English spoken				Sprechen etwas Deutsch	

Den Blå Dør (The Blue Door) is a pleasant place to stay at Kampen, one of the most attractive parts of Oslo. You will find closely built, old timber houses in a popular neighborhood where the owners have taken pride in restoring their homes over the decades.
The Blue Door is 10 minutes by bus from Oslo Central Station, close to Tøyen and the Munch Museum. Take bus No. 60, get off at Kampen Church. Skedsmogata is two blocks from the bus stop, along Bøgata.

Den Blå Dør er et sjarmerende overnattingssted på Kampen, en av de triveligste bydelene i Oslo. Her står gamle trehus tett i tett, et populært område hvor omsorgsfulle huseiere har pusset opp og restaurert i årtier.
Stedet ligger 10 min. med buss fra Oslo Sentralstasjon, nær Tøyen og Munchmuseet. Ta buss nr. 60 til Kampen kirke. Skedsmogata ligger to kvartaler fra kirken, langs Bøgata.

Den Blå Dør (Die Blaue Tür) ist eine gemütliche Übernachtungsmöglichkeit in Kampen, einem der schönsten Stadtteile Oslos. Dort findet man alte Holzhäuser dicht aneinander gereiht in einem populären Bezirk, wo umsichtige Besitzer seit Jahrzehnten ihre Häuser liebevoll restaurieren. Das Haus liegt in der Nähe des Munch-Museums und der U-Bahn Station Tøyen und ist nach 10 Min. Busfahrt vom Osloer Zentrum aus zu erreichen. Nehmen Sie Bus Nr. 60 bis Kampen Kirche. Die Skedsmogata befindet sich zwei Häuserblocks von der Kirche entfernt, entlang der Bøgata.

Enerhaugen

Your host:
Terje Hansen

Address:
Enerhauggata 3
N - 0651 Oslo
Phone: **22 19 02 15**
Mobile: **90 09 06 82**
E-mail: **tehahan@gmail.com**
Web: **http://oslo.steinarweb.com**

Best time to call:
08.00 - 23.00
GPS: 59°54'47"N 10°46'4"E

Room for 1 pers.:	**300,-**	Rom for 1 pers.:	**300,-**	Zimmer für 1 Pers.:	**300,-**
Extra person, (mattress):	**50,-**	Ekstra person (madrass):	**50,-**	Extra Pers. (Matratze):	**50,-**
Bed linen included		Sengetøy er inkludert		Inkl. Bettwäsche	
Shared bath and kitchen		Delt bad og kjøkken		Gemeins. Bad u. Küche	
Prices valid for 2011		Priser gyldig for 2011		Preise gültig für 2011	
TV/Internet (wireless) available		TV/Internett (trådløs) tilgjengelig		TV/Internet (W-Lan) vorhanden	
Open year round		Åpent hele året		Ganzjährig geöffnet	
English spoken				Sprechen etwas Deutsch	

If you want to live in the center of Oslo for a reasonable price, this is the place. Enerhaugen is on a knoll jutting out over the rest of the city center. The apartment boasts a panoramic view of the city . Here it's peaceful and quiet while the hustle and bustle of the city is within walking distance, as are the Oslo Bus Terminal, Central Station and the main street, Karl Johans gate. Just on the other side of Enerhaugen are the Munch Museum and Botanical Garden.

Hvis du ønsker å bo sentralt og rimelig, så er dette stedet. Enerhaugen er en knause i sentrum og rager over den øvrige sentrumsbebyggelsen. Leiligheten har panoramautsikt over byen. På Enerhaugen er det rolig og stille, med yrende liv i bystrøkene nedenfor. Det er gangavstand til Oslo Bussterminal, Oslo Sentralstrasjon og hovedgaten Karl Johans gate. På andre siden av Enerhaugen ligger Botanisk hage og Munchmuseet.

Wenn Sie gerne zentral und preiswert wohnen möchten, dann sind Sie hier genau richtig. Enerhaugen liegt im Zentrum auf einer Anhöhe und ragt über die anderen städtischen Bebauungen hinaus. Wohnung mit Panoramaaussicht auf die Stadt. Enerhaugen ist ruhig und still gelegen, und dennoch mitten im pulsierenden Leben der Stadt. Kurzer Fussmarsch zum Osloer Bustbahnhof, dem Hauptbahnhof und der Hauptstraße Karl Johans Gate. Auf der anderen Seite von Enerhaugen liegen der botanische Garten und das Munch Museum.

> The traveler is active; he goes strenuously in search of people, of adventure, of experience. The tourist is passive; he expects interesting things to happen to him. He goes "sight-seeing."
> ~Daniel J. Boorstin~

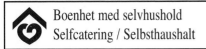
Frogner Guestroom

Your host:
Ingvild Holm

Address:
Baldersgate 11A
N - 0263 Oslo
Phone: 22 55 21 30
Mobile: 90 92 99 44
E-mail: i-holm@online.no
Web: www.baktruppen.org/
frogner_guestroom.html

Best time to call:
09.00 - 22.00
GPS: 59°55'9"N 10°42'40"E

Room for 1-4 persons:		Rom for 1-4 personer:		Zimmer für 1-4 Personen:	
Price for 1 pers.:	**500,-**	Pris for 1 pers.:	**500,-**	Preis für 1 Pers.:	**500,-**
Price for 2 pers.:	**700,-**	Pris for 2 pers.:	**700,-**	Preis für 2 Pers.:	**700,-**
Price for 3 pers.:	**900,-**	Pris for 3 pers.:	**900,-**	Preis für 3 Pers.:	**900,-**
Price for 4 pers.:	**1100,-**	Pris for 4 pers.:	**1100,-**	Preis für 4 Pers.:	**1100,-**

No. of rooms: 1
Kitchenette
Shared bath
Bed linen included
Breakfast service available: **50,-**
Discount for children
Prices valid for 2011/12/13
Minimum 2 nights
TV/radio/Internet available
Open year round
English spoken

Antall rom: 1
Kjøkkenkrok
Delt bad
Sengetøy er inkludert
Frokost kan serveres: **50,-**
Rabatt for barn
Priser gyldig for 2011/12/13
Minimum 2 netter
TV/radio/Internett tilgjengelig
Åpent hele året

Anzahl Zimmer: 1
Küchenecke
Gemeinsames Bad
Inkl. Bettwäsche
Frühstück auf Bestellung: **50,-**
Ermäßigung für Kinder
Preise gültig für 2011/12/13
Mindestaufenthalt 2 Nächte
TV/Radio/Internet vorhanden
Ganzjährig geöffnet
Sprechen Deutsch

Welcome to a bright room in classical style in a 1901 building located in a quiet street at Frogner. The house is centrally located with walking distance to all central attractions, museums, cinemas, theatres and shops. A few minutes by tram, bus or subway will take you to beaches and museums at Bygdøy, to Holmenkollen and the forests, or to the boats and the Oslofjord Islands.

Velkommen til et lyst og hyggelig rom i klassisk stil i en stille gate på Frogner. Bygården fra 1901 ligger i gangavstand til alle sentrale turistmål, butikker, caféer, restauranter, teatre og kinoer. Få minutter med buss, trikk eller T-bane tar deg til strender og muséer på Bygdøy, til Holmenkollen og Nordmarka, eller til båtene og øyene i Oslofjorden.

Willkommen in unserem hellen und freundlichen Raum in einem klassizistischen Haus von 1901. Das Haus liegt in einer zentralen aber ruhigen Strasse in Frogner. Nur wenige Gehminuten zu den Museen, Kinos u. Theatern im Zentrum. Mit den öffentlichen Verkehrsmitteln ist man schnell am Strand und bei den Museen auf Bygdøy, dem Holmenkollen und den umliegenden Wäldern oder bei den Booten und den Inseln im Oslofjord.

Frogner Bed & Breakfast

Your host:
Cecilie & Anders Due

Address:
Kirkeveien 5
N - 0266 Oslo
Mobile: 92 42 03 65
E-mail: post@frognerbb.no
Web: www.frognerbb.no

Best time to call:
09.00 - 22.00
GPS: 59°55'22"N 10°42'20"E

Double-/twin room:	**750,-**	Dobbelt-/tosengsrom:	**750,-**	Doppel-/Zweibettzi.:	**750,-**
No. of rooms: 3		Antall rom: 3		Anzahl Zimmer: 3	
Extra bed:	**150,-**	Ekstraseng:	**150,-**	Extrabett:	**150,-**
Baby bed:	**75,-**	Babyseng:	**75,-**	Babybett:	**75,-**
Breakfast service available:	**70,-**	Frokostbrett kan serveres:	**70,-**	Frühstück auf Bestellung:	**70,-**
or in one of the many cafés nearby		eller på kafé i nærheten		oder in einem der vielen Cafés	
Selfcatering possible		Selvhushold er mulig		Selbstverpflegung möglich	
Parking in the court yard:	**50,-**	Parkering i gårdsrommet:	**50,-**	Parken im Innenhof:	**50,-**
Prices valid for 2011		Priser gyldig for 2011		Preise gültig für 2011	
Internet available		Internett tilgjengelig		Internet verfügbar	
Terrace/deck/yard		Terrasse/uteplass/hage		Terrasse/Außenbereich/Garten	
Open year round		Åpent hele året		Ganzjährig geöffnet	
English spoken				Sprechen Englisch, etwas Deutsch	

Set in one of the city's finest areas you can live in a well-lit, peaceful and inviting rooms of a private, brick villa, with access to a tasteful and roomy bathroom. The house is at Frogner plass, right across the road from Vigeland Park. Coffee bars and restaurants nearby. Walking distance to vital tourist destinations and popular shopping areas Bogstadveien and Aker Brygge. Very good public transit direct to the ski jump and ski museum at Holmenkollen and Frognerseteren, or the harbor attractions such as Viking Ship Museum and Folk Museum at Bygdøy.

I et av byens flotteste strøk, i en privat murvilla, kan du bo i lyse, rolige og trivelige rom med romslig og delikat bad tilgjengelig. Huset ligger ved Frogner plass, rett over veien fra Vigelandsparken. Kaffebarer og restauranter i umiddelbar nærhet. Gangavstand til sentrale turistmål og populære handlesteder som Bogstadveien og Aker Brygge. Meget god offentlig kommunikasjon direkte til eksempelvis skihoppet, skimuseet og Frognerseteren i Holmenkollen, eller til sjøen med Vikingskip- og Folkemuseet på Bygdøy.

In einer der schönsten Stadtteile Oslos wohnen Sie in einer privaten Villa in hellen, ruhigen und gemütlichen Zimmern mit Zugang zu einem geräumigen und geschmackvoll eingerichteten Bad. Das Haus befindet sich am Frogner Plass, direkt gegenüber vom Vigelandspark. Cafés und Restaurants in unmittelbarer Nähe. Kurzer Fußweg zu den zentralen Sehenswürdigkeiten sowie den beliebten Einkaufsstätten 'Bogstadveien' oder 'Aker Brygge'. Direkte Verkehrsverbindung zum Holmenkollen, Skimuseum und Frognerseteren oder zu den Museen auf Bygdøy.

Residence Kristinelund

Your host:
Lennart Hansen
& Synne Tveitan

Address: Kristinelundveien 2
N - 0268 Oslo
Phone: 40 00 24 11
E-mail: booking@kristinelund.no
Web: www.kristinelund.no

Best time to call:
09.00 - 12.00 / 16.00 - 20.00
GPS: 59°55'10"N 10°41'49"E

Double-/twin room: **690,- to 990,-**	Dobbelt-/tosengsrom: **690,- til 990,-**	DZ/Zweibettzi.: **690,- bis 990,-**
Single room: **590,- to 790,-**	Enkeltrom: **590,- til 790,-**	Einzelzimmer: **590,- bis 790,-**
No. of rooms: 19	Antall rom: 19	Anzahl Zimmer: 19
Breakfast buffet	Frokostbufffét	Frühstücksbüfett
Prices valid for 2011	Priser gyldig for 2011	Preise gültig für 2011
TV available	TV tilgjengelig	TV vorhanden
Terrace/patio/yard	Terrasse/uteplass/hage	Terrasse/Außenbereich/Garten
Phone/fax/Internet available	Tilgang til telefon/fax/Internett	Tel., Fax und Internet vorhanden
Pets welcome	Kjæledyr velkommen	Haustiere willkommen
VISA, MC accepted	Vi tar VISA, MC	Wir akzeptieren VISA, MC
Open year round	Åpent hele året	Ganzjährig geöffnet
English & French spoken		Sprechen Deutsch

At Residence Kristinelund, Frogner, doors are open for guests who prefer closeness to the city center and easy access to several sights; 10-15 min. walk to the Royal Palace, 5 min. walk to the Vigeland park and short bus-trip to beaches and the museums at Bygdøy. Buses and trams stop right outside the building, which is an old, elegantly decorated and protected building in a very nice neighborhood. The area also offers restaurants, coffeehouses and small shops.

På Frogner er dørene åpne for turister som ønsker sentrumsnær beliggenhet. Her er det 10-15 min. gange til slottet og 5 min. til Vigelandsparken. Kort vei til strand og museer på Bygdøy. Det er også gode buss- og trikkeforbindelser med stoppested rett utenfor bygningen som er elegant i gammel stil og vernet.
Rett utenfor dørene finnes også et hyggelig strøk med restauranter, kaféer og små butikker.

Touristen, die zentrumsnah wohnen möchten, sollten sich nach Frogner orientieren. Von dort sind es nur ca. 10-15 Minuten Fußweg bis zum Schloss und 5 Minuten bis zum Vigelandpark. Kurze Entfernung zum Strand und zu den Museen auf Bygdøy. Ebenfalls gute Bus- und Straßenbahnverbindung.
Haltestelle direkt vor der Haustür. Elegantes älteres Gebäude unter Denkmalschutz. Unweit des Hauses gemütliches Viertel mit Restaurants, Cafés und kleinen Geschäften.

Tourists don't know where they've been,
travelers don't know where they're going. ~Paul Theroux~

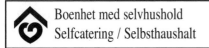
Bygdøy
Bed & Breakfast

Your host:
Jo Brønlund

Address:
Mellbyedalen 3
N - 0287 Oslo
Mobile: 97 56 13 79
E-mail: jo-br@online.no

Best time to call:
10.00 – 12.00 / 17.00 – 20.00
GPS: 59°54'25"N 10°41'25"E

Apt., 30m² for 2-3 pers.: **750,-**	Leil., 30m² for 2-3 pers.: **750,-**	Wohng., 30m² für 2-3 Pers.: **750,-**
Apt., 40m² for 4-5 pers.: **900,-**	Leil., 40m² for 4-5 pers.: **900,-**	Wohng., 40m² für 4-5 Pers.: **900,-**
Apt., 50m² for 4-6 pers.: **1100,-**	Leil., 50m² for 4-6 pers.: **1100,-**	Wohng., 50m² für 4-6 Pers.: **1100,-**

Applies to all rental units:	For alle enheter gjelder:	Für alle Einheiten gilt:
Apt. consist of kitchen, bath, LR, bedroom or sleeping alcove	Leil. med kjk., bad, stue, soverom eller sovealkove	Wohnung mit Küche, Bad, Stube, Schlafzi. oder Schlafnische
Breakfast available	Frokost kan serveres	Frühstück auf Bestellung
Prices valid for 2011/12	Priser gyldig for 2011/12	Preise gültig für 2011/12
TV/Internet	TV/Internett	TV/Internet
Garden/terrace access	Hage/terrasse	Garten/Terrasse
Free private parking	Gratis parkering i privat gård	Kostenloses Parken im Hof (privat)
Open year round	Åpent hele året	Ganzjährig Geöffnet
English & some French spoken		Sprechen Deutsch

Bygdøy Apartments is located on the green peninsula Bygdøy, only 12 min. by bus from Oslo town center. The house is 2 min. from the bus stop and the passenger boat to central Oslo. Here are large houses with large rooms and lush gardens, beaches, parks and many museums.
Walking distance to the Viking-skip-house, Folk-museum, Kontiki-museum, Fram-museum, Maritim museum and the Holocaust center. In the nearby neighbourhood you also find cafes and restaurants overviewing the fjord and the boats passing to/from Oslo harbour.

Bygdøy Apartments ligger på den grønne, frodige halvøyen Bygdøy, bare 12 min. med buss fra Karl Johans gate. Huset ligger 2 min. fra bussholdeplass og rutebåt til Oslo sentrum. Her er store hus med store rom og frodige hager, strender, friluftsområder og mange museer. Gangavstand til Viking-skipshuset, Folkemuseet, Kontiki-museet, Frammuseet, Maritimt museum og Holocaustsentret.
I nærheten finner du også cafeer og restauranter med utsikt mot fjorden og båtene som går til og fra Oslo havn.

Bygdøy Apartments liegt auf der grünen Halbinsel Bygdøy, nur 12 min vom Osloer Zentrum mit dem Bus. Das Haus liegt nur 2 min von der Bushaltestelle entfernt. Hier findet man große Häuser mit gro-ßen Zimmern u. blühenden Gärten, Strände, Erholungsgebiete und vie-le Museen. Vikingerschiff-, Volks-, Kontiki-, Fram-, Maritimmuseum und Holocaustcenter zu Fuß zu erreichen. In der Nähe befinden sich auch Cafés, Restaurants mit Aussicht auf den Fjord und die ein-und auslaufenden Schiffe.

Janesplace B&B

Your host:
Jane E. Dunn Børresen

Address:
Doktor Baches vei 4
N - 0284 Oslo
Phone: 21 69 65 25
Mobile: 91 15 98 78
E-mail: jane.boerresen@hotmail.com
Web: www.janesplace.no

Best time to call:
08.00 - 22.00
GPS: 59°55'23"N 10°38'33"E

Double-/twin room:	**850,-**	Dobbelt-/tosengsrom:	**850,-**	Doppel-/Zweibettzi.:	**850,-**
1 person in double room:	**700,-**	En pers. i dbl. rom:	**700,-**	1 Pers. im DZ:	**700,-**
One night stay only; add:	**150,-**	Ettdøgnstillegg:	**150,-**	Zuschlag für nur 1 ÜN:	**150,-**
Extra bed for child:	**150,-**	Ekstraseng for barn:	**150,-**	Extrabett für Kinder:	**150,-**

No. of rooms: 1	Antall rom: 1	Anzahl Zimmer: 1
Discount for children	Rabatt for barn	Ermäßigung für Kinder
Discount for longer stay	Rabatt for lenger tids opphold	Erm. für Langzeitaufenthalte
Breakfast; self-service	Frokost; selvbetjening	Frühstück: Selbstbedienung
Selfcatering possible	Selvhushold er mulig	Selbstverpflegung möglich
Prices valid for 2011	Priser gyldig for 2011	Preise gültig für 2011
TV, DVD, Internet available	TV, DVD, Internett tilgjengelig	TV, DVD, Internet
Terrace/patio/yard	Terrasse/uteplass/hage	Terrasse/Außenbereich/Garten
Suitable for handicapped	Handikaptilgjengelig	Behindertengerecht
Open year round	Åpent hele året	Ganzjährig geöffnet
English spoken		Sprechen Englisch

Artist and second-hand shop enthusiast Jane is a native of England, but she has lived in Norway for 30 years. She has a modern duplex at Lilleaker and rents out a one-room apartment on the lower floor.
Along the nearby Lysaker River you'll find foot paths and bicycle lanes leading to the famous Bygdøy peninsula. Tram / bus to Oslo center in immediate vicinity. 15 min. walk to airport train. You'll also find shopping center and cafes near Jane's Place.

Jane er opprinnelig fra England, men har vært bosatt i Norge i 30 år. Hun er kunstner og bruktmarkedentusiast. I en moderne tomannsbolig på Lilleaker leier hun ut en ettromsleilighet i underetasjen. Langs Lysakerelven er det fine turområder og en sykkelsti leder til Bygdøy. Det går trikk og buss til Oslo sentrum. 15 min. gange til flytoget. Kjøpesenter med butikker og kaféer i nærheten.

Jane kommt ursprünglich aus England, aber lebt seit 25 Jahren in Norwegen. Sie ist Künstlerin und Flohmarkt-Fan. In einem modernen Zweifamilienhaus in Lilleaker vermietet sie eine Einzimmerwohnung im EG. Es gibt tolle Ausflugsmöglichkeiten entlang des Lysaker Flusses und auch einen Radweg, der auf Bygdøy führt. Straßenbahn- und Busverbindungen ins Osloer Zentrum, sowie Geschäfte und Cafès in unmittelbarer Nähe. Nur 15 Gehminuten zur Haltestelle des Zuges zum Flughafen.

Garden Suite, Oslo west

Your host:
Ami Krogsæter

Address:
Finnhaugveien 36
N - 0760 Oslo
Phone: 21 91 23 66
Mobile: 91 30 40 89
E-mail: ami.krogsater@getmail.no
Best time to call: 18 - 21 (weekdays)
              10 - 18 (weekend)
GPS: 59°56'46"N 10°38'30"E

Main house:
Double-/twin room: **850,-**
1 pers. in double room: **700,-**
No. of rooms: 2
Discount for children under 7 yrs

Annex:
Apartment for 1-2 persons
1 BR, LR, kitchennook, bathroom
Whole unit: **1500,-**
Own garden w/ flowers and herbs

Breakfast tray
Prices valid for 2011
Sauna - ask for price
Open year round
English and French spoken

Hovedhus:
Dobbelt-/tosengsrom: **850,-**
En person i dobbeltr.:   **700,-**
Antall rom: 2
Rabatt for barn under 7 år

Annex:
Leilighet for 1-2 personer
1 soverom, stue, kjk.krok, bad
Hele enheten: **1500,-**
Egen hage med blomster og urter

Frokostbrett
Priser gyldig for 2011
Sauna - spør om pris
Åpent hele året

Haupthaus:
Doppel-/Zweibettzi.:   **850,-**
1 Pers. im DZ.:   **700,-**
Anzahl Zimmer: 2
Ermässigung für Kinder unter 7 J.

Annex:
Wohnung für 1-2 Personen
1 Schlafzi., Stube, Kü.ecke, Bad
Ganze Einheit: **1500,-**
Eig. Garten mit Blumen u. Kräutern

Frühstückstablett
Preise gültig für 2011
Sauna - Preis auf Anfrage
Ganzjährig geöffnet
Sprechen etwas Deutsch

The host is a health-worker/artist with Finnish roots. She welcomes you to a wooden house from 1934 in a quiet neighborhood conveniently located in Røa, at the foot of Holmenkollen. Finnish sauna by appointment. Pleasant walking tour along the Lysaker River including rapids and falls.
1 minute to metro railway and buses. 12 minutes to Oslo center. Near shops, bank and post office. Bus direct from Gardermoen Airport.

Vertinnen er kunstner og helse-arbeider med finske aner. Hun øns-ker deg velkommen til sitt trehus fra 1934 som ligger i et rolig strøk sentralt på Røa, ved foten av Holmenkollen. Finsk sauna etter avtale. Fin turvei langs Lysakerelva med fosser og stryk.
1 min. til T-bane og busser. 12 min. til Oslo sentrum. Nær butikker, bank og postkontor. Buss direkte fra Gardermoen flyplass.

Die Gastgeberin ist Künstlerin und Krankenschwester mit finnischen Wurzeln. Sie begrüßt Sie herzlich in ihrem Holzhaus von 1934, das ruhig und dennoch zentral im Stadtteil Røa am Fuße des Holmen-kollens liegt. Finnische Sauna nach Absprache. Schöner Wanderweg entlang des Lysaker Flusses mit Stromschnellen und Wasserfällen. Metro-, Bushaltestelle nur 1 min entfernt - 12 min ins Osloer Zen-trum. Unweit v. Geschäften, Bank, Post. Flughafenbus von/nach Gar-dermoen hält gleich in der Nähe.

Vinderen Bed & Breakfast

Your host:
Eva Engelhardt

Address:
Borgenveien 25A
N - 0370 Oslo
Phone: 22 14 45 28
Mobile: 48 27 46 16
E-mail: evaengel@vikenfiber.no

Best time to call:
08.00 - 22.00
GPS: 59°56'20"N 10°42'2"E

Double room:	950,-	Dobbeltrom:	950,-	Doppelzimmer:	950,-
One person in double room:	700,-	En pers. i dobbeltrom:	700,-	1 Pers. im DZ:	700,-
Single room:	600,-	Enkeltrom:	600,-	Einzelzimmer:	600,-
Extra bed for child:	250,-	Ekstraseng for barn:	250,-	Extrabett für Kinder:	250,-

No. of rooms: 3

Breakfast: Self-service in rooms

Prices valid for 2011/12

Selfcatering possible

Internet available

Terrace/deck access/yard

Pets welcome

Open year round

Closed Christmas and New Year

English and some French spoken

Antall rom: 3

Frokost: Selvbetjening på rom

Priser gyldig for 2011/12

Selvhushold er mulig

Internett tilgjengelig

Terrasse/uteplass/hage

Kjæledyr velkommen

Åpent hele året

Stengt jul og nyttår

Anzahl Zimmer: 3

Frühstück: Selbstbedienung im Zi.

Preise gültig für 2011/12

Selbstverpflegung möglich

Internet verfügbar

Terrasse/Außenbereich/Garten

Haustiere willkommen

Ganzjährig geöffnet

Weihnachten und Neujahr geschl.

Sprechen Deutsch

Vinderen B&B, a wooden house from 1986, lies in a quiet area with a cozy atmosphere within walking distance to Vigeland Park and the metro rail. The host is a journalist who has traveled much and enjoys having guests from around the world. She will gladly take guests on tours of Oslo in her own car by appointment.

Vinderen Bed & Breakfast, et trehus fra 1986, ligger i et rolig strøk med hyggelig atmosfære, med gangavstand til Vigelandsparken og til to T-bane-linjer.
Vertinnen er journalist, har reist mye og gleder seg til å ta imot gjester fra hele verden. Hun kan gjerne guide i Oslo med egen bil etter nærmere avtale.

Vinderen Bed & Breakfast empfängt seine Gäste in einem gemütlichen Holzhaus aus dem Jahre 1986. Das Gebäude liegt in einem ruhigen Viertel. Fußweg zum Vigelandpark und zwei U-Bahn-Linien. Die Wirtin ist Journalistin, viel gereist und freut sich auf Gäste aus der ganzen Welt.
Nach Absprache unternimmt sie gern mit dem eigenen Auto Führungen durch die Stadt.

Travel and change of place impart new vigor to the mind.

~Seneca~

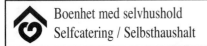
Villa May

Your host:
Marit Rafoss

Address:
Holmenveien 22 A
N - 0374 Oslo
Mobile: **92 81 71 81**
E-mail: **marit.rafoss@gmail.com**

Best time to call:
08.00 - 22.00
GPS: 59°56'37"N 10°41'48"E

Double room:	**650,-**	Dobbeltrom:	**650,-**	Doppelzimmer:	**650,-**
Single room:	**550,-**	Enkeltrom:	**550,-**	Einzelzimmer:	**550,-**
Large double room		Stort dobbeltrom		Großes Doppelzimmer	
w/priv. veranda and view:	**800,-**	m/egen veranda og utsikt:	**800,-**	m. priv. Veranda u. Aussicht:	**800,-**
One night stay only, add.:	**100,-**	Ettdøgnstillegg:	**100,-**	Zuschlag für nur 1 ÜN:	**100,-**
Extra bed:	**100,-**	Ekstraseng:	**100,-**	Extrabett:	**100,-**
No. of rooms: 3		Antall rom: 3		Anzahl Zimmer:3	
Guest kitchen included		Gjestekjøkken inkludert		Gästeküche inbegriffen	
Terrace/yard		Terrasse/hage		Terrasse/Garten	
Prices valid for 2011		Prisene gjelder for 2011		Preise gültig für 2011	
Internet available		Internett tilgjengelig		Internet verfügbar	
Open year round		Åpent hele året		Ganzjährig geöffnet	
English & some French spoken				Sprechen etwas Deutsch	

Villa May is located in West Oslo, and is a pleasant wooden house built in 1905. The rooms facing south have a lovely view of the Oslo fjord. With only 10 min. by tram from the city centre, and with other public transportation very close at hand, guests have easy access to all parts of the city.

Villa May ligger på Oslos vestkant, og er et hyggelig trehus fra 1905. De sydvendte rommene har en flott utsikt over Oslofjorden. Trikketur fra sentrum til Vindern tar 10 min., og andre nærliggende kommunikasjonsmidler gir enkel tilgang til alle deler av byen.

Die Villa May liegt im Westen von Oslo und ist ein gemütliches Holzhaus aus dem Jahre 1905. Die Räume gen Süden haben eine tolle Aussicht auf den Oslofjord. Alle Stadtteile Oslos sind leicht zu erreichen; öffentliche Verkehrsmittel gleich in der Nähe. Mit der Straßenbahn nur 10 min zum Stadtzentrum.

> What you've done becomes the judge of what you're going to do -
> especially in other people's minds. When you're traveling,
> you are what you are right there and then. People don't have your
> past to hold against you. No yesterdays on the road.
> ~William Least Heat Moon, Blue Highways~

Solveig's Bed & Breakfast

Your host:
Roy Everson

Address:
Tåsen Terrasse 11
N - 0873 Oslo
Phone: 22 23 60 41
Mobile: 96 50 85 84
E-mail: raeverso@online.no
Web: http://solveigs.com

Best time to call: 08.00 - 21.00
GPS: 59°57'18"N 10°45'12"E

Double-/twin room:	550,-	Dobbelt-/tosengsrom:	550,-	Doppel-/Zweibettzi.:	550,-
3-bedded room:	675,-	3-sengs room:	675,-	3-Bettzimmer:	675,-
Single room:	350,-	Enkeltrom:	350,-	Einzelzimmer:	350,-
One night stay only; add:	50,-	Ettdøgnstillegg:	50,-	Zuschlag für nur 1 ÜN:	50,-
No. of rooms: 3		Antall rom: 3		Anzahl Zimmer: 3	
Laid breakfast table		Dekket frokostbord		Gedeckter Frühstückstisch	
Prices valid for 2011		Priser gyldig for 2011		Preise gültig für 2011	
Terrace/patio/yard		Terrasse/uteplass/hage		Terrasse/Außenbereich/Garten	
Open most of the year		Åpent det meste av året		Fast ganzjährig geöffnet	
English spoken		Snakker litt norsk		Sprechen Englisch	

Solveig's B&B has its name from mother Solveig who emigrated to America in 1948 after growing up in the house. Her son Roy, your host, comes from America to Norway to open the doors of Solveig's house for guests from far and near. The house lies on a hillside 5 km north of downtown and enjoys a nice view of the city and fjord. Quiet neighborhood near Sognsvann lake and Nordmarka forest, 2 blocks from public transport, airport bus stop and local shopping center.

Solveigs B&B har navn etter mor Solveig som utvandret til Amerika i 1948 etter å ha vokst opp i huset under 2. verdenskrig. Verten Roy, hennes sønn, har nå utvandret fra Amerika til Norge og har åpnet dørene i Solveigs hus for gjester fra fjern og nær.
Huset ligger i en åsside i nordre del av Oslo og har fin utsikt over byen og fjorden. Det er et stille boligstrøk nær Sognsvann og Nordmarka. Det er god offentlig transport og kort vei til lokalt kjøpesenter.

Solveigs Bed and Breakfast wurde nach der Mutter Solveig benannt, die während des 2. Weltkriegs in diesem Haus aufwuchs und im Jahre 1948 nach Amerika auswanderte. Der Gastgeber Roy, ihr Sohn, ist nun von Amerika nach Norwegen gezogen und hat die Pforten in Solveigs Haus wieder für Gäste aus nah und fern geöffnet.
Das Haus liegt an einem Hügel im nördlichen Teil Oslos und bietet eine reizvolle Aussicht auf Stadt und Fjord. Es liegt in einer ruhigen Wohngegend nahe des Waldgebiets Nordmarka und des Sees Sognsvann. Kurze Entfernung zu öffentlichen Verkehrsmitteln sowie zum nächsten Einkaufszentrum.

Anna's Place

Your host:
Anna Borg

Address:
Myrveien 2B
N - 1358 Jar
Phone: **67 58 92 68**
Mobile: **93 69 56 14**
E-mail:
annasplacenorway@hotmail.com

Best time to call:
08.00 - 22.00
GPS: 59°55'35"N 10°36'47"E

Apartment w/own bath, kitchen	Leilighet m/eget bad, kjøkken	Wohnung mit eig. Bad, Küche
LR with double bed & bunk-beds	stue med dbl-seng og køyesenger	Stube mit Doppelbett u. Kojenb.
1 bedroom w/double bed	1 soverom m/dobbelseng	1 Schlafzimmer mit Doppelbett
Price for 2 pers.: **800,-**	Pris for 2 pers.: **800,-**	Preis für 2 Pers.: **800,-**
Price for family of 4: **1000,-**	Pris for fam. på 4: **1000,-**	Preis für Familie, 4 Pers.: **1000,-**
Price for 4 adults: **1200,-**	Pris for 4 voksne: **1200,-**	Preis für 4 Erw.: **1200,-**
Price for 4 adults + 2 ch.: **1500,-**	Pris for 4 voksne + 2 barn: **1500,-**	Preis f. 4 Erw. + 2 Kinder: **1500,-**
Laid breakfast table	Dekket frokostbord	Gedeckter Frühstückstisch
Prices valid for 2011/12	Priser gyldig for 2011/12	Preise gültig für 2011/12
Selfcatering possible	Selvhushold er mulig	Selbstverpflegung möglich
TV in appartment	TV i leiligheten	TV in der Wohnung
Yard/terrace/patio	Hage/terrasse/uteplass	Garten/Terrasse/Außenbereich
Open year round	Åpent hele året	Ganzjährig geöffnet
English and Czeck spoken		Sprechen Deutsch

This modern and spacious detached home is situated in a quiet neighborhood in Bærum, just outside Oslo's city limits, 15 min. drive by car or trolley from downtown. You will enjoy a full-featured and very comfortable basement apartment. You have your own entrance and a private garden and sitting area. A ping-pong table on the patio may be used. Your hostess is Swiss and her husband Norwegian. They have settled down in Norway after many years in Switzerland.

I et rolig villastrøk i Bærum, like utenfor Oslo's bygrense, 15 min. med bil eller trikk fra sentrum, ligger denne moderne og romslige eneboligen. Her tilbys en fullt utstyrt og meget komfortabel utleieleilighet i underetasjen . Den har egen inngang og egen hageflekk med sitteplass. Et ping-pong bord på terrassen kan også benyttes. Vertinnen er sveitsisk og mannen norsk. De har nå slått seg ned i Norge etter mange år i Sveits.

Das moderne, geräumige Einfamilienhaus liegt in einer ruhigen Wohngegend in Bærum, direkt hinter der Stadtgrenze Oslos; mit dem Auto bzw. der Straßenbahn ca. 15 min vom Zentrum entfernt. Den Gast erwartet eine sehr gut ausgestattete, komfortable Einlieger-Ferienwohnung mit eigenem Eingang und einem kleinen Garten mit Sitzgelegenheit. Auf der Terrasse steht eine Tischtennisplatte zur freien Verfügung. Die Gastgeberin stammt aus der Schweiz, ihr Mann ist Norweger. Nach vielen Jahren in der Schweiz haben sie sich nun in Norwegen niedergelassen.

The Blue Room

Your host:
Tone K. & Asgeir Mamen

Address:
Nesåsen 11C
N - 1394 Nesbru
Phone: 66 84 90 10
Mobile: 90 86 12 03
E-mail: tmamen@attglobal.net
Web:
http://pws.preserv.net/theblueroom

Best time to call:
10.00 - 20.00
GPS: 59°51'54"N 10°30'1"E

Double-/twin room:	**900,-**	Dobbelt-/tosengsrom:	**900,-**
1 pers. in double room:	**700,-**	1 person i dobbeltrom:	**700,-**

Double-/twin room: **900,-**
1 pers. in double room: **700,-**
No. of rooms: 2
Discount for children
Laid breakfast table
Prices valid for 2011/12
Terrace/patio/yard
Open 1 May - 1 September
Winter open: reserve at least
  2 weeks in advance
English spoken

Dobbelt-/tosengsrom: **900,-**
1 person i dobbeltrom: **700,-**
Antall rom: 2
Rabatt for barn
Dekket frokostbord
Priser gyldig for 2011/12
Terrasse/uteplass/hage
Åpent 1. mai - 1. sept.
Vinteråpent ved forhåndsbestilling
  min. 2 uker i forveien.

Doppel-/Zweibettzi.: **900,-**
1 Pers. im Doppelzi.: **700,-**
Anzahl Zimmer: 2
Ermässigung für Kinder
Gedeckter Frühstückstisch
Preise gültig für 2011/12
Terrasse/Aussenplatz/Garten
Geöffnet 1. Mai - 1. Sept.
Im Winter geöffnet - Reservierung
  mind. 2 Wochen im Voraus
Sprechen etwas Deutsch

On the outskirts of Oslo, Tone and Asgeir offer you airy, pleasant rooms with view in their large, modern manor home. Ample parking next to the house. Nesåsen is a residential area featuring detached homes with gardens and greenery. This allows you to combine a city holiday with outdoor activities. It is a short way to public transport and the marina.

I utkanten av Oslo tilbyr Tone og Asgeir lyse og trivelige rom med utsikt i deres store moderne villa. Gode parkeringsmuligheter ved huset. Nesåsen er et boligområde bestående av eneboliger med hager og grøntareal. På denne måten kan man kombinere storbyferien med friluftsopplevelser.
Det er kort vei til offentlig kommunikasjon og båthavn.

Am Rande Oslos vermieten Tone und Asgeir in ihrer großen und modernen Villa helle und einladende Zimmer mit Aussicht. Gute Parkmöglichkeiten direkt am Haus. Nesåsen ist eine Wohngegend, in der Einfamilienhäuser mit Vorgärten und viel Grün dominieren. Der ideale Ort, um einen Großstadturlaub mit Erholung im Grünen zu kombinieren.
Kurze Entfernung zu öffentlichen Verkehrsmitteln sowie zum Bootshafen.

> ## To travel is to discover that everyone is wrong about other countries.
> ~Aldous Huxley~

Niskinn
Bed & Breakfast

Your host:
Kate & Odd Thrana

Address:
Niskinnveien
N - 3538 Sollihøgda
Phone: 32 15 76 66
Mobile: 92 66 70 80
E-mail: annekatethrana@yahoo.no

Best time to call:
08.00 - 23.00
GPS: 59°58'15"N 10°21'39"E

A: One-room cabin for 2-4 persons	**A:** Ettromshytte for 2-4 personer	**A:** 1-Raum-Hütte für 2-4 Pers.
Loft, Kitchen-nook, bath	Hems, kjøkkenkrok, bad	Schlafboden, Küchenecke, Bad
Whole unit for 2-4 pers.: **650,-**	Hele enhet for 2-4 pers.: **650,-**	Ganze Einheit für 2-4 Pers.: **650,-**
1 pers. in whole unit: **450,-**	1 pers. i hele enheten: **450,-**	1 Pers. in ganzer Einheit: **450,-**
B: House for 2-5 persons	**B:** Hus for 2-5 personer	**B:** Haus für 2-5 Personen
2 bedrooms, bath, LR, kitchen-nook	2 soverom, bad, stue, kjk.-krok	2 Schlafzi., Bad, Stube, Kü.-ecke
Price for 2 pers.: **650,-**	Pris for 2 pers.: **650,-**	Preis für 2 Pers.: **650,-**
Price for 5 pers.: **750,-**	Pris for 5 pers.: **750,-**	Preis für 5 Pers.: **750,-**
Breakfast; self-service	Frokost; selvbetjening	Frühstück: Selbstbedienung
Selvcatering possible	Selvhushold er mulig	Selbstverpflegung möglich
Prices valid for 2011	Priser gyldig for 2011	Preise gültig für 2011
Terrace/patio/yard	Terrasse/uteplass/hage	Terrasse/Außenbereich/Garten
Boat and bike available	Båt og sykkel tilgjengelig	Boot u. Fahrrad vorhanden
Jacuzzi for rent	Uteboblebad til leie	Außenwhirlpool zu mieten
Pets welcome	Kjæledyr tillatt	Haustiere willkommen
Open year round	Åpent hele året	Ganzjährig geöffnet
English spoken		Sprechen etwas Deutsch

Niskinn B&B is a small but charming and picturesque lakeside log cabin situated by Niskinn Lake, a summer paradise. The chickens wandering outside contribute eggs for breakfast.

In the winter skiers race past the door while the host stokes up the fireplace before the guests arrive.

Niskinn B&B er en sjarmerende liten laftet hytte som ligger vakkert til ved Niskinnvannet, et paradis om sommeren. Hønene går fritt utenfor og ved frokosten vanker det hjemmeverpede egg.

Om vinteren går fine skiløyper rett utenfor døren og vertskapet fyrer opp i peisovnen før gjestene kommer.

Niskinn B&B ist eine charmante Holzblockhütte, die sich sehr schön gelegen am See 'Niskinnvann' befindet. Ein Paradies im Sommer. Die Hühner laufen frei im Garten umher und zum Frühstück gibt es täglich frische Eier.

Im Winter befinden sich die Skiloipen direkt vor der Tür und die Gastgeber feuern den Kaminofen für ihre Gäste an, bevor diese bei ihnen eintreffen.

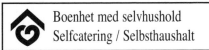
Linda's Place

Your host:
Linda Bouyssou

Address:
Lysgata 13
N - 1482 Nittedal
Phone/mobile: 95 78 61 77
E-mail:
linda.bouyssou@hotmail.com

Best time to call:
16.00 - 23.00
GPS: 60°3'20"N 10°51'44"E

Room/apartment for 2 persons:	Rom/leilighet for 2 personer	Zimmer/Wohnung für 2 Personen
1 bedroom, bath,	1 soverom, bad,	1 Schlafräume, Bad,
kitchen- and dining nook	kjøkken- og spisekrok	Küchen- und Essecke
Price for whole unit: **650,-**	Pris for hele enheten: **650,-**	Ganze Einheit: **650,-**

Bed linen included	Sengetøy inkludert	Inkl. Bettwäsche
Breakfast available on week-ends	Frokost kan serveres i helgene	Frühstück am WE auf Bestellung
Prices valid for 2011/12/13	Priser gyldig for 2011/12/13	Preise gültig für 2011/12/13
Internet available	Internett tilgjengelig	Internet verfügbar
Deck/yard	Uteplass/hage	Außenbereich/Garten
Bike for rent	Sykkelutleie	Fahrrad zu mieten
Pets welcome	Kjæledyr velkommen	Haustiere willkommen
Open year round	Åpent hele året	Ganzjährig geöffnet
English/French/some Spanish spoken		Sprechen etwas Deutsch u. Französt.

A red-painted house on a dead-end street tucked into a corner of the Nordmarka forest. You'll find peace and fresh air on walking trails suitable for winter and summer alike. 300 m to the metro rail which takes you into Oslo in 30 minutes or 10 minutes to one of eastern Norway's best alpine runs.
Linda's background includes many international experiences in the travel industry. She and her family of four welcome guests from near and far for peace and quiet in the nature with access to urban culture and restaurants.

Linda's Place finner du i et rødmalt hus innerst i en blindvei nesten helt i skogkanten av Nordmarka. Her kan du finne roen og frisk luft i nærheten av turløyper sommer som vinter. Det er 300 m til toget som tar deg til Oslo på 30 min. eller til et av Østlandets beste alpinanlegg på 10 min.
Linda har bakgrunn fra reiseliv og flere utenlandsopphold. Hun og familien på fire ønsker gjester velkommen fra både inn- og utland til fred og ro i naturnære omgivelser med kort vei til storbyens kultur- og restaurantliv.

Linda's Place ist ein rot gestrichenes Haus, das am Ende einer Sackgasse am Waldrand der Nordmarka liegt. Hier finden Sie Ruhe und frische Luft mit Wanderwegen und Loipen gleich in der Nähe. 300 m zum Zug, der Sie in 30 min ins Osloer Zentrum oder in 10 min zum besten Alpinskigebiet Ostnorwegens bringt. Linda kommt aus der Tourismusbranche und hat mehrfach im Ausland gelebt. Sie und ihre vierköpfige Familie heißen Gäste aus Nah und Fern willkommen in der ruhigen naturnahen Umgebung, nur einen Katzensprung von der Großstadt mit Kultur und Restaurants entfernt.

Smedstad Gård

Your host:
Randi & Ole Kristian Skallerud

Address:
Gjeriveien 76
N - 2022 Gjerdrum
Phone: 63 99 10 90
E-mail:
smedstad.gaard@online.no
Web: www.smedstadgaard.no

Best time to call:
08.00 - 21.00
GPS: 60°5'7"N 11°4'45"E

Twin room:	**760,-**	Tosengsrom:	**760,-**	Zweibettzimmer:	**760,-**
Single room:	**600,-**	Enkeltrom:	**600,-**	Einzelzimmer:	**600,-**
No. of rooms: 8		Antall rom: 8		Anzahl Zimmer: 8	
Breakfast buffet		Frokost buffét		Frühstücksbüfett	
Prices valid for 2011		Priser gyldig for 2011		Preise gültig für 2011	
TV/Internet available		TV/Internett tilgjengelig		TV/ Internet vorhanden	
Terrace/yard		Terrasse/hage		Terrasse/Garten	
Common smoking room available		Felles røykerom tilgjengelig		Gemeins. Raucherzi. vorhanden	
Phone/fax available		Tilgang på tlf./fax		Tel., Fax verfügbar	
Hot meals: min. 8 persons		Varme måltider: min. 8 personer		Warme Mahlzeiten: min. 8 Pers.	
Open 1 Jan. - 20 Dec.		Åpent 1. jan. - 20. des.		Geöffnet 1. Jan. - 20. Dez.	
English spoken				Sprechen Englisch	

Three generations welcome you to Smedstad Farm which is in the country side, 30 km north of Oslo, and approx. 20 km south of Oslo Airport Gardermoen.
The rooms are in the Main House, where the guests also have a common sitting-room. Eight rooms share two bathrooms. Washbasin with hot/cold water in each room. The farm has livestock which can be experienced at close hand.

Tre generasjoner ønsker velkommen til Smedstad gård som ligger i landlige omgivelser, 3 mil nord for Oslo og ca. 20 km sør for Oslo Lufthavn Gardermoen.
Rommene er i hovedhuset hvor gjestene også har en felles gjestestue. Åtte rom deler to bad, det er vaskeservant med varmt og kaldt vann på alle rom.
Det er dyr på gården som kan oppleves på nært hold.

Der Bauernhof Smedstad liegt in ländlicher Natur, 30 km nördlich von Oslo und etwa 20 km südlich vom Osloer Flughafen Gardermoen. Die drei Generationen des Hofes heißen ihre Gäste herzlich willkommen. Die Zimmer sowie ein gemeinsamer Aufenthaltsraum befinden sich im Haupthaus. 2 Bäder für insgesamt 8 Zimmer, Waschbecken (fl. w. u. k. Wasser) auf allen Zimmern. Bauernhofurlaub mit vielen Tieren zum Entdecken.

Half the fun of the travel is the esthetic of lostness.
~Ray Bradbury~

Room for 2 pers.:	**600,-**	Rom for 2 pers.:	**600,-**	Zimmer für 2 Pers.:	**600,-**
Room for 1 pers.:	**520,-**	Rom for 1 pers.:	**520,-**	Zimmer für 1 Pers.:	**520,-**

Shared bath, kitchen, DR and LR
Bed linen included
Prices valid for 2011
TV available
Yard/terrace/patio
Common smoking room available
Open 1 Jan. - 20 Dec.
English spoken

Delt bad, kjøkken, spisestue, stue
Sengetøy er inkludert
Priser gyldig for 2011
TV tilgjengelig
Hage/terrasse/uteplass
Felles røykerom
Åpent 1. jan. - 20. des.

Gem. Bad, Küche, Esszi.u. Stube
Inkl. Bettwäsche
Preise gültig für 2011
TV vorhanden
Garten/Terrasse/Außenbereich
Gemeins. Raucherzi. vorhanden
Geöffnet 1. Jan. - 20. Dez.
Sprechen Englisch

Close by the farm you have Romeriksåsen which has some lovely walks, cycle paths, fishing and swimming. In the winter there is a lit Nordic skiing circuit and downhill skiing. 18-hole golf course recently completed - 5 km from farm.

I nærheten av gården ligger Romeriksåsen med fine turstier for fotturer og sykkelturer, fiskemuligheter og badevann. På vinteren er det lysløype og alpin-bakke. 5 km unna ligger en nylig anlagt 18-hulls golfbane.

In der Nähe der Unterkunft liegt das Gebiet Romeriksåsen, wo man Wanderen, Radfahren, Angeln und Baden kann. Im Winter Flutlichtloipe und Alpinanlage. 5 km entfernt befindet sich ein neu angelegter 18-Loch-Golfplatz.

Directions:
From Oslo: Take E-6 north towards Hamar/Trondheim. Exit in Skedsmokorset and then take RV 120 towards Nannestad and Gjerdrum until you reach Ask. Turn right towards Kløfta and the Gjerdrum church. Look for a sign marked 'Smedstad Gård' about 3 km from Ask on the left-hand side.

From Hamar or Oslo Airport:
Follow E-6 towards Oslo and exit towards Kløfta. Turn right in the roundabout and continue towards Kløfta town center. Drive straight ahead through two roundabouts and stay on this road until it ends. Then turn left towards Ask and drive for about 1 km. Look for the sign for Smedstad Gård on the right side of the road.

Veibeskrivelse:
Fra Oslo: Følg E-6 nordover i retning Hamar/Trondheim. Ta av i Skedsmokorset og følg RV 120 mot Nannestad og Gjerdrum helt til du kommer til Ask. Ta til høyre mot Kløfta og Gjerdrum kirke. Ca. 3 km fra Ask finner du skiltet "Smedstad Gård" inn til venstre.

Fra Hamar eller Oslo lufthavn:
Følg E-6 i retning Oslo og ta av mot Kløfta, ta til høyre i rundkjøringen og fortsett mot Kløfta sentrum. Kjør rett fram i to rundkjøringer og følg denne veien helt til enden. Ta så til venstre mot Ask og etter ca. 1 km vil du se skiltet med Smedstad Gård på høyre side av veien.

Wegbeschreibung:
Ab Oslo: Folgen Sie der E-6 in Richtung Norden (Hamar/Trondheim). Bei Skedsmokorset biegen Sie ab auf die Str.120 in Richtung Nannestad und Gjerdrum. Im Ort Ask geht es rechts nach Kløfta bzw. Gjerdrum kirke. 3 km nach Ask links dem Schild 'Smedstad Gård' folgen.

Aus Richtung Hamar oder Flughafen Oslo: Folgen Sie der E-6 in Richtung Oslo und fahren Sie dann bei Kløfta ab. Im Kreisverkehr zweigen Sie nach rechts in Richtung Kløfta Zentrum ab. Halten Sie sich die nächsten zwei Kreisverkehre geradeaus und folgen Sie der Straße ganz bis zum Ende. Dort geht es nach links in Richtung Ask, nach ca. 1 km sehen Sie das Schild 'Smedstad Gård' auf der rechten Straßenseite.

Gardermoen Hotel Bed & Breakfast

Address:
Gardermoveien 42
N - 2030 Nannestad
Phone: 63 93 00 50
E-mail: hotel@gardermoenbb.no
Web: www.gardermoenbb.no

Best time to call:
08.00 - 23.00
GPS: 60°12'39"N 11°4'32"E

Double-/twin room:	**845,-**	Dobbelt-/tosengsrom:	**845,-**	Doppel-/Zweibettzi.:	**845,-**
Single room:	**745,-**	Enkeltrom:	**745,-**	Einzelzimmer:	**745,-**
Family room:	**1200,-**	Familierom:	**1200,-**	Familienzimmer:	**1200,-**
No. of rooms: 42		Antall rom: 42		Anzahl Zimmer: 42	
Breakfast buffet		Frokostbuffét		Frühstücksbüfett	
Prices valid for 2011/12		Priser gyldig for 2011/12		Preise gültig für 2011/12	
TV/Internet available		TV/Internett tilgjengelig		TV/Internet vorhanden	
Patio/yard		Uteplass/hage		Außenbereich/Garten	
Pets welcome		Kjæledyr velkommen		Haustiere willkommen	
VISA, MC, DC, AmEx accepted		Vi tar VISA, MC, DC, AmEx		VISA, MC, DC, AmEx	
Open year round		Åpent hele året		Ganzjährig geöffnet	
English spoken				Sprechen Deutsch	

A small homey hotel next to Oslo Airport Gardermoen. Guests can be picked up when arriving by plane, train or bus, and delivered back to the airport. Long-term parking available.

Directions:
E-6 exit to Gardermoen, take RV 35 toward Nannested to the 'Nannestad' community sign. In the round-about right after the sign turn right. (The round-about is called Vigsteinkrysset.) A few meters up you'll see the sign for Gardermoen Hotel Bed & Breakfast.

Et hjemmetrivelig hotell like ved Oslo Lufthavn Gardermoen. Gjester kan bli hentet ved ankomst med fly, tog eller buss og kan bli kjørt tilbake til flyplassen. Tilbyr også langtidsparkering.

Veibeskrivelse:
E-6: ta av mot Gardermoen, ta RV 35 mot Nannestad, kjør denne inntil kommuneskilt Nannestad. I rundkjøringen rett etter skiltet ta til høyre. (Rundkjøringen heter Vigsteinkrysset.) Noen meter lenger opp ser du skiltet Gardermoen Hotell Bed & Breakfast.

Gardermoen B&B ist ein gemütliches Hotel direkt in der Nähe des Osloer Flughafens Gardermoen. Als Gast können Sie nach Ihrer Ankunft mit Flug, Bus oder Bahn abgeholt und für die Rückreise zum Flugahfen gefahren werden. Auch Langzeitparken möglich.

Wegbeschreibung:
E-6 Ri. Gardermoen abfahren, dann Ri. Nannestad auf die Str. 35. Dieser bis zum Ortsschild Nannestad folgen. Direkt dahinter im Kreisverkehr "Vigsteinkrysset" nach rechts fahren. Kurz darauf sehen Sie das Schild Gardermoen Hotel Bed & Breakfast.

Styri Gård

Your host:
Jo Holdhus

Address:
Nesveien 17
N - 2080 Eidsvoll
Mobile: **90 91 00 48**
E-mail: **mullahjo@yahoo.com**

Best time to call:
10.00 - 24.00
GPS: 60°19'4"N 11°17'6"E

Twin room:	**600,-**	Tosengsrom:	**600,-**	Zweibettzimmer:	**600,-**
Single room:	**350,-**	Enkeltrom:	**350,-**	Einzelzimmer:	**350,-**
No. of rooms: 8		Antall rom: 8		Anzahl Zimmer: 8	
Breakfast; self-service		Frokost; selvbetjening		Frühstück: Selbstbedienung	
Selfcatering possible		Selvhushold er mulig		Selbstverpflegung möglich	
Prices valid for 2011/12		Priser gyldig for 2011/12		Preise gültig für 2011/12	
TV/Internet available		TV/Internett tilgjengelig		TV/Internet vorhanden	
Terrace/deck/yard		Terrasse/uteplass/hage		Terrasse/Außenbereich/Garten	
Boat and bike for rent		Båt- og sykkelutleie		Boot und Fahrrad zu mieten	
Pets welcome		Kjæledyr velkommen		Haustiere willkommen	
Open year round		Åpent hele året		Ganzjährig geöffnet	
English and some French spoken				Sprechen Englisch	

At Styri Gård eco-friendly horticulture is the rule. The animals on the farm include two cats and three dogs. The main building dates from the early 1800s and was remodelled to Swiss chalet style around 1880. From the beginning the farm was a social gathering place for eastern Eidsvoll. The author Henrik Wergeland was a frequent guest.

Directions:
Along E-6 take exit RV 181 toward Eidsvoll (not Eidsvoll Verk). Cross the bridge over Volma River continuing through the first roundabout, then at 2nd roundabout turn right on RV 177. After another 2.5 km, Styri is first farm on the right.

På Styri Gård drives det økologisk planteproduksjon. Dyrene på gården teller to katter og tre hunder. Hovedbygningen er fra tidlig på 1800-tallet og ombygd til Sveitserstil ca. 1880. Gården var fra tidlige tider et sosialt samlingspunkt for det østre området av Eidsvoll. Henrik Wergeland var en hyppig gjest her og skrev Styrivisa herfra.

Veibeskrivelse:
Fra E-6 ta RV 181 mot Eidsvoll, (ikke Eidsvoll Verk). Etter brua over Vorma (elv) kjører du rett fram i første rundkjøring og til høyre i andre rundkjøring. Du er nå på RV 177 og etter 2,5 km ser du gården, den første gården på høyre side.

Auf dem Styri Hof wird ökologisch Gemüse angebaut. Zu den Tieren auf dem Hof zählen 2 Katzen und 3 Hunde. Das Hauptgebäude ist aus dem frühen 19. Jh. und wurde um ca. 1880 im Schweizerstil umgebaut. Schon seit jeher ist der Styri Hof ein Treffpunkt in der östlichen Gegend Eidsvolls. Henrik Wergeland war ein häufiger Gast und schrieb hier sein Werk "Styrivisa".

Wegbeschreibung:
Von der E-6 die Str. 181 Ri. Eidsvoll (nicht Eidsvoll Værk). Hinter der Brücke über den Fluss Vorma im 1. Kreisverkehr geradeaus und im 2. nach rechts auf die Str. 177 ausfahren. Nach 2,5km ist es der erste Hof auf der rechten Seite.

Bjerknes Gård

Your host:
Ingeborg Ree & Jon Wenger

Address:
Bjerknes Gård
N - 2092 Minnesund
Phone: 63 96 80 20
Mobile: 92 40 21 60
E-mail: jon@wenger.no
Web: www.bjerknes-bb.no

Best time to call:
08.00 - 21.00
GPS: 60°23'25"N 11°14'33"E

Double-/twin room:	**550,-**	Dobbelt-/tosengsrom:	**550,-**	Doppel-/Zweibettzi.:	**550,-**
Single room:	**350,-**	Enkeltrom:	**350,-**	Einzelzimmer:	**350,-**
No. of rooms: 4		Antall rom: 4		Anzahl Zimmer: 4	
Discount for children		Rabatt for barn		Ermäßigung für Kinder	
Breakfast tray		Frokostbrett		Frühstückstablett	
Selfcatering possible		Selvhushold er mulig		Selbstverpflegung möglich	
Prices valid for 2011/12/13		Priser gyldig for 2011/12/13		Preise gültig für 2011/12/13	
TV/Internet available		TV/Internett tilgjengelig		TV/Internet vorhanden	
Terrace/patio/yard		Terrasse/uteplass/hage		Terrasse/Außenbereich/Garten	
Boat for rent		Båtutleie		Boot zu mieten	
Bike for rent		Sykkelutleie		Fahrrad zu mieten	
Open year round		Åpent hele året		Ganzjährig geöffnet	
English spoken				Sprechen etwas Deutsch	

At Bjerknes Gård guests will be received by the hosts Ingeborg and Jon. The farm is located at the far south end of Mjøsa Lake. 10 km away is 'Riksbygningen' which is very famous for historic events when the Constitution was signed in 1814. The oldest steamboat in the world, Skibladner, also called the swan of Mjøsa, is plying by three times per week.
The area offers inviting forest-walks. Two old mines are within reach. The farm is 35 km/30 min. from Oslo Airport Gardermoen.

På Bjerknes gård er det vertskapet Ingeborg og Jon som tar imot gjestene. Gården ligger i søndre ende av Mjøsa og 10 km fra Riks-bygningen som er så kjent for hendelsene i 1814 da Grunnloven ble undertegnet. Verdens eldste hjul-damper, Skibladner, som også blir kalt Mjøsas svane, passerer tre ganger pr. uke.
Området er fint til skogsturer, to gamle gruver er innen rekkevidde. Stedet ligger ca. 35 km/30 min. fra Oslo Flyhavn Gardermoen.

Auf dem Hof Bjerknes erwarten Ingeborg und Jon ihre Gäste. Der Hof befindet sich am südlichen Ende des Mjøsa-Sees, 10 km vom Reichsgebäude entfernt, in dem 1814 das norwegische Grundgesetz formuliert und unterzeichnet wur-de. Auf dem Mjøsa verkehrt noch heute dreimal pro Woche der ältes-te Raddampfer der Welt, der Ski-bladner (auch „weißer Schwan des Mjøsa" genannt).
Die Gegend eignet sich gut zum Wandern, außerdem sind zwei sehenswerte alte Gruben in Reich-weite. Der Bjerknes Hof liegt ca. 35 km/30 min. vom Osloer Flug-hafen Gardermoen entfernt.

Ullershov Gård

Your host:
Inger Marie Ødegaard

Address:
Ullershovvegen 45
N - 2160 Vormsund
Phone: 63 90 27 40
Mobile: 95 04 42 41
E-mail: ullerhov@online.no
Web: www.ullershov.no

Best time to call:
08.00 - 23.00
GPS: 60°9'26"N 11°27'9"E

Double room:	900,-	Dobbeltrom:	900,-	Doppelzimmer:	900,-
Single room:	450,-	Enkeltrom:	450,-	Einzelzimmer:	450,-

No. of rooms: 20
Discount for children
Laid breakfast table
Prices valid for 2011
TV/Internet available
Terrace/patio/yard
Boat and bike for rent
Pets welcome by agreement
Open year round
English spoken

Antall rom: 20
Rabatt for barn
Dekket frokostbord
Priser gyldig for 2011
TV/Internett tilgjengelig
Terrasse/uteplass/hage
Båt- og sykkelutleie
Kjæledyr velkommen etter avtale
Åpent hele året

Anzahl Zimmer: 20
Ermäßigung für Kinder
Gedeckt. Frühstückstisch
Preise gültig für 2011
TV/Internet verfügbar
Terrasse/Außenbereich/Garten
Boot u. Fahrrad zu mieten
Haustiere nach Absprache willk.
Ganzjährig geöffnet
Sprechen Deutsch

Ullershov farm lies at the point where the Vorma and Glomma rivers meet. A farm in continuous use since 600 A.D., it has been an administrative and religious center, counsil meeting place and the site of worship and sacrifices to the Norse god Ullr. The farm today boasts 15 buildings, mostly from the period 1725-1923. In the main building you'll find a big collection of textiles and folk costumes with women's clothes and accessories from childhood to granny-hood. Farm store on premises.

Ullershov gård ligger på neset der elvene Vorma og Glomma møtes. Gården har vært fast bosted siden år 600 og har vært et administrativt og religiøst senter, tingsted og kult- og offersted for den norrøne guden Ullr. Gården har i dag 15 bygninger, de fleste fra perioden 1725 - 1923. I hovedbygningen finner du en stor tekstil- og drakthistorisk samling med kvinners klær og utstyr fra barndom til alderdom. Gårdsbutikk.

Der Hof Ullershov liegt an der Landzunge der Flüsse Vorma u. Glomma, die sich hier treffen. Der Hof wird seit dem Jahre 600 fest bewohnt und war ein administratives und religöses Zentrum, Richtplatz sowie Kult- und Opferstätte für den altnordischen Gott Ullr. Zum Hof gehören heute 15 Gebäude, die meisten aus der Periode von 1725-1923. Im Haupthaus befindet sich eine große historische Textil- und Trachtensammlung von Frauenkleidung sowie Ausstattungsgegenständen von Jung und Alt. Ein Hofladen ist ebenfalls vorhanden.

Heggelund's rom og frokost

Your host:
Berit & Lars Petter Heggelund

Address:
Negardssvingen 3
N - 2270 Flisa
Mobile: 91 19 15 59
E-mail: berit@negarden.no
Web: www.negarden.no

Best time to call:
08.00 - 20.00
GPS: 60°36'48"N 12°00'34"E

Double-/twin room: **700,-/800,-**	Dobbelt-/tosengsrom: **700,-/800,-**	Doppel-/Zweibettzi.: **700,-/800,-**
1 pers. in dbl room: **450,-/650,-**	En pers. i dobbeltrom: **450,-/650,-**	1 Pers. im Doppelzi.: **450,-/650,-**
No. of rooms: 3	Antall rom: 3	Anzahl Zimmer: 3
Laid breakfast table	Dekket frokostbord	Gedeckter Frühstückstisch
Prices valid for 2011/12	Priser gyldig for 2011/12	Preise gültig für 2011/12
TV/Internet available	TV/Internett tilgjengelig	TV/Internet vorhanden
Terrace/patio/yard	Terrasse/uteplass/hage	Terrasse/Außenbereich/Garten
Open year round	Åpent hele året	Ganzjährig geöffnet
English and some French spoken		Sprechen etwas Deutsch

Berit and Lars Petter bid you welcome to their newly restored Swiss villa from the early 1900s in a large garden at Flisa, between Kongsvinger and Elverum. They are determined to preserve the house's uniqueness and style, and the dining room is all original. Excellent opportunities for hiking tours, including nearby Finnskogen woods. If desired and weather permitting, breakfast may be served on the terrace or in the garden.

I en stor hage på Flisa, mellom Kongsvinger og Elverum, ønsker vertskapet Berit og Lars Petter deg velkommen til sin nyrestaurerte sveitservilla fra århundreskiftet. De har satset på å bevare husets stil og særpreg, og spisestua er helt uendret.
Det er fine muligheter for turgåing med blant annet Finnskogen i nærheten.
Om ønskelig og om været tillater det, kan frokosten serveres på terrassen eller i hagen.

In Flisa, zwischen Kongsvinger und Elverum, heißen Sie die Gastgeber Berit und Lars Petter in ihrer frisch renovierten Villa im Schweizer Stil aus der Jahrhundertwende willkommen. Das Ehepaar hat es verstanden, den besonderen Stil des Hauses zu bewahren, so ist z.B. das Esszimmer nahezu unverändert geblieben.
Die Region bietet mit dem in der Nähe liegenden Waldgebiet Finnskogen sehr gute Wandermöglichkeiten. Nach Absprache und wenn das Wetter es zulässt, kann das Frühstück auch im Garten oder auf der Terrasse serviert werden.

Like all great travellers, I have seen more than I remember, and remember more than I have seen.
~Benjamin Disraeli~

Solvår's Bed & Breakfast

Your host:
Solvår & Jan Viggo Oppegård

Address:
Barbra Ringsvei 14
N - 2407 Elverum
Phone: 62 41 49 48
Mobile: 99 61 20 26
elverumbedandbreakfast@gmail.com
Web: www.elverumbb.com
Best time to call: 08.00 - 23.00
GPS: 60°51'39"N 11°34'31"E

Double room:	**600,-**	Dobbeltrom:	**600,-**	Doppelzimmer:	**600,-**
Single room:	**450,-**	Enkeltrom:	**450,-**	Einzelzimmer:	**450,-**

No. of rooms: 2	Antall rom: 2	Anzahl Zimmer: 2
Discount for children	Rabatt for barn	Ermäßigung für Kinder
Laid breakfast table	Dekket frokostbord	Gedeckter Frühstückstisch
Selfcatering possible	Selvhushold mulig	Selbstverpflegung möglich
Prices valid for 2011/12	Priser gyldig for 2011/12	Preise gültig für 2011/12
TV available	TV tilgjengelig	TV vorhanden
Terrace/patio/yard	Terrasse/uteplass/hage	Terrasse/Außenbereich/Garten
Bike available	Sykkel kan lånes	Fahrrad verfügbar
Pets welcome	Kjæledyr velkommen	Haustiere willkommen
Open year round	Åpent hele året	Ganzjährig geöffnet
English, some French & some Greek spoken		Sprechen etwas Deutsch

Rentals include a double room and a large family room (up to 6 persons). In Elverum, Solvår's Bed & Breakfast is within walking distance of the Forestry Museum and Glomdal Museum. Behind the property lies a forest area with good hiking terrain. The rooms are in the host's own home. A hosthome well known for good homemade breakfast.

Directions:
Follow RV 20 towards Kongsvinger. Look for a sign marked B&B 1 km after passing Norsk Skogmuseum and proceed to follow the sign.

Det leies ut et dobbeltrom, og et stort familierom (opptil 6 personer). Solvårs Bed & Breakfast ligger i Elverum med gangavstand til Norsk Skogmuseum og Glomdalsmuseet. Bak eiendommen ligger skogen med turterreng. Utleierommene er i vertskapets egen bolig. Stedet er kjent for god hjemmelaget frokost.

Veibeskrivelse:
Følg RV 20 mot Kongsvinger. 1 km etter at du har passert Norsk Skogmuseum; se etter B&B-skilt, følg skilt videre.

Es stehen ein DZ und ein großes FZ für bis zu 6 Pers. zur Verfügung. Solvårs Bed & Breakfast liegt in Elverum, in Reichweite des Forstwirtschafts- und des Glomdalsmuseums. Wandermöglichkeiten im Wald hinterm Haus. Die zu vermietenden Räume befinden sich im eigenen Wohnhaus der Wirtsleute. Bekannt für gutes hausgemachtes Frühstück.

Wegbeschreibung:
Folgen Sie der Straße 20 in Richtg. Kongsvinger. 1 km hinter dem Norsk Skogmuseum auf das B&B-Schild achten und diesem folgen.

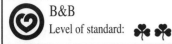
Solbakken Gjestegård

Your host:
Karen & Rolf Rønnekleiv

Address:
Fangbergsveien 99
N - 2380 Brumunddal
Phone: 62 35 55 43
Mobile: 47 02 75 61
E-mail: roennek@online.no
Web: http://roennek.home.online.no
Best time to call: 15.00 - 23.00
GPS: 60°53'53"N 10°52'34"E

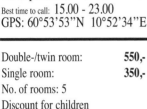

Double-/twin room:	550,-	Dobbelt-/tosengsrom:	550,-	Doppel-/Zweibettzi.:	550,-
Single room:	350,-	Enkeltrom:	350,-	Einzelzimmer:	350,-
No. of rooms: 5		Antall rom: 5		Anzahl Zimmer: 5	
Discount for children		Rabatt for barn		Ermäßigung für Kinder	
Laid breakfast table		Dekket frokostbord		Gedeckter Frühstückstisch	
Selfcatering possible		Selvhushold er mulig		Selbstverpflegung möglich	
Prices valid for 2011/12		Priser gyldig for 2011/12		Preise gültig für 2011/12	
TV available		TV tilgjengelig		TV vorhanden	
Terrace/yard		Terrasse/hage		Terrasse/Garten	
Open 1 April - 15 October		Åpent 1. april - 15. oktober		Geöffnet 1. April - 15. Oktober	
English spoken				Sprechen Deutsch	

Solbakken Guest House was once a pension. The Guest House is beautifully situated at Veldre in Ringsaker Municipality, 3 km from highway E-6 and 5 km from Brumunddal railway station. The poet Alf Prøysen's childhood home is only 6 km. away. Close by is a beach for swimming. Ringsaker Mountain and Sjusjøen ski slopes and hiking terrain are 30-40 minutes away by car.

Solbakken gjestegård har tidligere vært drevet som pensjonat. Gjestegården ligger idyllisk til i Veldre i Ringsaker kommune, 3 km fra E-6 og 5 km fra Brumunddal jernbanestasjon. Alf Prøysens barndomshjem, Prøysenstua, er bare 6 km unna. Det er kort vei til badestrand. Ringsakerfjellet og Sjusjøen, flott ski- og turterreng, kan man nå på 30-40 min. med bil.

Solbakken gjestegård wurde früher als Pension betrieben. Das Haus liegt idyllisch in Veldre bei Ringsaker, 3 km von der E-6 und 5 km vom Bahnhof Brumunddal entfernt. Bis zum Elternhaus des norwegischen Poeten Alf Prøysen sind es 6 km. Unweit zum Badestrand. 30-40 min Autofahrt zu den Bergen von Ringsaker und Sjusjøen mit herrlichem Wander- und Skigelände.

The traveler sees what he sees. The tourist sees what he has come to see.
~G.K. Chesterton~

We wander for distraction, but we travel for fulfillment.
~Hilaire Belloc~

Kvebergsøya Gard

Your host:
Eris Davids &
Martin Kjønsberg

Address:
Grimsbu
N - 2580 Folldal
Phone: 62 49 03 33
Mobile: 41 61 39 41 / 95 24 15 71
E-mail: post@kvebergsoeya.com
Web: www.kvebergsoeya.com

Best time to call:
09.00 - 22.00
GPS: 62°8'54"N 10°10'41"E

Double/twin room:	**960,-**	Dobbelt-/tosengsrom:	**960,-**	Doppel-/Zweibettzi.:	**960,-**
4-bed room:	**1260,-**	4-sengsrom:	**1260,-**	4-Bettzimmer:	**1260,-**
Single room:	**550,-**	Enkeltrom:	**550,-**	Einzelzimmer:	**550,-**
No. of rooms: 4		Antall rom: 4		Anzahl Zimmer: 4	
Laid breakfast table		Dekket frokostbord		Gedeckter Frühstückstisch	

Cabin "Eldhus"		Hytte "Eldhus"		Hütte "Eldhus"	
3 beds, bath, kitchenette		3 senger, bad, kjk.krok		3 Betten, Bad, Küchenecke	
Price for whole unit:	**800,-**	Pris for hele enhet:	**800,-**	Preis für ganze Einheit:	**800,-**

Discount for children	Rabatt for barn	Ermäßigung für Kinder
Prices valid for 2011/12	Priser gyldig for 2011/12	Preise gültig für 2011/12
TV/Internet available	TV/Internett tilgjengelig	TV/Internet vorhanden
Terrace/deck/yard	Terrasse/uteplass/hage	Terrasse/Außenbereich/Garten
Boat, canoe, bike for rent nearby	Båt-, kano-, sykkelutleie i nærheten	Boot/Kanu/Fahrradvermietung nah
Horseback and horse-wagon riding, sleighing	Rideturer/kjøring med hest og vogn, kanefart	Reittouren, Kutsch-/Schlittenfahrten
Pets welcome	Kjæledyr velkommen	Haustiere willkommen
Open year round	Åpent hele året	Ganzjährig geöffnet
English spoken		Sprechen Deutsch

Kvebergsøya is an old farm with roots back to the 1600's situated near Rondane national park and the touristroads 27 and 29, ca. 100 km from Røros. The hosts offer a unique atmosphere, where one can feel the "soul" and peace of times past in the old buildings. Norwegian farm style breakfast and dinner, made from local ingredients. Enjoy nature's tranquillity and life on the farm with horses, sheep and lambs.

Kvebergsøya er en gammel gard med røtter tilbake til 1600-tallet med beliggenhet ved Rondane nasjonalpark og turistvei RV 27 og 29 og ca. 100 km fra Røros. Vertskapet tilbyr et unikt miljø, der en i de gamle husene føler stemning, "sjel" og ro fra gamle dager. Norsk bondekost til frokost og middag, laget av råvarer fra regionen. Spesielt tilbud i advent- og juletider. Nyt naturen og livet på garden med hester, sauer og lam.

Kvebergsøya ist ein alter Holf mit Ursprung im 17.Jh. in der Nähe des Rondane Nationalparks u. der Touristenstr. RV 27 u. 29, ca. 100 km v. Røros. Die Gastgeber bieten ein besonderes Ambiente und das Gefühl ein "lebendes Museum" und die alten Zeiten zu erleben. Frühstück, traditionelles warmes Abendessen aus der norwegischen Küche und Rohwaren der Region. Natur u. Leben auf dem Bauernhof mit Lämmern, Schafen, Pferden.

Kronviksætra
Bed & Breakfast

Your host:
Geir Raaum &
Marianne Olaisen
Address: Landåsveien 949
N - 2861 Landåsbygda
Phone: 61 12 68 85
Mobile: 92 68 88 50
E-mail: post@kronviksetra.com
Web: www.kronviksetra.com
Best time to call: 17.00 - 23.00
GPS: 60°49'31"N 10°20'33"E

Double-/twin room:	650,-	Dobbelt-/tosengsrom:	650,-	Doppel-/Zweibettzi.:	650,-
Single room:	400,-	Enkeltrom:	400,-	Einzelzimmer:	400,-
No. of rooms: 5		Antall rom: 5		Anzahl Zimmer: 5	
Laid breakfast table		Dekket frokostbord		Gedeckter Frühstückstisch	
Selfcatering possible		Selvhushold er mulig		Selbstverpflegung möglich	
Prices valid for 2011/12/13		Priser gyldig for 2011/12/13		Preise gültig für 2011/12/13	
TV/Internet available		TV/Internett tilgjengelig		TV/Internet vorhanden	
Terrace/patio		Terrasse/uteplass		Terrasse/Außenbereich	
Boat and bike for rent		Båt- og sykkelutleie		Boot u. Fahrrad zu mieten	
Open year round		Åpent hele året		Ganzjährig geöffnet	
Some English spoken				Sprechen etwas Deutsch	

Kronviksætra lies quietly situated 20 km west of Gjøvik. There is a view over Landås Lake, hiking, swimming or fishing. For winter sports enthusiasts: crosscountry ski trails.
Kronviksætra was originally built as a boarding house in 1936. It is now fully renovated in its original style with the atmosphere still intact. Charming wood stoves in the rooms. Cozy living room, fireplace and TV. This farm features dogs.

Directions:
From Gjøvik: follow RV 33 towards Fagernes/Dokka 14 km. Exit in direction Kronviksætra/ Landåsbygda and drive 6 km on road 132. Follow posted signs.

Kronviksætra ligger landlig og fredelig til 20 km vest for Gjøvik. Det er fin utsikt ned til Landåsvannet med bade- og fiskemuligheter. For vintersportsinteresserte har Landåsbygda lysløype og flott turterreng.
Kronviksætra ble bygd i 1936 som pensjonat, nå restaurert, hvor stil og atmosfære er bevart. Gamle vedovner i alle rom. Peisestue og TV-stue disponible for gjester. Det er hunder på gården.

Veibeskrivelse:
Fra Gjøvik; følg RV 33 mot Fagernes/Dokka 14 km. Ta av mot Kronviksætra/Landåsbygda på fylkesvei 132, følg denne 6 km. Det er skiltet helt frem.

Kronviksætra liegt ländlich und ruhig, 20 km westl. von Gjøvik. Herrliche Aussicht auf den See Landåsvann mit Bade- und Angelmöglichkeiten. Schönes Gelände zum Skiwandern mit Flutlichtloipe. Kronviksætra wurde 1936 als Pension gebaut, nun modernisiert, aber Stil und Atmosphäre wurden bewahrt. Kamin- und TV-Stube für Gäste. Auf dem Hof gibt es Hunde.

Wegbeschreibung:
Von Gjøvik: der Str. 33 Ri. Fagernes/Dokka auf 14 km folgen, dann abbiegen auf Str. 132 Ri. Kronviksætra/Landåsbygda. Etwa 6 km weiter auf dieser Straße. Der Hof ist ausgeschildert.

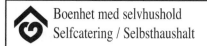
Øvergaard

Your host:
Egil Sorgendal & Åse Skarbø

Address:
Jernbanegaten 24
N - 2609 Lillehammer
Phone: 61 25 99 99
Mobile: 92 61 47 00 / 92 22 28 93
E-mail: oevergaard@gmail.com
Web:
http://oevergaard.com
Best time to call:
10.00 - 22.00
GPS: 61°6'57"N 10°28'15"E

Double room: from **600,-** to **700,-**	Dobbeltrom: fra **600,-** til **700,-**	Doppelzimmer: von **600,-** bis **700,-**
Single room: from **350,-** to **400,-**	Enkeltrom: fra **350,-** til **400,-**	Einzelzimmer: von **350,-** bis **400,-**
No. of rooms: 4	Antall rom: 4	Anzahl Zimmer: 4
The rooms share kitchen and LR	Rommene deler kjøkken og stue	Zimmer teilen Küche und Wohnzi.
Prices valid for 2011	Priser gyldig for 2011	Preise gültig für 2011
TV/Internet available	TV/Internett tilgjengelig	TV/Internet verfügbar
Discount for fam. and longer stay	Rabatt: fam. og ved lengre opphold	Ermäß. f. Familien u. Langzeitaufenth.
Patio/yard	Uteplass	Außenbereich
Open year round	Åpent hele året	Ganzjährig geöffnet
English spoken		Sprechen Deutsch

Øvergaard features a tastefully renovated, luxurious farmhouse dating from around 1850 and is located in quiet and peaceful surroundings in the middle of the town center. It is a 2 min. walk to the pedestrian-only shopping street. Good parking facilities. The property has shielded and roomy area for play and recreation. Lillehammer is popular and tourist attractions includes: "Maihaugen", an open-air museum and craftshop museum, the old steamboat, "Skibladner", touring on Mjøsa Lake. For skiing enthusiasts Olympic City '94 has an enviable assortment of lit tracks for both Nordic and alpine skiing.

Øvergaard med deres restaurerte herskapelige gårdsbygning fra 1850-tallet ligger i stille og rolige omgivelser midt i sentrum av byen. Det er 2 min. gangavstand til gågaten. Gode parkeringsmuligheter. Eiendommen har romslig og skjermet uteområde for lek og opphold.
Lillehammer er en typisk turistby med mange og varierte turistattraksjoner; Maihaugen med friluftsmuseum og De Sandvigske Samlinger. Skibladner, den gamle dampbåten, går i turisttrafikk på Mjøsa. OL-byen er godt utstyrt med lysløyper og slalåmbakker.

Der Hof Øvergaard mit seinem restaurierten herrschaftlichen Wohnhaus aus den1850ern liegt im Zentrum der Stadt in ruhiger und friedlicher Umgebung. In nur 2 Minuten gelangt man in die Fußgängerzone. Gute Parkmöglichkeiten. Zum Haus gehört ein weitläufiges abgeschirmtes Grundstück, das zum Spielen oder Verweilen einlädt.
Lillehammer ist ein typischer Touristenort mit vielerlei Angeboten: das Maihaugen Freilichtmuseum, die Sandvigschen Sammlungen etc. Das alte Dampfschiff Skibladner verkehrt im Sommer auf dem Mjøsa-See. Für Wintersportler bietet die Olympia-Stadt Flutlichtloipen und Alpinpisten.

Lillehammer Vandrerhjem

Address:
Jernbarnetorvet 2
N - 2609 Lillehammer
Phone: 61 26 00 24
E-mail: post@stasjonen.no
Web: www.stasjonen.no

Best time to call:
07.00 - 22.00
GPS: 61°6'53"N 10°27'42"E

Double room:	from **950,-**	Dobbeltrom:	fra **950,-**	Doppelzimmer:	ab **950,-**
Single room:	from **695,-**	Enkeltrom:	fra **695,-**	Einzelzimmer:	ab **695,-**
3-bedded room:	from **1080,-**	3-sengsrom:	fra **1080,-**	3-Bettzimmer:	ab **1080,-**
4-bedded room:	from **1190,-**	4-sengsrom:	fra **1190,-**	4-Bettzimmer:	ab **1190,-**
Bed in multibedded r.:	from **330,-**	Seng i flersengsrom:	fra **330,-**	Bett in Mehrbettzi.:	ab **330,-**
No. of rooms: 28		Antall rom: 28		Anzahl Zimmer: 28	
Breakfast buffet		Frokostbuffét		Frühstücksbüfett	
Selfcatering possible		Selvhushold er mulig		Selbstverpflegung möglich	
Prices valid for 2011/12/13		Priser gyldig for 2011/12/13		Preise gültig für 2011/12/13	
Discount for members HI hostels		Rabatt ved medlemskap HI hostels		Rabatt für HI-hostels-Mitglieder	
Kitchen available		Kjøkken tilgjengelig		Küchenbenutzung möglich	
TV/Internet available		TV/Internett tilgjengelig		TV/Internet vorhanden	
Pets welcome		Kjæledyr velkommen		Haustiere willkommen	
VISA, MC, DC, AmEx accepted		Vi tar VISA, MC, DC, AmEx		Wir akzept. VISA, MC, DC, AmEx	
Open year round		Åpent hele året		Ganzjährig geöffnet	
English spoken				Sprechen etwas Deutsch	

You'll find Lillehammer Vandrerhjem hostel upstairs at the Lillehammer train station. You can go right from the train to your room. Centrally located only 100 m from the walking street. The bus to Hunderfossen is just outside the door. The hostel sells tickets to the famous Maihaugen outdoor folkmuseum, Lilleputthammer, Hunderfossen, Bjerkebæk, the OL Olympics Museum and Aulestad.

Du finner Lillehammer Vandrerhjem, Stasjonen i 2. etasje på Lillehammer jernbanestasjon. Du kan gå rett fra toget og inn på rommet ditt.
Sentralt beliggende bare 100 m fra gågaten. Buss til Hunderfossen like utenfor døra. Vandrerhjemmet selger billetter til Maihaugen, Lilleputthammer, Hunderfossen, Bjerkebæk, OL-museet og Aulestad.

Sie finden das Lillehammer Vandrerhjem im 1. Stock des Lillehammer Bahnhofs. Erreichen Sie Lillehammer mit dem Zug, können Sie unmittelbar nach der Ankunft hinauf zu Ihrem Zimmer gehen. Das Vandrerhjem ist zentral gelegen, nur 100 m von der Fußgängerzone entfernt. Bus nach Hunderfossen fährt direkt vor der Tür. Das Vandrerhjem verkauft Karten für das Maihaugen Freiclichtmuseum, Lilleputthammer, Hunderfossen, Bjerkebæk, das Olympia-Museum und Aulestad.

Skåden Gård

Your host:
Anne Marie & Trond Skåden

Address:
Skåden Gård
N - 2636 Øyer
Phone: 61 27 81 60
Mobile: 97 65 93 01
E-mail: am-skaad@frisurf.no
Web: www.skaaden-gaard.no

Best time to call:
08.00 - 16.00 / 18.00 - 23.00
GPS: 61°17'2"N 10°24'29"E

Apt. and cabins for 2-6 persons	Leil. og hytter for 2-6 personer	Wohnungen u. Hütten für 2-6 Pers.
No. of units: 5	Antall boenheter: 5	Anzahl Wohneinheiten: 5
A: Dwelling for up to 3 pers.: **300,-**	A: Boenhet for inntil 3 pers.: **300,-**	A: Wohng. für bis zu 3 Pers.: **300,-**
B: Dwelling for up to 4 pers.: **550,-**	B: Boenhet for inntil 4 pers.: **550,-**	B: Wohng. für bis zu 4 Pers.: **550,-**
C: Dwelling for up to 6 pers.: **850,-**	C: Boenhet for inntil 6 pers.: **850,-**	C: Wohng. für bis zu 6 Pers.: **850,-**
All rental units: bath, kitchen, LR	Alle enheter: bad, kjøkken, stue	Alle Einheiten: Bad, Küche, Stube
Shared bath for smallest units	De minste enhetene deler bad	Gemeins. Bad f. die kleinsten Einh.
Bed linen fee: **75,-**	Tillegg for sengetøy: **75,-**	Mieten von Bettw.: **75,-**
Cleaning fee: **50,-** to **500,-**	Sluttrengjøring: **50,-** til **500,-**	Endreinigung: **50,-** bis **500,-**
Prices valid for 2011	Priser gyldig for 2011	Preise gültig für 2011
TV in most rental units	TV i de fleste enheter	TV in den meisten Einheiten
Terrace/patio/yard	Terrasse/uteplass/hage	Terrasse/Außenbereich/Garten
Discount off-season	Rabatt utenom sesong	Ermäßigung in der Nebensaison
Open year round	Åpent hele året	Ganzjährig geöffnet
Some English spoken		Sprechen etwas Englisch

Skåden Gard is located 20 km north of Lillehammer, lying high up in the valley with an incredible view of the valley and the Øyer community. The farm is steeped in tradition tracing its family roots back to 1734. Through many generations artifacts have been collected and today are exhibited in a small farm museum in the old store house. The hosts emphasize the importance of coziness and cleanliness in the cabins and apartments.
The Trondheim pilgrim route passes through the farm courtyard.

Skåden Gard finner du 20 km nord for Lillehammer, høyt oppe i dalsiden med storslått utsikt over Øyerbygda. Den gamle og tradisjonsrike gården har slektsrøtter tilbake til 1734. Gjennom flere generasjoner er det samlet gamle bruksgjenstander som idag utgjør et lite gårdsmuseum i det gamle stabburet. Vertskapet legger vekt på at hytter og leiligheter er hjemmekoselige og rene.
Pilegrimsleden Oslo - Trondheim går gjennom gardstunet.

Skåden Gard liegt 20 km nördlich von Lillehammer, hoch oben am Hang mit einer großartigen Aussicht über die Landschaft der Gemeinde Øyer. Die Wurzeln dieses alten, traditionsreichen Hofs reichen zurück bis ins Jahr 1734. Über mehrere Generationen wurden historische Gebrauchsgegenstände gesammelt, die heute ein kleines Bauernhofmuseum füllen und in einem historischen Vorratshaus ausgestellt sind. Die Gastgeber legen großen Wert auf gemütliche und saubere Hütten/ Wohnungen.
Der Pilgerpfad Oslo-Trondheim geht mitten durch den Hof.

Skarsmoen Gård

Your host:
Marit & Anders Bleka

Address:
N - 2635 Tretten
Phone: **61 27 63 13**
Mobile: **95 79 43 13**
E-mail: **info@skarsmoen.no**
Web: **www.skarsmoen.no**

Best time to call:
08.00 - 22.00
GPS: 61°16'35"N 10°19'3"E

Double-/twin room:	**990,-**	Dobbelt-/tosengsrom:	**990,-**	Doppel-/Zweibettzi.:	**990,-**
Single room:	**670,-**	Enkeltrom:	**670,-**	Einzelzimmer:	**670,-**
No. of rooms: 8		Antall rom: 8		Anzahl Zimmer: 8	
Discount for children,		Rabatt for barn,		Ermäßigung für Kinder,	
children under 3 yrs. free		barn under 3 år gratis		Kinder unter 3 Jahren gratis	
Breakfast tray or -buffet		Frokostbrett eller buffét		Gedeckter Frühstückstisch/büffet	
Prices valid for 2011		Priser gyldig for 2011		Preise gültig für 2011	
TV		TV		TV	
Yard/garden		Hage		Garten	
VISA, MC accepted		Vi tar VISA, MC		Wir akzeptieren VISA, MC	
Open year round		Åpent hele året		Ganzjährig geöffnet	
Some English spoken				Sprechen etwas Deutsch	

Selfcatering units:		Enheter med selvhushold:		Einheiten mit Selbstverpflegung:	
Cabins:	from **500,-** to **1200,-**	Hytter:	fra **500,-** til **1200,-**	Hütten:	von **500,-** bis **1200,-**
Bed linen fee:	**100,-**	Sengetøy:	**100,-**	Mieten von Bettwäsche:	**100,-**
Breakfast available:	**90,-**	Frokost kan serveres:	**90,-**	Frühstück auf Bestellung:	**90,-**
Cleaning fee:	**100,-** to **400,-**	Sluttrengjøring:	**100,-** til **400,-**	Endreinigung:	**100,-** bis **400,-**

The Skarsmoen Farm is located in an idyllic wilderness area between Øyer and Tretten. The main house, from 1760, is now fully restored and renovated. The farm has a dairy herd. On marked walking trails you chance sightings of elk and deer. The flora is exceptional. 500 m from farm is Lågen in which you can fish trout and pike. In the winter there are prepared Nordic skiing trails. This is the place for quiet contemplation, in inviting and well equipped rooms and huts.

I et idyllisk skogområde mellom Øyer og Tretten ligger gården Skarsmoen, med hovedhus fra 1760, nå restaurert og ombygd. På gården er det melkeproduksjon. På merkede turstier kan du møte elg og småvilt. Floraen kan by på mange overraskelser. Det er 500 m til Lågen, hvor du kan fiske ørret, sik og harr. Oppkjørte skiløyper på vinteren. Vil du ha det stille og fredelig, ønsker vi deg velkommen til hyggelige og velutstyre rom og hytter.

Der Hof Skarsmoen liegt idyllisch in einer Waldgegend zwischen Øyer und Tretten und wird mit Milchwirtschaft betrieben. Das restaurierte, angebaute Haupthaus stammt von 1760. Auf markierten Wanderpfaden mit reicher Flora kann man Elchen und Kleinwild begegnen. 500 m zum Angelfluss Lågen mit Forellen, Maränen und Äschen. Präparierte Loipen im Winter. Ruhiger, friedlicher Ferienplatz mit gemütlichen, gut ausgestatteten Zimmern und Hütten.

Glomstad Gård

Your host:
Janna & Odd Glomstad
Address:
Nord Trettenveien 465
N - 2635 Tretten
Phone: 61 27 62 57
Mobile: 91 79 98 50
E-mail: glogap@online.no
Web: www.glomstadgjestehus.no
Best time to call:
09.00 - 21.00
GPS: 61°21'24"N 10°18'25"E

Double room:	760,-/960,-	Dobbeltrom:	760,-/960,-	Doppelzimmer:	760,-/960,-
Single room:	435,-/630,-	Enkeltrom:	435,-/630,-	Einzelzimmer:	435,-/630,-

Extra bed, ask for price
No. of rooms: 26
Discount for children
Breakfast buffet
Dinner available
Prices valid for 2011/12
Yard/garden
TV available
VISA accepted
Open year round
English & Dutch spoken

Ekstraseng, spør om pris
Antall rom: 26
Rabatt for barn
Frokostbuffét
Mulighet for kjøp av middag
Priser gyldig for 2011/12
Hage
TV tilgjengelig
Vi tar VISA
Åpent hele året

Extrabett, Preis auf Anfrage
Anzahl Zimmer: 26
Ermäßigung für Kinder
Frühstücksbüfett
Abendessen möglich
Preise gültig für 2011/12
Garten
TV vorhanden
Wir akzeptieren VISA
Ganzjährig geöffnet
Sprechen Deutsch

Glomstad Gård, 5 km from Tretten, has traditions dating back to the 16th century. Janna is the 12th generation on the farm. Janna's mother started hosting guests in 1942.

Today you find a modern vacation spot characterized by Gudbrandsdalen's rich village heritage, and Norwegian tradition is present in both interior design and local cuisine. The delicious food has been featured in newspaper articles. Friendly, homey and relaxed atmosphere. Short distance to Lillehammer, Hunderfossen Family Park, ski centers, Rondane and Jotunheimen.

Glomstad Gård, 5 km fra Tretten, har tradisjoner tilbake til det 16. århundre, og Janna er 12. generasjon på gården. Jannas mor startet å ta imot gjester i 1942.
I dag er det et moderne feriested preget av Gudbrandsdalens rike bygdekultur, og norsk tradisjon preger såvel interiøret som kokkekunsten. Den gode maten har også ført til reportasjer i ukepressen. Her er det en vennlig, hjemmekoselig og avslappet atmosfære. Kort avstand til Lillehammer, Hunderfossen familiepark, skianlegg, som Rondane og Jotunheimen.

Glomstad Gård, 5 km von Tretten entfernt, ist ein Traditionsbetrieb mit Wurzeln bis ins 16. Jahrhundert. Übernachtungsgäste kamen erstmals 1942.
Heute ist Glomstad ein moderner Urlaubsort, geprägt von der bäuerlichen Kultur des Gudbrandstals. Norwegische Tradition ebenfalls bei Interieur und Kochkunst. Das schmackhafte Essen wurde sogar in der Wochenpresse vorgestellt. Freundliche und gemütliche Atmosphäre. Unweit nach Lillehammer, zum Hunderfossen-Fam.park, zu Skigebieten sowie zu den Nationalparks Rondane und Jotunheimen.

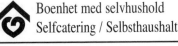
Sygard Romsås
på Stortann seter

Your host:
Aase Mork Borgedal
& Simen Borgedal

Address:
Brekkom, N - 2634 Fåvang
Phone: 61 28 24 15
Mobile: 91 18 92 00
E-mail: aas-b@online.no
Web: www.sygard-romsas.no
Best time to call: 16.00 - 23.00
GPS: 61°28'10"N 10°14'2"E

A: Cabin for 2-6 persons
2 bedrooms, kitchenette, LR, DR
No plumbing, outhouse
Price for whole unit: **700,-**

B: Cabin for 2-4 persons
1 bedroom, big loft with bed,
komb. kitchen/LR
No plumbing, outhouse
Price for whole unit: **700,-**

Applies to both rental units:
Bed linen fee: **100,-**
Breakfast svc available: **100,-/50,-**
Prices valid for 2011/12
Terrace/yard
Open year round
Board only July- ca. 15 Aug.
English spoken

A: Hytte for 2-6 personer
2 soverom, tekjøkken, stue, sp.st.
Ikke innlagt vann, utedo
Pris for hele enheten: **700,-**

B: Hytte for 2-4 personer
1 soverom, stor hems for 2-3 pers.,
komb. kjøkken/stue
Ikke innlagt vann, utedo
Pris for hele enheten: **700,-**

For begge enhetene gjelder:
Tillegg for sengetøy: **100,-**
Frokost kan serveres: **100,-/50,-**
Priser gyldig for 2011/12
Terrasse/uteplass
Åpent hele året
Servering kun juli - ca. 15. aug.

A: Hütte für 2-6 Personen
2 Schlafzi., Teeküche, Stube, Esszi.
Kein fl. Wasser, Plumpsklo
Ganze Einheit: **700,-**

B: Hütte für 2-4 Personen
1 Schlafzi., 1 großer Schlafboden
für 2-3 Pers.,Küchen-/Wohnzi.
Kein fl. Wasser, Plumpsklo
Ganze Einheit: **700,-**

Für beide Einheiten gilt:
Mieten von Bettwäsche: **100,-**
Frühst. auf Bestellung: **100,-/50,-**
Preise gültig für 2011/12
Terrasse/Außenbereich
Ganzjährig geöffnet
Verfplegung nur Juli - Mitte Aug.
Sprechen etwas Deutsch

Cabins A and B sit on a charming old mountain pasture. Rich cultural heritage and a beautiful view. In the summer livestock graze freely. Fine trails for hiking, bicycling and horseback riding. Good hunting. In winter great skiing trails. Short way to Kvitfjellalpinanlegg.

Både hytte A og B ligger på fjellet på en sjarmerende, gammel seter-grend. Setra er rik på kulturminner og har flott utsikt. Om sommeren går mange husdyr fritt omkring på beite her. Fint turterreng både til fots, på sykkel og på hesteryggen. Gode jaktmuligheter. Om vinteren er det flott skiterreng. Kort vei til Kvitfjellalpinanlegg.

Beide Hütten liegen auf einem charmanten, alten Almenhof in den Bergen. Die Alm ist reich an Kulturgütern und bietet eine tolle Aussicht. Im Sommer laufen viele Tiere auf der Weide frei umher. Tolles Gebiet für Touren zu Fuß, mit dem Fahrrad oder auf dem Pferderücken. Im Winter ist das Gebiet gut zum Skifahren geeignet; die Skipisten rund um Kvitfjell sind nicht weit.

Valbjør Gard

Your host:
Live Hosar & Kai Valbjør

Address:
Øvre Nordheradsvegen 486
N - 2680 Vågå
Phone: 61 23 70 59
Mobile: 90 82 29 89
E-mail: post@valbjoer.no
Web: www.valbjoer.no

Best time to call:
09.00 - 22.00
GPS: 61°52'18"N 9°1'28"E

A: 'Vetlestugu' for 2 pers.
Bath, kitchen, LR, sleeping alcove

B: 'Nørdre stugu' for 4-8 pers.
3 bedrooms, bath, kitchen, LR

C: 'Aasheimstugu' for 4-5 pers.
2 bedrooms, bath, kitchen, LR

A-C: Pris per pers.:   **400,-** to **500,-**

D: 2 loft rooms, pr. pers: **300,-**

Bed linen included
Discount for children
Prices valid for 2011 & 2012
TV available
Terrace/patio/yard
Open year round
English spoken

A: 'Vetlestugu' for 2 pers.
Bad, kjk., stue, sovealkove

B: 'Nørdre stugu' for 4-8 pers.
3 soverom, bad, kjøkken, stue

C: 'Aasheimstugu' for 4-5 pers.
2 soverom, bad, kjøkken, stue

A-C: Pris pr. pers.:   **400,-** til **500,-**

D: 2 loftsrom, pr. pers: **300,-**

Sengetøy er inkludert
Rabatt for barn
Priser gyldig for 2011 & 2012
TV tilgjengelig
Hage/terrasse/uteplass
Åpent hele året

A: 'Vetlestugu' für 2 Pers.
Bad, Küche, Stube, Schlafnische

B: 'Nørdre stugu' für 4-8 Pers.
3 Schlafzi., Bad, Küche, Stube

C: 'Aasheimstugu' für 4-5 Pers.
2 Schlafzi., Bad, Küche, Stube

A-C: Preis p.P.:   **400,-** bis **500,-**

D: 2 Schlafböden, p.P.:   **300,-**

Inkl. Bettwäsche
Ermässigung für Kinder
Preise gültig für 2011 & 2012
TV vorhanden
Garten/Terrasse/Außenbereich
Ganzjährig geöffnet
Sprechen etwas Deutsch

At Valbjør Farm you are staying at a heritage building featuring many old timber houses. A burial mound bears witness to a settlement of 1,000 years ago. Your hosts focus on organic farm operations. The farm has sheep, goats, horses, dogs, cats and pigs and hens in the summer. The farm's store has food and handicrafts, and a pub in an old grain shed. The farm is on a sunny hillside with a view of snowy peaks and green Lake Vågå. Hiking terrain.

På Valbjør Gard får du bo på en fredet gard med mange gamle tømmerhus. En gravhaug vitner om bosetning her for 1000 år siden. Vertskapet driver økologisk gårdsdrift. På gården er det sau og geit, hester, hund og katter, om sommeren; griser og høner. Egen gårdsbutikk med mat og husflidsvarer, og pub i en gammel kornbu. Gården ligger høyt oppe i solsiden med utsikt mot snøkledde fjell og grønt Vågåvann. Fint turterreng.

Auf dem denkmalgeschützten Hof wohnt man in historischen Blockhütten. Ein Hügelgrab erinnert an eine mehr als 1000-jährige Besiedelung. Öko-Landwirtschaft. Schafe, Ziegen, Pferde, Hunde u. Katzen auf dem Hof, im Sommer auch Schweine u. Hühner. Hofladen mit Lebensmitteln u. Kunstgewerbe, Pub in der alten Getreidekate. Der Hof liegt hoch oben (Sonnenseite) mit schöner Aussicht auf schneebedeckte Berge u. den türkisfarbenen See Vågåvann. Tolles Wandergebiet.

Kvila Turistheim

Your host:
Rikke & Erling Hegge

Address:
N - 2685 Garmo
Phone: 61 21 24 20
Mobile: 90 64 46 61 / 95 12 43 79
E-mail: kvila1@online.no
Web: www.kvila.info

Best time to call:
09.00 - 23.00
GPS: 61°50'47"N 8°49'43"E

Double/twin room:	**675,-**	Dobbelt-/tosengsrom:	**675,-**	Doppel-/Zweibettzi.:	**675,-**
Triple room:	**825,-**	3-sengsrom:	**825,-**	Dreibettzimmer:	**825,-**
Single room:	**450,-**	Enkeltrom:	**450,-**	Einzelzimmer:	**450,-**
No. of rooms: 4		Antall rom: 4		Anzahl Zimmer: 4	
Breakfast buffet		Frokost buffét		Frühstücksbüfett	
Prices valid for 2011		Priser gyldig for 2011		Preise gültig für 2011	
TV/Internet available		TV/Internett tilgjengelig		TV/Internet vorhanden	
Terrace/deck/yard		Terrasse/uteplass/hage		Terrasse/Außenbereich/Garten	
Boat and bike for rent		Båt- og sykkelutleie		Boot und Fahrrad zu mieten	
Pets welcome		Kjæledyr velkommen		Haustiere willkommen	
VISA, MC, AmEx accepted		Vi tar VISA, MC, AmEx		Wir akzeptieren VISA, MC, AmEx	
Open year round		Åpent hele året		Ganzjährig geöffnet	
English, some French & Spanish		Snakker norsk og dansk		Sprechen Deutsch	

A Norwegian/Danish family of four live at and run Kvila. Cabins and rooms are situated in beautiful panorama of mountains and waterways. Good fishing nearby, boat, canoe and kayaks for rent. Breakfast, lunch and dinner are served in a cozy cafe in the main house. Enjoy the TV room with books and games. Possibilities for mountain hikes in Jotunheimen and motoring to famous tourist destinations such as Besseggen, Geiranger, Trollstigen and Galdhøpiggen. In Lom you can visit 'Bakeren' geology museum, a stave church, mountain museum. Knut Hamsun's birthplace 500m.

En norsk/dansk familie på fire driver og bor på Kvila. Hyttene og rommene ligger i naturskjønne omgivelser med flott utsikt over fjell og vann. Godt fiskevann like ved og båt, kano og kajakker til utleie. Frokost, lunsj og middag serveres i den hyggelige kaféen i hovedhuset. Kos deg i TV-stue med bøker og spill.
Mange muligheter for fjellturer i Jotunheimen og bilturer til kjente turmål som Besseggen, Geiranger, Trollstigen og Galdhøpiggen. I Lom kan du besøke "Bakeren" steinmuseum, stavkirken og Fjellmuseet. Hamsunstugu kun 500 m.

Eine vierköpfige norwegisch-dänische Familie betreibt und wohnt auf dem Kvila Hof. Die Hütten und Zimmer liegen in naturschöner Umgebung mit toller Aussicht auf Berg und See. Angelsee gleich nebenan; Boot, Kanu und Kajaks zum Ausleihen. Frühstück, Mittag u. Abendbrot werden in dem gemütlichen Kaffé im Haupthaus serviert. TV-Stube mit Büchern und Spielen. Viele Wandermöglichkeiten im Jotunheimen Nationalpark. Populäre Ausflugsziele wie Besseggen, Galdhøppigen, Geiranger, Trollstigen gut mit dem Auto zu erreichen. In Lom kann man z.B. das Geburtshaus Knut Hamsuns besuchen.

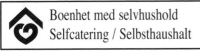

A: Cabin 'Heks 1' for 6 persons
2 bedrooms, own bath, kitchen, LR
Price for whole unit: **675,-**

B: Cabin 'Hulder 1' for 4 persons
1 bedroom, own bath, kitchen, LR
Price for whole unit: **575,-**

C: Cabins "Heks 2" and "Hulder 2"
for 4 persons
1 room, own bath, kitchen
Price for whole unit: **525,-**

D: Cabins "Spekebua", "Tusse",
"Troll", "Nøkken" for 4 pers.
1 room, shared bath,kitchen
Price for whole unit: **350,-/375,-**

A: Hytte "Heks 1" for 6 personer
2 soverom, eget bad, kjøkken, stue
Pris for hele enheten: **675,-**

B: Hytte "Hulder 1" for 4 personer
1 soverom, eget bad, kjøkken, stue
Pris for hele enheten: **575,-**

C: Hyttene "Heks 2" og "Hulder 2"
for 4 personer
1 rom, eget bad, kjøkken
Pris for hele enheten: **525,-**

D: Hyttene "Spekebua", "Tusse",
"Troll", "Nøkken" for 4 pers.
1 rom, delt bad, kjøkken
Pris for hele enheten: **350,-/375,-**

A: Hütte "Heks 1"für 6 Personen
2 Schlafzi., eig. Bad, Küche, Stube
Ganze Einheit: **675,-**

B: Hütte "Hulder 1" für 4 Personen
1 Schlafzi., eig. Bad, Küche, Stube
Ganze Einheit: **575,-**

C: Hütten "Heks 2" u. "Hulder 2"
für 4 Personen
1 Zimmer, eig. Bad, Küche
Ganze Einheit: **525,-**

D: Hütten "Spekebua", "Tusse",
"Troll", "Nøkken" für 4 Pers.
1 Zimmer, geteiltes Bad, Küche
Ganze Einheit: **350,-/375,-**

Bed linen fee: **50,-**
Breakfast service available
Prices valid for 2011
TV/Internet available
Terrace/deck/yard
Boat for rent
Bike for rent
Pets welcome
VISA, MC, AmEx accepted
Open 1 May - 30. Nov.
English, some French & Spanish

Directions:
Kvila is at Garmo, along RV 15
between Vågå and Lom. Follow
signs.

Tillegg for sengetøy: **50,-**
Frokost kan serveres
Priser gyldig for 2011
TV/Internett tilgjengelig
Terrasse/uteplass/hage
Båtutleie
Sykkelutleie
Kjæledyr velkommen
Vi tar VISA, MC, AmEx
Åpent 1. mai - 30. nov.
Snakker norsk og dansk

Veibeskrivelse:
Kvila ligger i Garmo, ved RV 15,
mellom Vågå og Lom. Det er godt
skiltet.

Mieten von Bettwäsche: **50,-**
Frühstück auf Bestellung
Preise gültig für 2011
TV/Internet vorhanden
Terrasse/Außenbereich/Garten
Boot zu mieten
Fahrrad zu mieten
Haustiere willkommen
Wir akzeptieren VISA, MC, AmEx
Geöffnet 1. Mai - 30. Nov.
Sprechen Deutsch

Wegbeschreibung:
Der Kvila Hof liegt in Garmo entlang der Str. 15 zwischen Vågå und
Lom. Der Hof ist gut ausgeschildert.

Teigen Gard

Your host:
Kari & Bjørn Teigen

Address:
Teigen gård
N - 2686 Lom
Phone: 61 21 14 88
Mobile: 90 10 00 72
E-mail: bjteig@hotmail.com
Web: www.teigen-gard.no

Best time to call:
08.00 - 23.00
GPS: 61°49'10"N 8°31'53"E

A: "Stabburet" for 2-4 persons
1 bedroom, bath, LR w/kitchenette
Price for whole unit: **650,-**

B: "Gamlestugu" for 4-10 pers.
3 bedrooms, bath, kitchen, LR
Ask for price

C: "Brekkøya" for 2-4 persons
2 bedrooms, kitchen, LR,
   outhouse, bath w/shower inside
Price for whole unit: **700,-**

D: "Setra" at Hovde, 2-4 pers.
1 bedroom, kitchen, LR, outhouse
Gas stove, paraphine lamps, no el.
Price for whole unit: **400,-**

Bed linen fee: **60,-**
Prices valid for 2011
Weekly price on request
Terrace/yard
Open 1 May - 1 October
Some English spoken

A: "Stabburet" for 2-4 personar
1 soverom, bad, stove m/tekjøken
Pris for heile eininga: **650,-**

B: "Gamlestugu" for 4-10 pers.
3 soverom, bad, kjøken, stove
Spør om pris

C: "Brekkøya" for 2-4 personar
2 soverom, utedo, dusjbad inne,
   kjøken og stove
Pris for heile eininga: **700,-**

D: "Setra" på Hovde, 2-4 pers.
1 soverom, kjk., stove, utedo
gasskomfyr, parafinlampar, ikkje el.
Pris for heile eininga: **400,-**

Tillegg for sengeklede: **60,-**
Prisar gjeld for 2011
Vekesutleige - spør om pris
Terrasse/uteplass
Ope 1. mai - 1. oktober

A: "Stabburet" für 2-4 Personen
1 Schlafzi., Bad, Stube u. Teeküche
Ganze Einheit: **650,-**

B: "Gamlestugu" für 4-10 Pers.
3 Schlafzi., Bad, Küche, Stube
Preis bitte erfragen

C: "Brekkøya" für 2-4 Personen
2 Schlafzi., Plumpsklo, Bad mit
   Dusche innen, Küche und Stube
Ganze Einheit: **700,-**

D: "Setra", Almhütte für 2-4 Pers.
1 Schlafzi., Kü., Stube, Plumpsklo, Gas-
herd, Petroleumlampen, kein Strom
Ganze Einheit: **400,-**

Mieten von Bettwäsche: **60,-**
Preise gültig für 2011
Wochenmiete - Preis erfragen
Terrasse/Außenbereich
Geöffnet 1. Mai - 1. Oktober
Sprechen etwas Englisch

At Teigen Gard sheep are raised. Guest facilities/rooms in outbuildings on the farm. Brekkøya lies along the river about 6 km up in the valley, an ideal small farmstead with fine old log-cabin. Beautiful location. You can also rent the mountain cabin where the sheep are out at feed. Good fishing in river and lakes, mountain hiking.

På Teigen Gard driv dei med sau. To utleigeeiningar, Stabburet og Gamlestugu, er på garden. Brekkøya ligg langs elva 6 km lenger oppe i dalen, eit idyllisk lite småbruk med ei fin gamal laftestove. Flott beliggenhet. Også setra leiges ut. Her går sauene på sommerbeite. Gode høve for fiske i elva og i fjellvatn, fotturar i fjellet.

Auf dem Teigen Hof wird Schafzucht betrieben. Die Einheiten A und B befinden sich auf dem Hof. Brekkøya liegt entlang des Flusses 6 km weiter hinten im Tal, ein idyllischer kleiner Hof mit einem alten Blockhaus. Die Almhütte steht auf der Sommerweide der Schafe. Möglichk. zum Angeln in Fluss u. Bergsee und Wandern.

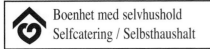

Strind Gard

Your host:
Anne Jorunn & Trond Dalsegg

Address:
Strind Gard
N - 2686 Lom
Phone: 61 21 12 37
Mobile: 91 87 52 48
E-mail: post@strind-gard.no
Web: www.strind-gard.no

Best time to call:
16.00 - 23.00
GPS: 61°49'06"N 8°31'37"E

A: 'Låvebrua' for 5 persons
Price for whole unit: **450,-**
Extra per pers. over 3 pers.: **40,-**

B: 'Eldhuset' for 2 persons
Price for whole unit: **250,-**

C: 'Stabburet' for 2-3 persons
Price for whole unit: **350,-**

D: 'Gammelstugu' 1.fl. for 5 pers.
Price for whole unit: **450,-**
Extra per pers. over 3 pers.: **40,-**

E: 'Gammelstugu' 2.fl. for 3 pers.
Price for whole unit: **350,-**

F/G: Apt./Cabin for 4-6 persons
Price for whole unit: **700,-**
Extra per pers. over 4 pers.: **50,-**

Applies to all rental units:
Bed linen fee: **60,-**
A-E: Common sanitary fac. & ktch.
Prices valid for 2011
Internet available
Terrace/garden and grill
Bike for rent / Sauna available
Open year round
English spoken

A: 'Låvebrua' for 5 personer
Pris for hele enheten: **450,-**
Tillegg pr. pers. over 3 pers.: **40,-**

B: 'Eldhuset' for 2 personer
Pris for hele enheten: **250,-**

C: 'Stabburet' for 2-3 personer
Pris for hele enheten: **350,-**

D: 'Gammelstugu', 1. etg., 5 pers.
Pris for hele enheten: **450,-**
Tillegg pr. pers. over 3 pers.: **40,-**

E: 'Gammelstugu', 2. etg., 3 pers.
Pris for hele enheten: **350,-**

F/G: Leil./hytte for 4-6 personer
Pris for hele enheten: **700,-**
Tillegg pr. pers. over 4 pers.: **50,-**

For alle enhetene gjelder:
Tillegg for leie av sengetøy: **60,-**
A-E: felles sanitæranlegg & kjk.
Priser gyldig for 2011
Internett tilgjengelig
Terasse/uteplass/hage og grill
Sykkelutleie / Badstu tilgjengelig
Åpent hele året

A: 'Låvebrua' für 5 Pers.
Ganze Einheit: **450,-**
Mehr als 3 P., Zuschlag p.P.: **40,-**

B: 'Eldhuset' für 2 Pers.
Ganze Einheit: **250,-**

C: 'Stabburet' für 2-3 Personen
Ganze Einheit: **350,-**

D: 'Gammelstugu', 1. Etg., 5 Pers.
Ganze Einheit: **450,-**
Mehr als 3 P., Zuschlag p.P.: **40,-**

E: 'Gammelstugu', 2. Etg., 3 Pers.
Ganze Einheit: **350,-**

F/G: Wohng./Hütten für 4-6 Pers.
Ganze Einheit: **700,-**
Mehr als 4 P., Zuschlag p.P.: **50,-**

Für alle Einheiten gilt:
Mieten von Bettwäsche: **60,-**
A-E: Gem. Sanitäranlage & Küche
Preise gültig für 2011
Internet verfügbar
Terrasse/Außenbereich und Grill
Fahrrad zu mieten; Sauna
Ganzjährig geöffnet
Sprechen etwas Deutsch

Cozy farmyard with a pleasant
mix of old and new structures.
Great base for day-trips, by foot or
car, to Jotunheimen. Livestock
includes sheep, hens and horses.

Koselig gardstun med blanding av
eldre og nyere bebyggelse. Fint utgangspunkt for dagsturer i Jotunheimen til fots eller bilturer. Det er
sau, høner og hest på garden.

Gemütl. Bauernhof mit älteren und
neueren Gebäuden. Guter Ausgangspunkt f. Tagestouren ins Jotunhei-
men-Gebirge zu Fuß o. mit d. Auto.
Hier gibt es Schafe, Hühner, Pferde.

Storhaugen

Your host:
Joar Slettede

Address:
Storhaugen
N - 2687 Bøverdalen
Phone: 61 21 20 69
Mobil: 91 10 89 42
E-mail: info@storhaugengard.no
Web: www.storhaugengard.no

Best time to call:
10.00 - 22.00
GPS: 61°42'52"N 8°20'58"E

Cabin 'Jotunheim' for 16 pers.	Jotunheimhytta for 16 pers.	Jotunheimhütte für 16 Pers.
Price for whole unit: **2000 - 2750,-**	Pris for hele enheten: **2000 - 2750,-**	Ganze Einheit: **2000 - 2750,-**
Cabin 'Märtha' for 6 pers.	Märthahytta for 2-6 pers.	Märthahütte für 6 Pers.
Price for whole unit: **600 - 1100,-**	Pris for hele enheten: **600 - 1100,-**	Ganze Einheit: **600 - 1100,-**
Apt. no. 1 & 2 for 5 pers.	Leilighet nr. 1 & 2 for 2-5 pers.	Wohnung 1 & 2 für 5 Pers.
Price for whole unit: **600 - 950,-**	Pris for hele enheten: **600 - 950,-**	Ganze Einheit: **600 - 950,-**
Apt. no. 3 for 7 pers.	Leilighet nr. 3 for 2-7 pers.	Wohnung 3 für 7 Pers.
Price for whole unit: **600 - 1100,-**	Pris for hele enheten: **600 - 1100,-**	Ganze Einheit: **600 - 1100,-**
Apt. no. 4 for 9 pers.	Leilighet nr. 4 for 2-9 pers.	Wohnung 4 für 9 Pers.
Price for whole unit: **600 - 1350,-**	Pris for hele enheten: **600 - 1350,-**	Ganze Einheit: **600 - 1350,-**
Apt. no. 5 for 14 pers.	Leilighet nr. 5 for 14 pers.	Wohnung 5 für 14 Pers.
Price for whole unit: **1500 - 2500,-**	Pris for hele enheten: **1500 - 2500,-**	Ganze Einheit: **1500 - 2500,-**
Apt. no. 6 for 10 pers.	Leilighet nr. 6 for 10 pers.	Wohnung 6 für 10 Pers.
Price for whole unit: **1000 - 1850,-**	Pris for hele enheten: **1000 - 1850,-**	Ganze Einheit: **1000 - 1850,-**
Bed linen fee: **100,-**	Tillegg for sengetøy: **100,-**	Mieten von Bettwäsche: **100,-**
Cleaning fee: **350 - 600,-**	Sluttrengjøring: **350 - 600,-**	Endreinigung: **350 - 600,-**
Prices valid for 2011/12	Priser gyldig for 2011/12	Preise gültig für 2011/12
TV/Internet available	TV/Internett tilgjengelig	TV/Internet verfügbar
Deck/yard	Hage/uteplass	Garten/Außenbereich
Pets: **150,-**	Kjæledyr: **150,-**	Haustiere: **150,-**
VISA, MC accepted	Vi tar VISA, MC	Wir akzeptieren VISA, MC
Open Easter - 1 Nov.	Åpent påske - 1. nov.	Geöffnet Ostern - 1. Nov.
Some English spoken		Sprechen etwas Deutsch

To get away from one's working environment is,
in a sense, to get away from one's self;
and this is often the chief advantage of travel and change.
~Charles Horton Cooley~

Storhaugen gard is at the foot of Galdhøpiggen, 700 m above sea level, surrounded by high peaks and impressive nature. Fantastic location. Storhaugen is a fully operating goat and cattle farm with milk and meat production.

Storhaugen gard ligger ved foten av Galdhøpiggen, 700 meter over havet, omkranset av høye fjell og mektig natur. Fantastisk beliggenhet. Storhaugen er en gård i full drift med melk- og kjøttproduksjon av geiter og kjøttfe.

Storhaugen liegt am Fuße des Galdhøppigen, 700 m ü. NN., umgeben von hohen Bergen und beeindruckender Natur - fantastische Lage! Auf Storhaugen ist die Milch- und Fleischproduktion von Ziegen und anderem Vieh in vollem Gange.

Cabins and apartments boast a very high standard. All are built in traditional timber style.
Our location between and Jotunheimen and Breheimen national parks is an ideal starting point for visitors who want mountains, glacier tours, skiing or simply to enjoy the epic nature. The farm includes Oppland's highest water fall, Veslegjuvfossen, just a footpath away.
One can also enjoy Klimapark 2469, a spectacular ice tunnel built in the glacier featuring an exhibit of archeological artifacts found in the area.
Also not too far away is Galdhøpiggen, north Europe's highest mountain at 2,469 m. above sea level, or visit Dummdalsgrottene, north Europe's highest limestone caves.

Hytter og leiligheter har meget god standard. Alle er bygd i tradisjonell stil med tømmer.
Vår beliggenhet midt mellom Jotunheimen nasjonalpark og Breheimen nasjonalpark, gjør Storhaugen til et utmerket utgangspunkt for dem som vil gå i fjellet, gå på bretur, skitur, eller rett og slett bare vil oppleve den storslåtte naturen i området. På gården har vi også Opplands høyeste foss, Veslegjuvfossen. Det går sti dit fra gården .
Andre ting du kan oppleve er klimapark 2469, en spektakulær istunnel i isbreen, med utstilling av arkeologiske funn fra området. Videre kan du gå til Galdhøpiggen, Nord-Europas høyeste fjell med sine 2469 m.o.h. eller besøke Dummdalsgrottene, Nord-Europas høyest beliggende kalksteinsgrotter.

Die Hütten und Wohnungen haben sehr hohen Standard und sind alle im traditionellen Holzblockstil erbaut. In der Mitte zwischen dem Jotunheimen und Breheimen Nationalpark gelegen, ist Storhaugen der ideale Ausgangspunkt für Wander-, Gletscher-, Skitouren oder einfach Ausflüge in die grandiose Natur ringsherum. Zum Hof gehört übrigens Opplands höchster Wasserfall, der Veslegjuvfoss. Ein Weg führt Sie vom Hof aus dorthin. Ganz andere Erlebnisse bietet der Klimapark 2469 - ein spektakulärer Eistunnel im Gletscher, in dem archäologische Funde der Umgegend ausgestellt sind. Weiterhin kann man auf den Galdhøppigen, Nordeuropas höchsten Berg mit 2469 m, wandern oder die Dummdals-Grotten, Nordeuropas höchstgelegene Kalksteingrotten, besuchen.

Sørre Hemsing

Your host:
Berit & Arne Nefstad

Address:
Heensgarda
N - 2975 Vang i Valdres
Phone: 61 36 72 70
Mobile: 97 16 84 58
E-mail: post@sorrehemsing.no
Web: www.sorrehemsing.no

Best time to call:
09.00 - 22.00
GPS: 61°9'50"N 8°40'15"E

Double room:	**1065,-**	Dobbeltrom:	**1065,-**	Doppelzimmer:	**1065,-**
Single room:	**625,-**	Enkeltrom:	**625,-**	Einzelzimmer:	**625,-**
Children under 12:	**350,-**	Barn under 12:	**350,-**	Kinder unter 12:	**350,-**

No. of rooms: 6
Laid breakfast table
Prices valid for 2011
TV/Internet available
Terrace/patio
Boat for rent
Open year round
Some English spoken

Antall rom: 6
Dekket frokostbord
Priser gyldig for 2011
TV/Internett tilgjengelig
Terrasse/uteplass
Båtutleie
Åpent hele året

Anzahl Zimmer: 6
Gedeckter Frühstückstisch
Preise gültig für 2011
TV/Internet vorhanden
Terrasse/Außenbereich
Boot zu mieten
Ganzjährig geöffnet
Sprechen etwas Englisch

Sørre Hemsing is a beautiful exam-
ple of a Norwegian historical landmark. The farm consists of two
farmhouses, barn, stall, millhouse,
smithy and drying hut. Awarded
"Olavsrosa" for its historic quality.
Some of the structures are newly
renovated while others are not
quite finished. The farm's unique
character is well preserved in its
interiors and furnishings. The kitch-
en and bathrooms are both modern
and comfortable. Vang is a mountain village whose main activities
are sheep, goat and cattle raising.
Mountain dairy farming is a summertime activity that often brings
livestock to Sørre Hemsing.

Sørre Hemsing er et vakkert
eksempel på norsk kulturhistorie.
Gården består av to våningshus,
fjøs, bu, låve, kvernhus, smie og
tørkehus. Tildelt Olavsrosa for sin
historiske miljøkvalitet.
Noen av husene er nyrestaurerte,
mens noen ikke er helt ferdige
ennå. Det unike særpreget ved
gården er godt bevart i interiør og
møblement, dog er kjøkken og bad
både moderne og lekre.
Vang er ei fjellbygd der nærings-
veien er sau, geit og ku. På som-
merst id er det en del stølsdrift, og
da er det gjerne dyr på Sørre Hemsing.

Das Gehöft ist ein schönes Beispiel
Norwegischer Kulturgeschichte.
Zwei Wohnhäuser, Stall, Speicher,
Scheune, Mühle, Schmiede und
Darre (hist. Trockenanlage für
Getreide). Aufgrund der Qualität
dieses historischen Ensembles mit
der Olavsrose ausgezeichnet. Die
meisten Gebäude wurden in den
letzten Jahren restauriert. Die besondere Atmosphäre wurde auch
bei der Möblierung beibehalten.
Modern und einladend sind Küche
und Bad.
Vang ist eine Berggegend mit
Schaf-, Ziegen- und Viehwirtschaft.
Während der bewirtschafteten Zeit
im Sommer sind auf Sørre Hemsing
viele Tiere zu sehen.

Herangtunet

Your host:
Marco & Marie-José Robeerst

Address:
Herangtunet
N - 2940 Heggenes
Phone: 61 34 16 65
Mobile: 97 63 33 10
E-mail: info@herangtunet.com
Web: www.herangtunet.com

Best time to call:
10.00 - 21.00
GPS: 61°7'49"N 9°4'55"E

Double room: from **1140,-**	Dobbeltrom: fra **1140,-**	Doppelzimmer: ab **1140,-**
No. of rooms: 9	Antall rom: 9	Anzahl Zimmer: 9
Discount for children	Rabatt for barn	Ermäßigung für Kinder
Laid breakfast table	Dekket frokostbord	Gedeckter Frühstückstisch
Dinner possible	Mulighet for middag	Abendessen auf Wunsch
Selfcatering available	Selvhushold er mulig	Selbstverpflegung möglich
Prices valid for 2011	Priser gyldig for 2011	Preise gültig für 2011
Internet available	Internett tilgjengelig	Internet verfügbar
Terrace/patio/yard	Terrasse/uteplass/hage	Terrasse/Außenbereich/Garten
VISA, MC accepted	Vi tar VISA, MC	Wir akzeptieren VISA, MC
Open year round	Åpent hele året	Ganzjährig geöffnet
English, Dutch & French spoken		Sprechen Deutsch

At Herangtunet Marco and Marie-José are welcoming you. Marie-José is an interior designer and Marco is a graphic designer. A few years ago they decided to set up a high-standard boutique hotel in Norway. Step by step Herangtunet has been transformed into a pleasant environment with beautiful and charming stylish interiors. Herangtunet is an ideal starting point for holidays in Norway through all seasons. The village is situated in one of Norway's sunniest regions, close to lakes, a ski resort and the Jotunheimen National Park.

På Herangtunet vil Marco og Marie-José ønske deg velkommen. Marie-José er interiørdesigner og Marco er grafisk formgiver. For noen år siden bestemte de seg for å starte et boutique hotell med høyt standard i Norge. Skritt for skritt har Herangtunet blitt omskapt til et sjarmerende sted med koselige og stilig dekorerte rom og suiter. Herangtunet er et ideelt utgangspunkt for ferie i Norge til alle årstider. Heggenes ligger i et av de mest solrike områdene i Norge, nært til innsjøer, nært skianlegg og Jotunheimen nasjonalpark.

Marco und Marie-José heißen Sie herzlich auf Herangtunet willkommen. Marie-José ist Innenarchitektin und Marco Grafikdesigner. Vor einigen Jahren beschlossen die beiden ein Boutique-Hotel mit gehobenem Standard in Norwegen zu eröffnen. Schritt für Schritt wurde Herangtunet zu einem charmanten Haus mit gemütlichen und stilvollen Zimmern und Suiten umgebaut. Zu jeder Jahreszeit ist Herangtunet ein idealer Ausgangspunkt für Urlaub in Norwegen. Heggenes liegt in einer der sonnigsten Gegenden des Landes, in der Nähe von Seen, einer Alpin-Skianlage und dem Jotunheimen Nationalpark.

Furulund Pensjonat

Your host:
Rob & Betty van Kruining

Address:
N - 2960 Røn (Valdres)
Phone: 61 42 33 39
Mobile: 90 96 56 69
info@furulundpensjonat.com
Web: www.furulundpensjonat.com

Best time to call:
08.00 - 22.00
GPS: 61°2'00"N 9°3'26"E

Double room:	**760,-**	Dobbeltrom:	**760,-**	Doppelzimmer:	**760,-**
Twin room:	**710,-**	Tosengsrom:	**710,-**	Zweibettzimmer:	**710,-**
Single room:	**600,-**	Enkeltrom:	**600,-**	Einzelzimmer:	**600,-**
Family room:	**1350,-**	Familierom:	**1350,-**	Familienzimmer:	**1350,-**
No. of rooms: 9		Antall rom: 9		Anzahl Zimmer: 9	
Laid breakfast table or buffet		Frokostbord eller buffét		Frühstückstisch o. Büffet	
Dinner, today's special:	**240,-**	Middag, dagens rett:	**240,-**	Abendessen, Tagesgericht:	**240,-**
Prices valid for 2011		Priser gyldig for 2011		Preise gültig für 2011	
TV/Internet available		TV/Internett tilgjengelig		TV/Internet vorhanden	
Terrace/patio/yard		Terrasse/uteplass/hage		Terrasse/Außenbereich/Garten	
Rowing boat available		Robåt kan lånes		Ruderboot zu leihen	
Bike for rent		Sykkelutleie		Fahrrad zu mieten	
VISA, MC accepted		Vi tar VISA, MC		Wir akzeptieren VISA, MC	
Open year round		Åpent hele året		Ganzjährig geöffnet	
English/Dutch/some French spoken				Sprechen Deutsch	

Furulund has been a tourist mecca for the past hundred years. In the beautiful Valdres valley you'll find a bountiful cultural landscape, forests and lakes. At nearby Jotunheimen mountains peaks rise to altitude over 2,000 m. There are numerous possibllities for outdoor activities the year round. Large open-air museum at Fagernes, stave churches, ancient stone carvings, runesones and burial sites are but a few. Furulund is a cozy place where you can relax and meet other guests by the fireplace in the lounge.

Furulund har vært drevet som turiststed siden begynnelsen av 1900-tallet. I vakre Valdres finner du frodige kulturlandskap, skoger og innsjøer. I Jotunheimen kan du oppleve topper på over 2000 m. Utallige muligheter for utendørsaktiviteteter året rundt. Stort friluftsmuseum på Fagernes (14 km). Stavkirker, helleristninger, runestein og gravrøyser i området. Furulund er et hyggelig sted hvor du kan slappe av og møte andre gjester. Salong og peisestue.

Seit Beginn des 20. Jh. ist Furulund ein Ziel für Touristen. Im schönen Valdres finden Sie eine üppige Kulturlandschaft, Wälder und Seen. In Jotunheimens Berglandschaft können Sie Gipfel auf über 2000 m erleben. Unzählige Möglichkeiten für Aussenaktivitäten das ganze Jahr über. Stabkirchen und Felszeichnungen, Runesteine und Grabsteinhaufen in der Umgebung. Großes Freiluftmuseum in Fagernes (14 km). Furulund ist ein gemütlicher Ort, wo man ausspannen und andere Gäste treffen kann, z.B. in der Kaminstube.

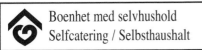

Grønebakke Gard i Valdres

Your host:
Mette Irene Johansen

Address:
Grønebakke
N - 2917 Skautvål
Phone: 61 36 37 87
Mobile: 97 57 49 10
E-mail: gronebakke@online.no

Best time to call:
09.00 - 21.00
GPS: 61°2'25"N 9°23'20"E

Guesthouse for 2-8 persons	Gjestehus for 2-8 personer	Gästehaus für 2-8 Personen
3 bedrooms, bath, kitchen, LR	3 soverom, bad, kjøkken, stue	3 Schlafzi., Bad, Küche, Stube
Price for whole unit: **850,-**	Pris for hele enheten: **850,-**	Ganze Einheit: **850,-**
Bed linen fee: **100,-**	Tillegg for sengetøy: **100,-**	Mieten von Bettwäsche: **100,-**
Prices valid for 2011/12	Priser gyldig for 2011/12	Preise gültig für 2011/12
TV available	TV tilgjengelig	TV vorhanden
Patio/yard	Uteplass/hage	Außenbereich/Garten
Pets welcome	Kjæledyr velkommen	Haustiere willkommen
Reservations required	Forhåndsbestilling nødvendig	Vorbestellung nötig
At weekly rent, final cleaning	Ved ukesleie kan slutt-	Wochenleihe: Endreinigung
can be ordered: **400,-**	rengjøring bestilles: **400,-**	auf Bestellung: **400,-**
Open year round	Åpent hele året	Ganzjährig geöffnet
English & Dutch spoken		Sprechen etwas Deutsch

Grønebakke Gard is an inviting farmyard with main building, storehouse and barn from the 1850s. The guesthouse was fully restored in 1997-98. It sits alone and peaceful with a view of other farmsteads lower in the valley and toward the Jotenheimen mountains and to the south toward Fagernes. The distance to Fagernes is 7 km. There are many activities available both summer and winter. Valdres ski center, with lighted ski trails and large network of maintained trails in forest and mountain terrain, is only 1 km. away.

Grønebakke gard er et trivelig tun med hovedbygning, stabbur og stall fra 1850-tallet. Utleiehuset ble fullstendig restaurert i 1997/98. Det ligger fritt og fredelig og litt for seg selv med flott utsikt mot bygda nede i dalen og mot fjellene i Jotunheimen og sørover mot Fagernes. Avstand til Fagernes er 7 km.
Mange muligheter for spennende og varierte dager både sommer og vinter. 1 km til Valdres skisenter med lysløype og et stort nett av preparerte løyper i skogs- og fjellterreng.

Grønebakke ist ein gemütlicher Hof aus den 1850ern mit Wohnhaus, Stabbur (Lebensmittelspeicher) und Stall. Das Gästehaus wurde 1997/98 vollständig restauriert. Es ist ein frei und etwas abseits stehendes Haus, mit schöner Aussicht auf das Dorf im Tal, die Berge in Jotunheimen und Richtung Süden nach Fagernes. Bis Fagernes sind es 7 km.
Viele Möglichkeiten für spannende und abwechslungsreiche Tage im Sommer wie im Winter. 1 km bis zum Skizentrum Valdres mit Flutlichtpiste und einem grossen Netz von präparierten Loipen durch den Wald.

Ulsåkstølen

Your host:
Anne & Gunnar
Ulsaker Bækken

Address:
Ulsåk
N - 3560 Hemsedal
Mobile: 92 23 14 13
E-mail: anne@ulsaakstolen.com
Web: www.ulsaakstolen.com
Best time to call:
09.00 - 22.00
GPS: 60°52'8"N 8°42'26"E

B&B in 'Fjellstugu':
Double-/single room: **900,-/540,-**
No. of rooms: 5
Discount for children under 12 yrs
Breakfast buffet

Selfcatering:
A: "Gamlebua" for 4-8 persons
3 BR, bath, kichen, LR w/fireplace
Price for whole unit: **700,-** to **850,-**

B: "Stølsbua" for 2-6 persons
2 BR, bath, kichen., LR, outhouse
Price for whole unit: **390,-** to **500,-**

Applies to all rooms and cabins:
Prices valid for 2011/12
Available: TV, terrace/deck/yard
Sauna available, boat for rent
Pets welcome
Suitable for handicapped
VISA, MC, DC, AmEx accepted
B&B rooms is open year round
Cabins: open 20 June - 28 Aug.
Some English spoken

B&B i Fjellstugu:
Doppelt-/enkeltrom: **900,-/540,-**
Antal rom: 5
Rabatt for born under 12 år (40%)
Frukostbuffét

Sjølvhushald på Stølen:
A: "Gamlebua" for 4-8 personar
3 soverom, bad, kjøken, peisestove
Pris for heile eininga: **700,-** til **850,-**

B: "Stølsbua" for 2-6 personar
2 soverom, bad, kjk., stove, utedo
Pris for heile eininga: **390,-** til **500,-**

For alle rom og hytter gjeld:
Prisar gjeld for 2011/12
TV tilgjengeleg, uteplass/hage
Badstu gratis, båtutleige
Kjæledyr velkomne
Handikaptilgjengeleg
Vi tek VISA, MC, DC, AmEx
Fjellstugu er ope heile året
Stølen open 20. juni - 28 august.

B&B in der "Fjellstugu":
Doppel-/Einzelzi.:   **900,-/540,-**
Anzahl Zimmer: 5
40% Erm. für Kinder unter 12 J.
Frühstücksbüfett

Selbsthaushalt:
A: "Gamlebua" für 4-8 Personen
3 Schlafzi., Bad, Kü., Stube m. Kamin
Ganze Einheit: **700,-** bis **850,-**

B: "Stølsbua" für 2-6 Personen
2 Schafzi., Bad, Kü.., Stube, Plumpsklo
Ganze Einheit: **390,-** bis **500,-**

Für alle Zimmer und Hütten gilt:
Preise gültig für 2011/12
TV, Außenbereich/Garten
Sauna gratis, Boot zu mieten
Haustiere willkommen
Behindertengerecht
Wir akzept. VISA, MC, DC, AmEx
Berghütte (B&B) ganzjähr. geöffnet
Hütten: Geöffnet 20. Juni - 28. Aug.
Sprechen etwas Deutsch

In beautiful nature with the formidable Skogshorn (1728 m) behind, lies Ulsåkstølen. Cozy ancient farm atmosphere offering hobnobbing with farm animals, flat-bread baking, tending the livestock. Traditional food, sale of farm produce. Mountain trips and lake fishing.

I flott høgfjellsnatur med det mektige Skogshorn (1728m) i bakgrunn ligg Ulsåkstølen. Koseleg gamalt stølsmiljø som tilbyr klapp og kos av dyr, flatbrødbaking, dyrestell, servering av tradisjonsmat, sal av gardsprodukt og Hallingkost, toppturar og fiske med robåt.

In herrlicher Hochgebirgsnatur mit dem mächtigen Skogshorn (1728m) im Hintergrund liegt Ulsåkstolen. Gemütliche, urige Almatmosphäre: Tiere zum Streicheln u. Versorgen, traditionelle Gerichte, "Flatbrød"-Backen, Verkauf v. Hof- u. regionalen Produkten; Wandern, Angeln.

Laa Gjestestugu

Your host:
Lisa Laa

Address:
Øvre Ål
N - 3570 Ål
Phone/Fax: 32 08 12 12
Mobile: 93 86 82 99

Best time to call:
08.00 - 23.00
GPS: 60°37'52"N 8°31'36"E

Double- and single rooms	Doble og enkle rom	Doppel- und Einzelzimmer
Price per person: **380,-**	Pris pr. pers.: **380,-**	Preis pro Pers.: **380,-**
No. of rooms: 2	Antall rom: 2	Anzahl Zimmer: 2
Discount for children	Rabatt for barn	Ermäßigung für Kinder
Breakfast tray	Frokostbrett	Frühstückstablett
Selfcatering possible	Selvhushold er mulig	Selbstverpflegung möglich
Prices valid for 2011	Priser gyldig for 2011	Preise gültig für 2011
TV available	TV tilgjengelig	TV vorhanden
Terrace/patio	Terrasse/uteplass	Terrasse/Außenbereich
Bike for rent	Sykkelutleie	Fahrrad zu mieten
Open year round	Åpent hele året	Ganzjährig geöffnet
English spoken		Sprechen etwas Deutsch

In the country farm courtyard are 9 houses: the oldest being from 1706. For rent is a recent wooden guesthouse which offers high standard with a fireplace and Jacuzzi, washing machine and dish washer. Large common-room. The farm is situated 720 m. above sea level on the sunny side of the valley with a view. Neighboring farm offers horseback riding, sleigh ride in the winter and use of carriage in summer. Hiking facilities with marked trails.

Nybygget gjestehus i tømmer. Gårdstunet har ni hus; det eldste er fra 1706. Hytten/gjestehuset har høy standard med peis og boble-bad, vaskemaskin og oppvask-maskin. Stor fellesstue. Gården ligger på solsiden av dalen, på 720 m.o.h, med fin utsikt. Det er muligheter for å ri på hester hos en nabo, kanefart om vinteren og med vogn om sommeren. Muligheter for fotturer på merkede stier.

Neuerbautes Blockhaus auf einem Gehöft mit 9 Gebäuden; das älteste von 1706. Hütte bzw. Gästehaus sind komfortabel eingerichtet und haben Kamin und Whirlpool, Wasch- u. Spülmaschine. Großes gemeinsames Wohnzimmer. Der Hof liegt auf der Sonnenseite des Tals auf 720 m ü.NN. mit schöner Aussicht. Ganzjährige Reitmöglichkeiten beim Nachbarn (exkl. Schulferien), Pferdekutsch-fahrten (im Winter Pferdeschlitten-touren). Markierte Wanderwege.

A journey is best measured in friends, rather than miles.
~Tim Cahill~

Hagaled Gjestegård

Your host:
Sigrunn Bæra Svenkerud

Address:
Alfarvegen 95
N - 3540 Nesbyen, Hallingdal
Phone: 32 07 10 07
Mobile: 41 41 92 16
E-mail: post@hagaled.no
Web: www.hagaled.no
Best time to call: 09.00 - 23.00
GPS: 60°33'47"N 9°6'44"E

Double room:	**950,-**	Dobbeltrom:	**950,-**	Doppelzimmer:	**950,-**
Single room:	**625,-**	Enkeltrom:	**625,-**	Einzelzimmer:	**625,-**
No. of rooms: 7		Antall rom: 7		Anzahl Zimmer: 7	
Bryggerhus/cabin m/kitchenette, fireplace, bath, BR w/ 4 beds		Bryggerhus/hytte med kjk.krok, peis, bad, soverom med 4 senger		Bryggerhus/Hütte mit Küchenecke, Kamin, Bad, Schlafzi. mit 4 Betten	
Price for 2 persons:	**1050,-**	Pris for 2 personer:	**1050,-**	Preis für 2 Personen:	**1050,-**
Extra bed:	**225,-**	Ekstra seng:	**225,-**	Extrabett:	**225,-**
Laid breakfast table		Dekket frokostbord		Gedeckter Frühstckstisch	
Selfcatering possible		Selvhushold er mulig		Selbstverpflegung möglich	
Prices valid for 2011		Priser gyldig for 2011		Preise gültig für 2011	
TV/Internet available		TV/Internett tilgjengelig		TV/Internet vorhanden	
Terrace w/BBQ/patio/yard		Tun/uteplass med grill/hage		Terrasse/Sitzecke m. Grill/Garten	
Sorry, no pets/smoking indoors		Dyr/røking inne ikke tillatt		Tiere/Rauchen im Haus nicht gest.	
Open year round		Åpent hele året		Ganzjährig geöffnet	
English spoken				Sprechen etwas Deutsch	

Hageled invites you to stay in historic buildings on a thriving farmstead in Gamle Nes near town. Rooms have distinctive and homey atmosphere in the main house, brewhouse and storehouse. Breakfast by the fireplace in a 17th century living room is a good way to start the day. Walking distance to eateries, shops, movies, museum, gallery, hiking and bicycle paths, outoor bathing, fishing. By car: marked hiking/ski trails in gorgeous mountain surroundings, mountain golf, horse center, alpine skiing, Langedrag nature and Vassfaret bear park.

Hagaled inviterer deg til å bo i historiske bygninger på et trivelig gårdstun i Gamle Nes nær sentrum. Rom med særpreg og hjemlig atmosfære i våningshus, bryggerhus og stabbur. Frokost ved peisen i Hallingstugu fra 1600-tallet kan være en god start på en ny dag. Gangavstand til spisested, butikk, kino, museum, galleri, tur-/sykkelstier, friluftsbad, fiske, lysløype, m.m.
Med bil: merkede tur-/skiløyper i "snille fjell" med flott utsikt, fjellgolf, ridesenter, alpinanlegg, Langedrag natur-/Vassfaret bjørnepark.

Hagaled lädt Sie ein, in historischen Gebäuden auf einem gemütlichen Bauernhof in Zentrumsnähe der kulturhistorischen Stadt Gamle Nes zu wohnen. Stilvolle, gemütliche Zimmer. Ein Frühstück am Kamin in der Halling-Stube aus dem 17. Jh. ist der ideale Start in den Tag. Kurzer Fußweg zu Restaurants, Geschäften, Kino, Museum, Galerie, Freibad, Wander-/Radwegen, Loipen uvm. Mit dem Auto zu erreichen: Wander-/Skigebiet "snille fjell", Golf, Reiten, Langedrag Natur-, Vassfaret Bärenpark.

Sevletunet

Your host:
Gro Sevle

Address:
N - 3630 Rødberg
Phone: 32 74 15 86
Mobile: 97 66 56 38
E-mail: post@sevletunet.no
Web: www.sevletunet.no

Best time to call:
08.00 - 23.00
GPS: 60°14'27"N 9°00'34"E

Double room:	**800,-/850,-**	Dobbeltrom:	**800,-/850,-**	Doppelzimmer:	**800,-/850,-**
Single room:	**550,-/650,-**	Enkeltrom:	**550,-/650,-**	Einzelzimmer:	**550,-/650,-**
Family room, for 4 p.:	**1200,-/1300,-**	Familierom for 4 p.:	**1200,-/1300,-**	Familienzi. für 4 P.:	**1200,-/1300,-**
No. of rooms: 8		Antall rom: 8		Anzahl Zi.: 8	
Breakfast buffet		Frokostbuffé		Frühstücksbüfett	
Selfcatering: 4 Cabins: from **500,-**		Selvhushold: 4 hytter: fra **500,-**		Selbsthaushalt: 4 Hütten: ab **500,-**	
Prices valid for 2011		Priser gyldig for 2011		Preise gültig für 2011	
Available: TV, patio/yard		Tilgjengelig: TV, uteplass/hage		TV; Außenbereich/Garten	
Barbeque, hot tub, sauna		Grillhytte, badestamp, badstu		Grillhütte, Badezuber, Sauna	
Boat and bike for rent		Båt- og sykkelutleie		Boot u. Fahrrad zu mieten	
Open year round		Åpent hele året		Ganzjährig geöffnet	
English spoken				Sprechen Deutsch	

In three restored buildings you can stay in historic surroundings: the main house from 1850, a rebuilt barn and bathhouse, both from 1700, all with old-time atmosphere, timber walls and fireplace. Charming bedroom. Both the main house and guest-barn can be rented with room for multiple families. Large green farmyard offers family fun.
The family has lived on the farm since 1837. The hosts are happy to amuse the guests with stories like the famous folk tale about Sevleguten. Tours can be arranged for small and large groups. Wildlife park nearby. Fishing on the farm by the dam, river and fjord.

I tre restaurerte bygninger kan du bo i historiske omgivelser; hovedhuset fra 1850, en ombygd låve og badstua/Rallarstua – begge disse fra 1700, alle med gammeldags atmosfære, tømmervegger og peis. Sjarmerende soverom. Både hovedbygning og gjestelåven kan også leies som storhytte med plass til flere familier. Stort grønt tun som innbyr til gode aktiviteter. Familien har bodd på gården siden 1837. Vertinnen tar seg tid til gjestene og har historier å fortelle. Arrangerer også omvisninger og forteller for små og store grupper. Hør bl.a. den spennende historien om Sevleguten. Nær villmarksparken Langedrag. Fiske på gården både i dam, elv og fjord.

In drei restaurierten Gebäuden wohnen Sie in historischer Umgebung: dem Haupthaus von 1850, der umgebauten Scheune und der Rallarstua, beide von 1700. Die Gebäude, alle mit Holzwänden und Kamin, versprühen eine altertümliche Atmosphäre. Haupthaus und Gästescheune können jeweils auch als große Hütten mit Platz für mehrere Fam. gemietet werden. Großer, grüner Hof. Die Familie wohnt seit 1837 auf dem Hof. Die Gastgeberin nimmt sich Zeit für ihre Gäste und hat einige Geschichten parat. Sie arrangiert auch Führungen für kleine und große Gruppen. Der Wildpark Langedrag ist nicht weit. Angeln vom Hof aus möglich.

Eggedal Borgerstue

Your host:
Elisabeth &
Henriette Koren Bøle

Address:
N - 3359 Eggedal
Phone: 32 71 46 18
Mobile: 92 63 94 63
E-mail: post@eggedal-borgerstue.no
Web: www.eggedal-borgerstue.no
Best time to call: 10.00 - 21.00
GPS: 60°14'42"N 9°21'25"E

Double room:	**690,- / 850,-**	Dobbeltrom:	**690,- / 850,-**	Doppelzimmer:	**690,- / 850,-**
Single room:	**450,- / 650,-**	Enkeltrom:	**450,- / 650,-**	Einzelzimmer:	**450,- / 650,-**

No. of rooms: 15
Breakfast buffet
Prices valid for 2011
VISA, MC, DC accepted
Discount for children
TV/Internet available
Terrace/patio
Open year round
English, some Spanish & French

Antall rom: 15
Frokostbufffét
Priser gyldig for 2011
Vi tar VISA, MC, DC
Rabatt for barn
TV/Internett tilgjengelig
Terrasse/uteplass
Åpent hele året

Anzahl Zimmer: 15
Frühstücksbüfett
Preise gültig für 2011
Wir akzeptieren VISA, MC, DC
Ermäßigung für Kinder
TV/Internet vorhanden
Terrasse/Außenbereich
Ganzjährig geöffnet
Sprechen etwas Deutsch

Eggedal Borgerstue is a small, family-run hotel, owned by the Koren Bøle family for over 40 years. The old house from 1919 was originally a transit and community center. The oldest rooms are named for their former functions, such as "Doctors office", "Priest's room", "Sherrif's office" and "Waiting room".
Borgerstue is in scenic "artists' valley" just two hours from Oslo. At Eggedal Borgerstue they take time to prepare home-made Norwegian food with ingredients gathered from the local nature. There's always moose, trout and reindeer on the menu.

Eggedal Borgerstue er et lite familiedrevet hotell, eid av familien Koren Bøle i over 40 år. Det gamle huset fra 1919 var opprinnelig skysstasjon og kommunehus. De eldste rommene har fortsatt navnet til sin tidligere funksjon som for eksempel "Legekontoret", "Prestestua", "Forliksrådet", "Lensmannsrommet" og "Venteværelset".
Borgerstua ligger midt i vakre "kunstnerdalen" – bare 2 timer fra Oslo.
På Eggedal Borgerstue er de opptatt av hjemmelaget norsk mat, råvarene hentes helst i naturen omkring. Til enhver tid er det elg, ørret og rein på menyen.

Eggedal Borgerstue ist ein kleines, familienbetriebenes Hotel, das sich seit über 40 Jahren im Besitz der Familie Koren Bøle befindet. Das alte Haus von 1919 war ursprünglich Pferdewechselstation und Gemeindehaus. Die ältesten Zimmer sind nach ihren damaligen Funktionen benannt, z.B. Arztpraxis, Pfarrraum, Wartezimmer und Wache. Die Borgerstue liegt mitten im schönen 'Künstlertal', nur zwei Stunden von Oslo entfert. Hier in der Eggedal Borgerstue legen wir sehr viel Wert auf hausgemachte norwegische Speisen. Die Zutaten dafür holen wir uns am liebsten aus der umliegenden Gegend. Elch, Lachsforelle u. Rentier stehen bei uns jederzeit auf d. Karte.

Bjørke gård

Your host:
Kristin Farden Bjella
& Knut Bjella

Address:
Bjørkeveien 25
N - 3512 Hønefoss
Phone: 32 16 01 20
Mobile: 95 45 01 55 / 90 86 13 66
E-mail: post@bjorkegard.no
Web: www.bjorkegard.no

Best time to call:
09.00 - 23.00
GPS: 60°06'46"N 10°16'29"E

Store-house for up to 6 persons		Stabbur for inntil 6 personer		"Stabbur" für bis zu 6 Personen	
Price for 1 person:	**540,-**	Pris for 1 person:	**540,-**	Preis für 1 Person:	**540,-**
Price for 2 Persons:	**680,-**	Pris for 2 personer:	**680,-**	Preis für 2 Personen:	**680,-**
Price for 3 persons:	**820,-**	Pris for 3 personer:	**820,-**	Preis für 3 Personen:	**820,-**
Price per additional pers.:	**240,-**	Pris pr. tilleggsperson:	**240,-**	Jede weitere Person:	**240,-**

Discount for children: ask
Breakfast tray
Selfcatering possible
Prices valid for 2011/12
Terrace/deck/yard
Pets welcome by agreement
Open 1 April - 10 Oct.
English spoken

Rabatt for barn: spør
Frokostbrett
Selvhushold er mulig
Priser gyldig for 2011/12
Terrasse/uteplass/hage
Kjæledyr: spør
Åpent 1. april - 10. okt.

Ermäßigung f. Kinder auf Anfrage
Frühstückstablett
Selbstverpflegung möglich
Preise gültig für 2011/12
Terrasse/Außenbereich/Garten
Haustiere auf Nachfrage willk.
Geöffnet 1. April - 10. Okt.
Sprechen etwas Deutsch

Bjørke gård is on high ground surrounded by a beautiful panorama. The farm produces grain, vegetables and corn. They provide a pick-your-own produce service in August and September. There are also sheep, chickens and horses on the farm.
In the storehouse for rent, the old corn crib has been converted into beds. There is a bath in the barn.
Within reach are Oslo, Nordmarka, Hadeland Glassverk, Kistefosmuseet, Kjerratmuseet, Hringariki kulturminnepark, Ringerikbadet, Tyrifjorden and Steinsfjorden.

Bjørke gård ligger på en høyde, midt i kulturlandskapet, med flott utsikt. På gården driver vertskapet med produksjon av korn, grønnsaker og mais. De driver en gårdsbutikk med selvplukk i august og september. Det er også hester, sauer og høner på gården.
I stabburet som leies ut, er de gamle kornbingene gjort om til senger. Badet ligger i låven.
Innen rekkevidde er Oslo, Nordmarka, Hadeland Glassverk, Kistefosmuseet, Kjerratmuseet, Hringariki kulturminnepark, Ringerikbadet, Tyrifjorden og Steinsfjorden.

Der Bjørke Hof liegt mitten in der Kulturlandschaft auf einer Anhöhe mit toller Aussicht. Der Hof ist ein Getreide-, Gemüse- und Maisbetrieb. Im Hofladen können Sie alle Produkte kaufen oder im August und September auch selber vom Feld ernten. Auf dem Hof gibt es Pferde, Schafe und Hühner. Im zu vermietenden ehemaligen "Stabbur" (Lebensmittelspeicher) wurden die alten Kornspeichernischen zu Betten umgebaut. Das Bad befindet sich in der Scheune. Vom Hof gut zu erreichen sind Oslo, die Nordmarka, das Hadeland Glaswerk, das Kristefoss-Industrie-, das Kjerrat-Handwerksmuseum uvm.

Frøhaug Gård

Your host:
Ellen & Arne Fjeldstad

Address:
Røyseveien 531
N - 3530 Røyse
Phone/Fax: 32 15 71 09
E-mail: d-fjeld@online.no

Best time to call:
15.00 - 21.00
GPS: 60°5'20"N 10°12'54"E

Double-/Twin-/Triple room		Dbl.rom/2-sengsrom/3-sengsrom		Doppel-/Zweibett-/Dreibettzi.	
Price per person:	**350,-**	Pris pr. pers.:	**350,-**	Preis pro Pers.:	**350,-**
No. of rooms: 5		Antall rom: 5		Anzahl Zimmer: 5	
Breakfast buffet		Frokostbuffét		Frühstücksbüfett	
or laid breakfast table		eller dekket frokostbord		oder gedeckter Frühstückstisch	
Prices valid for 2011		Priser gyldig for 2011		Preise gültig für 2011	
TV available		TV tilgjengelig		TV vorhanden	
Terrace/patio/yard		Terrasse/uteplass/hage		Terrasse/Außenbereich/Garten	
Open year round		Åpent hele året		Ganzjährig geöffnet	
Some English spoken				Sprechen etwas Deutsch	

Frøhaug Farm, located in a quiet area 5 km from Vik in Hole, with view of Tyrifjorden and Krokskogen forest. The "Main House," from 1766, the second floor room is in Biedermeier style. A large farm kitchen offers large farm style breakfasts. The hosts' son runs the farm. There are farm animals and a large quiet yard, safe for children.

Directions:
Follow E-16 to Vik about 10 km south of Hønefoss. Take the exit towards Røyse and proceed straight ahead 5 km. Look for the sign alongside the highway.

Frøhaug gård, 5 km fra Vik i Hole, ligger høyt og fritt med utsikt over Tyrifjorden og med Krokskogen i bakgrunnen. Hovedbygningen er fra 1766, TV-stuen i 2. etg. er i biedermeierstil.
Stor frokost serveres i stort gårdskjøkken.
Vertskapets sønn har overtatt driften av gården. Det er noen dyr.
Stor hage og uteplass ved husene, stille og barnevennlig.

Veibeskrivelse:
Kjør E-16 til Vik ca. 10 km sør for Hønefoss. Ta av mot Røyse og kjør rett frem 5 km. Det står skilt ved veien.

Der Hof Frøhaug, 5 km von Vik in Hole, liegt hoch und frei mit Aussicht über den See Tyrifjord, umgeben vom Waldgebiet Krokskogen. Das Haupthaus ist aus 1766, die TV-Stube im OG im Biedermeierstil. In der großen Bauernküche gibt es ein reichhaltiges Frühstück. Der Sohn hat den Hof mit einigen Tieren übernommen. Großer Garten, ruhig u. kinderfreundlich.

Wegbeschreibung:
Fahren Sie die E-16 bis Vik, ca. 10 km südlich von Hønefoss. Dort biegen Sie ab in Richtung Røyse und fahren 5 km geradeaus. Der Hof ist von der Straße aus ausgeschildert.

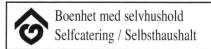

Hamremoen Gård

Your host:
Diana Wijnans-Ewalds
Address:
Bøveien 1
N - 3618 Skollenborg
Phone: **32 76 88 59**
Mobile: **32 76 88 59**
E-mail: **post@hamremoen.no**
Web: **www.hamremoen.no**
Best time to call:
07.00 - 21.00
GPS: 59°34'25"N 9°46'51"E

One-room cabin for 2-4 persons	Ettromshytte for 2-4 personer	1-Raum-Hütte für 2-4 Personen
Kitchen nook	Kjøkkenkrok	Küchenecke
WC & shower in sanitary facilities	WC og dusj i sanitæranlegg	WC u. Dusche in Sanitäranlage
Price per 1 unit: **550,-**	Pris pr. enhet: **550,-**	Preis pro Einheit: **550,-**
No. of units: 7	Antall enheter: 7	Anzahl Einheiten: 7
Bed linen: **75,-**	Tillegg for sengetøy: **75,-**	Bettwäsche: **75,-**
Breakfast service available: **115,-**	Frokost kan serveres: **115,-**	Frühstück auf Bestellung: **115,-**
Prices valid for 2011	Priser gyldig for 2011	Preise gültig für 2011
Internet available	Internett tilgjengelig	Internet verfügbar
Terrace/patio/yard	Terrasse/uteplass/hage	Terrasse/Außenbereich/Garten
Pets welcome	Kjæledyr velkommen	Haustiere willkommen
VISA, MC accepted	Vi tar VISA, MC	Wir akzeptieren VISA, MC
Open April - October	Åpent april - oktober	Geöffnet April - Oktober
English, Dutch & some Fr. spoken		Sprechen Deutsch

Hamremoen Gård is operated by a family of five from the Netherlands. On the farmsite are a store and restaurant to satisfy guests' needs from breakfast to dinner to late-night snack. The store sells locally made goods such as preserves, honey, eggs, ecological herbs, tea and craft items. Besides the cabins there is a campground with tent rental. Here is a playground for children and fenced-in farm animals. The nearby Skrimfjell mountains can be easily hiked by the entire family. Norway's longest 18-hole golf course is 5 km from Hamremoen farm, which is 15 km. south of Kongsberg on the RV 40.

Hamremoen Gård drives av en familie på fem fra Nederland. På gården er det både gårdsbutikk og restaurant som dekker alle gjestenes behov fra frokost til middag. I butikken selges lokalt produserte varer som syltetøy, honning, egg, økologiske urter, te og en del lokalt håndverk. I tillegg til hyttene er her også campingplass med utleie av lavvuer. Her er lekeplass for barna og en innhegning med dyr. Skrimfjellene er et lett tilgjengelig turområdet for hele familien. 5 km til Norges lengste 18-hulls golfbane. Alt dette; 15 km sør for Kongsberg langs RV 40.

Hamremoen Gård wird von einer fünfköpfigen Familie aus den Niederlanden betrieben. Ein Hofladen und ein Restaurant decken alle kulinarischen Bedürfnisse der Gäste. Lokal produzierte Waren wie Marmelade, Honig, Eier, ökologische Kräuter, Tee etc. werden angeboten. Ein Campingplatz mit der Möglichkeit Zelte auszuleihen ist vorhanden, sowie ein Spielplatz für Kinder und ein Tiergehege. Die Skrimfjellene sind ein familienfreundliches Wandergebiet. 5 km bis zur längsten 18-Loch-Golfbahn Norwegens. All dies 15 km südl. von Kongsberg entlang der Str. 40.

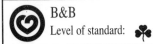
Hvasser B&B

Your host:
Christine Tønnessen

Address:
Hvasserveien 211
N - 3148 Hvasser
Phone: 33 39 33 42
Mobile: 95 21 65 99
E-mail:
christineslampe@hotmail.com

Best time to call:
16.00 - 22.00
GPS: 59°04'52"N 10°26'45"E

Double room:	**800,-**	Dobbeltrom:	**800,-**	Doppelzimmer:	**800,-**
1 pers. in double room:	**400,-**	1 pers. i dobbeltrom:	**400,-**	1 Pers. im DZ:	**400,-**
Extra bed:	**200,-**	Ekstraseng:	**200,-**	Extrabett:	**200,-**

No. of rooms: 2
Laid breakfast table/breakfast tray
Prices valid for 2011/12
Discount for children
Selfcatering possible
Terrace/patio/yard
Pets welcome
Open year round
English spoken

Antall rom: 2
Dekket frokostbord el. frokostkurv
Priser gyldig for 2011/12
Rabatt for barn
Selvhushold er mulig
Terrasse/uteplass/hage
Kjæledyr tillatt
Åpent hele året

Anzahl Zimmer: 2
Frühstückstisch oder -tablett
Preise gültig für 2011/12
Ermäßigung für Kinder
Selbstverpflegung möglich
Terrasse/Außenbereich/Garten
Haustiere willkommen
Ganzjährig geöffnet
Sprechen Englisch

Hvasser is a little place on the island community Tjøme in Vestfold with unique contact with skerries and sea. Here is fantastic bicycle and hiking trails with many bathing beaches and rock slabs for sun bathing. Hvasser B&B has one double and one single room with a sunny outdoor area suitable for grilling and food preparation.
From the house it's about 200 m to Sandøsund with harbour, bathing beach, general store, fish shop, restaurant and gallery.

Hvasser er et lite sted i øykommunen Tjøme i Vestfold og har unik kontakt med skjærgården og havet. Her er et fantastisk sykkel- og turterreng med flere badestrender og svaberg for solbading.
Hvasser B&B har et dobbelt og et enkeltrom, samt solrik uteplass for med mulighet for grilling og matlaging.
Fra huset er det ca 200 meter til Sandøsund med båthavn, badestrand, kolonialforretning, fiskebutikk, samt restauranter og gallerier.

Hvasser ist ein kleiner Ort in der Inselkommune Tjøme und hat einmaligem Zugang zum Meer und den Schären. Das Gebiet ist fantastisch zum Radfahren und Wandern und bietet mehrere Badestrände und Felsen zum Sonnenbaden.
Im Hvasser B&B finden Sie ein Doppel- und ein Einzelzimmer zusammen mit einem sonnenreichen Garten, in dem auch gegrillt werden kann.
Vom Haus sind es ca. 200 m zum Sandøsund mit Bootshafen, Badestrand, Lebensmittelgeschäft, Fischladen, sowie Restaurants und Galerien.

Lavendela B&B

Your host:
Øivind Sande

Address:
Gamle Kongevei 22B
N - 3269 Larvik
Mobile: 98 82 55 65 / 45 21 31 25
E-mail: lavendela22b@live.no
Web: www.lavendela.com

Best time to call:
08.00 - 23.00
GPS: 59°3'42"N 10°1'55"E

Prices low season / high season:		Priser lavsesong / høysesong:		Preis: Nebensaison / Hochsaison:	
Double room:	750,-/850,-	Dobbeltrom:	750,-/850,-	Doppelzimmer:	750,-/850,-
Single room:	650,-/750,-	Enkeltrom:	650,-/750,-	Einzelzimmer:	650,-/750,-

No. of rooms: 2 | Antall rom: 2 | Anzahl Zimmer: 2
Laid breakfast table | Dekket frokostbord | Gedeckter Frühstückstisch
Prices valid for 2011/12 | Priser gyldig for 2011/12 | Preise gültig für 2011/12
TV/Internet available | TV/Internett tilgjengelig | TV/Internet vorhanden
Terrace/deck/yard | Terrasse/uteplass/hage | Terrasse/Außenbereich/Garten
Suitable for handicapped | Handikapvennlig | Behindertengerecht
Open year round | Åpent hele året | Ganzjährig geöffnet
English spoken | Sprechen Englisch

Lavendela is a friendly and informal B&B offering light and comfortable rooms in a newly renovated 1920s-era house. It lies near Larvik centrum, a popular stop for travelers going by ferry to/from Denmark or flight passengers from Torp airport. Larvik district boasts forest and mountain, beaches and coastline, a bounty of vacation experiences.

Directions:
Turn off E-18 to follow signs to Nanset. At the third roundabout turn right on Gamle Kongevei.

Lavendela er et vennlig og uformelt B&B som tilbyr lyse og komfortable rom i nyoppusset hus fra 1920-årene. Det ligger nær Larvik sentrum, et populært stopp for reisende både med båt til/fra Danmark og flyreisende som reiser via Torp flyplass. Larvikdistriktet kan by på både skog og fjell, strender og skjærgård, et mangfold av ferieopplevelser.

Veibeskrivelse:
Ta av fra E-18 og følg skilt mot Nanset. Ved 3dje rundkjøring tar du til høyre som er Gamle Kongevei.

Lavendela - ein freundliches und offenes B&B - bietet helle und komfortable Zimmer in einem neurenovierten Haus aus den 1920ern. Das Haus befindet sich nahe des Zentrums von Larvik und ist daher ein beliebter Halt für Reisende mit der Fähre von/nach Dänemark oder mit dem Flugzeug ab/nach Torp Flughafen.
Das Gebiet um Larvik kann mit Wäldern und Bergen, Stränden und Schären, und einer Vielfalt an Ferienerlebnissen aufwarten.

Wegbeschreibung:
Von der E-18 abfahren und den Schildern nach Nanset folgen. Am dritten Kreisverkehr rechts in den Gamle Kongevei ausfahren.

Nordbø Pensjonat

Your host:
Patrick & Marieke Clijsters

Address:
N - 3690 Hjartdal
Phone: 35 60 70 46
Mobile: 98 08 17 84
E-mail: info@nordbopensjonat.com
Web: www.nordbopensjonat.com

Best time to call:
09.00 - 22.00
GPS: 59°35'59"N 8°39'22"E

Double room:	**795,-**	Dobbeltrom:	**795,-**	Doppelzimmer:	**795,-**
Twin room:	**745,-**	Tosengsrom:	**745,-**	Zweibettzimmer:	**745,-**
Single room:	**585,-**	Enkeltrom:	**585,-**	Einzelzimmer:	**585,-**
No. of rooms: 5		Antall rom: 5		Anzahl Zimmer: 5	
Breakfast buffet		Frokost buffét		Frühstücksbüfett	
Prices valid for 2011		Priser gyldig for 2011		Preise gültig für 2011	
TV/Internet available		TV/Internett tilgjengelig		TV/Internet vorhanden	
Terrace/deck/yard		Terrasse/uteplass/hage		Terrasse/Außenbereich/Garten	
VISA, MC accepted		Vi tar VISA, MC		Wir akzeptieren VISA, MC	
Open year round		Åpent hele året		Ganzjährig geöffnet	
English, Dutch spoken				Sprechen Deutsch	

Nordbø Pension is a guesthouse with a lively, cozy atmosphere tucked in the heart of Telemark. Guest rooms are newly renovated. Cafe serves full dinners or just coffee; gift shop offers locally made products.
Surrounding mountains offer recreation year-round.
One of Norway's most beautiful mountains, Gaustatoppen, is nearby. From the top you can see one-sixth of Norway on a clear day. Telemark is specially known for rich cultural traditions including museums, Telemark canal and canal lock, and Norway's largest stave church at Heddal.

Nordbø Pensjonat er et gjestehus fylt med god stemning og koselig atmosfære som ligger i hjertet av Telemark. Gjesterommene er nyoppussede. I kaféen kan du få servert full middag eller bare ta en kaffe, eller du kan handle lokale produkter i gavebutikken.
Fjellene rundt gir muligheter for aktiviteter både sommer og vinter. Gaustatoppen er et av Norges vakreste fjell. Fra toppen kan du i klarvær se 1/6 av Norges land. Telemark er særlig kjent for sine rike kulturelle tradisjoner. I regionen kan du finne museer, Telemarkskanalen med sitt sluseanlegg og i Heddal Norges største stavkirke.

Mitten im Herzen Telemarks gelegen besticht die Nordbø Pension durch ihre freundliche und gemütliche Atmosphäre.Die Gästezimmer sind neu renoviert. In unserem Café können sie ein Abendessen erhalten oder auch nur einen Kaffee trinken. In unserem kleinen Geschenkeladen halten wir lokale Produkte für Sie bereit. Die Berge ringsherum bieten Möglichkeiten für Sommer- u. Winteraktivitäten. Der Gaustatoppen ist einer der schönste Berge Norwegens. Von der Spitze kann man hier bei klarem Wetter 1/6 des ganzen Landes sehen. Die Telemark ist besonders für ihre kulturellen Traditionen bekannt - hier finden sich Museen, der Telemarkkanal mit seinen Schleusenanlagen u. Norwegens größte Stabkirche in Heddal.

Huldrehaugen

Your host:
Lisbeth & John Arthur Haugen

Address:
Flatdalsvegen 1231
N - 3841 Flatdal
Phone: 35 05 22 75
Mobile: 95 21 03 35
E-mail:
lisbethshaugen@hotmail.com

Best time to call:
20.00 - 22.00
GPS: 59°34'18"N 8°33'28"E

Double room: double bed, desk	**780,-**	Dobbeltrom: dobbeltseng, skrivebord	**780,-**	Doppelzimmer: Doppelbett, Schreibtisch	**780,-**
Double room: convertible double bed sofa	**700,-**	Dobbeltrom: dobbel sovesofa	**700,-**	Doppelzimmer: Doppelschlafcouch	**700,-**
1 pers. in double room:	**450,-**	1 pers. i dobbeltrom:	**450,-**	1 Pers. in Doppelzi.:	**450,-**
Extra bed:	**100,-**	Ekstraseng:	**100,-**	Extrabett:	**100,-**
Children's bed available		Barneseng tilgjengelig		Kinderbett auf Anfrage	
No. of rooms: 2		Antall rom: 2		Anzahl Zimmer: 2	
Laid breakfast table		Dekket frokostbord		Gedeckter Frühstückstisch	
Prices valid for 2011/12		Priser gyldig for 2011/12		Preise gültig für 2011/12	
Common LR with TV/radio		Gjestestue med TV/Radio		Aufenthaltsraum mit TV/Radio	
Patio/yard		Uteplass/hage		Außenbereich/Garten	
Pets welcome, pls. ask beforehand		Kjæledyr velk. ved forespørsel		Haustiere nach Absprache willk.	
Open year round		Åpent hele året		Ganzjährig geöffnet	
English spoken				Sprechen etwas Deutsch	

Flatdal is a distinctive valley, completely flat between steep mountain walls. Huldrehaugen is located on a mountain slope with beautiful view of Lifjell, Skorve and Melefjell.
You are in the midst of Telemark's many cultural and historical attractions; only 200 m. from Nutheim, with a café and gallery. Possibility to visit the studio of the famous Norwegian artists the brothers Grøstad.
Hiking in the forest, fields and mountains.

Flatdal er en særegen dal og er, som navnet forteller, helt flat i bunnen. På begge sider stiger fjellene bratt opp. Huldrehaugen ligger oppe i dalsiden med en fantastisk flott utsikt til Lifjell, Skorve og Melefjell.
Her befinner du deg midt blandt Telemarks mange kulturelle og historiske opplevelsestilbud. Like ved ligger Nutheim, med kafé og galleri. Muligheter for å besøke atelieret til de kjente norske kunstnerne brødrene Grøstad.
Turer i skog, mark og fjell.

Flatdal ist ein besonderes Tal und, wie der Name andeutet, ganz flach mit zu beiden Seiten steil aufragenden Bergen. Von Huldrehaugen haben Sie eine fantastische Aussicht auf die Berge Lifjell, Skorve und Melefjell. Günstiger Ausgangspunkt zu den vielen kulturellen und historischen Erlebnissen in Telemark. Gleich nebenan liegt Nutheim mit Galerie und. Café. Hier können Sie das Atelier der bekannten norwegischen Künstlerbrüder Grøstad besuchen. Gute Ausflugsmöglichkeiten in die umliegenden Wälder, Felder und Gebirge.

Solheim Overnatting

Your host:
Kari Seliussen
& Tore Sognefest
Address: Seljordvegen 1225
N - 3800 Bø i Telemark
Phone: 35 95 00 15
Mobile: 91 34 81 40
E-mail: torefest@c2i.net
Web: www.mitt.no/solheim
Best time to call: 08.00 - 22.00
GPS: 9°26'11"N 8°51'48"E

Double room:	**700,-**	Dobbeltrom:	**700,-**	Doppelzimmer:	**700,-**
Triple room:	**800,-**	Trippelrom:	**800,-**	Dreibettzimmer:	**800,-**
No. of rooms: 2		Antall rom: 2		Anzahl Zimmer: 2	
Breakfast served		Frokost serveres		Frühstück wird serviert	
Other meals served upon request		Andre måltider mulig, vegetarisk		Weitere Mahlzeiten mgl., vegetar.	
Prices valid for 2011/12		Priser gyldig for 2011/12		Preise gültig für 2011/12	
DVD/Internet available		DVD/Internett tilgjengelig		DVD/Internet verfügbar	
Terrace/patio/yard		Terrasse/uteplass/hage		Terrasse/Außenbereich/Garten	
Jacuzzi, steam shower, massage and infrared sauna		Boblebad, steamdusj, massasje og IR-sauna		Whirlpool, Dampfdusche, Massage und Infrarotsauna	
Open year round		Åpent hele året		Ganzjährig geöffnet	
English spoken				Sprechen etwas Deutsch	

Directions:
RV 36 between Bø and Seljord; 13 km from Bø and 16 km from Seljord. Look for signs "Kunst og håndverk" and "Eden Glassdesign", a large yellow house.
(Hegna Camping across the street.)

Veibeskrivelse:
RV 36 mellom Bø og Seljord; 13 km fra Bø og 16 km fra Seljord. Se etter skiltene "Kunst og håndverk" og "Eden Glassdesign", et stort gult hus.
(Hegna Camping ligger på motsatt side av veien).

Wegbeschreibung:
Strasse 36 zwischen Bø und Seljord; 13 km von Bø und 16 km von Seljord entfernt. Achten Sie auf die Schilder "Kunst og håndverk" und "Eden Glassdesign", bzw. auf ein grosses gelbes Haus. (Hegna Camping liegt auf der gegenüberliegenden Straßenseite).

Twenty years from now you will be more disappointed by
the things you didn't do than by the ones you did do.
So throw off the bowlines, sail away from the safe harbor.
Catch the trade winds in your sails. Explore. Dream. Discover.
~Mark Twain~

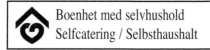
Apartment for 4 (-6) persons	Leilighet for 4 (-6) personer	Wohnung für 4 (-6) Personen
1 bedroom, bath, kitchen, dinette	1 soverom, bad, kjk., sittegruppe	1 Schlafzi., Bad, Küche, Essecke
Price for whole unit (4 p.): **950,-**	Pris for hele enheten (4p.): **950,-**	Ganze Einheit (4 P.): **950,-**
Price per pers. exeeding 4 p.: **50,-**	Pr. pers. utover 4 p.: **50,-**	Jede weitere Pers.: **50,-**
No. of apartments: 2	Antall leiligheter: 2	Anzahl Wohnungen: 2
Bed linen included	Sengetøy er inkludert	Inkl. Betwäsche
Bed linen extra bed: **75,-/50,-**	Sengetøy ekstra seng: **75,-/50,-**	Bettwäsche f. Extrabett: **75,-/50,-**
Breakfast svc. avail.: **100,-/50,-**	Frokost kan serveres: **100,-/50,-**	FR auf Bestellung: **100,-/50,-**
Other meals served upon request	Andre måltider mulig, vegetarisk	Weitere Mahlzeiten mgl., vegetar.
Prices valid for 2011/12	Priser gyldig for 2011/12	Preise gültig für 2011/12
TV/Internet available	TV/Internett tilgjengelig	TV/Internet verfügbar
Terrace/patio/yard	Terrasse/uteplass/hage	Terrasse/Außenbereich/Garten
Jacuzzi, steam shower, massage	Boblebad, steamdusj, massasje	Whirpool, Dampfdusche, Massage
and infrared sauna	og IR-sauna	und Infrarotsauna
Pets welcome by agreement	Kjæledyr velkommen etter avtale	Haustiere nach Absprache willk.
Open year round	Åpent hele året	Ganzjährig geöffnet
English spoken		Sprechen etwas Deutsch

Solheim Overnatting is in a building which formerly has housed both a boarding house and a store. The hosts are teachers in arts and crafts and music. Kari runs a shop in the house with craftworks for sale and she produces modern leaded glass. The property also comprises a barn, greenhouse and ball field.

Solheim lies in a beautiful area between Bø and Seljord in the heart of Telemark near the east side of Seljord Lake, which is famous for the sea serpent Selma. Good possibilities for swiming, fishing and hiking in the forest and mountains. Short way to Sommarland swimming park in Bø, Telemarkskanalen and Lifjell. There are good connections with trains and express buses. The Torp airport bus and 'Haukeliexpress' Oslo/Bergen stop nearby.

Solheim Overnatting er et stort hus som tidligere har vært både pensjonat og butikk. Vertskapet er lærere i kunst/håndverk og musikk. Kari har egen butikk i huset med håndverksprodukter for salg og hvor hun produserer moderne blyglass.
Eiendommen omfatter også låve, drivhus og ballplass.
Solheim ligger i et vakkert område mellom Bø og Seljord i hjertet av Telemark, like ved enden av Seljordvannet som er kjent for sjøormen Selma. Her er gode muligheter for bading, fiske og turer i skog og fjell. Kort vei til Sommarland badepark i Bø, Telemarkskanalen og Lifjell.
Det er gode forbindelser med tog og ekspressbuss. Buss fra Torp flyplass og Haukeliekspressen Oslo/Bergen stopper like ved.

Solheim Overnattting ist ein großes Haus, in dem früher eine Pension und ein Geschäft untergebracht waren. Die Wirtsleute sind Lehrer für Kunsthandwerk und Musik. Kari betreibt im Haus ein eigenes Geschäft mit Handwerksprodukten und stellt modernes Bleiglas her. Zum Hof gehören zusätzlich eine Scheune, ein Gewächshaus und Fußballplatz.
Solheim liegt in reizvoller Umgebung zwischen Bø und Seljord im Herzen der Telemark, direkt am Ende des Sees Seljordvatn, der bekannt für sein Seeungeheuer „Selma" ist. Gute Möglichkeiten zum Baden, Angeln und Wandern. Unweit entfernt sind der „Sommarland Badepark" in Bø, der Telemarkkanal und das Lifjell Wander- und Skigebiet. Gute Anbindung (Bahn und Expressbus). Der Flughafenbus Torp sowie der 'Haukeliexpress' Oslo/Bergen halten gleich in der Nähe.

Nordigard Bjørge

Your host:
Solrunn & Leiv Bjørge

Address:
N - 3840 Seljord
Phone: 35 05 00 40
E-mail: vbjoerge@online.no
Web: www.nord-bjoerge.no

Best time to call:
08.00 - 23.00
GPS: 59°29'24"N 8°38'51"E

Double-/twin room:	**850,-**	Dobbelt-/tosengsrom:	**850,-**	Doppel-/Zweibettzi.:	**850,-**
Single room:	**525,-**	Enkeltrom:	**525,-**	Einzelzimmer:	**525,-**

No. of rooms: 8
Discount for children/families
Laid breakfast table
Selfcatering possible
Prices valid for 2011
TV available
Terrace/patio/yard
Boat and canoe for rent
Pets welcome
VISA accepted
Open year round
Winter: Book in advance, min. 4 p.
English spoken

Antal rom: 8
Rabatt for born/familiar
Dekka frukostbord
Høve til sjølvhushald
Priser gjeld for 2011
TV tilgjengeleg
Terrasse/uteplass/hage
Båt- og kanoutleige
Kjæledyr velkomne
Vi tek VISA
Ope heile året
Vinter: best. på førehand, min. 4 p.

Anzahl Zimmer: 8
Ermäßigung für Kinder/Familien
Gedeckter Frühstückstisch
Selbstverpflegung möglich
Preise gültig für 2011
TV vorhanden
Terrasse/Außenbereich/Garten
Boot und Kanu zu mieten
Haustiere willkommen
Wir akzeptieren VISA
Ganzjährig geöffnet
Winter: Vorausbestellung, mind. 4 P.
Sprechen etwas Deutsch

Nordigard Bjørge has a natural bucolic farm atmosphere. Milk cows stay outside the entire summer while the hens roam freely behind the barn. Ice cream is produced on the farm from milk contributed by Telemark cows. Here there is an abundance of activities to offer. Children may enjoy a fine playground and it's only a 5-min. walk to the beach. Guests may use a rowboat or canoe on the lake, where they can also fish for freshwater herring and trout. Marked trails leading to mountains in the area, and on Lifjell there are other lakes teeming with fish.

Nordigard Bjørge har eit roleg og naturleg gardsmiljø. Mjølkekyrne går ute heile sumaren og bak fjøset trippar hønene. Produksjon av iskrem på garden med mjølk frå ku-rasen Telemarksku.
Her er rikeleg med aktivitetstilbod. Borna har fin leikeplass, og det er berre 5 min. å gå til badestrand. På vatnet ligg ein robåt og ein kano som kan nyttast og kor ein kan fiske sik og aure. Frå garden og frå bygda ellers er det merka turløyper til fjellområda rundt. På Lifjell er det rike fiskevatn.

Nordigard Bjørge ist ein ruhiger Hof umgeben von schöner Natur. Kühe und Hühner laufen den Sommer über frei auf dem Hof umher.. Aus der Milch der Telemark-Kuh wird hier hausgemachte Eiscreme hergestellt. Reichhaltige Aktivitätsangebote für Gäste. Schöner Spielplatz für Kinder und es sind nur 5 Gehminuten bis zum Badestrand. Ruderboot und Kanu stehen dort zur Verfügung, auch Angeln ist möglich. Ausgeschilderte Wanderwege in die Berge vom Hof und auch vom Ort aus. Im Lifjellgebiet finden sich viele Angelseen.

Mjonøy

Your host:
**Ellen B. Nordstoga &
Darius Jasmantavicius**
Address:
N - 3890 Vinje
Phone: **35 07 25 53**
Mobile: **97 57 40 84**
Fax: **35 07 26 33**
E-mail: **ellen@mjonoy.no**
Web: **www.mjonoy.no**

Best time to call:
08.00 - 20.00
GPS: 59°38'4"N 7°48'2"E

A: 4 rental units w/high standard
   ask for price

B: 9 rental units with simple std.
   Kitchenette, no running water
   WC & shower in sanitary facilities
   Price per unit for 2 pers.:   **300,-**
   Price per unit for 4 pers.:   **400,-**

Bed linen fee: **100,-**
Breakfast available: from **85,-**
Prices valid for 2011/12
Internet available
Pets welcome
Terrace/patio/yard
VISA, MC accepted
A-units: Open year round
B-units: Open 1 June - 1 October
English spoken

A: 4 einingar med høg standard
   spør om pris

B: 9 einingar med enkel standard
   Kjøkenkrok, ikkje innlagt vatn
   Delt WC og dusj i sanitæranlegg
   Pris pr. eining for 2 pers.:   **300,-**
   Pris pr. eining for 4 pers.:   **400,-**

Tillegg for sengeklede: **100,-**
Frukost: frå **85,-**
Priser gjeld for 2011/12
Internett tilgjengeleg
Kjæledyr velkomne
Terrasse/uteplass/hage
Vi tek VISA, MC
A-einingar: ope heile året
B-einingar: ope 1. juni - 1. okt.

A: 4 Einheit mit hohem Standard
   Preis auf Anfrage

B: 9 Einheiten, einfacher Standard
   Küchenecke, kein fl. Wasser
   WC u. Dusche in Sanitäranlage
   Preis pro Einheit, 2 Pers.:   **300,-**
   Preis pro Einheit, 4 Pers.:   **400,-**

Mieten von Bettwäsche: **100,-**
Frühstück: ab **85,-**
Preise gültig für 2011/12
Zugang zu Internet
Haustiere willkommen
Terrasse/Außenbereich/Garten
Wir akzeptieren VISA, MC
A: Ganzjährig geöffnet
B: Geöffnet 1. Juni - 1. Okt.
Sprechen etwas Deutsch

Mjonøy is an island surrounded by the rivers Klevastøylåi and Smørkleppåi. Old timber houses from the area were erected on Mjonøy. Then later came construction of a residence, a wood-fired stone-oven bakery; a 'eldhus', now the reception and food outlet, a russet mill was built and finally Alvstoga with fireplace for those who need to get warm when it's cold outside. Bakery on premises. Cultural events in the summer.

Mjonøy er ei øy, elvane Klevastøylåi og Smørkleppåi renn rundt øya. Gamle tømmerhus frå området blei satt dei opp på Mjonøy. Etter kvart vart det bygd bustadhus, eit vedfyrt steinomnbakeri, eldhus som nå er resepsjon og matutsal, ei vadmålstampe blei bygd, og til slutt Alvstoga til bruk for grupper og andre som har trong for å varme seg ved peisvarmen når det er kaldt ute. Eige bakeri. Kulturarrangement om somrane.

Mjonøy ist eine Insel, umgeben von den Flüssen Klevastøylåi und Smørkleppåi. Alte Blockhäuser aus der Gegend wurden hier aufgestellt. Nach und nach kamen ein Wohnhaus, eine Steinofenbäckerei, ein Koch-/Backhaus, das jetzt als Rezeption und Speisesaal genutzt wird, eine Walkmühle und zum Schluss die Alvstoga hierher.. Dort können sich die Gruppen am Kamin wärmen. Eigene Bäckerei. Angebot an Kulturveranstaltungen.

Dalen
Bed & Breakfast

Your host:
Delphine & Oliver Desmet

Address:
Aasmund Nordgaardsveg 6
N - 3880 Dalen
Phone: 35 07 70 80
Mobile: 92 81 70 12
E-mail: info@dalenbb.com
Web: www.dalenbb.com

Best time to call: 07.30 - 22.00
GPS: 59°26'42"N 8°0'33"E

Single room:	**890,-**	Enkeltrom:	**890,-**	Einzelzi.:	**890,-**
Double room:	**980,- to 1260,-**	Dobbeltrom:	**980,- til 1260,-**	Doppelzi.:	**980,- bis 1260,-**
3-bedded room:	**1340,-**	3-sengsrom:	**1340,-**	3-Bettzimmer:	**1340,-**
4-bedded room:	**1490,-**	4-sengsrom:	**1490,-**	4-Bettzimmer:	**1490,-**
Luxury room:	**1530,-**	Luksusrom:	**1530,-**	Luxuszimmer:	**1530,-**

No. of rooms: 13	Antall rom: 13	Anzahl Zimmer: 13
Breakfast buffet	Frokost buffét	Frühstücksbüfett
Selfcatering possible	Selvhushold er mulig	Selbstverpflegung möglich
Prices valid for 2011	Priser gyldig for 2011	Preise gültig für 2011
TV available	TV tilgjengelig	TV vorhanden
Terrace/patio/yard	Terrasse/uteplass/hage	Terrasse/Außenbereich/Garten
Canoe, boat and bike for rent	Kano-, båt- og sykkelutleie	Kanu, Boot und Fahrrad zu mieten
Small pets welcome	Små kjæledyr velkommen	Kleinere Haustiere willkommen
Open year round	Åpent hele året	Ganzjährig geöffnet
English, French and Dutch spoken		Sprechen etwas Deutsch

In the heart of Telemark, after a rather spectacular drive down steep hills, you can take a deep breath in Dalen and relax in newly renovated rooms at the Desmet's, the Belgian couple Delphine and Olivier. Next morning you will be surprised by Delphine's extraordinary homemade breakfast.
All rooms have own bath and access to a common room. Deluxe room has canopy bed and massage shower.

I hjertet av Telemark, etter en nokså spektakulær kjøretur ned de bratte fjellsidene, kan du puste lettet ut i Dalen og slappe av i nyoppusede rom hos det belgiske paret Delphine og Olivier. Neste morgen kan du bli overrasket av Delphines nydelige hjemmelagde mat.
Alle rom har eget bad og adgang til et felles oppholdsrom. Luksusrommet har himmelseng og massasjedusj.

Mitten im Herzen der Telemark, nach einer spektakulären Autofahrt über steile Bergstraßen, können Sie es sich in den frisch renovierten Zimmern der Wirtsleute Delphine und Olivier so richtig gemütlich machen. Und am nächsten Morgen überrascht Sie Delphine mit schmackhaftem, selbst gemachtem Frühstück. Alle Zimmer mit eigenem Bad. Gemeinschaftsraum ebenfalls vorhanden. Das Luxuszimmer hat ein Himmelbett und eine Massagedusche.

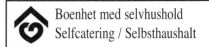

Naper Gård

Your host:
Solveig & Ådne A. Naper

Address:
Vråvegen 1752
N - 3849 Vråliosen
Phone: 47 75 56 75
Mobile: 90 23 35 26
E-mail: anaper@telefiber.no

Best time to call:
09.00 - 21.00
GPS: 59°21'27"N 8°10'18"E

Guesthouse for 2-7 persons	Gjestehus for 2-7 personer	Gästehaus für 2-7 Personen
2 bedrooms, bath, kitchen, LR	2 soverom, bad, kjk., stue	2 Schlafzi., Bad, Küche, Stube
Price for whole unit: **700,-**	Pris for hele enheten: **700,-**	Ganze Einheit: **700,-**
Bed linen fee: **70,-**	Tillegg for sengetøy: **70,-**	Mieten von Bettwäsche: **70,-**
Prices valid for 2011/12/13	Priser gyldig for 2011/12/13	Preise gültig für 2011/12/13
Patio	Uteplass	Außenbereich
Boat: free use	Båt kan brukes fritt	Boot zur freien Benutzung
Open July & August	Åpent juli og august	Geöffnet Juli & August
English spoken		Sprechen Deutsch

Old ancestral farm next to Vråvann lake situated in a beautiful area for walking tours in nearby forests and meadows. Fishing/boat trips and swimming. The only residents are the couple who run the farm and they enjoy meeting the nice people who come to visit the farm.

Directions:
E-134 from Drammen towards Brunkeberg. Exit onto RV 41 towards Kvitseid/Vrådal. From Vrådal: RV 38 towards Vråliosen. Turn left just after passing Vråliosen (towards Nordbø). From here it is only 500 m to Naper Gård.

Gammel slektsgård ved Vråvann i flott område for turer i skog og mark. Fiske/båtturer og bading. Kun ekteparet som driver gården bor der nå, og de syntes det er hyggelig å treffe nye mennesker som kommer på besøk på gården.

Veibeskrivelse:
E-134 fra Drammen til Brunkeberg. Ta av mot Kvitseid/Vrådal, RV 41. Fra Vrådal RV 38 til Vråliosen. Ta til venstre rett etter Vråliosen (mot Nordbø). Da er det ca 500 m til Naper Gård.

Alter Familienbetrieb in reizvoller Lage am Vråvann See. Tolle Umgebung für Ausflüge durch Wald und Flur. Angeln, Bootstouren und Baden möglich. Auf dem Hof wohnt heute nur noch das Gastgeber-Ehepaar. Beide freuen sich auf neue Leute, die den Hof besuchen.

Wegbeschreibung:
Fahren Sie die Str. 134 von Drammen in Richtung Brunkeberg. Biegen Sie anschließend auf die Str. 41 nach Kviteseid/Vrådal ab. Ab Vrådal geht es weiter auf der Str. 38, bis Sie Vråliosen erreichen. Direkt hinter der Siedlung zweigen Sie in Richtung Nordbø ab. Ab hier sind es nur noch rund 500 m zum Hof.

Fossum Kurs- & Feriesenter

Your host:
Dierk & Brigitte Rengstorf

Address:
Hauggrend
N - 3870 Fyresdal
Phone: 35 04 25 14
E-mail: fossum@fyresdal.online.no
Web: www.fossumferie.com

Best time to call:
08.00 - 09.00 / 19.00 - 22.00
GPS: 59°19'12"N 8°8'12"E

Double-/twin room:	**850,-**	Dobbelt-/tosengsrom:	**850,-**	Doppel-/Zweibettzimmer:	**850,-**
1 pers. in double room:	**500,-**	1 pers. i dobbeltrom:	**500,-**	1 Pers. in Doppelzimmer:	**500,-**

No. of rooms: 9
Discount for children u. 13 yrs.
Laid breakfast table
Other meals served by agreement
Prices valid for 2011
Access to telephone/fax
Terrace/patio/yard
Boat for rent
Sauna, outdoor hot tub
VISA, MC, AmEx accepted
Open year round
English and French spoken

Antall rom: 9
Rabatt for barn u. 13 år
Dekket frokostbord
Andre måltider etter avtale
Priser gyldig for 2011
Tilgang på tlf./faks/internett
Terrasse/uteplass/hage
Båtutleie
Sauna, badestamp
Vi tar VISA, MC, AmEx
Åpent hele året

Anzahl Zimmer: 9
Ermäßigung für Kinder u. 13 J.
Gedeckter Frühstückstisch
Andere Mahlzeiten auf Best.
Preise gültig für 2011
Telefon/Fax/Internet verfügbar
Terrasse/Außenbereich/Garten
Boot zu mieten
Sauna, Badezuber
Wir akzeptieren VISA, MC, AmEx
Ganzjährig geöffnet
Sprechen Deutsch

Holiday center on the lake with plenty of indoor and outdoor activities. Workshop for arts and handicraft, weaving/weaving looms, courses in Yoga, Reiki, and meditation. Skiing, climbing, survival, horseback riding. Sightseeing nearby: stave church, Telemark canal, museums and mines. Geologically interesting area.

Directions:
Via RV 355, 15 km north of Fyresdal.

Ferieanlegg ved sjøen med et bredt spekter aktivitetstilbud. Atelierer for kunst og håndverk, veving, meditasjon/yogakurs. Svært gode friluftslivmuligheter sommer og vinter. Betydelige severdigheter i nærområdet, blant annet stavkirke, Telemarkskanalen, gruver, museer og interessante geologiske formasjoner.

Veibeskrivelse:
Ved RV 355, 15 km nord for Fyresdal.

Ferienhof am See mit breit gefächertem Aktivitätenangebot. Atelier für Kunst und Kunsthandwerk, Webstube. Kursangebot für Yoga, Reiki, Meditation. Gute Möglichkeiten für naturnahe Freizeitgestaltung. Sehenswürdigkeiten in der Nähe, u.a. Stabkirche, Bergwerke, Museen und der Telemarkkanal. Geologisch interessantes Gebiet.

Wegbeschreibung:
An der Str. 355 gelegen, 15 km nördlich von Fyresdal.

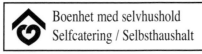

A: 3 cabins for 4 persons	**A:** 3 hytter for 4 personer	**A:** 3 Hütten für 4 Personen
LR w/kitchen nook	Stue m/kjøkkenkrok	Stube mit Küchenecke
Price for whole unit: **400,-**	Pris for hele enheten: **400,-**	Ganze Einheit: **400,-**
B: 2 cabins for 2 persons	**B:** 2 hytter for 2 personer	**B:** 2 Hütten für 2 Personen
LR w/kitchen nook	Stue m/kjøkkenkrok	Stube mit Küchenecke
Price for whole unit: **500,-**	Pris for hele enheten: **500,-**	Ganze Einheit: **500,-**
C: 3 cabins for 3 persons	**C:** 3 hytter for 3 personer	**C:** 3 Hütten für 3 Personen
1 room w/kitchen nook	1 rom m/kjøkkenkrok	1 Raum mit Küchenecke
Price for whole unit: **450,-**	Pris for hele enheten: **450,-**	Ganze Einheit: **450,-**
D: 2 cabins for 4 persons	**D:** 2 hytter for 4 personer	**D:** 2 Hütten für 4 Personen
1 bedroom, LR w/kitchen nook	1 soverom, stue m/kjøkkenkrok	1 Schlafzi., Stube mit Küchenecke
Price for whole unit: **650,-**	Pris for hele enheten: **650,-**	Ganze Einheit: **650,-**
E: 1 cabin for 5-6 persons	**E:** 1 hytte for 5-6 personer	**E:** 1 Hütte für 5-6 Personen
2 bedrooms, LR w/kitchen nook	2 soverom, stue m/kjøkkenkrok	2 Schlafzi., Stube mit Küchenecke
Price for whole unit: **800,-**	Pris for hele enheten: **800,-**	Ganze Einheit: **800,-**
F: 2 cabins for 6 persons	**F:** 2 hytter for 6 personer	**F:** 2 Hütten für 6 Personen
3 bedrooms, LR w/kitchen nook	3 soverom, stue m/kjøkkenkrok	3 Schlafzi.,Stube mit Küchenecke
Price for whole unit: **900,-**	Pris for hele enheten: **900,-**	Ganze Einheit: **900,-**
G: 1 cabin for 10 persons	**G:** 1 hytte for 10 personer	**G:** 1 Hütte für 10 Personen
5 bedrooms, LR w/kitchen nook	5 soverom, stue m/kjøkkenkrok	5 Schlafzi., Stube mit Küchenecke
Price for whole unit: **1250,-**	Pris for hele enheten: **1250,-**	Ganze Einheit: **1250,-**
H: Apartment for 2 persons	**H:** Leilighet for 2 personer	**H:** Wohnung für 2 Personen
Own bath, kitchen, LR, DR	Eget bad, kjøkken, stue, spiserom	Eig. Bad, Küche, Stube, Esszi.
No pets please	Merk: ikke husdyr	Keine Haustiere
Price for whole unit: **1000,-**	Pris for hele enheten: **1000,-**	Ganze Einheit: **1000,-**
Applies to all rental units:	For alle enhetene gjelder:	Für alle Einheiten gilt:
Bed linen fee: **100,-**	Tillegg for sengetøy: **100,-**	Mieten von Bettwäsche: **100,-**
Breakfast service available	Frokost kan serveres	Frühstück auf Bestellung
Cabins A-G: no indoor plumbing	Hyttene A-G har ikke innlagt vann	Kein fl. Wasser in den Hütten A-G
Common sanitary facility, kitchen	Felles sanitæranlegg og storkjk.	Gemeins. Sanitäranl. u. Grossküche
Terrace/patio/yard	Terrasse/uteplass/hage	Terrasse/Außenbereich/Garten

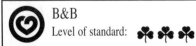
Fyresdal
Bed & Breakfast

Your host:
Ron & Joke Petrych

Address:
N - 3870 Fyresdal
Phone: 35 04 26 66
Fax: 35 04 26 67
E-mail: post@fyresdalbb.com
Web: www.fyresdalbb.com

Best time to call:
08.00 - 23.00
GPS: 59°11'2"N 8°5'34"E

Room for 1 pers.:	**550,-**	Rom for 1 pers.:	**550,-**	Zimmer für 1 Pers.:	**550,-**
Room for 2 pers.:	**710,-**	Rom for 2 pers.:	**710,-**	Zimmer für 2 Pers.:	**710,-**
No. of rooms: 2		Antall rom: 2		Anzahl Zimmer: 2	
Discount for children		Rabatt for barn		Ermäßigung für Kinder	
Laid breakfast table		Dekket frokostbord		Gedeckter Frühstückstisch	
Priser gyldig for 2011/12		Priser gyldig for 2011/12		Priser gyldig for 2011/12	
TV/Internet available		TV/Internett tilgjengelig		TV/Internet vorhanden	
Terrace/patio/yard		Terrasse/uteplass/hage		Terrasse/Außenbereich/Garten	

Selfcatering (without bed linen):		Selvhushold (uten sengetøy):		Selbsthaushalt (ohne Bettwäsche):	
Apartment for 6 pers.:	**800,-**	Leil. for 6 pers.:	**800,-**	Wohnung für 6 Pers.:	**800,-**
Apartment for 2 pers.:	**600,-**	Leil. for 2 pers.:	**600,-**	Wohnung für 2 Pers.:	**600,-**
Open year round		Åpent hele året		Ganzjährig geöffnet	
English & Dutch spoken				Sprechen Niederl. / etwas Deutsch	

Fyresdal Bed & Breakfast has a long traditon. The house was totally renovated in 1985 to its original 'Swiss style' but remained empty until the new host, Petrych, came in 2004 from the Netherland to breathe new life into the inn.
In 2010 we made a transition from traditional guesthouse to a bed and breakfast. Here there is emphasis on a personal and intimate atmosphere and good homemade food.
The area has many possiblities for mountain tours by foot or bicycle. Good fishing as well.
Welcome to calm and peaceful Fyresdal Bed & Breakfast.

Fyresdal Bed & Breakfast har lange tradisjoner. Huset ble i 1985 totalrenovert til opprinnelig sveitserstil, men ble så stående tomt inntil vertskapet Petrych kom fra Nederland og blåste nytt liv i vertshuset i 2004. Fra 2010 har vi bygged om fra et tradisjonelt vertshus til et Bed & Breakfast. Her legges det vekt på en personlig og intim atmosfære og god hjemmelaget mat.
Området har flotte muligheter for fjellturer til fots eller på sykkel.
Fine fiskevann.
Velkommen til et stille og rolig opphold på Fyresdal Bed & Breakfast.

Fyresdal Bed & Breakfast hat eine lange Geschichte. 1985 wurde das Haus im ursprünglichen schweizer Stil renoviert, stand allerdings bis 2004 leer. Gastgeber Petrych aus den Niederlanden hat dem Haus neues Leben eingehaucht. Seit 2010 wurde dann das traditionelle Gasthaus zu einem B&B umgebaut. Hier wird auf eine persönliche Atmosphäre und hausgemachtes Essen Wert gelegt.
Ausflüge in die schöne Bergumgebung zu Fuss oder mit dem Fahrrad möglich. Gute Angelmöglichkeiten am See. Fyresdal Bed & Breakfast heißt Sie zu einem ruhigen Aufenthalt willkommen.

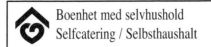

Ettestad Gård

Your host:
Nina Ettestad Herfoss

Address:
Ettestad
N - 3750 Drangedal
Phone: 35 99 64 53
Mobile: 91 64 87 13
E-mail: post@ettestad-gard.no
Web: www.ettestad-gard.no

Best time to call:
10.00 - 22.00
GPS: 59°7'5"N 8°54'33"E

Guesthouse for 2-10 persons	Gjestehus for 2-10 personer	Gästehaus für 2-10 Personen
1 bedroom, 1 loft w/bed, bath, kitchen, LR	1 soverom m/hems, bad, kjk., stue	1 Schlafzi. mit Schlafboden, Bad, Küche, Stube
Price for whole unit: **700,-**	Pris for hele enheten: **700,-**	Ganze Einheit: **700,-**
Bed linen fee: **50,-**	Tillegg for sengetøy: **50,-**	Mieten von Bettwäsche: **50,-**
Cleaning fee: **300,-**	Sluttrengjøring: **300,-**	Endreinigung: **300,-**
Prices valid for 2011	Priser gyldig for 2011	Preise gültig für 2011
TV	TV	TV
Patio/yard	Uteplass/hage	Außenbereich/Garten
Boat and bike for rent	Båt- og sykkelutleie	Boot und Fahrrad zu mieten
Pets welcome	Kjæledyr velkommen	Haustiere willkommen
Open year round	Åpent hele året	Ganzjährig geöffnet
English spoken		Sprechen etwas Deutsch

The small 'eldhus'-cabin from the 1700s was restored in 1998 and is now available to guests. It's on the outskirts of the farm only 50 m from Bjårvann lake where you can swim and relax. The house has a fine natural stone fireplace besides fully equipped kitchen and modern bathroom.

There are three horses, one goat, dog, cat and rabbit. There is fine terrain for hiking, bicycling and canoeing.

Huset som leies ut er det gamle eldhuset på gården. Det er fra 1700-tallet og ble restaurert i 1998. Det ligger i utkanten av gården og bare 50 m fra et vann, Bjårvann, hvor man kan bade og slappe av. Huset har en flott peis i naturstein og forøvrig et fullt utstyrt kjøkken og et moderne bad.

På gården er det 3 hester, 1 geit, hund, katt og kanin. Det er flott turterreng man kan ta fatt på både til fots, på sykkel eller i kano.

Auf dem Hof wird das ehemalige "Backhaus" vermietet. Es stammt aus dem 18. Jh. und wurde 1998 restauriert. Das Haus liegt am Rande des Hofes, nur 50 m vom Bjårvann See entfernt, wo man sich erholen und baden kann. Das Haus hat einen schönen Naturstein-Kamin, eine voll ausgestattete Küche und ein modernes Bad. Auf dem Hof befinden sich 3 Pferde, 1 Ziege, Hunde, Katzen und Kaninchen. Schöne Ausflugsumgebung, die zu Fuss, mit dem Fahrrad oder dem Kanu erkundet werden kann.

A journey is best measured in friends, rather than miles. ~Tim Cahill~

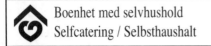
Hulfjell Gård og Hytteutleie

Your host:
Tellef Moland & Britt Eide
Address: Hulfjell Gård
N - 3750 Drangedal
Phone: 35 99 92 54
Mobile: 41 30 90 52
E-mail: tollak@c2i.net
Web: www.hulfjell.no

Best time to call:
08.00 - 22.00
GPS: 59°4'9"N 9°5'22"E

A: 'Gubbens ork', hus for 2-9 p.
2 bedrooms, 1 loft w/bed
Bath/WC, kitchen, LR
Price for whole unit: **800,-**

B: 'Fruens vilje', Cabin for 2-8 p.
2 bedrooms, bath/WC, kitchen, LR
This cabin lies 5 m from the water
w/ large terrace adjacent to the water
Price for whole unit: **800,-**

C: 'Nordeatoppen', hytte for 2-5 p.
2 bedr., bath/WC, kitchenette, LR
Located on a top with nice view
Pris for hele enheten: **800,-**

Bed linen fee: **75,-**
Prices valid for 2011
TV in all cabins w/many channels
Terrace, patio, yard
Boat for rent / Pets welcome
Suitable for handicapped
Open year round
Some English spoken

A: 'Gubbens ork', hus for 2-9 p.
2 soverom, 1 sovehems
Bad/WC, kjøkken, stue
Pris for hele enheten: **800,-**

B: 'Fruens vilje', hytte for 2-8 p.
2 soverom, bad/WC, kjøkken, stue
Denne hytten ligger 5 m fra vannet
med stor terrasse mot vannet.
Pris for hele enheten: **800,-**

C: 'Nordeatoppen', hytte for 2-5 p.
2 soverom, bad/WC, kjk-krok, stue
Ligger på en topp med fin utsikt
Pris for hele enheten: **800,-**

Sengetøy kan leies: **75,-**
Priser gyldig for 2011
TV på alle hytter m/mange kanaler
Terrasse, uteplass
Båtutleie / Kjæledyr velkommen
Handikaptilgjengelig
Åpent hele året
Sprechen etwas Englisch

A: 'Gubbens ork', Haus für 2-9 P.
2 Schlafzimmer, 1 Schlafboden
Bad/WC, Küche, Stube
Ganze Einheit: **800,-**

B: 'Fruens vilje', Hütte für 2-8 P.
2 Schlafzi., Bad/WC, Küche, Stube
Diese Hütte liegt direkt am See mit
großer Terrasse Richtung See.
Ganze Einheit: **800,-**

C: 'Nordeatoppen', Hütte für 2-5 P.
2 Schlafzi., Bad/WC, Kü-ecke., Stube
Auf einem Hügel m. toller Aussicht.
Ganze Einheit: **800,-**

Mieten von Bettwäsche: **75,-**
Preise gültig für 2011
TV in allen Hüten m. vielen Sendern
Terrasse, Außenbereich
Boot zu mieten / Haustiere willk.
Behindertengerecht
Ganzjährig geöffnet
Sprechen etwas Englisch

Hulfjell is a pleasant farm w/ lots of animals: cows, horses, ponies, miniature pigs, goats, sheep, rabbits and geese. Enjoy excellent swimming in a lake that gets nice and warm during summertime. Guests can also fish; the farm rents out canoes and boats. Also pheasant, peafowl, llama, dog and cat on the farm. Great place for families.

Hulfjell er en trivelig gård med mange dyr: ku, hest, ponni, minigris, geit, sau, kanin, and, kalkun og gjess. Her er det fine bademuligheter i vann som blir godt og varmt om sommeren. Gjestene kan også fiske, og gården leier ut kanoer og båter. Det er også fasan, lama, esel, påfugl, hund og katt på gården. Flott sted for familier.

Gemütl. Bauernhof m. vielen Tieren: Kühe, Pferde, Ponys, Ziegen, Minischweine, Schafe, Hasen, Enten u. Gänse. Tolle Bademöglk. im See, der im Sommer schön warm wird. Gäste können Fischen u. der Hof leiht Kanus u. Boote aus. Außerdem auf dem Hof: Fasan, Lama, Esel, Pfau, Truthahn, Hund u. Katze. Ein toller Ort für Familien.

Templen
Bed & Breakfast

Your host:
Britt Egeland

Address:
Vestre Bievei 6
N - 4825 Arendal
Phone: 37 09 59 81
Mobile: 90 75 02 88

Best time to call:
08.00 - 22.30
GPS: 58°26'46"N 8°43'45"E

Double-/twin room:	**800,-**	Dobbelt-/tosengsrom:	**800,-**	Doppel-/Zweibettzi.:	**800,-**
1 pers. in double room:	**500,-**	En pers. i dobbeltrom:	**500,-**	1 Pers. im DZ:	**500,-**

No. of rooms: 2	Antall rom: 2	Anzahl Zimmer: 2
Discount for children	Rabatt for barn	Ermäßigung für Kinder
Laid breakfast table	Dekket frokostbord	Gedeckter Frühstückstisch
Prices valid for 2011/12/13	Priser gyldig for 2011/12/13	Preise gültig für 2011/12/13
Internet available	Internett tilgjengelig	Internet verfügbar
Terrace/patio/yard	Terrasse/uteplass/hage	Terrasse/Außenbereich/Garten
Parking	Parkeringsplass	Parkplatz
Open year round	Åpent hele året	Ganzjährig geöffnet
Some English spoken		Sprechen etwas Deutsch

Templen, a small farming complex on 95 hectares, is situated among peaceful surroundings about 4 km west of Arendal.There is excellent hiking in the nearby woods, and a short distance to nice beaches, golf course and museums. Kristiansand Dyrepark (zoo) is about a 45 min drive. Easy ferry connections to the continent, including Denmark.

Templen, et lite gardsbruk på 95 mål, ligger i rolige omgivelser ca. 4 km vest for Arendal. Her er fine turmuligheter i skogen like ved, og det er kort avstand til fine badestrender, golfbane og museer. Til Kristiansand Dyrepark tar det ca 45 min. med bil.
Gode ferjeforbindelser til Danmark og kontinentet.

Templen ist ein kleiner Bauernhof mit 9,5 Hektar, der in ruhiger Umgebung ca. 4 km westlich von Arendal liegt. Schöne Wandermöglichkeiten im nahegelegenen Wald, kurze Entfernung zu reizvollen Badestränden, Golfplatz und Museen. 45 Minuten mit dem Auto bis zum Tierpark in Kristiansand. Gute Fährverbindungen nach Dänemark und Mitteleuropa.

Travel is more than the seeing of sights; it is a change
that goes on, deep and permanent, in the ideas of living.
~Miriam Beard~

One's destination is never a place, but a new way of seeing things.
~Henry Miller~

Ibsens Bed & Breakfast

Your host:
Anita Nicolaysen

Address:
Løkkestredet 7
N - 4876 Grimstad
Phone: 37 27 57 63
Mobile: 90 91 29 31
E-mail: post@cafeibsen.no

Best time to call:
08.00 - 22.00
GPS: 58°20'32"N 8°35'40"E

Double room:	**900,-**	Dobbeltrom:	**900,-**	Doppelzi.:	**900,-**
Single room:	**500,-**	Enkeltrom:	**500,-**	Einzelzi.:	**500,-**

Breakfast is served in the café	Frokost serveres i caféen	FR wird im Café serviert
Discount for longer stay	Rabatt ved lengre opphold	Ermäßigung bei längerem Aufenth.
Prices valid for 2011/12	Priser gyldig for 2011/12	Preise gültig für 2011/12
LR and kitchen available	Stue og kjøkken tilgjengelig	Stube und Küche zugänglich
TV/Internet available	TV/Internett tilgjengelig	TV/Internet verfügbar
Terrace	Terrasse	Terrasse
Pets welcome	Kjæledyr velkommen	Haustiere willkommen
Open year round	Åpent hele året	Ganzjährig geöffnet
English and some Spanish spoken		Sprechen etwas Deutsch

Ibsen's Bed & Breakfast is located in the old town center of Grimstad. The rental rooms are in different old wooden houses, all elegantly refurbished and furnished in old style.
The host is also running Café Ibsen, which has been elected Norway's most cozy café by the readers of KK, a weekly magazine. Grimstad is a charming small coastal town with typical white painted houses, surrounded by hilltops.
The author Henrik Ibsen lived here in his young years when he was an apprentice pharmacist in the 1840s.

Ibsens Bed & Breakfast finner du i det gamle sentrum av Grimstad. Utleierommene ligger i ulike gamle trehus som er lekkert nyoppusset og innredet i gammel stil.
Vertskapet driver også Café Ibsen som har blitt kåret til Norges koseligste café av KK's lesere.
Grimstad er en idyllisk liten sørlandsby med hvitmalte små hus mellom knatter og knauser. Her bodde Henrik Ibsen i sin ungdom, på 1840-tallet hvor han gikk i apotekerlære.

Ibsens Bed & Breakfast liegt im alten Zentrum von Grimstad. Die zu vermietenden Zimmer befinden sich in verschiedenen alten Holzhäusern, die hübsch renoviert und im traditionellen Stil eingerichtet wurden. Die Gastgeberin betreibt auch das Café Ibsen, welches von den Lesern der Zeitschrift KK zu Norwegens gemütlichstem Café gekürt wurde.
Grimstad ist eine idyllische kleine Stadt an der Südküste Norwegens, mit weiß gestrichenen Häusern, umgeben von Bergkuppen. In den 1840ern lebte Henrik Ibsen hier in seiner Jugend als er seine Apothekerlehre absolvierte.

Døblane
Bed & Breakfast

Your host:
Egil & Liv Tone D. Larsen
Address: Tvidøblane 46
N - 4700 Vennesla
Phone Egil: 40 20 20 25
Phone Liv Tone: 90 74 55 75
E-mail: egil.lars@live.no
Web:
www.doblanebed-breakfast.com
Best time to call: 08.00 - 22.00
GPS: 58°16'21"N 7°58'35"E

Large family room:		Stort familierom:		Großes Familienzimmer:	
For 2 persons:	**1100,-**	For 2 personer:	**1100,-**	Für 2 Personen:	**1100,-**
Extra bed, adult:	**550,-**	Ekstraseng, voksne:	**550,-**	Extrabett, Erwachsene:	**550,-**
Extra bed, child:	**275,-**	Ekstraseng, barn:	**275,-**	Extrabett, Kinder:	**275,-**
Children under 3 yrs no charge		Barn under 3 år gratis		Kinder unter 3 Jahren gratis	
No. of rooms: 2		Antall rom: 2		Anzahl Zimmer: 2	
Laid breakfast table		Dekket frokostbord		Gedeckter Frühstückstisch	
Prices valid for 2011		Priser gyldig for 2011		Preise gültig für 2011	
Terrace/deck access		Terrasse/uteplass		Terrasse/Außenbereich	
Internet available		Internett tilgjengelig		Internet vorhanden	
Open year round		Åpent hele året		Ganzjährig geöffnet	
English spoken				Man spricht Englisch	

A friendly and sympathetic couple enjoy having guests at their newly renovated home in Vennesla centrum. Several enriching vacations spent in private homes inspired them and now they are the ones providing accommodations. Their dream has been realized and you are heartily welcome.
Vennesla is a community at the entrance to Setesdal valley, 18 km north of Kristiansand.
In Setesdalen you can fish for salmon and enjoy beautiful nature in mountain hikes. In Kristiansand you and your family experience exotic animals and rumors of pirates in Norway's only zoo.

Et hyggelig og imøtekommende ektepar gleder seg til å ta imot gjester i sin nyrenoverte enebolig i Vennesla sentrum. Etter flere berikende ferier med overnatting i private hjem ble drømmen skapt om å åpne et liknende sted hjemme. Drømmen har nå gått i oppfyllelse og du ønskes hjertelig velkommen. Vennesla er ei bygd i inngangen til Setesdalen, 18 km nord for Kristiansand.
I Setesdalen finner du muligheter for laksefiske og fjellturer i flott natur. I Kristiansand kan du og din familie oppleve eksotiske dyr og skumle sjørøvere i dyreparkens fantastiske verden.

Ein freundliches und zuvorkommendes Ehepaar freut sich, Sie als Gäste in ihrem frisch renovierten Einfamilienhaus, im Zentrum von Vennesla, begrüßen zu dürfen. Nach vielen bereichernden Ferien, mit Übernachtungen bei Familien zu Hause, ist der Traum entstanden, etwas Vergleichbares selber zu betreiben. Der Traum ist jetzt in Erfüllung gegangen und Sie sind herzlich willkommen. Vennesla ist ein Dorf an der Einfahrt zum Setesdalen, 18 km nördl. von Kristiansand. Im Setesdalen kann man Lachsangeln und wandern. Die fantastische Welt des Tierparks in Kristiansand bietet exotische Tiere und unheimliche Seeräuber.

Liane Gård

Your host:
Wenche Kjær

Address:
Liane 19
N - 4640 Søgne
Phone: 38 16 77 32
Mobile: 91 34 02 146
E-mail: wenche@liane-gaard.com
Web: www.liane-gaard.com

Best time to call:
15.00 - 23.00
GPS: 58°4'38"N 7°42'45"E

Per person:	**500,-**	Pr. person:	**500,-**	Pro Person:	**500,-**
No. of rooms: 5		Antall rom: 5		Anzahl Zimmer: 5	
No. of beds: 10		Antall senger: 10		Anzahl Betten: 10	
Breakfast basket or -buffet		Frokostbrett eller -buffet		Frühstückstablett oder -büffet	
Prices valid for 2011/12/13		Priser gyldig for 2011/12/13		Preise gültig für 2011/12/13	
TV/Internet available		TV/Internett tilgjengelig		TV/Internet vorhanden	
Terrace/patio/yard		Terrasse/uteplass/hage		Terrasse/Außenbereich/Garten	
Bike for rent		Sykkelutleie		Fahrrad zu mieten	
Open year round		Åpent hele året		Ganzjährig geöffnet	
English spoken				Sprechen etwas Deutsch	

In old, typical houses for the area, friendly and helpful hosts offer accommodation, located in the end of a fjord. Good possibilities for fishing or swimming. The area is well suitable for any outdoor activities, a family-friendly location, a beautiful garden surrounding the house. Landscape with forest for hiking trips, a quiet destination for recreation.

Directions:
Along E-39, 15 km west of Kristiansand; take off toward Trysnes. After 4 km you'll see a new sign to Trysnes, but here you go straight, go another 1 km, take then private road marked 'Liane', then straight 350 m to the house.

I eldre sørlandshus møter du her et vennlig og hjelpsomt vertskap og tilbys overnatting i naturskjønne omgivelser. Husene ligger vakkert til i enden av en fjordarm med fine fiske- og bademuligheter. Stort og flott uteareal som kan brukes til lek og spill. Stor vakker omkringliggende hage. I skogsområdet rundt er det flott turterreng. Et rolig og nydelig sted for rekreasjon.

Veibeskrivelse:
Langs E-39, 15 km vest for Kristiansand; ta av mot Trysnes. Etter 4 km kommer nytt skilt mot Trysnes, men da ta rett fram, kjør 1 km, ta så privat vei merket 'Liane', derfra: rett fram 350 m til huset.

Die freundlichen und hilfsbereiten Gastgeber bieten Ihnen eine Übernachtung in landschaftlich reizvoller Umgebung. Die Häuser liegen sehr schön am Ende eines Fjordarms (gute Angel- und Bademöglichkeiten). Großes und schönes Außenareal, sehr gut geeignet für Spiel und Spaß. Großer Garten rundherum. Umgeben von reizvollem Wandergebiet. Ein ruhiger und gemütlicher Ort, wie geschaffen zur Erholung.

Entlang der E-39, 15 km westlich von Kristiansand. Ri. Trysnes abfahren. Nach 4 km kommt ein neues Schild Ri. Trysnes, dem folgen Sie aber nicht sondern fahren geradeaus. Nach 1 km dem privaten Weg (Schild "Liane") zum Haus folgen (350 m geradeaus).

Mones Feriesenter

Your host:
Vidar Bergheim

Address:
Skogsfjordveien 134
N - 4513 Mandal
Phone: 38 26 49 00
Mobile: 90 51 95 57
E-mail: mones@postnorge.no
Web: mones-feriesenter.no

Best time to call:
07.00 - 21.00
GPS: 58°02'22"N 7°26'03"E

Low seasong: 15/8 - 23/6:
A: Standard apt. for 2-5 persons
2 bedrooms, bath, kitchen, LR
Price for 2 pers.:	**795,-**
Per extra pers.:	**200,-**

B: Luxus apt. for 4-10 persons
4 bedrooms, 2 baths, kitchen, LR
Price for 4 pers.:	**1395,-**
Per extra pers.:	**200,-**

Breakfast tray
Selfcatering possible
Prices valid for 2011/12
TV/Internet available
Terrace/deck/yard
Boat for rent
Suitable for handicapped
VISA, MC, DC, AmEx accepted

High season: 23/6-15/8: Weekly rent
Daily rent on short notice if available
Open year round
English spoken

Lavsesong: 15/8 - 23/6:
A: Standardleilighet for 2-5 pers.
2 soverom, bad, kjøkken, stue
Pris for 2 pers.:	**795,-**
Pr. ekstra pers.:	**200,-**

B: Luksusleilighet for 4-10 pers.
4 soverom, 2 bad, kjøkken, stue
Pris for 4 pers.:	**1395,-**
Pr. ekstra pers.:	**200,-**

Frokostbrett
Selvhushold er mulig
Priser gyldig for 2011/12
TV/Internett tilgjengelig
Terrasse/uteplass/hage
Båtutleie
Handikapvennlig
Vi tar VISA, MC, DC, AmEx

Høysesong: 23/6-15/8: Ukesleie
Døgnutleie på kort varsel hvis ledig
Åpent hele året

Nebensaison: 15/8 - 23/6:
A: Wohnung für 2-5 Personen
2 Schlafräume, Bad, Küche, Stube
Preis für 2 Pers.:	**795,-**
Jede weitere Pers.:	**200,-**

B: Luxuswohnung für 4-10 Pers.
4 Schlafzi., 2 Bäder, Küche, Stube
Preis für 4 Pers.:	**1395,-**
Jede weitere Pers.:	**200,-**

Frühstückstablett
Selbstverpflegung möglich
Preise gültig für 2011/12
TV/Internet vorhanden
Terrasse/Außenbereich/Garten
Boot zu mieten
Behindertengerecht
Wir akzept. VISA, MC, DC, AmEx

Hochsaison: 23/6-15/8: Wochenmiete
Wenn frei, Tagesmiete kurzfristig mgl.
Ganzjährig geöffnet
Sprechen etwas Deutsch

Mones Feriesenter has 15 bright
and pleasant seaside apartments.
Beautiful view of the fjord. Private
beach with play area, sand volley-
ball, common pier and grilling.
Child friendly. Skogsfjorden is
known for warm weather and good
swimming temperature. Fishing
and golfing nearby.

Mones Feriesenter har 15 lyse og
trivelige leiligheter helt i sjøkanten.
Flott utsikt utover fjorden. Egen
strand med lekeplass, sand-
volleybane, fellesbrygge og grill-
plasser. Barnevennlig. Skogsfjorden
er kjent for lun beliggenhet og
gode badetemperaturer. Fiskemuligheter og golfbane i nærheten.

Mones Feriencenter hat 15 helle
und gemütliche Wohnungen direkt
am Wasser. Tolle Aussicht über den
Skogsfjord. Eigener Strand mit
Spiel-, Beachvolleyball-, Grillplatz
und Bootssteg. Kinderfreundlich,
windgeschützt und mit angenehmer
Wassertemperatur. Angelmöglichkeiten und Golfplatz in der Nähe.

Heddan Gard

Your host:
Erling Stokkeland

Address:
Heddan Gard
N - 4595 Tingvatn
Phone: 38 34 88 37
E-mail: post@heddan-gard.no
Web: www.heddan-gard.no

Best time to call:
08.00 - 23.00
GPS: 58°25'38"N 7°9'53"E

Double-/twin room:	**1090,-**	Dobbelt-/tosengsrom:	**1090,-**	Doppel-/Zweibettzi.:	**1090,-**
Single room:	**845,-**	Enkeltrom:	**845,-**	Einzelzimmer:	**845,-**
No. of rooms: 15		Antall rom: 15		Anzahl Zimmer: 15	
Breakfast tray or -buffet		Frokostbrett eller buffét		Frühstückstablett oder -büfett	
Other meals served upon request		Andre måltider kan bestilles		Andere Mahlzeiten nach Vereinb.	
Prices valid for 2011		Priser gyldig for 2011		Preise gültig für 2011	
Terrace/patio/yard		Terrasse/uteplass/hage		Terrasse/Außenbereich/Garten	
Boat and bike for rent		Båt- og sykkelutleie		Boot u. Fahrrad zu mieten	
Suitable for handicapped		Handikaptilgjengelig		Behindertengerecht	
VISA, MC accepted		Vi tar VISA, MC		Wir akzeptieren VISA, MC	
Open year round		Åpent hele året		Ganzjährig geöffnet	
English spoken				Sprechen Deutsch	

This culturally historic guest-farm in the middle of Vest Agder provides personal service, exciting food experiences, accessible mountainous hiking trails and fishing possibilities. The rooms are in well-maintained old buildings offering private shower/wc. Heddan Gard is well situated to make it a getaway but is also centrally located with nearby towns and points of interest; and easy to reach by car, plane and train. Nature is on duty year round at Heddan Garden, whether by foot, bicycle or skis.

Kulturhistorisk gjestegård midt i Vest Agder. Vi tilbyr personlig service, spennende matopplevelser, turstier i lett tilgjengelig fjellområde og gode fiskemuligheter. Rommenen er i velholdte gamle bygninger med egen dusj/wc. Heddan Gard, med sin beliggenhet, legger grunnlaget for et spennende opphold, et sted å trekke seg tilbake til, men er samtidig sentralt beliggende med kort avstand til byer og tettsteder, og lett å nå bade med bil, fly og tog. Naturen holder åpent hele aret på Heddan Garden, enten til fots, på sykkel eller ski.

Ein kulturhistorischer Bauernhof inmitten der Provinz Vest Agder. Wir bieten persönlichen Service, spannende Essenserlebnisse, Wanderwege in sanfter Bergumgebung und gute Angelmöglichkeiten. Die Zimmer befinden sich in gut erhaltenen alten Gebäuden mit eigener Dusche/WC. Heddan Gard ist mit seiner Lage ein Ort um sich zurückzuziehen, aber gleichzeitig auch der ideale Ausgangspunkt für einen spannenden Aufenthalt. Kurzer Weg zu den nächsten Ortschaften/ Städten sowie leicht mit dem Auto, Flugzeug und Zug zu erreichen. Das ganze Jahr über lädt die Natur hier zum Erkunden ein - zu Fuß, mit dem Fahrrad oder auf Skiern.

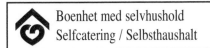

Magne Handeland

Your host:
Magne Handeland

Address:
Handeland
N - 4462 Hovsherad

Phone: 51 40 21 24

Best time to call:
08.00 - 22.00
GPS: 58°30'35"N 6°31'14"E

Guesthouse for 2-6 persons	Gjestehus for 2-6 personer	Gästehaus für 2-6 Personen
No. of bedrooms: 2	Antall soverom: 2	Anzahl Schlafzimmer: 2
Own bath, kitchen, LR	Eget bad, kjøkken, stue	Eig. Bad, Küche, Stube
Price per pers.: **300,-**	Pris pr. pers.: **300,-**	Preis pro Pers.: **300,-**
Bed linen included	Sengetøy er inkludert	Inkl. Bettwäsche
Prices valid for 2011/12/13	Priser gyldig for 2011/12/13	Preise gültig für 2011/12/13
TV available	TV tilgjengelig	TV vorhanden
Terrace/garden	Terrasse/uteplass/hage	Terrasse/Außenbereich/Garten
Rowboat and canoe available	Robåt- og kanoutlån	Ruderboot und Kanu zu leihen
Open year round	Åpent hele året	Ganzjährig geöffnet
English spoken		Sprechen Englisch

Magne Handeland's guest house was built in 1978 and is well equipped with freezer, washing machine, telephone, and a full kitchen. It has a private outdoor terrace, grill and garden furniture.
Handeland is a short way from E-39, just north of the village of Moi. Fresh-water swimming and fishing opportunities nearby.
The farm has cows, hens and cats and guests may arrange to assist in tending. Magne also has a wood workshop where beautiful bowls and candlesticks are designed and handcrafted.

Gjestehuset hos Magne Handeland ble bygget i 1978 og er godt utstyrt med både fryseboks, vaskemaskin, telefon, fullt utstyrt kjøkken og en terrasse med grill og utemøbler som er til gjestenes disposisjon.
Handeland ligger på en liten avstikker fra E-39, like nord for Moi. Badeplasser i ferskvann og muligheter for fiske.
På gården er det både kyr og høns og gårdskatter. Etter nærmere avtale kan gjestene få være med på å stelle husdyrene.
Magne har også et tredreiingsverksted og lager vakre staker og boller.

Das Gästehaus wurde 1978 gebaut und ist gut ausgestattet mit Tiefkühltruhe, Waschmaschine, Telefon und komplett eingerichteter Küche. Eigene Terrasse mit Grill und Sitzmöbeln.
Handeland liegt einen kleinen Abstecher von der E-39, nördlich von Moi. Badeplätze am See und Möglichkeit zum Angeln.
Der Hof hat Kühe, Hühner und Katzen. Die Gäste können nach Absprache an der Tierpflege teilnehmen.
Magne hat auch eine Drechselwerkstatt, wo die schönsten Schüsseln und Kerzenhalter entstehen.

Go for it now. The future is promised to no one. ~Wayne Dyer~

Skjerpe Gard Hytter

Your host:
Magne Leirflåt & Jorunn Skjerpe
Address: Heskestad
N - 4463 Ualand
Phone/Fax: 51 40 09 62
Mobile: 90 94 54 64
E-mail: kjeleir@online.no
Web: www.skjerpegardhytter.no
Best time to call:
08.00 - 23.00 (mob.)
GPS: 58°29'47"N 6°21'34"E

A: Cabin for 2-6 persons	**A:** Hytte for 2-6 personer	**A:** Hütte für 2-6 Personen
2 bedrooms and 1 sleeping loft	2 soverom og 1 sovehems	2 Schlafzimmer u. 1 Schlafboden
Bath, kitchen, LR	Bad, kjøkken, stue	Bad, Küche, Stube
Whole unit for 2 pers.: **700,-**	Hele enheten for 2 pers.: **700,-**	Ganze Einheit für 2 Pers.: **700,-**
Price per additional pers.: **50,-**	Pris pr. tilleggsperson: **50,-**	Aufschl. pro weiterer Pers.: **50,-**
No. of cabins: 2	Antall hytter: 2	Anzahl Hütten: 2
B: Cabin 'Lillebu' for 2 pers.	**B:** Hytte 'Lillebu' for 2 pers.	**B:** Hütte 'Lillebu' für 2 Pers.
1 bedroom w/doublebed, WC	1 soverom m/dobbeltseng, WC	1 Schlafzi. mit Doppelbett, WC
Price for whole unit: **500,-**	Pris for hele enheten: **500,-**	Preis für ganze Einheit: **500,-**
Bed linen fee: **65,-**	Tillegg for sengetøy: **65,-**	Mieten von Bettwäsche: **65,-**
Guests clean prior to checkout,	Gjestene står for sluttrengjøring,	Gäste verantw. f. d. Endreinigung,
or cleaning fee: **300,-**	ellers: **300,-**	oder Endreinigung gegen: **300,-**
Prices valid for 2011	Priser gyldig for 2011	Preise gültig für 2011
Terrace/patio/yard	Terrasse/uteplass/hage	Terrasse/Außenbereich/Garten
Boat for rent	Båtutleie	Boot zu mieten
Open year round	Åpent hele året	Ganzjährig geöffnet
English spoken		Sprechen etwas Deutsch

At Skjerpe Gård the hosts operate a farm with sheep. The cabins are on the outskirts of the farm with a fine view of the valley. It's quiet and peaceful with grazing animals on the other side of the cattle pen. The hosts consist of two persons now that the children have grown and moved away.
Marked trails are near the cabins, and there is a fishing lake about 20-min. walk. Free fishing.

På Skjerpe Gård driver vertsfolket med sau. Hyttene ligger litt i utkanten av gården, på en høyde med fin oversikt over dalen. Her er det rolig og fredfylt med beitende dyr på andre siden av gjerdet. Vertsfamilien består nå av to personer da alle tre barna har flyttet ut. Merkede turstier går forbi hyttene, 20 min. å gå til fiskevann. Gratis fiske.

Auf Skjerpe Gård wird Schafzucht betrieben. Die Hütten liegen auf einer Anhöhe, ein wenig am Rand des Hofes, mit schöner Aussicht über das Tal. Hier ist es ruhig und friedlich mit weidenden Tieren ringsherum. Die Gastgeberfamilie besteht nun aus zwei Personen, da alle drei Kinder bereits ausgezogen sind. Markierte Wanderwege führen an den Hütten vorbei. 20 min zu Fuß zum See; dort kostenfreies Angeln.

Bjørg's Bed & Breakfast

Your host:
Bjørg Sunde

Address:
Nordsjøveien 1215 B
N - 4343 Orre
Phone: 51 42 87 05
Mobile: 95 91 15 04
E-mail: mazu@kleppnett.no

Best time to call:
09.00 - 22.00
GPS: 58°42'53"N 5°31'42"E

Double room:	**600,-**	Dobbeltrom:	**600,-**	Doppelzimmer:	**600,-**
1 pers. in double room:	**400,-**	1 pers. i dobbeltrom:	**400,-**	1 Pers. in Doppelzimmer:	**400,-**
No. of rooms: 2		Antall rom: 2		Anzahl Zimmer: 2	
Discount for children		Rabatt for barn		Ermäßigung für Kinder	
Breakf.: selfservice in common LR		Frokost: selvbetjening i gjestestue		Frühstück: SB in der Gästestube	
Prices valid for 2011		Priser gyldig for 2011		Preise gültig für 2011	
TV available		TV tilgjengelig		TV vorhanden	
Terrace/patio/yard		Terrasse/uteplass/hage		Terrasse/Außenbereich/Garten	
Bike for rent		Sykkelutleie		Fahrrad zu mieten	
Commonroom with ocean-view		Loftstue med havutsikt		Dachzimmer mit Meerblick	
Open year round		Åpent hele året		Ganzjährig geöffnet	
English spoken				Sprechen Englisch	

Your hosts at Bjørg's B&B, a couple in their late 50's, are always happy to receive new guests in their newly built home at Vik, near Orre. They were previously full-time farmers and still reside in the middle of the important agricultural region at Jæren. The view from the house is of the sea and up towards the mountains on the other side. The coastline along Jæren and Orre is specially known for its splendid white, sandy beaches and sand dunes. Walking distance to the beach. There is also excellent terrain for walking tours and bicycling.

Vertskapet i Bjørg's B&B, et par i slutten av 50-årene, tar hjertelig imot gjester i sitt nybygde hus på Vik, ved Orre. De har tidligere vært aktive bønder og bor fremdeles midt i det viktige jordbruksområdet på Jæren. Fra huset er det utsikt ut mot havet og opp mot fjellene på andre siden. Kysten langs Jæren og Orre spesielt er kjent for sine storslagne sandstrender med hvit sand og sand-dyner. Gangavstand til stranden. Forøvrig fint tur- og sykkelterreng.

Die Gastgeber, ein Paar von ca. Ende 50, freuen sich in ihrem neu erbauten Haus in Vik (bei Orre) auf ihre Gäste. Früher waren sie der Landwirtschaft verbunden und wohnen noch heute gern in Jæren, einer landwirtschaftlich wichtigen norwegischen Region. Vom Haus hat man einen schönen Blick aufs Meer und die Berge auf der gegenüberliegenden Seite. Die Küstenregion um Jæren und Orre ist besonders für ausgezeichnete Strände aus weißem Sand und Dünen bekannt. Kurzer Abstand zum Strand. Darüber hinaus hat man hier gute Wander- und Radelmöglichkeiten.

The Thompsons' Bed & Breakfast

Your host:
Sissel & Roger Thompson
Address: Musègaten 79
N - 4010 Stavanger
Phone: 51 52 13 29
Mobile: 97 15 05 20
E-mail: sthompso@online.no
Web: www.thompsonsbedand
breakfast.com
Best time to call: 08.00 - 23.00
GPS: 58°57'31"N 5°44'13"E

Double room:	**480,-**	Dobbeltrom:	**480,-**	Doppelzimmer:	**480,-**
Single room:	**325,-**	Enkeltrom:	**325,-**	Einzelzimmer:	**325,-**
No. of rooms: 4		Antall rom: 4		Anzahl Zimmer: 4	
Laid breakfast table		Dekket frokostbord		Gedeckter Frühstückstisch	
Prices valid for 2011/12		Priser gyldig for 2011/12		Preise gültig für 2011/12	
TV in all rooms		TV i alle rom		TV in allen Zimmern	
Terrace/yard/garden		Terrasse/hage		Terrasse/Garten	
Open year round		Åpent hele året		Ganzjährig geöffnet	
English spoken				Sprechen Deutsch	

English/Norwegian couple invites you to a lovely old villa from 1910 about 10 min. walk from city center. Large rooms, high ceiling. 5 min. walk to lovely walking areas. Close to museums, shops, harbor etc. Sissel and Roger are both classic car enthusiasts. They maintain a very hospitable family home. Breakfast is served in family dining room. TV, hairdryer, tea/coffee in rooms.
Cyclists welcome.

Directions:
From Stavanger city center to Musègate: Straight up the hill, with Rogaland theater and the Stavanger Museum on your left-hand side. Look for the beige house with green trim, about 800 m from city center.

Engelsk/norsk ektepar ønsker deg velkommen til en nydelig gammel villa fra 1910, ca. 10 min. spasertur fra sentrum. Store rom med stor takhøyde. Fem minutters gange til vakkert turterreng. Nær museer, butikker, havnen etc. Sissel og Roger er begge veteranbilentusiaster. De driver et meget gjestfritt hjem. Frokost serveres i familiens spisestue. TV, hårtørker og kaffe/te på rommene.
Syklister ønskes velkommen.

Veibeskrivelse:
Fra Stavanger sentrum til Musègaten: Opp bakken, med Rogaland Teater og Stavanger Museum på venstre side. Se etter beige hus med grønne lister, ca. 800 m fra sentrum.

Das Englisch/Norwegische Gastgeber-Ehepaar heisst seine Gäste in einer gemütlichen alten Villa von 1910 willkommen, die nur 10 min vom Stadtzentrum liegt. Große Zimmer mit hohen Decken. 5 min bis zu einem schönen Wandergebiet. In der Nähe Museen, Geschäfte, Hafen usw. Sissel u. Roger sind "Oldtimerfans". Sie haben ein sehr gastfreundliches Haus. Frühstück im Esszimmer der Familie. TV, Fön und Kaffee/Tee auf allen Zimmern.
Radfahrer willkommen.

Wegbeschreibung:
Stavanger Zentrum bis Musègata: den Hang hinauf (Rogaland Theater und Stavanger Museum linkerhand). Achten Sie auf ein beigefarbenes Haus mit grünen Fensterrahmen; ca. 800 m vom Zentrum entfernt.

Bed, Books & Breakfast

Your host:
Janken Robberstad
& Otto Bjelland

Address:
Byfoged Christensensgate 12
N - 4011 Stavanger
Phone: 51 52 50 50 / 90 82 35 26
E-mail: bioaroma@hotmail.com

Best time to call:
12.00 - 13.00 / 16.00 - 23.00
GPS: 58°57'27"N 5°44'9"E

Double room:	750,-	Dobbeltrom:	750,-	Doppelzimmer:	750,-
1 pers. in double room:	600,-	1 pers. i dobbeltrom:	600,-	1 Pers. im Doppelzi.:	600,-
Extra bed:	200,-	Ekstraseng:	200,-	Extrabett:	200,-

1 room with bath, kitchen, LR	1 rom med bad, kjøkken, stue	1 Zimmer mit Bad, Küche, Stube
Breakfast tray	Frokostbrett	Frühstückstablett
Selfcatering possible	Selvhushold er mulig	Selbsthaushalt möglich
Prices valid for 2011/12	Priser gyldig for 2011/12	Preise gültig für 2011/12
TV/Internet available	TV/Internett tilgjengelig	Zugang zu TV/Internet
Terrace/patio/yard	Terrasse/uteplass/hage	Terrasse/Außenbereich/Garten
Open year round	Åpent hele året	Ganzjährig geöffnet
English spoken		Sprechen etwas Deutsch

You're invited to a bed and breakfast with a private library of 400 books and music collection. The hosts enjoy books, music, good food and people from different cultures. Janken is a teacher of aroma therapy and feng shui. Otto is a sociologist and kinesiologist. Together they run a little school in natural therapy. 10-15 min. walk from Stavanger center.

Du inviteres her til en liten utleieleilighet med et eget bibliotek med 400 bøker og en musikksamling. Vertskapet er glad i bøker, musikk, god mat og mennesker fra ulike kulturer. Janken er lærer i aromaterapi og feng shui. Otto er sosiolog og kinesiolog. Sammen driver de en liten skole innen naturterapier. 10 - 15 min. å gå fra Stavanger sentrum.

Seien Sie herzlich eingeladen bei Janken und Otto zu übernachten. Beide sind Buch- und Musikenthusiasten, lieben gutes Essen und freuen sich über Gäste unterschiedlicher Kulturen. Sie besitzen eine Bibliothek mit über 400 Büchern und eine Musiksammlung. Janken ist Lehrerin für Aromatherapie und Feng Shui, Otto ist Soziologe und Kinesiologe. Zusammen betreiben sie eine kleine Schule für Naturtherapie. Bis zum Zentrum von Stavanger sind es nur 10-15 Min. zu Fuss.

I travel not to go anywhere, but to go.
I travel for travel's sake. The great affair is to move.
~Robert Louis Stevenson~

Byhaugen

Your host:
Harald Asche

Address:
Bruveien 6
N - 4024 Stavanger
Phone: **51 53 57 85**
Mobile: **97 62 12 00**
E-mail: **booking@byhaugen.no**
Web: **www.byhaugen.no**

Best time to call:
08.00 - 22.00
GPS: 58°58'18"N 5°42'18"E

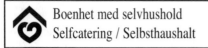

Apartment for 1-4 persons	Leilighet for 1-4 personer	Wohnung für 1-4 Personen
2 rooms, bath, kitchen	2 rom, bad, kjøkken	2 Zimmer, Bad, Küche
1 double bed & 2 single beds	1 dobbeltseng og 2 enkeltsenger	1 Doppelbett & 2 einzelne Betten
Price for 1 pers.: **550,-**	Pris for 1 pers.: **550,-**	Preis für 1 Pers.: **550,-**
Price for 2 pers.: **600,-**	Pris for 2 pers.: **600,-**	Preis für 2 Pers.: **600,-**
Price for 3 pers.: **750,-**	Pris for 3 pers.: **750,-**	Preis für 3 Pers.: **750,-**
Price for 4 pers.: **850,-**	Pris for 4 pers.: **850,-**	Preis für 4 Pers.: **850,-**
Extra bed: **100,-**	Ekstra seng: **100,-**	Extrabett: **100,-**
Minimum stay 2 nights	Minimum 2 netter	Mindestaufenthalt 2 Nächte
Prices valid for 2011/12/13	Priser gyldig for 2011/12/13	Preise gültig für 2011/12/13
TV/Internet available	TV/Internett tilgjengelig	TV/Internet verfügbar
Washing machine	Vaskemaskin	Waschmaschine
Terrace/patio	Terrasse/uteplass	Terrasse/Außenbereich
Open year round	Åpent hele året	Ganzjährig geöffnet
English, some French and Italian		Sprechen etwas Deutsch

Near both downtown and nature. Your host is glad to assist with reservations for tours, transportation, etc. Member of B&B Circle Stavanger. The unit was built in 2000 and is of high standard. Car parking in yard and bicycle parking i garage.
From the center of Stavanger: Take local bus no. 25 to Byhaugen or no. 27 to Egenes kolonihage.

Nær både sentrum og naturen. Eieren er behjelpelig med å bestille turer, transport etc. Medlem av B&B Circle Stavanger. Boenheten ble ferdig i 2000 og holder høy standard. Bilparkering i gården og sykkelparkering i garasje.
Fra Stavanger sentrum ta bybuss nr. 25 til Byhaugen eller nr. 27 til Egenes kolonihage.

Gute Lage in Zentrums- und Naturnähe. Der Besitzer hilft gern beim beim Buchen von Touren, Transport usw. Mitglied des B&B Kreises Stavanger. Die Wohnung bietet einen hohen Standard. Parkplätze im Innenhof und Garage für Fahrräder vorhanden.
Vom Zentrum Stavanger: Nehmen Sie den lokalen Stadtbus Nr. 25 bis Byhaugen oder Bus Nr. 27 bis Egenes kolonihage.

A good vacation is over when you begin to yearn for your work.
~Morris Fishbein~

Åmøy Fjordferie

Your host:
Lillian & Jan-Thor Holgersen

Address:
Varebergveien 47
N - 4152 Vestre Åmøy
Phone: 51 72 40 77
Mobile: 97 76 63 50
E-mail: post@amoyfjordferie.no
Web: www.amoyfjordferie.no

Best time to call:
08.00 - 19.00
GPS: 59°2'0"N 5°41'52"E

Double-/twin room:	**930,-**	Dobbelt-/tosengsrom:	**930,-**	Doppel-/Zweibettzi.:	**930,-**
Single room:	**660,-**	Enkeltrom:	**660,-**	Einzelzimmer:	**660,-**
Family room: ask for price		Familierom: spør om pris		Familienzimmer: Preis auf Anfrage	
No. of rooms: 11		Antall rom: 11		Anzahl Zimmer: 11	
Discount for children		Rabatt for barn		Ermäßigung für Kinder	
Laid breakfast table		Dekket frokostbord		Gedeckter Frühstückstisch	
Selfcatering possible		Selvhushold er mulig		Selbsthaushalt möglich	
Prices valid for 2011		Priser gyldig for 2011		Preise gültig für 2011	
TV/Internet available		TV/Internett tilgjengelig		TV/Internet verfügbar	
Terrace/patio/yard		Terrasse/uteplass/hage		Terrasse/Außenbereich/Garten	
Boat for rent		Båtutleie		Boot zu mieten	
Open year round		Åpent hele året		Ganzjährig geöffnet	
English spoken				Sprechen etwas Deutsch	

Åmøy Fjordferie lies by the sea with a panoramic view of the fjord towards Stavanger. It's possible to fish or tour the small islands in the area. For children it's exciting to hunt for small crabs under the beach rocks. Here one can find balm for the soul on a bicycle tour or from the stillness of an evening walk along the beach. Maybe you'd like to join the host in collecting the crab traps?

Åmøy Fjordferie ligger ved sjøen med panoramautsikt utover fjorden og mot Stavanger. Her er muligheter for å fiske, og turer til holmene i området.
For barna kan det være spennende å gå på jakt etter småkrabber under fjæresteinene. Her kan man oppleve balsam for sjelen på en sykkeltur eller gjennom stillheten på en kveldstur langs stranden.
Kanskje ønsker du å være med vertskapet å trekke krabbeteiner?

Åmøy Fjordferie liegt am See mit Panoramaaussicht hinaus auf den Fjord Ri. Stavanger. Sie können angeln und Ausflüge zu den kleinen Inseln in der Umgebung unternehmen. Kinder werden bei der Jagd nach Kleinenkrebsen, die sich unter den Steinen am Strand verstecken, viel Spass haben. Eine Fahrradtour oder ein Abendspaziergang am Strand sind Balsam für die Seele.
Vielleicht wollen Sie auch dabei sein, wenn die Gastgeber die Krebsreusen einholen?!

Spend the afternoon. You can't take it with you. ~Annie Dillard~

Høiland Gård

Your host:
Synnøve & Sigbjørn Vadla

Address:
Årdal
N - 4137 Årdal i Ryfylke
Phone: 51 75 27 75
Mobile: 97 12 90 36
E-mail: post@hoiland-gard.no
Web: www.hoiland-gard.no

Best time to call:
09.00 - 19.00
GPS: 59°9'29"N 6°12'53"E

Double room:	800,-/1000,-	Dobbeltrom:	800,-/1000,-	Doppelzimmer:	800,-/1000,-
Single room:	650,-/750,-	Enkeltrom:	650,-/750,-	Einzelzimmer:	650,-/750,-

Double room: **800,-/1000,-**
Single room: **650,-/750,-**
No. of rooms: 30
Breakfast buffet
Selfcatering possible
Houses and cabins also for rent
Prices valid for 2011
TV/Internet available
Terrace/patio/yard
VISA, MC, DC, AmEx accepted
Open year round
English spoken

Dobbeltrom: **800,-/1000,-**
Enkeltrom: **650,-/750,-**
Antall rom: 30
Frokost buffét
Selvhushold er mulig
Hus og hytter også til leie
Priser gyldig for 2011
TV/Internett tilgjengelig
Terrasse/uteplass/hage
Vi tar VISA, MC, DC, AmEx
Åpent hele året

Doppelzimmer: **800,-/1000,-**
Einzelzimmer: **650,-/750,-**
Anzahl Zimmer: 30
Frühstücksbüfett
Selbstverpflegung möglich
Auch Häuser/Hütten zu vermieten
Preise gültig für 2011
TV/Internet vorhanden
Terrasse/Außenbereich/Garten
Wir akzept. VISA, MC, DC, AmEx
Ganzjährig geöffnet
Sprechen Deutsch

Høiland Gard lies at the foot of Årdalsheiene with panoramic view of the rural settlements of Årdal and Årdal fjord. These culturally historic buildings are ideally positioned in rural surroundings and together with the characteristic farmyard tree they create a wonderful atmosphere.
The Vadla family bought the farmstead in 1995 and have since done restoration work, renovated, moved in a whole building and built from scratch. Today they have 70 sleeping places in assorted categories of accommodations.

Høiland Gard ligger ved foten av Årdalsheiene med panoramautsikt over bygda Årdal og Årdalsfjorden. De kulturhistoriske bygningene har en fin beliggenheten i landlige omgivelser, og sammen med det karakteristiske tuntreet, skapes en flott atmosfære.
Familien Vadla kjøpte garden i 1995 og har siden den gang restaurert, pusset opp, flyttet et hus til garden og bygget nytt. De har idag ialt 70 sengeplasser i ulike feriehus og hotellrom.

Høiland Gard liegt am Fuss von Årdalsheien mit Panoramaaussicht auf den Ort Årdal und den Årdalsfjord. Die kulturhistorischen Gebäude sind eingebettet in ländliche Natur und schaffen eine außergewöhnliche Atmosphäre.
Die Familie Vadla kaufte 1995 den Hof und hat ihn seitdem restauriert und renoviert. Ein ganzes Haus wurde sogar auf den Hofplatz umgesiedelt und wieder neu aufgebaut. Heute hat Familie Vadla 70 Betten in unterschiedlichen Ferienhäusern und Hotelzimmern.

Laughter is an instant vacation. ~Milton Berle~

Hotel Nøkling
Hjelmeland Camping

Your host:
Per Anker Bergh Nøkling
& Åse Tone Nøkling

Address:
Postboks 4, Hjelmeland
N - 4148 Hjelmeland
Phone/Fax: 51 75 02 30

Best time to call:
08.00 - 24.00
GPS: 59°14'00"N 6°10'13"E

Double room:	**1000,-**	Dobbeltrom:	**1000,-**	Doppelzimmer:	**1000,-**
Single room:	**700,-**	Enkeltrom:	**700,-**	Einzelzimmer:	**700,-**

No. of rooms: 24
Discount for children
Laid breakfast table or buffet
Other meals served on request
Self-catering possible (+ 8 cabins)
Prices valid for 2011/12/13
TV available
Access to telephone/fax
Terrace/patio/yard/garden
Boat and bike for rent
Pets welcome
Open year round
English and French spoken

Antall rom: 24
Rabatt for barn
Dekket frokostbord el. -buffet
Andre måltider serveres
Selvhushold er mulig (+ 8 hytter)
Priser gyldig for 2011/12/13
TV tilgjengelig
Tilgang på telefon/faks
Terrasse/uteplass/hage
Båt- og sykkelutleie
Kjæledyr velkommen
Åpent hele året

Anzahl Zimmer: 24
Ermäßigung für Kinder
Ged. Frühstückstisch oder -büfett
Andere Mahlzeiten nach Vereinb.
Selbsthaushalt mögl. (+ 8 Hütten)
Preise gültig für 2011/12/13
TV vorhanden
Telefon/Fax verfügbar
Terrasse/Außenbereich/Garten
Boot und Fahrrad zu mieten
Haustiere willkommen
Ganzjährig geöffnet
Sprechen Deutsch

Centrally, yet beautifully situated near the fjord in Hjelmeland. Excellent fishing spots and hiking trails. Row boats, swimming area. Local attractions: Breathtaking Preikestolen, Skomakernibba. Meals served to overnight guests.

Directions:
About 300 m from ferry quay in Hjelmeland along RV 13. Signposts lead to hotel. Travel time from Stavanger via Tau: about 75 min.

Stedet ligger vakkert til ved fjorden sentralt i Hjelmeland. Gode fiskemuligheter og turterreng. Robåter, badestrand. Attraksjoner i nærområdet: Preikestolen, Skomakernibba. Servering for overnattingsgjester.

Veibeskrivelse:
Ca. 300 m fra fergekaien i Hjelmeland ved RV 13. Skiltanvisning til hotellet. Reisetid fra Stavanger via Tau: ca. 75 min.

Landschaftlich reizvolle Lage am Fjord, zentral in Hjelmeland. Gute Angelmöglichkeiten. Wandergebiet, Ruderboote, Badestrand. Sehenswürdigkeiten in der Umgebung: Die Berges Preikestolen und Skomakernibba. Bewirtung für Übernachtungsgäste.

Wegbeschreibung:
Ca. 300 m vom Fähranleger in Hjelmeland entfernt (entlang der Str. 13). Der Beschilderung bis zum Hotel folgen. Fahrzeit ab Stavanger über Tau (Fähre!): ca. 75 min.

Fossane

Your host:
Kari og Sven E. Sørensen

Address:
Fossane, Vormedalen
N - 4130 Hjelmeland
Phone: 51 75 15 32
Mobile: 92 06 80 96
E-mail: post@fossane.no
Web: www.fossane.no

Best time to call:
08.00 - 23.00
GPS: 59°15'39"N 6°22'41"E

Double room:	**600,-**	Dobbeltrom:	**600,-**	Doppelzimmer:	**600,-**
Single room:	**300,-**	Enkeltrom:	**300,-**	Einzelzimmer:	**300,-**
Children:	**200,-**	Born:	**200,-**	Kinder:	**200,-**

No. of rooms: 3
Laid breakfast table
For updated prices, see web-page
Terrace/patio/yard/garden
Open year round
English spoken

Antal rom: 3
Dekka frukostbord
For oppdaterte priser, se web-side
Terrasse/uteplass/hage
Ope heile året

Anzahl Zimmer: 3
Gedeckter Frühstückstisch
Aktuelle Preise auf unserer Website
Terrasse/Außenbereich/Garten
Ganzjährig geöffnet
Sprechen Deutsch

The farm features Bed & Breakfast as well as 3 restored houses available for rent on a self-catering basis. The farm is a place that is full of culture and history. There are numerous cascades with old-style and modern hydroelectric stations and a restored grinding mill. The river includes an exciting swimming spot and you can fish in your host's own part of the waterway. Tour the lake in our rowboat or canoe. Fossane is situated in a beautiful wilderness area, near both fjord and mountain.
1.5 hour drive to the starting point for walking tours to Preikestolen.

På garden tilbys B&B-overnatting i tillegg til tre restaurerte hus som er til leige med sjølvhushald.
Garden er fylt med kultur og historie. Her er det fossefall med gamalt og nytt elektrisitetsverk, og eit restaurert kvernhus. I elva er det ein spennande badeplass og tilbod om stangfiske i eigars del av vassdraget. Robåt og kano kan nyttast til turar på vatnet.
Fossane ligg i eit flott naturområde, nært både fjord og fjell. Det er 1,5 time med bil til utgangspunktet for fottur til Preikestolen.

Auf dem Hof weden Bed & Breakfast sowie 3 renovierte Ferienhäuser mit Selbstverpflegung angeboten. Ein Aufenthalt auf dem Hof ist kulturell und geschichtlich sehr reizvoll. Sehenswürdigkeiten: ein Wasserfall, ein altes und ein neues E-Werk sowie historische, restaurierte Mühlen. Schöne Badestelle. Der dem Besitzer gehörige Flussabschnitt lädt zum Angeln ein; außerdem stehen Ruderboot und Kanu zur Verfügung. Fossane ist in eine sehr reizvolle Landschaft eingebettet; in der Nähe von Fjorden und Gebirgen. Der Ausgangspunkt zur Wanderung auf den Preikestolen ist mit dem Auto nur ca. 1,5 Stunden entfernt.

Why always "not yet"? Do flowers in spring say "not yet"? ~Norman Douglas~

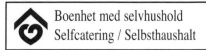

A: "Johnsenhuset"
Guesthouse for 2-8 persons:
3 bedrooms, bath, kitchen, LR

B: "Folgå"
Guesthouse for 2-10 persons:
3 bedrooms, bath, kitchen, LR

C: "Bjødlandsfolgå"
Guesthouse for 2-6 persons:
2 bedrooms, bath, kitchen, LR

Applies to all rental units:
For updated prices, see:
   www.fossane.no
Garden/yard/terrace/patio
Boat for rent
Open year round
English spoken

A: "Johnsenhuset"
Gjestehus for 2-8 personar:
3 soverom, bad, kjøken, stove

B: "Folgå"
Gjestehus for 2-10 personar:
3 soverom, bad, kjøken, stove

C: "Bjødlandsfolgå"
Gjestehus for 2-6 personar:
2 soverom, bad, kjøken, stove

Gjeld alle einingar:
For oppdaterte prisar sjå:
   www.fossane.no
Hage/terrasse/uteplass
Båtutleige
Ope heile året

A: "Johnsenhuset"
Gästehaus für 2-8 Personen
3 Schlafzi., Bad, Küche, Stube

B: "Folgå"
Gästehaus für 2-10 Personen
3 Schlafzi., Bad, Küche, Stube

C: "Bjødlandsfolgå"
Gästehaus für 2-6 Personen:
2 Schlafzi., Bad, Küche, Stube

Für alle Einheiten gilt:
Aktualisierte Preise hier:
   www.fossane.no
Garten/Terrasse/Außenbereich
Boot zu mieten
Ganzjährig geöffnet
Sprechen Deutsch

Directions:
From Stavanger: Take the ferry to Tau, then follow RV 13 to Hjelmeland. Turn toward Vormedalen, you see the sign just before the ferry quay at Hjemeland. To Vormedalen the distance is ca. 20 km drive and turn right over the bridge towards Fundingsland for 1 km or turn right on the 3rd road after the bridge.

Veibeskrivelse:
Frå Stavanger. Ta ferge til Tau, følg RV 13 til Hjelmeland.
Du finn skilt til Vormedalen rett før fergekaia i Hjelmeland. Kjøyr mot Vormedalen, ca. 20 km, veg over bru til høgre (Fundingsland) 1 km mot Fundingsland eller 3dje veg til høgre etter bru.

Wegbeschreibung:
Ab Stavanger: Nehmen Sie die Fähre nach Tau, und folgen der Str. 13 nach Hjelmeland. Direkt vor dem Fähranleger ist der Weg nach Vormedalen ausgeschildert Fahren Sie Ri. Vormedalen, ca. 20 km. Dann geht es rechts über eine Brücke nach Fundingsland. Nehmen Sie die 3. Straße hinter der Brücke nach rechts (nach ca. 1 km) Ri. Fundingsland.

Kleivå Gårdscamping

Your host:
Torstein Alvestad
Address: Lodavegen 323
N - 5561 Bokn
Phone: 52 74 84 13
Mobile: 97 15 56 27
E-mail: camping@kleivaa.no
Web: www.kleivaa.no

Best time to call:
09.00 - 23.00
GPS: 59°11'43"N 5°25'28"E

A: Apartment for 2-8 persons
3 bedrooms, bath, sauna, kitchen
Price for whole unit: **700,-**

B: One-room cabin for 2-4 pers.
w/kitchenette, shared bath
Price for whole unit: **275,-**

C: Cabin for 2-5 persons
2 bedrooms, bath in sanitary facilities
Price for whole unit: **380,-**

Additional bed linen fee
Breakfast tray available
Prices valid for 2011
TV/Internet available
Large outdoor area, grill shelter
Boat and bike for rent
Pets welcome
Open year round
English spoken

A: Husvære for 2-8 personar
3 soverom, bad, badstu og kjøken
Pris for heile eininga: **700,-**

B: Eitromshytte for 2-4 personar
m/kjøkenkrok, bad i sanitæranlegg
Pris for heile eininga: **275,-**

C: Toromshytte for 2-5 personer
m/kjøkenkrok, bad i sanitæranlegg
Pris for heile eininga: **380,-**

Leige av sengeklede kjem i tillegg
Frukost kan bestellast
Prisar gjeld for 2011
TV/Internett tilgjengeleg
Stor uteplass, grillhytte
Båt- og sykkelutleige
Kjæledyr velkomen
Ope heile året

A: Wohnung für 2-8 Personen
3 Schlafzi., Bad, Sauna, Küche
Ganze Einheit: **700,-**

B: Einraumhütte für 2-4 Personen
Küchenecke, Bad in Sanitäranlage
Ganze Einheit: **275,-**

C: Zweiraumhütte für 2-5 Pers.
Küchenecke, Bad in Sanitäranlage
Ganze Einheit: **380,-**

Zusätzliche Gebühr für Bettwäsche
Frühstück auf Bestellung
Preise gültig für 2011
TV/Internet vorhanden
Großer Außenbereich, Grillhütte
Boot und Fahrrad zu mieten
Haustiere willkommen
Ganzjährig geöffnet
Sprechen etwas Deutsch

Kleivå farm camping is approx. 3.5 km from E-39, on the island of Vestre Bokn.
Plentiful opportunity for hiking, fishing, biking, canoeing. Guests can help with feeding the animals. The farm has cows, cats, lambs and rabbits.
Bokn is in in the heart of Rogaland, about 1 hr from Stavanger or Haugesund. Much to do in Haugalandet.

Kleivå Gardscamping finn du 3,5 km frå E-39, på øya Vestre Bokn. Her er det gode høve til fotturar, kanopadling, fiske og sykkelturar. Du kan og vere med på stell av dyr. På garden er det kyr, kattar, lam og kaniner.
Haugalandet kan by på mange aktiviteter. Bokn ligg sentralt i Rogaland. Det er ca. 1 times reise til Stavanger eller Haugesund.

Kleivå Hofcamping liegt 3,5 km von der E-39 auf der Insel Vestre Bokn. Toll zum Wandern, Kanu- u. Radfahren, Angeln. Auf dem Hof gibt es Kühe, Katzen, Lämmer und Kaninchen. Sie können die Tiere gerne mit betreuen und versorgen.
Bokn liegt zentral in der Provinz Rogaland, nur 1 h von Stavanger oder Haugesund entfernt.
Die Region bietet viele verschiedene Aktivitäten.

Dugneberg Bed & Breakfast

Your host:
Jan Arnstein Liknes
Address: Vestre Karmøyveg 435
N - 4270 Åkrehamn
Phone: 52 81 62 52
Mobile: 48 15 07 87
E-mail: dugneberg@c2i.net
Web:
http://home.c2i.net/dugneberg
Best time to call: 08.00 - 23.00
GPS: 59°14'15"N 5°11'56"E

Double room:	**500,-**	Dobbeltrom:	**500,-**	Doppelzimmer:	**500,-**
Single room:	**250,-**	Enkeltrom:	**250,-**	Einzelzimmer:	**250,-**
No. of rooms: 3		Antall rom: 3		Anzahl Zimmer: 3	

Laid breakfast table
Prices valid for 2011
TV/Internet available
Terrace/patio/yard
Pets welcome
Open year round
English & some French spoken

Dekket frokostbord
Priser gyldig for 2011
TV/Internett tilgjengelig
Terrasse/uteplass/hage
Kjæledyr velkommen
Åpent hele året

Gedeckter Frühstückstisch
Preise gültig für 2011
TV/Internet vorhanden
Terrasse/Außenbereich/Garten
Haustiere willkommen
Ganzjährig geöffnet
Sprechen Deutsch

Dugneberg is a small farm on Karmøy. From the top of Dugneberg one can see miles and miles of coastline and enjoy fantastic sunsets on clear summer nights. There are fine foot paths through heather purple and only 10 min. walk to the sea. The farm has an inviting look with meadows and fields. Everyone is welcome to putter around or find a bench and read a book. It's allowed to enjoy the fruit from berry bushes in the old garden.

Dugneberg er et lite gårdsbruk på Karmøy. Fra toppen av Dugneberg kan man se kilometervis langs kystlinjen og nyte en fantastisk solnedgang på klare sommerkvelder. Her er flotte turstier innover lyngheiene og bare 10 min. å gå ned til havet. Gården har et trivelig uteareal med plener og marker der alle er velkomne til å tusle rundt eller finne seg en benk for å lese litt i en bok. Det er også lov å forsyne seg fra bærbuskene i den gamle havnehagen.

Dugneberg ist ein kleiner Hof auf Karmøy. Man kann kilometerlang die Küste entlangsehen u. fantastische Sonnenuntergänge geniessen. Schöne Wanderwege führen durch die hügelige Heidelandschaft. Zu Fuss sind es nur 10 min bis zum Hafen. Der Hof hat einen gemütlichen Garten. Seien Sie herzlich zu einem Rundgang willkommen oder lesen Sie ein Buch auf einer der Gartenbänke. Sie dürfen gerne an den Beerensträuchern im alten Garten naschen.

Directions:
Situated on route RV 47, 13 km. north of Skudesneshavn and 2.5 km. south of Åkrehamn. At the Liknes busstop see the sign 'Rom', pointing to the farm yard.

Veibeskrivelse:
Langs RV 47, 13 km nord for Skudesneshavn og 2,5 km sør for Åkrehamn; like ved buss-stoppestedet på Liknes, se 'ROM'-skiltet som peker mot tunet.

Wegbeschreibung:
Entlang der Str. 47, 13 km nördlich v. Skudesneshavn u. 2,5 km südlich v. Åkrehamn; direkt bei der Bushaltestelle in Liknes sehen Sie das 'ROM'- Schild, das Ri. Hof zeigt.

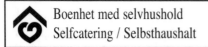
Anne Grete's Husrom

Your host:
Anne Grete Gausvik

Address:
Soldalveien 3
N - 5546 Røyksund
Phone: 52 83 65 93
Mobile: 90 88 14 35

Best time to call:
08.00 - 22.00
GPS: 59°20'6"N 5°21'53"E

Apartment for 2-4 persons	Leilighet for 2-4 personer	Wohnung für 2-4 Personen
Own bath, sleeping alcove and LR w/kitchen	Eget bad, sovealkove og stue m/kjøkken	Eig. Bad, Bettnische und Stube mit Küche
Price for whole unit: **350,-**	Pris for hele enheten: **350,-**	Ganze Einheit: **350,-**
Bed linen fee: **50,-**	Tillegg for sengetøy: **50,-**	Mieten von Bettwäsche: **50,-**
Prices valid for 2011/12/13	Priser gyldig for 2011/12/13	Preise gültig für 2011/12/13
TV available	TV tilgjengelig	TV vorhanden
Yard/terrace/patio	Hage/terrasse/uteplass	Garten/Terrasse/Außenbereich
Suitable for handicapped	Handikaptilgjengelig	Behindertengerecht
Pets welcome	Kjæledyr velkommen	Haustiere willkommen
Open May - October	Åpent mai - oktober	Geöffnet Mai - Oktober
Some English & Spanish spoken		Sprechen etwas Deutsch

Anne Grete is an experienced hostess, and you find her on the mainland, 12 km south of Haugesund. The house has a lovely view of the fjord and neighboring wilderness. Good hiking opportunities, abundant seasonal berry and mushroom picking, swimming and fishing. From Anne Grete's you can venture on day trips to visit the quaint villages of Skudenes and Kopervik with their historical wooden buildings, visit Avaldsnes Church, or take the boat from Haugesund to Utsira, an ocean island, Norway's most western settlement.

Anne Grete har tatt imot turister i mange år. Du finner stedet på fastlandet 12 km sør for Haugesund. Huset har fin utsikt over fjord og friområde.
I området er det fint turterreng, bra med skogsbær og sopp. Fine steder for bading og fisking i fjorden.
Fra Anne Gretes husrom kan man legge ut på dagsturer for å besøke de idylliske småstedene Skudenes og Kopervik med gammel trehusbebyggelse, beskue Avaldsnes kirke eller ta båten fra Haugesund til Utsira, et lite samfunn på ei øy ute i havgapet som er Norges vestligste bosetning.

Anne Grete nimmt seit vielen Jahren Gäste bei sich auf. Gausvik liegt 12 km südlich von Haugesund auf dem Festland. Das Haus hat eine schöne Aussicht über den Fjord und die Umgebung. Reizvolles Wandergelände, reich an Waldbeeren und Pilzen. Schöne Stellen zum Baden und Angeln im Fjord. Gute Lage für Ausflüge nach Skudenes oder Koppervik, kleine idyllische Orte mit Holzhäusern. Zu empfehlen sind der Besuch der Avaldsnes-Kirche und eine Fahrt mit Schiff von Haugesund nach Utsira, der westlichsten Siedling Norwegens auf einer Insel in der Nordsee.

Eide Gard

Your host:
Johanne Marie Heggebø

Address:
Eide
N - 5580 Ølen
Phone: 53 76 82 23
Mobile: 90 19 53 10
E-mail:
johanne.marie@eidegard.no
Web: www.eidegard.no
Best time to call:
09.00 - 22.00
GPS: 59°35'59"N 5°49'3"E

Double-/twin room:	**1000,-**	Dobbelt-/tosengsrom:	**1000,-**	Doppel-/Zweibettzimmer:	**1000,-**
1 pers. in double room:	**750,-**	1 pers. i dobbeltrom:	**750,-**	1 Pers. im Doppelzimmer:	**750,-**
No. of rooms: 3		Antal rom: 3		Anzahl Zimmer: 3	
Laid breakfast table		Dekka frukostbord		Gedeckter Frühstückstisch	
Prices valid for 2011		Priser gjeld for 2011		Preise gültig für 2011	
TV available		TV tilgjengeleg		TV vorhanden	
Terrace/patio/yard		Terrasse/uteplass/hage		Terrasse/Außenbereich/Garten	
Boat for rent.		Båtutleige		Boot zu mieten	
Open year round		Ope heile året		Ganzjährig geöffnet	
English spoken				Sprechen etwas Deutsch	

Eide Gard is the place for anyone who is seeking the uncomplicated, original atmosphere of Western Norway. Farm facilities dating from around 1800 are restored in the traditional Norwegian style. Here you will find an old cookhouse with a hearth and an old woodshed that has been converted for use as an old-style gathering hall.
Eide Gard has been awarded "Olavsrosa" for its historic quality. Fjord view from the rooms, walking distance to Ølen town center, marked walking trails.

Eide Gard er staden for deg som søkjer den enkle og tradisjonelle stemninga frå Vestlandet. Gardstunet, som stammer frå rundt år 1800 er satt i stand i tradisjonell norsk stil. På garden finn du óg eit eldhus med grue, og eit vedskjul som er omgjort til gildeskål (trad. selskapslokale).
Eide gard er tildelt Olavsrosa for sin historiske miljøkvalitet.
Fjordutsikt frå romma, gangavstand til Ølen sentrum, merka turløyper.

Der Hof Eide Gard ist genau der richtige Ort für alle Gäste, die die einfache und ursprüngliche Atmosphäre Westnorwegens mögen. Der Hof stammt ca. von 1800, die Gebäude sind im traditionellen norwegischen Stil erbaut und eingerichtet. Unter anderem gibt es ein altes Backhaus mit Feuerstelle sowie einen Holzschuppen, der zu einem sogenannten "Gildeskål" umgebaut wurde, einem trad. Gesellschaftsraum. Der Hof wurde aufgrund seiner historischen Bausubstanz mit der Olavsrose ausgezeichnet.
Fjordblick aus den Zimmern, Fußweg zum Zentrum von Ølen, markierte Wanderwege.

Guddalstunet

Your host:
Kirsten & Johannes Guddal

Address:
Guddalsvegen 181
N - 5470 Rosendal
Phone: 53 48 11 27
Mobile: 91 69 60 21
E-mail: post@guddalstunet.no
Web: www.guddalstunet.no

Best time to call:
08.00 - 22.00
GPS: 59°57'46"N 6°1'33"E

Double room:	**1000,-**	Dobbeltrom:	**1000,-**	Doppelzimmer:	**1000,-**
1 pers. in double room:	**700,-**	1 pers. i dobbeltrom:	**700,-**	1 Pers. im DZ:	**700,-**
No. of rooms: 2		Antall rom: 2		Anzahl Zimmer: 2	
Laid breakfast table		Dekket frokostbord		Gedeckter Frühstückstisch	

Cabins for 2-6 pers. (selfcatering)		Hytter for 2-6 pers. (selvhushold)		Hütten f. 2-6 Pers. (Selbsthaushalt)	
Own bath, kitchen, LR		Eget bad, kjøkken, stue		Eig. Bad, Küche, Stube	
Price per cabin:	**1100,-**	Pris pr. hytte:	**1100,-**	Preis pro Hütte:	**1100,-**
Bed linen fee:	**100,-**	Tillegg for sengetøy:	**100,-**	Mieten von Bettw.:	**100,-**

Prices valid for 2011/12/13
TV available
Terrace/patio/yard
Boat for rent
Open year round
English spoken

Priser gyldig for 2011/12/13
TVtilgjengelig
Terrasse/uteplass/hage
Båtutleie
Åpent hele året

Preise gültig für 2011/12/13
TV vorhanden
Terrasse/Außenbereich/Garten
Boot zu mieten
Ganzjährig geöffnet
Sprechen Deutsch

In old and new houses and huts you will be welcomed to a generation farm with traditions. The farm has been awarded the "Olavsrosa" by the national cultural foundation for the historic environmental quality which the place represents, through careful restoration. Rosendal is known for its renaissance/baroque chateau from the 17th century barony, which is now a museum.
Guddals lies just off the RV 13 on the southern side of the Hardangerfjord. Drive off at Seimsfoss, 3 km south of Rosendal.

I gamle og nye hus og hytter ønskes du velkommen til en generasjonsgård med tradisjoner. Guddalstunet er tildelt Olavsrosa fra den nasjonale kulturminnestiftelsen for den historiske miljøkvaliteten som anlegget representerer, gjennom pietetsfullt restaureringsarbeide.
Rosendal er kjent for sitt renessanse/barokkslott Baroniet, fra 1600-tallet, som nå er museum. Guddal ligger på en avstikker fra RV 13 på sørsiden av Hardangerfjorden. Ta av ved Seimsfoss, 3 km sør for Rosendal.

Auf dem traditionsreichen Erbhof werden Gäste in alten und neuen Häusern und Hütten willkommen geheißen. Der Hof wurde vom nationalen Kulturdenkmalsfond für pietätsvolle Restaurierung und geschichtliche Bauqualität ausgezeichnet. Der Ort Rosendal ist bekannt für sein Renaissance/ Barock Schloss aus dem 17. Jh., das jetzt ein Museum ist.
Guddal liegt an der Südseite des Hardangerfjords; einen Abstecher von der Str. 13. Abfahrt Seimsfoss, 3 km südlich von Rosendal.

Heradstveit Herberge

Your host:
An Riemslag
Address: Heradstveitvegen 244
N - 5620 Tørvikbygd
Phone: 56 56 46 64
Mobile: 97 54 92 40
E-mail: an.riemslag@kvamnet.no
Web: www.heradstveit-herberge.no

Best time to call:
08.00 - 22.00
GPS: 60°19'19"N 6°9'3"E

Double-/twin room:	950,-	Dobbelt-/tosengsrom:	950,-	Doppel-/Zweibettzi.:	950,-
Single room:	650,-	Enkeltrom:	650,-	Einzelzimmer:	650,-

Double-/twin room: 950,-
Single room: 650,-
No. of rooms: 5
Laid breakfast table
Dinner: 350,-
Priser gjeld for 2011
TV/Internet available
Terrace/patio/yard
Suitable for handicapped
Pets welcome
Open year round
English, Dutch & French spoken

Dobbelt-/tosengsrom: 950,-
Enkeltrom: 650,-
Antal rom: 5
Dekka frukostbord
Middag: 350,-
Priser gjeld for 2011
TV/Internett tilgjengeleg
Terrasse/uteplass/hage
Tilhøve for gjester med handikap
Kjæledyr velkomen
Ope heile året

Doppel-/Zweibettzi.: 950,-
Einzelzimmer: 650,-
Anzahl Zimmer: 5
Gedeckter Frühstückstisch
Abendessen: 350,-
Preise gültig für 2011
TV/Internet vorhanden
Terrasse/Außenbereich/Garten
Behindertengerecht
Haustiere willkommen
Ganzjährig geöffnet
Sprechen Deutsch

At 250 meters above sea level with a great view lies Heradstveit Herberge, a family farm with active operations including forestry, sawmill, woodwork, a store-house museum and more. The hostess is from Netherlands and welcome travelers. Guests can hike mountains up to 1000 m. altitude and wander to romantic forest lake; go horseback riding or use the neighborhood fitness center. The hosts offer mountain tours with guide and transport. Ask about price. Good food and a friendly atmosphere with culture and history. Heradstveit Herberge is also suitable for courses, meetings, surprise trips and other group activities.

På ei høgde 250 m.o.h. med fint utsyn ligg Heradstveit Herberge, ein slektsgard i aktiv drift med skog, sagbruk, treverkstad, stabbursmuseum og anna. Vertinna er frå Nederland og ynskjer reisande velkomen.
Fine høve til fjellturar opp til over 1000 m, turar til romantisk skogsvatn, hesteridning, treningsstudio i nærleiken.
Vertsfolket kan tilby fjellturar med guide og transport. Spør om pris.
God mat i ein venskapeleg atmosfære prega av kultur og historie. Heradstveit Herberge er óg egna til kurs, møter, blåturar, og andre gruppesamankomster.

Auf einer Höhe von 250 m ü.NN, mit schöner Aussicht befindet sich die Heradstveit Herberge. Der Familienhof wird voll betrieben mit Forstwirtschaft, Sägewerk, Holzwerkstatt, Speicher-Museum u.v.m. Die Gastgeberin aus den Niederlanden heißt ihre Gäste herzlich willkommen. Hier ist vieles möglich: Bergtouren bis auf über 1000 m, Ausflüge zum romantischen Waldsee, Reiten und auch ein Fitnessstudio ist in der Nähe. Gastgeber bieten auf Nachfrage geführte Bergtouren an. Geniessen Sie gutes Essen in einer gastfreundlichen Atmosphäre voller Kultur und Geschichte. Der Hof eignet sich auch für Kurse, Meetings und andere Gruppenveranstaltungen.

Lerkebo

Your host:
Klausen

Address:
Sætervegen 40
N - 5236 Rådal
Phone: 55 13 62 44
Mobil: 41 14 68 98
Fax: 55 13 38 50
E-mail: solveig@lerkebo.no
Web: www.lerkebo.no

Best time to call:
08.00 - 23.00

Double room:	**550,-/850,-**	Dobbeltrom:	**550,-/850,-**	Doppelzimmer:	**550,-/850,-**
Room for 3 pers.:	**700,-/850,-**	Rom for 3 pers.:	**700,-/850,-**	Zimmer für 3 Pers.:	**700,-/850,-**
Single room:	**350,-/450,-**	Enkeltrom:	**350,-/450,-**	Einzelzimmer:	**350,-/450,-**
Extra bed:	**50,-** up to **175,-**	Ekstraseng:	**50,-** opp til **175,-**	Extrabett:	**50,-** bis zu **175,-**

No. of rooms: 7	Antall rom: 7	Anzahl Zimmer: 7
Discount for children	Rabatt for barn	Ermässigung für Kinder
Breakfast buffet or self-service	Frokostbuffét el. selvbetjening	Frühstücksbüfett o. Selbstbedienung
Selfcatering possible	Selvhushold er mulig	Selbsthaushalt möglich
Prices valid for 2011/12/13	Priser gyldig for 2011/12/13	Preise gültig für 2011/12/13
TV/Internet available	TV/Internett tilgjengelig	Zugang zu TV/Internet
Terrace/patio/yard	Terrasse/uteplass/hage	Terrasse/Aussenplatz/Garten
Bike for rent	Sykkelutleie	Fahrrad zu mieten
Suitable for handicapped	Handikapvennlig	Behindertengerecht
BBQ and pool in the garden	Grill og basseng i hage	Grill und Pool im Garten
Weekly rate on request	Ukepris på forespørsel	Wochenpreis auf Anfrage
Open year round	Åpent hele året	Ganzjährig geöffnet
English & French spoken		Sprechen Deutsch

Lerkebo - where chirping birds may be heard during light summer nights - is a modern and spacious detached home that is located in a quiet, suburban area on a private cul-de-sac 12 km from downtown Bergen. Your hosts love to meet people and take pride in making conditions optimal for their guests. Here you are welcome to just relax after a hectic day of running between Bergen's many attractions.

Lerkebo - kanskje med litt fugle-kvitter gjennom lyse sommernetter - er en moderne og romslig enebo-lig som ligger i et stille forstads-område i en privat blindvei 12 km fra Bergen sentrum. Vertskapet liker å møte mennesker, og setter sin stolthet i å gjøre det best mulig for gjestene. Her er du velkommen til å slappe av etter en hektisk dag løpende mellom Bergens mange attraksjoner.

Lerkebo -mit Vogelgezwitscher in hellen Sommernächten- ist ein modernes und geräumiges Einfamilienhaus in einer privaten Sackgasse eines ruhigen Vororts. Nur 12 km bis Bergen. Die aufgeschlossenen Gastgeber legen sehr viel Wert auf das Wohl ihrer Gäste. Nach dem Besuch vieler Sehenswürdigkeiten in Bergen kann man sich hier bestens erholen.

EkerGarden

Your host:
**Christa-Lis Devangel
& Irene Evensen**

Address: Kyrkjeledvegen 7
Nordre Ekerhovd
N - 5360 Kolltveit
Phone: 56 33 03 34 / 56 32 15 10
Mobile: 95 05 19 61 / 93 22 84 34
E-mail: devangel@online.no
ireevens@online.no
Web: www.ekergarden.com
Best time to call: 08.00 - 22.00
GPS: 60°19'55"N 5°7'14"E

Twin room:	600,-	Tosengsrom:	600,-	Zweibettzimmer:	600,-
Single room:	350,-	Enkeltrom:	350,-	Einzelzimmer:	350,-
Familyroom for 4 pers.:	850,-	Familierom, 4 pers.:	850,-	Familienzimmer, 4 Pers.:	850,-

No. of rooms: 6
Shared bath and kitchen
Bed linen included
Tea/koffee available
Prices valid for 2011
Internet available
Terrace/patio/yard
Open year round
English & some French spoken

Antall rom: 6
Delt bad og kjøkken
Sengetøy er inkludert
Te og kaffe tilgjengelig
Priser gyldig for 2011
Internett tilgjengelig
Terrasse/uteplass/hage
Åpent hele året

Anzahl Zimmer: 6
Gemeins. Bad und Küche
Inkl. Bettwäsche
Tee/Kaffe zur Verfügung
Preise gültig für 2011
Internet verfügbar
Terrasse/Außenbereich/Garten
Ganzjährig geöffnet
Sprechen etwas Deutsch

EkerGarden lies snugly in natural and peaceful surroundings on the east side of Sotra. Near mountains and coast. EkerGarden is an oasis to visit when you need a holiday, to relax or recharge.
Besides a place to stay the hosts offer services such as massage, healing and guiding. EkerGarden is owned by two women who are experienced therapists and educators.

EkerGarden ligger nydelig til i fin natur og rolige omgivelser på østsiden av Sotra, nær fjell og sjø. EkerGarden er en oase når du trenger ferie, et sted å slappe av, eller når du trenger påfyll.
I tillegg til overnatting tilbyr vertskapet behandlinger som massasje, healing og veiledning. De driver også med kurs og foredrag.
EkerGarden eies av to kvinner som også bor på stedet, begge er erfarne terapeuter og undervisere.

EkerGarden liegt ruhig und von herrlicher Natur umgeben auf der Ostseite von Sotra. Die Berge und das Meer befinden sich in unmittelbarer Umgebung. EkerGarden ist eine Oase für alle Urlauber. Hier kann man sich erholen und neue Kräfte tanken.
Zusätzlich zur Übernachtung gehören Massagen, Geistiges Heilen, Wegbereitung, sowie verschiedene Kurse und Vorträge zum Angebotsspektrum. EkerGarden ist in Besitz zweier Frauen, die auch auf dem Hof wohnen; beide sind erfahrene Therapeuten und Lehrer.

Life is short, God's way of encouraging a bit of focus. ~Robert Brault~

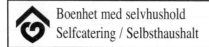
Klosteret 5 Gjestehus

Your host:
Elisabet Kaltenborn

Address:
Klosteret 5
N - 5005 Bergen
Phone: 55 31 55 50
Mobile: 95 05 14 30
E-mail: ekaltenb@online.no

Best time to call:
08.00 - 23.00
GPS: 60°23'42"N 5°18'58"E

Apartment for 5 persons	Leilighet for 5 personer	Wohnung für 5 Personen
2 bedrooms and bath	2 soverom og bad	2 Schlafzimmer und Bad
Kitchenette and LR w/fireplace	Tekjøkken og stue med peis	Küchenecke und Stube mit Kamin
Price for whole unit: **1200,-**	Pris for hele enheten: **1200,-**	Ganze Einheit: **1200,-**
4 nights or more, per night: **1000,-**	4 netter eller mer, pr. natt: **1000,-**	4 Nächte o. mehr, p. Nacht: **1000,-**
Double room: **500,-**	Dobbeltrom: **500,-**	Doppelzimmer: **500,-**
Single room: **400,-**	Enkeltrom: **400,-**	Einzelzimmer: **400,-**
Bed linen included	Sengetøy inkl.	Inkl. Bettwäsche
Tea and coffe available	Te og kaffe tilgjengelig	Tee und Kaffee erhältlich
Prices valid for 2011	Priser gyldig for 2011	Preise gültig für 2011
TV/Internet	TV/Internett	TV/Internet
Pets welcome by agreement	Kjæledyr velkommen etter avtale	Haustiere nach Vereinbarung willk.
Open year round	Åpent hele året	Ganzjährig geöffnet
English spoken		Sprechen Englisch

Klosteret 5 is situated in a cozy, old alley among old wooden houses on Nordnes, the peninsula that makes up part of downtown Bergen. Walking distance to all facilities. Parks, aquarium and swimming pool are nearby. Several good restaurants in the neighborhood.

Directions:
All routes into Bergen: Follow the signs towards "Akvariet", and continue back around towards downtown. Look for Klosteret 5, 100 m past the avenue which has trees along each side.

Klosteret 5 ligger i et koselig smau i gammel bebyggelse på Nordnes, en halvøy som utgjør en del av Bergen sentrum. Gangavstand til alle fasiliteter. Park, akvarium og svømmebasseng like i nærheten. Flere gode restauranter i nabolaget.

Veibeskrivelse:
Alle innkjørsler til Bergen: følg skilt til Akvariet, fortsett tilbake mot sentrum, se etter Klosteret 5, 100 m etter alléen.

Klosteret 5 liegt in einer niedlichen Gasse im Altstadteil Nordnes - einer Halbinsel, die einen Teil des Stadtzentrums Bergens ausmacht. Kurze Entfernung zu allen Angeboten wie Stadtpark, Aquarium und Schwimmbad. Mehrere gute Restaurants befinden sich in der Nachbarschaft.

Wegbeschreibung:
Aus allen Richtungen kommend: Folgen Sie der Beschilderung zum Aquarium, anschließend fahren Sie zurück Richtung Zentrum. Achten Sie 100 m hinter der Allee auf Klosteret 5.

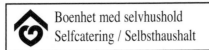
Anne's Gjestehus

Your host:
Anne Magnussen

Address:
Klostersmauet 6
N - 5005 Bergen
Mobile: 99 01 23 70
E-mail: anne@emblafilm.no
Web: http://
annmagnussen.googlepages.com

Best time to call:
18.00 - 23.00
GPS: 60°23'44"N 5°18'51"E

Apartment for 1-5 persons	Leilighet for 1-5 personer	Wohnung für 1-5 Personen
2 bedrooms,own bath and kitchen	2 soverom,eget bad og kjøkken	2 Schlafzi., eig. Bad und Küche
Whole unit (1-4 pers.): **1200,-**	For hele enheten (1-4 pers.): **1200,-**	Ganze Einheit (1-4 Pers.): **1200,-**
4 nights or more, per night: **1000,-**	4 netter el. mer, per. natt: **1000,-**	4 oder mehr Nächte, p.N.: **1000,-**
Price per additional pers.: **150,-**	Pris pr. tilleggsperson: **150,-**	Jede weitere Person: **150,-**
Babybed available	Babyseng tilgjengelig	Babybett verfügbar
Bed linen included	Sengetøy er inkludert	Inkl. Bettwäsche
Prices valid for 2011	Priser gyldig for 2011	Preise gültig für 2011
TV and Internet available	TV/Internett tilgjengelig	TV/Internet vorhanden
Patio/yard	Uteplass	Außenbereich/Sitzecke
Pets welcome by agreement	Kjæledyr velkommen etter avtale	Haustiere nach Absprache willk.
Open year round	Åpent hele året	Ganzjährig geöffnet
English spoken		Sprechen etwas Deutsch

Anne's Gjestehus is also situated in the cozy old neighborhood of Nordnes (see page 138). The house is 250 years old but the apartment is restored with new bathroom and kitchen with washing machine and dryer. One bedroom has a double sleeping sofa and a wood stove. This room can be used as living room.

Anne's Gjestehus ligger også i koselig gammel bebyggelse på Nordnes (se side 138). Huset er 250 år gammelt, men leiligheten er restaurert og har nytt kjøkken og bad med vaskemaskin og tørketrommel. Det ene soverommet har en dobbel sovesofa og en liten vedovn. Dette rommet kan brukes som stue.

Anne's Gjestehus liegt ebenfalls in der alten, gemütlichen Siedlung auf der Halbinsel Nordnes (vgl. Seite 138). Das Haus ist 250 Jahre alt, aber die Wohnung ist saniert und hat eine neue Küche und ein neues Bad mit Waschmaschine und Trockner. Eines der Schlafzimmer hat ein Schlafsofa für zwei Personen und einen kleinen Holzofen. Dieses Zimmer kann als Wohnzimmer genutzt werden.

> There are a million ways to lose a work day,
> but not even a single way to get one back.
> ~Tom DeMarco and Timothy Lister~

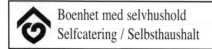
Skiven Gjestehus

Your host:
**Elisabeth Kvale
& Alf Magne Heskja**

Address:
Skivebakken 17
N - 5018 Bergen
Phone: 55 31 30 30
Mobile: 90 05 30 30
E-mail: skiven@skiven.no
Web: www.skiven.no

Best time to call:
08.00 - 22.00
GPS: 60°23'33"N 5°20'3"E

Double room:	**600,-**	Dobbeltrom:	**600,-**	Doppelzimmer:	**600,-**
1 pers. in double room:	**400,-**	1 pers. i dobbeltrom:	**400,-**	1 Pers. im Doppelzi.:	**400,-**
Extra bed:	**150,-**	Ekstraseng:	**150,-**	Extrabett:	**150,-**

Shared: bath, 2 WC and kitchen
No. of double rooms: 4
Bed linen included
Prices valid for 2011/12
TV/Internet available
VISA, MC accepted
Open year round
English and some Italian spoken

Deles: bad, 2 WC og kjøkken
Antall dobbeltrom: 4
Sengetøy er inkludert
Priser gyldig for 2011/12
TV/Internett tilgjengelig
Vi tar VISA, MC
Åpent hele året

Gemeins.: Bad, 2 WC u. Küche
Anzahl Dobbelzimmer: 4
Inkl. Bettwäsche
Preise gültig für 2011/12
TV/Internet vorhanden
Wir akzeptieren VISA, MC
Ganzjährig geöffnet
Sprechen etwas Deutsch

Skiven Gjestehus is conveniently located in the centre of Bergen, a charming area with old wooden houses and small paved streets. Skivebakken is a quiet street, without through traffic. It is said to be one of the most frequently painted streets in Bergen: here the artists have captured on canvas the charm of this lane and its views across nearby rooftops. The host family of 4 lives on the 2nd floor and the guest rooms are on the 1st.
It's a 10-minute walk to Torgallmenningen, Bryggen and the fish market. The railway station is just 5 minutes away.

Skiven Gjestehus ligger fint til i Bergen sentrum, i et sjarmerende boligområde med gammel trehusbebyggelse og smale brosteinsbelagte gater. Skivebakken er en rolig gate uten gjennomgangstrafikk, og sies å være Bergens mest malte gate. Her har kunstnere stått med sine staffelier og fanget bygatens idyll og den flotte utsikten over husrekkene. Utleierommene er i 1. etasje og vertskapet, en familie på fire, bor i 2. etasje. Kort gangavstand til Torgallmenningen, Bryggen og fisketorget. Jernbanestasjonen er bare 5-10 minutter unna.

Skiven Gjestehus finden Sie günstig gelegen im Zentrum von Bergen. Zauberhaftes Wohngebiet mit alten Holzhäusern und schmalen Pflastersteinstrassen. Skivebakken ist eine ruhige Strasse ohne Durchgangsverkehr. Es ist die am häufigsten gemalte Strasse in Bergen. Hier standen Maler, um die Idylle der Stadt und den herrlichen Blick über die Häuserreihen einzufangen. Die Mieträume befinden sich im Erdgeschoss, während die Gastgeber, eine vierköpfige Familie, den 1. Stock bewohnen. Kurzer Fussweg zum Torgallmenningen, Bryggen und Fischmarkt. HBF nur 5-10 Minuten entfernt.

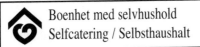
Skuteviken gjestehus

Your host:
Solveig & Eivind Rongved

Address:
Skutevikens smalgang 11
N - 5035 Bergen
Mobile: 93 46 71 63
solveig_rongved@hotmail.com
www.skutevikenguesthouse.com

Best time to call:
09.00 - 19.00
GPS: 60°24'8"N 5°19'16"E

A: Apartment for 1-3 persons
1 bedroom, bath, minikitchen, LR
Price for 2 pers.: **900,-**
Price for 3 pers.: **1100,-**
No. of apt.: 4

B: Loft apt. for 1-3 persons
1 bedroom, bath, minikitchen, LR
Price for 2 pers.: **1100,-**
Price for 3 pers.: **1300,-**

Bed linen included
Prices valid for 2011
Internet available
Open year round
English spoken

Skuteviken guesthouse lies in the Skuteviken neighborhood in Bergen. The area has developed through several centuries with small wooden houses snugly situated in the topography along cobbled alleys. Skuteviken guesthouse is among many protected wooden structures in the neighborhood. It has undergone extensive restoration work. The apartments are within walking distance of historic Bryggen and Bergen center.

A: Leilighet for 1-3 personer
1 soverom, bad, minikjøkken, stue
Pris for 2 pers.: **900,-**
Pris for 3 pers.: **1100,-**
Antall leiligheter: 4

B: Toppleilighet for 1-3 personer
1 soverom, bad, minikjøkken, stue
Pris for 2 pers.: **1100,-**
Pris for 3 pers.: **1300,-**

Sengetøy er inkludert
Priser gyldig for 2011
Internett tilgjengelig
Åpent hele året

Skuteviken gjestehus ligger i bydelen Skuteviken i Bergen. Husene her har utviklet seg gjennom flere hundre år med små terrengtilpassede trehus, trange smug og gater belagt med brostein. Skuteviken gjestehus er et av mange bevaringsverdige trehus i nabolaget, og har gjennomgått et omfattende restaureringsarbeid. Leilighetene ligger i gangavstand fra Bryggen og Bergen sentrum.

A: Wohnung für 1-3 Personen
1 Schlafzi., Bad, kl. Küche, Stube
Preis für 2 Pers.: **900,-**
Preis für 3 Pers.: **1100,-**
Anzahl Wohnungen: 4

B: Dachbodenwohnung für 1-3 P.
1 Schlafzi., Bad, kl. Küche, Stube
Preis für 2 Pers.: **1100,-**
Preis für 3 Pers.: **1300,-**

Inkl. Bettwäsche
Preise gültig für 2011
Internetzugang
Ganzjährig geöffnet
Sprechen Englisch

Skuteviken gjestehus liegt im Bergener Stadtteil Skuteviken. Die Häuser hier haben sich durch viele Jahrhunderte hindurch entwickelt; kleine Holzhäuser, die in das Stadtbild passen, enge Gassen und Straßen mit Kopfsteinpflaster. Skuteviken gjestehus ist eines der vielen Holzhäuser, die es Wert sind erhalten zu werden, und hat umfassende Restaurierungsarbeiten erfahren. Die Wohnungen liegen einen kurzen Fussweg von den Landungsbrücken (Bryggen) und dem Bergener Zentrum entfernt.

Bøketun overnatting

Your host:
Kari Daae

Address:
Postboks 73, N - 5326 Ask

Phone: 56 14 90 28 (norske henvendelser)
Mobile: 98 42 44 57 (norske henvendelser)
Reserv. in English: boketun@online.no
or text to mobile number

Best time to call:
09.00 - 23.00
GPS: 60°28'45"N 5°12'40"E

Single room/1 p. in dbl. room:	**400,-**	Enkeltr./1 pers. i dobbeltr.:	**400,-**	Einzelzi./1 Pers. im DZ:	**400,-**
Twin-/fam. room, per pers.:	**300,-**	Tosengs-/fam.rom, pr. pers.:	**300,-**	Zweibett-/Fam. zi., pro Pers.:	**300,-**
Children under 12 yrs:	**160,-**	Barn under 12 år:	**160,-**	Kinder unter 12 J.:	**160,-**
One night stay only; add:	**50,-**	Ettdøgnstillegg:	**50,-**	Zuschlag für nur 1 ÜN:	**50,-**
No. of rooms: 2		Antall rom: 2		Anzahl Zimmer: 2	
Own LR and bath		Egen stue og bad		Eigene Stube u. Bad	
Laid breakfast table or self-service		Dekket frokostbord el. selvbetj.		Gedeckter Frühstückstisch oder SB	
Prices valid for 2011/12		Priser gyldig for 2011/12		Preise gültig für 2011/12	
TV/Internet available		TV/Internett tilgjengelig		TV/Internet verfügbar	
Terrace/patio/yard/garden		Terrasse/uteplass/hage		Terrasse/Außenbereich/Garten	
Open year round		Åpent hele året		Ganzjährig geöffnet	
Very little English spoken				Sprechen sehr wenig Englisch	

Bøketun guest house is on Askøy island, about 30 minutes by car from Bergen. You'll find a big house with a big garden that includes outoor bonfire and play area and playhouse for children. Patios outside the rooms.
Askøy offers sightseeing through forested roads and mountain trails with a grand view toward Bergen. Fine swimming places by the seashore. Foodshop and postal service nearby. Nine km to shopping center at Kleppestø. It's 20 km. to the historical island of Herdla. There you find golfcourse with equipment rental and also boat rental.

Bøketun overnatting ligger på Askøy, ca. 30 min. med bil fra Bergen. Her finner du et stort hus med stor hage hvor det er utepeis og lekehus. Terrasser utenfor rommene. Askøy kan by på mange turmuligheter på skogsveier, stier og fjell med flott utsikt inn mot Bergen. Fine badeplasser ved sjøen. Matbutikk og post like ved. 9 km til kjøpesenteret på Kleppestø. Det er 20 km til den historiske øyen Herdla. Der er det golfbane med utleie av golfutstyr og båtutleie.

Bøketun overnatting liegt auf Askøy, ca. 30 Min. mit dem Auto von Bergen entfernt. Großes Haus mit riesigem Garten (Grill/Kamin und Spielhaus f. Kinder). Terrassen vor den Zimmern.
Askøy bietet schöne Wandermöglichkeiten durch Wald und Gebirge mit einer reizvollen Aussicht auf Bergen. Schöne Badestellen am See. Lebensmittelgeschäft und Post in unmittelbarer Nähe. 9 km zum Einkaufszentrum in Kleppestø. 20 km bis zur historischen Insel Herdla. Dort finden Sie einen Golfplatz mit Verleih von Golfausrüstung und einen Bootsverleih.

Fjordutleie
Solheim aktivitetsgard

Your host:
Norunn Stien

Address:
Heggernesvegen 150
N - 5314 Kjerrgarden
Mobile 91 18 26 47
E-mail: norsti@hotmail.com

Best time to call:
09.00 - 22.00
GPS: 60°31'21"N 5°6'3"E

Single room:	**400,-**	Enkeltrom:	**400,-**	Einzelzimmer:	**400,-**
Twin-/fam. room, per pers.:	**300,-**	Tosengs-/fam.rom, pr. pers.:	**300,-**	Zweibett-/Fam.zi., p. P.:	**300,-**
Children under 12 yrs:	**170,-**	Barn under 12 år:	**170,-**	Kinder unter 12 J.:	**170,-**
One night stay only; add:	**50,-**	Ettdøgnstillegg:	**50,-**	Zuschlag für nur 1 ÜN:	**50,-**
No. of rooms: 2		Antall rom: 2		Anzahl Zimmer: 2	
Own LR, kitchen and bath		Egen stue, kjøkken og bad		Eigenes Wohnzi., Küche u. Bad	
Breakfast tray		Frokostbrett		Frühstückstablett	
Prices valid for 2011		Priser gyldig for 2011		Preise gültig für 2011	
Terrace/patio/yard/garden		Terrasse/uteplass/hage		Terrasse/Außenbereich/Garten	
TV		TV		TV	
Canu, cayac and boat for rent		Utleie av kano, kajakk og båt		Kanu, Kajak u. Boot zu mieten	
Open year round		Åpent hele året		Ganzjährig geöffnet	
English spoken				Sprechen Englisch	

Fjordutleie Solheim activityfarm is located at Askøy, about 35 min. from Bergen. The farm is entirely adjacent to the sea and boasts its own bathing beach with a shallow child-friendly section. Around the farm you find a beautiful landscape with farm animals roaming about. Wonderful opportunities to explore the forested roads and trails. In the evening you can spot deer and other animals in the forest. The historic island of Herdla is 14 km away, where you find a golf course with rental of golf equipment. Stores and post office at Fromreide shopping center, 4 km from the farm. The community center, Kleppestø, 20 km.

Fjordutleie Solheim aktivitetsgård ligger på Askøy ca. 35 min. med bil fra Bergen. Gården ligger helt ved sjøen og har egen badestrand. Barnevennlig med langgrunne partier. Rundt gården er et flott kulturlandskap med dyr på beite. Fine turmuligheter på skogsveier og stier. På kveldstid kan man ofte se hjort og andre dyr i skogen. Det er 14 km til den historiske øya Herdla. Der er det golfbane med utleie av golfutstyr. Butikker og post finner du i Fromreide senter, 4 km fra gården. Til kommunesenteret Kleppestø er det 20 km.

Fjordutleie Solheim aktivitetsgård liegt auf Askøy, ca. 35 Min. mit dem Auto von Bergen entfernt. Der Hof liegt direkt am Meer, hat einen eigenen Badestrand mit flachen, kinderfreundlichen Abschnitten. Rund um den Hof finden Sie eine schöne Kulturlandschaft mit weidenden Tieren. Gute Wandermöglichkeiten in der Umgebung. Abends sind oft Hirsche im Wald anzutreffen. 14 km bis zur historischen Insel Herdla. Dort gibt es einen Golfplatz mit der Möglichkeit Golfausrüstung auszuleihen. Geschäfte und Post befinden sich im 'Fromreide Center', 4 km vom Hof entfernt. 20 km zum Gemeindezentrum 'Kleppestø'.

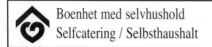
Fjordside Lodge

Your host:
Rita Ripman

Address:
Steinestøvegen 745
N - 5108 Hordvik
Phone: 55 19 08 12
Mobile: 99 25 52 41
E-mail: post@fjordside.no
Web: www.fjordside.no

Best time to call:
08.00 - 23.00
GPS: 60°31'15"N 5°19'17"E

A: Apartment for up to 4 persons
2 bedrooms, own bath, LR, kitchen
Price per pers.:   **400,- to 1000,-**
No. of apartments.: 2

B: Annex for 2 persons
used when extrabed is needed
Per person: **200,-**

Bed linen included
TV/DVD/Internet available
Parking, boathouse, pier
Discount for longer stay
Prices valid for 2011/12/13
Open year round
English spoken

A: Leilighet for intil 4 personer
2 soverom, eget bad, stue, kjøkken
Pris pr. person: **400,- til 1000,-**
Antall leiligheter: 2

B: Annex for 2 personer
brukes ved behov for ekstrasenger
Pr. person: **200,-**

Sengetøy inkludert
TV/DVD/Internett tilgjengelig
Parkering, naust, brygge
Rabatt ved lengre opphold
Priser gyldig for 2011/12/13
Åpent hele året

A: Wohnung für bis zu 4 Pers.
2 Schlafzi., eig.Bad, Stube, Küche
Preis pro Person: **400,- bis 1000,-**
Anzahl Wohnungen: 2

B: Annex für 2 Pers.
wenn extra Betten benötigt werden
Preis pro Person: **200,-**

Inkl. Bettwäsche
TV/DVD/Internet verfügbar
Parkplätze, Bootshaus, Bootssteg
Langzeitrabatt
Preise gültig für 2011/12/13
Ganzjährig geöffnet
Sprechen Englisch

Fjordside is in a red-painted house with turf roof and surrounded by hedges and trees. It lies on a hillside with a great view of the fjord and its islands.
Relax and enjoy the view, the breakfast or grilling. Chat with ducks, hens, cats or the host. Walk over to the water's edge, the dock or fishing spots.
You can drive to Bergen or take the road across a pontoon bridge where there is a fantastic untouched nature with high peaks, rivers and waterfalls to the east and countless fjord inlets and islands to the west.

Fjordside består av rødmalte hus med torvtak som er omkranset av hekk og trær. Det ligger på en høyde med nydelig utsikt til fjorden og øyene rundt.
Slapp av, nyt utsikten, frokosten eller grillen. Slå av en prat med ender, høns, katter eller vertskap. Tur til stranden, marinaen eller fiskeplasser. Du kan kjøre til Bergen sentrum eller du kan ta veien over flytebroen som fører til en fantastisk urørt natur med høye fjell, elver og fossefall i øst, utallige fjordarmer og øyer i vest.

Fjordside - das sind rot angestrichene Hütten mit Naturdach, umgeben von Hecken und Bäumen. Das Grundstück liegt auf einer Anhöhe und bietet eine prachtvolle Aussicht auf den Fjord und die Inseln. Entspannen, die Aussicht genießen, sich das Frühstück oder etwas Gegrilltes schmecken lassen... Enten, Hühner, Katzen auf dem Hof. Strand, Marina, Angelplätze in der Nähe. Von hier aus sind Sie sowohl schnell in Bergen als auch in unberührter Natur mit hohen Bergen, Flüssen und Wasserfällen im Osten sowie unzähligen Fjordarmen und Inseln im Westen.

Skjerping Gård

Your host:
Ellinor Skjerping
& Jan Inge Wold

Address:
Skjerping
N - 5282 Lonevåg
Phone: 56 39 02 91
Mobile: 91 34 99 25
E-mail: info@skjerping.net
Web: www.skjerping.net
Best time to call:
08.00 - 23.00
GPS: 60°29'2"N 5°33'24"E

A: Guesthouse for 2-5 persons
2 bedrooms, bath, kitchen, LR
Price for whole unit: **700,-/750,-**

B: Apartment for 3-9 persons
Loft w/3 beds, bath, kitchen, LR
Price for whole unit: **700,-**
Price for extra room, 1-6 p.:   **250,-**

C: In old main house, w/kitch., LR
Double room, shared bath: **700,-**

D: Apt. in Bergen center, 4-5 pers.
3 bedrooms, bath, kitchen, LR, deck
Price for whole unit: **1500,-**

Bed linen fee: **70,-**
Prices valid for 2011/12
TV/Internet available
Patio/yard
Bike and canoes for rent
Open year round
English spoken

A: Gjestehus for 2-5 personer
2 soverom, bad, kjøkken, stue
Pris for hele enheten: **700,-/750,-**

B: Leilighet for 3-9 personer
Hems til 3 pers., bad, kjk., stue
Pris for hele enheten: **700,-**
Pris for ekstra rom, 1-6 pers.:   **250,-**

C: Rom i gml. hovedhus m/kjk., stue
Dobbeltrom, delt bad: **700,-**

D: Leil. i Bergen sentrum, 4-5 pers.
3 soverom, bad, kjk, stue, terrasse
Pris for hele enheten: **1500,-**

Tillegg for sengetøy: **70,-**
Priser gyldig for 2011/12
TV/Internett tilgjengelig
Uteplass/hage
Sykkel- og kanoutleie
Åpent hele året

A: Gästehaus für 2-5 Personen
2 Schlafzi., Bad, Küche, Stube
Ganze Einheit: **700,-/750,-**

B: Wohnung für 3-9 Personen
Schlafboden, Bad, Küche, Stube
Ganze Einheit: **700,-**
Preis für extra Zi., 1-6 Pers.:   **250,-**

C: Im alten Haupthaus, Küche, Stube
Doppelzi. mit Gemeins.Bad: **700,-**

D: Wohnung in Bergens zentrum
3 Schlafzi., Bad, Küche, Stube
Ganze Einheit: **1500,-**

Mieten von Bettwäsche: **70,-**
Preise gültig für 2011/12
TV/Internet vorhanden
Außenbereich/Garten
Fahrrad- u. Kanuvermietung
Ganzjährig geöffnet
Sprechen etwas Deutsch

The farm is located on Osterøya, Norway's largest landlocked island surrounded by fjords. Three generations live on the farm, also many animals: sheep, horse, calves, goats, hens, ducks, rabbits, dogs and cats. Lovely hiking areas with freshwater fishing and a salmon river. Nice farm village museum and other cultural attractions.

Gården ligger på Osterøya, Norges største innlandsøy omgitt av fjorder, 30 min. fra Bergen. Det bor tre generasjoner på gården. Her er også mange dyr; sauer, hest, kalver, geiter, høns, ender, kaniner, hund og katt. Stor trampoline i hagen. Nydelig turterreng med fiskemuligheter i fjellvann og lakseelv. Flott bygdemuseum og andre kulturtilbud.

Der Hof liegt auf Osterøya, der größten Binneninsel des Landes umgeben von Fjorden. 3 Generationen leben auf dem Hof, sowie viele Tiere: Schafe, Pferde, Kälber, Ziegen, Hühner, Enten, Kaninchen, Hunde, Katzen. Goßes Trampolin im Garten. Wandern, Angeln in Bergseen u. Lachsflüssen möglich. Interessantes Freilichtmuseum sowie weitere kulturelle Angebote.

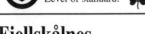
Fjellskålnes
Bed & Breakfast

Your host:
John Egil Hilt

Address:
N - 5282 Lonevåg
Mobile: 98 62 20 42
E-mail: johhil@hfk.no

Best time to call:
09.00 - 22.00
GPS: 60°34'12"N 5°27'53"E

Double room:	**680,-**	Dobbeltrom:	**680,-**	Doppelzimmer:	**680,-**
1 pers. in double room:	**360,-**	1 pers. i dobbeltrom:	**360,-**	1 Pers. im Doppelzi.:	**360,-**
No. of rooms: 3		Antall rom: 3		Anzahl Zimmer: 3	
Breakfast tray		Frokostbrett		Frühstückstablett	
Sauna: 80,-/20 min.		Badstu: 80,-/20 min.		Sauna: 80,-/20 Min.	
Trim-room: 60,-/hour		Trimrom: 60,-/time		Fitnessraum: 60,-/Stunde	
Prices valid for 2011		Priser gyldig for 2011		Preise gültig für 2011	
TV available		TV tilgjengelig		TV vorhanden	
Terrace/garden		Hage		Garten	
Boat for rent		Båtutleie		Boot zu mieten	
Open 22 June - 14 Aug.		Åpent 22. juni - 14. aug.		Geöffnet 22. Juni - 14. Aug.	
English spoken				Man spricht Englisch	

Fjellskålnes Bed & Breakfast is along the fjord by Hosanger on Ostorøy's north side. Good fishing, convenient to fjord and mountains. Walk to bathing beach in 7 min.

Directions:
Along E-16 follow signs toward Osterøybrua, RV 566. Cross the bridge and follow signs toward Lonevåg/Hosanger. Just before Hosanger turn left toward Fjellskålnes. Take first road to right. Big white house on the hill.

Fjellskålnes Bed & Breakfast ligger ut mot fjorden ved Hosanger på Osterøys nordside. Gode fiskemuligheter, nærhet til fjord og fjell. Til badevik er det 7 min. gange.

Veibeskrivelse:
Langs E-16 tar du av ved skilt mot Osterøybrua, RV 566. Kjør over broen og følg skilt i retning Lonevåg/Hosanger. Like før Hosanger tar du til venstre mot Fjellskålnes. Ta så første vei opp til høyre. Stort hvitt hus på toppen.

Fjellskålnes Bed & Breakfast liegt am Fjord bei Hosanger auf der Nordseite der Insel Osterøy. Gute Angelmöglichkeiten; nah zum Fjord und zu den Bergen. 7 min Fußweg zur Badebucht.

Wegbeschreibung:
Auf der E-16 fahrend biegen Sie bei der Osterøy-Brücke auf die Str. 566 ab. Fahren Sie über die Brücke und folgen Sie den Schildern Ri. Lonevåg/Hosanger. Kurz vor Hosanger fahren Sie nach links Ri. Fjellskålnes. Nehmen Sie dann den ersten Weg nach rechts, der hinauf führt. Das große weiße Haus ganz oben ist ihr Ziel.

Bergsdalstunet

Your host:
Olaug Fagerbakke
& Helge Terje Fosse

Address:
Lid i Bergsdalen
N - 5722 Dalekvam
Phone: 56 59 89 34
Mobile: 93 21 32 13
E-mail: post@bergsdalstunet.no
Web: www.bergsdalstunet.no

Best time to call:
08.00 - 22.00
GPS: 60°34'12"N 5°57'40"E

Guesthouse for 2-9 persons	Gjestehus for 2-9 personar	Gästehaus für 2-9 Personen
No. of bedrooms: 3	Antal soverom: 3	Anzahl Schlafzimmer: 3
Own bath, kitchen, DR, LR	Eige bad, kjøken, spisestove, stove	Eig. Bad, Küche, Esszi., Stube
Price per pers., 1-2 pers.: **300,-**	Pris pr. pers., 1-2 personar: **300,-**	Preis pro Pers., 1-2 Pers.: **300,-**
Price for whole unit, 3-5 p.: **900,-**	Pris for heile eininga, 3-5 p.: **900,-**	Ganze Einheit, 3-5 Pers.: **900,-**
Surcharge per pers. over 5p.: **100,-**	Tillegg pr. pers. over 5p.: **100,-**	Zuschlag pro pers. über 5 P.: **100,-**
Bed linen fee: **100,-**	Tillegg for sengeklede: **100,-**	Mieten von Bettwäsche: **100,-**
Breakfast service available: **95,-**	Frukost kan serverast: **95,-**	Frühstück auf Bestellung: **95,-**
Prices valid for 2011/12	Priser gjeld for 2011/12	Preise gültig für 2011/12
Yard/terrace/patio	Terrasse/uteplass	Terrasse/Aussenplatz/Garten
Boat for rent	Båtutleige	Boot zu mieten
No pets from other countries	Norske kjæledyr velkomen	Keine Haustiere aus dem Ausland
Suitable for handicapped	Tilhøve for gjester med handikap	Behindertengerecht
Open year round	Ope heile året	Ganzjährig geöffnet
Some English spoken		Sprechen etwas Deutsch

Lid in Bergsdalen valley is situated between Dale and Voss. The farm is about 450 meters above sea level. The house was renovated and expanded in 1998. Child-friendly outdoor environment. Excellent terrain for mountain excursions by foot or bicycle. Fishing in rivers or lakes. Good skiing areas.

Directions:
Along E-16 at Dale in Vaksdal; take FV 314 toward Bergsdalen and drive 11.5 km. Vikinghuset is located at Lid, on your left hand side of the road.

Lid i Bergsdalen ligg mellom Dale og Voss, og garden Lid ligg ca. 450 meter over havet.
Huset er bygd ca. 1930, og vart restaurert og påbygd i 1998. Bornevennleg utemiljø. Gode høve til turar i fjellet, til fots eller på sykkel. Fiske i elvar og vatn. Godt skiterreng.

Veibeskrivelse:
Langs E-16 ved Dale i Vaksdal; ta FV 314 mot Bergsdalen og køyr 11,5 km, på Lid ligg Vikinghuset på venstre side av vegen.

Das ca. 1930 erbaute Gehöft Lid liegt auf 450 m Höhe in Bergsdalen zwischen Dale und Voss. 1998 wurde die Anlage renoviert, außerdem hat man angebaut. Kinderfreundliche Umgebung. Möglichkeiten zum Bergwandern und Radfahren. Angeln in Flüssen und Seen. Gutes Skigebiet.

Wegbeschreibung:
Entlang E-16 bei Dale in der Kommune Vaksdal; nehmen Sie Str. 314 (Landstr.) in Ri. Bergsdalen und fahren Sie 11,5 km. Vikinghuset liegt auf der linken Straßenseite.

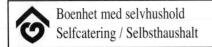
Bergagarden / Skomakarhuset

Your host:
Turid & Karl Magne Bolstad

Address:
Øyravegen 30
N - 5723 Bolstadøyri
Mobile: 41 32 24 45
E-mail: post@bergagarden.no
Web: www.bergagarden.no

Best time to call:
09.00 - 22.00
GPS: 60°38'21"N 5°57'25"E

Guesthouse for 1-6 persons	Feriehus for 1-6 personar	Gästehaus für 1-6 Personen
2 bedrooms, bath, kitchen, LR	2 soverom, bad, kjøken, stove	2 Schlafzi., Bad, Küche, Stube
Price for 1 person: **600,-**	Pris for 1 person: **600,-**	Preis für 1 Person: **600,-**
Price for 2 persons: **700,-**	Pris for 2 personar: **700,-**	Preis für 2 Personen: **700,-**
Price for 4 persons: **900,-**	Pris for 4 personar: **900,-**	Preis für 4 Personen: **900,-**
Price per add. pers. over 4: **50,-**	Pris pr. tilleggspers. over 4: **50,-**	Jede weitere Person: **50,-**
High season 10.07 - 28.08: **+15%**	Høgsesong 10.07 - 28.08: **+15%**	Hochsaison 10.07 - 28.08: **+15%**
Bed linen included	Omfattar sengeklede	Inkl. Bettwäsche
Weekly rent, ask for price	Vekeleige, spør om pris	Wochenmiete möglich
Prices valid for 2011/12	Priser gjeld for 2011/12	Preise gültig für 2011/12
TV available, yard/patio	TV tilgjengeleg, hage/uteplass	TV vorh., Garten/Außenbereich
Rowboat free	Fri robåt	Ruderboot gratis - Außenmotor u.
For rent: outboard motor & canoe	Utleige av påhengsmotor og kano	Kanu können gemietet werden
Open year round	Ope heile året	Ganzjährig geöffnet
English spoken		Sprechen Englisch

Tourists have been visiting the farm since 1910, and were mostly British salmon fishermen. Skomakarhuset (shoemaker's house) is a comfortable, newly restored vacation home in peaceful environment. It's one of 6 white-painted Vestland houses and a little church which lies in a cluster down by the fjord. Outside the house is a flat lawn with spacious terrace and view of the fjord. The property stretches down to the beach where one can enjoy bonfires and grilling. The house is literally surrounded by breathtakingly beautiful Norwegian landscapes - hills, mountains, waterfalls and rapids.

På Bergagarden har det vore turistar sidan 1910, den gongen engelske lakseturistar. 'Skomakarhuset' som leiges ut er eit komfortabelt, nyrestaurert, feriehus i rolege omgjevnader. Dette er eit av 6 kvitmåla vestlandshus og ei lita kyrkje som ligg i ei husklynge nede ved fjorden der det tidlegare var bygdesenter med tingstove, landhandel, vertshus og skipsekspedisjon. Attmed huset er det flat plen og ein romsleg terasse med utsyn mot fjorden. Tomta går vidare ned til stranda ved fjorden der ein kan brenna bål og grilla. Her er det flott vestlandsnatur heilt inntil dørene.

Seit 1910 begrüßt Bergagarden Touristen; anfangs waren es britische Lachsfischer. Das "Schuhmacherhaus" ist ein komfortables, neurestauriertes Ferienhaus in ruhiger Umgebung. Es ist eines von 6 weißgestrichenen Vestland-Häusern und einer Kirche, die direkt unten am Fjord liegen. An das Haus schließt eine weite Rasenfläche und eine geräumige Terasse, die Aussicht auf den Fjord bietet. Das Grundstück reicht bis hinunter zum Strand, wo man ein Lagerfeuer machen oder Grillen kann. Hier beginnt die spektakuläre Landschaft Westnorwegens direkt vor der Tür.

Haugo Utleige

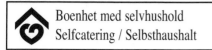

Your host:
Mona & Knut Haugo

Address:
Gamle Bordalsvei 54
N - 5700 Voss
Mobile: 97 56 29 52
E-mail: post@haugo.net
Web: www.haugo.net

Best time to call:
08.00 - 22.00
GPS: 60°37'28"N 6°26'20"E

A: Rooms in large house
12 rooms, 4 baths, 2 LR, sauna
Large communal kitchen
Double room: **500,-**
Single room: **350,-**

B: Cabin for 2-5 persons
2 bedrooms, bath, kitchen, LR
Whole unit, 2 pers.: **800,-**
Whole unit, 3-5 pers.: **1000,-**

C: Cabin for 3 persons
3 beds, basic standard
Price for whole unit: **500,-**

Applies to all rental units:
Bed linen fee: **50,-**
Prices valid for 2011/12/13
TV/Internet available
Large terrace
Pets welcome
Open year round
English spoken

A: Rom i stort utleigehus
12 rom, 4 bad, 2 stover, badstove
Stort felleskjøken
Dobbeltrom: **500,-**
Enkeltrom: **350,-**

B: Hytte for 2-5 personar
2 soverom, bad, kjøken, stove
Heile eininga, 2 pers.: **800,-**
Heile eininga, 3-5 pers.: **1000,-**

C: Hytte for 3 personar
3 sengeplassar, enkel standard
Pris for heile eininga: **500,-**

For alle einingar gjeld:
Tillegg for sengeklede: **50,-**
Priser gjeld for 2011/12/13
TV/Internett tilgjengeleg
Stor terrasse
Kjæledyr velkomen
Ope heile året

A: Zimmer im großen Mietshaus
12 Zi., 4 Bäder, 2 Wohnzi., Sauna
Große gemeinsame Küche
Doppelzimmer: **500,-**
Einzelzimmer: **350,-**

B: Hütte für 2-5 Personen
2 Schlafzi., Bad, Küche, Stube
Ganze Einheit, 2 Pers.: **800,-**
Ganze Einheit, 3-5 Pers.: **1000,-**

C: Hütte für 3 Personen
3 Schlafplätze, einfacher Standard
Ganze Einheit: **500,-**

Für alle Einheiten gilt:
Mieten von Bettwäsche: **50,-**
Preise gültig für 2011/12/13
TV/Internet vorhanden
Große Terrasse
Haustiere willkommen
Ganzjährig geöffnet
Sprechen etwas Deutsch

Haugo Utleige is 1.5 km from Voss center. Here it's rural, quiet and sunny with beautiful scenery. At Voss you'll have many experiences with nature and culture, many possible outdoor activities in summer and winter: alpine skiing and walking areas, horseback riding, air sports and mountain climbing.

Haugo Utleige ligg 1,5 km frå Voss sentrum. Her er det landleg og roleg, solrikt og med flott utsikt. På Voss møter du eit mangfald av opplevingar basert på natur og kultur, mange tilbod for utandørs aktiviteter både sommar og vinter; alpinanlegg, turløyper, rafting, hesteridning, luftsportsenter og fjellvandring.

Hier können Sie in ländlicher und ruhiger Umgebung mit schöner Aussicht entspannen. Nur 1,5 km bis ins Zentrum von Voss. Dort erwartet Sie ein reichhaltiges Angebot an kulturellen Aktivitäten und viel Natur. Sommer wie Winter kann man sich hier im Freien aufhalten: Skigebiet, Langlaufrouten, Rafting, Reiten, Bergwanderungen.

Brandseth Fjellstove

Your host:
Erling Brandseth

Address:
Haugsvik
N - 5713 Vossestrand
Phone: 56 53 05 00
Mobile: 93 20 67 51
E-mail: mail@brandseth.no
Web: www.brandseth.no
Best time to call: 09.00 - 21.00
GPS: 60°47'41"N 6°41'18"E

Double room:	750,-/900,-	Dobbeltrom:	750,-/900,-	Doppelzimmer:	750,-/900,-
Single room:	450,-/550,-	Enkeltrom:	450,-/550,-	Einzelzimmer:	450,-/550,-

No. of rooms: 7 — Antal rom: 7 — Anzahl Zimmer: 7

Discount for children	Rabatt for born	Ermäßigung für Kinder
Breakfast buffet	Frukostbuffét	Frühstücksbüfett
Other meals served upon request	Andre måltid kan bestellast	Andere Mahlzeiten nach Vereinb.
Prices valid for 2011/12/13	Prisar gjeld for 2011/12/13	Preise gültig für 2011/12/13
TV/Internet available	TV/Internett tilgjengeleg	TV/Internet vorhanden
Terrace/patio	Terrasse/uteplass	Terrasse/Außenbereich
VISA, MC accepted	Vi tek VISA, MC	Wir akzeptieren VISA, MC
Open 15 Febr. - 25 April	Ope 15. febr. - 25. april	Geöffnet 15. Febr. - 25. April
and 15 June - 30 Aug.	og 15. juni - 30. aug.	und 15. Juni - 30. Aug.
English spoken		Sprechen Deutsch

Charming mountain lodge halfway between Voss and Flåm, in the heart of fjord country, 2.5 km from E-16 and the "Norway in a Nutshell"-route. The Brandseth Fjellstove lodge is nicely situated with a view of the town and near good terrain for walks. An excellent starting point for fjord tours. The lodge kitchen is known for its tasty home-style cooking. All rooms include shower and WC.

Directions:
From Voss: Look for the sign to Brandseth Fjellstove after you pass Haugsvik.
From Flåm: Look for the sign after the tunnel near Stalheim.

Triveleg fjellstove midt mellom Voss og Flåm, i hjartet av fjord-Noreg, 2,5 km frå E-16 og "Norway in a Nutshell"-ruta. Fjellstova ligg fint til med utsyn over bygda og med flott turterreng. Godt utgangspunkt for turar til fjordane. Kjøkenet er kjend for god heimelaga mat.
Alle rom har dusj og WC.

Vegforklaring:
Frå Voss: Etter Haugsvik; sjå etter skilt til Brandseth Fjellstove. Frå Flåm: Sjå etter skiltet etter tunnellane ved Stalheim.

Gemütlicher Berggasthof im Herzen Fjordnorwegens, auf halbem Weg zwischen Voss und Flåm. Nur 2,5 km zur Hauptstraße E-16 und der bekannten Rundreiseroute "Norway in a Nutshell". Der Berggasthof bietet eine sehr schöne Aussicht über die Ortschaft; reizvolles Wandergebiet ringsherum. Guter Ausgangspunkt für Touren zu den Fjorden. Der Gasthof ist bekannt für gute hausgemachte Speisen. Alle Zimmer mit Dusche und WC.

Wegbeschreibung:
Ab Voss: hinter Haugsvik ist "Brandseth Fjellstove" ausgeschildert.
Ab Flåm: Ausschilderung beginnt hinterm Tunnel bei Stalheim.

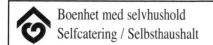

Solund Gjestegaard

Your host:
Nina Bauge &
Tom Erling Bahus

Address:
N - 6924 Hardbakke
Phone: 95 06 73 63
Mobile: 90 05 58 91
E-mail: nb@baugeogbahus.no
Web: www.solundgjestegaard.no
Best time to call: 08.00 - 21.00
GPS: 61°4'33"N 4°50'18"E

Apartments for up to 5 pers.:	Leiligheter for inntil 5 pers.:	Wohnungen für bis zu je 5 Pers.:
1 person in the apt.: **750,-**	1 pers. i hele enheten: **750,-**	1 Pers. in der Einheit: **750,-**
Price per following pers.: **150,-**	Hver av de påfølgende pers.: **150,-**	Jede weitere Person: **150,-**
Own bath, kitchen,dining-/LR	Eget bad, kjk, spiseplass, stue	Eig. Bad, Küche, Ess-/ Wohnzi.
No. of apts: 4	Antall leiligheter: 4	Anzahl Einheiten: 4
"Lars": double bed and a bed sofa	"Lars": dobbeltseng og sovesofa	"Lars": Doppelbett und Schlafsofa
"Mari": double bed	"Mari": dobbeltseng	"Mari": Doppelbett
"Ida": double bed and a bunkbed	"Ida": dobbeltseng og køyeseng	"Ida": Doppel- und ein Kojenbett
"Lotta": double bed and a bed sofa	"Lotta": dobbeltseng og sovesofa	"Lotta": Doppelbett u. Schlafsofa
Bed linen incl.	Sengetøy inkludert	Inkl. Bettwäsche
Prices valid for 2011/12	Priser gyldig for 2011/12	Preise gültig für 2011/12
TV/Internet available	TV/Internett tilgjengelig	TV/Internet verfügbar
Dekk with furniture	Møblert uteplass	Sitzecke mit Gartenmöbeln
Bike for rent at tourist information	Sykkelutleie hos turistinformasjonen	Fahrradverm. bei der Touristinfo
VISA, MC accepted	Vi tar VISA, MC	Wir akzeptieren VISA, MC
Open year round	Åpent hele året	Ganzjährig geöffnet
English & some French spoken		Sprechen etwas Deutsch

Solund Gjestegaard is centrally located in Hardbakke, in walking distance to nearly everything. The apartments are individually furnished in a personal style. Quality is based on the hosts' own expectations of great travel experiences. Enjoy the beach and the fjords with its small and big adventures. You can go fishing, swimming, paddling, sailing, bicycling, climbing, hiking. Reams of skerries.

Solund Gjestegaard ligger sentralt i Hardbakke med gangavstand til det meste. Leilighetene har fått en personlig stil og individuell innredning. Kvalitetsnivået er basert på vertskapets egne forventninger til gode reiseopplevelser. Opplev kysten og fjordane med sine små og store eventyr! Du kan fiske, bade, ro, segle, sykle, padle, klatre og gå på tur i fjellet. Tusenvis av holmer og skjær.

Solund Gjestegaard liegt zentral in Hardbakke; das meiste ist zu Fuß zu erreichen. Die Wohnungen haben einen persönlichen, individuellen Stil. Die Qualität wird dabei ausgerichtet an den eigenen Erwartungen der Gastgeber an einen guten Urlaubsaufenthalt. Erleben Sie die Küsten und Fjorde mit ihren kleinen und grossen Abenteuern. Sie können angeln, baden, rudern, segeln, Fahrrad fahren, paddeln, klettern, wandern. Unzählige kleine Inseln und Schären.

Flesje Gard

Your host:
Rune Andersen

Address:
Flesje
N - 6899 Balestrand
Mobile: **41 50 72 48**
E-mail: ruande5@online.no

Best time to call:
08.00 - 10.00 / 16.00 - 22.00
GPS: 61°10'30"N 6°32'30"E

Double room:	**900,-/950,-**	Dobbeltrom:	**900,-/950,-**	Doppelzimmer:	**900,-/950,-**
Extra bed:	**200,-**	Ekstraseng:	**200,-**	Extrabett:	**200,-**
No. of rooms: 1		Antal rom: 1		Anzahl Zimmer: 1	
Laid breakfast table		Dekka frukostbord		Gedeckter Frühstückstisch	
Prices valid for 2011/12		Prisar gjeld for 2011/12		Preise gültig für 2011/12	
Large yard/garden		Stor hage		Grosser Garten	
Bike and sail boat for rent		Sykkel- og seglbåtutleige		Fahrrad und Segelboot zu mieten	
Open 15 June - 20 August		Ope 15. juni - 20. august		Geöffnet 15. Juni - 20. August	
English spoken				Sprechen etwas Deutsch	

Flesje is an idyllic place in Balestrand community. It's the gateway to touring the mountains and fjords. Or you can just enjoy the peace and lovely surroundings with a good book t teh waterfront. If there is a good wind try sailing on the fjord. If you're an experienced sailor you can rent a boat, a 26' J80, but you may also join the host's crew. Flesje lies 4 km from Balestrand center. The farm is from the 1700s with the houses directly down by the Sognefjord. In the old days the house was used by sheriffs and military. Among the famous names who have stayed here are Henrik Wergeland, Hans Fredrik Gude and Helge Ingstad. The 9 old buildings on the farm include a restored millhouse.A family of four welcomes you: father and three children.

Flesje er ein idyllisk plass i Balestrand. Her har du eit fint utgangspunkt for turar til fjells og på fjorden. Eller kanskje berre nyta freden i vakre omgivnader med ei god bok på bryggekanten. Om det er fin vind kan det kanskje freista med ein segltur på fjorden. Er du erfaren seglar kan du leiga ein 26' J80, du kan også få med vertskapet som mannskap. Flesje ligg 4 km frå Balestrand sentrum. Garden er fra 1700-talet med husa liggande i ei klyngje heilt nede ved Sognefjorden. I gamle dager var Flesje bustad for både futar og militærfolk. Av dei som har vore på besøk her kan nemnast Henrik Wergeland, Hans Fredrik Gude og i nyare tid Helge Ingstad. Det er no att 9 gamle hus på garden, blant dei eit restaurert kvernhus. Familien på fire ynskjer dykk velkommen; far og tre born.

Flesje ist ein idyllischer Platz in der Gemeinde Balestrand. Guter Ausgangspunkt für Berg- u. Fjordtouren; oder vielleicht entspannen Sie sich bei einem guten Buch am Bootssteg. Bei gutem Wind bietet sich eine Segeltur auf dem Fjord an. Wenn Sie erfahrener Segler sind, können Sie eine 8 m J80 ausleihen oder als Teil der Mannschaft mitsegeln. Flesje liegt 4 km von Balestrand Zentrum. Der Hof aus dem 18. Jh. umfasst mehrere Häuser, die direkt unten am Sognefjord liegen. Bekannte Persönlichkeiten, die hier zu Besuch waren: Henrik Wergeland, Hans Fredrik Gude und in neuerer Zeit Hele Ingstad. Heute finden sich auf dem Hof 9 alte Häuser, unter diesen ein restauriertes Mühlhaus. Die vierköpfige Familie, der Vater mit seinen drei Kindern, heißt Sie herzlich willkommen.

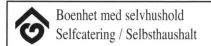
Thue appartement

Your host:
Britt Thue Olsen
& Jan Henry Olsen
Address: Kong Beles veg 2
N - 6898 Balestrand
Phone: 57 69 15 95
Mobile: 97 19 92 63 / 41 32 07 60
E-mail: j-holse@online.no

Best time to call:
17.00 - 23.00
GPS: 61°12'36"N 6°32'5"E

Double room/twin room w/ own bath & kitchenette **750,-**	Dobbelt-/tosengsrom med eige bad og mini-kjk. **750,-**	Doppel-/Zweibettzimmer mit eig. Bad u. Mini-Küche **750,-**
Familyroom for 4 persons w/own bath & kitchenette **850,-**	Familierom for 4 personer med eige bad og mini-kjk. **850,-**	Familienzi. für 4 Personen mit eig. Bad u. Mini-Küche **850,-**
Bed linen fee: **50,-**	Tillegg for sengeklede: **50,-**	Mieten von Bettwäsche: **50,-**
No. of rooms: 5	Antal rom: 5	Anzahl Zimmer: 5
Prices valid for 2011	Prisar gjeld for 2011	Preise gültig für 2011
Balcony	Balkong	Balkon
Boat and bike for rent	Båt-/Sykkelutleige	Boot u. Fahrrad zu mieten
Open 15 May - 15 Sept.	Ope 15. mai - 15. sept.	Geöffnet 15. Mai - 15. Sept.
English spoken		Sprechen etwas Deutsch

Thue appartement is next to the fjord in central Balestrand, near tourist information center. See sign "Thue-appartement". All rooms were renovated in 2010. The nearest neighbor is a beautiful aquarium that's home to fish and shell-fish from Sognefjorden. Balestrand is known as an artist's quarter and for the gold and stately Kvikne Hotel. Here are many fine wooden houses in the Kaiser Wilhelm-style built in the early 1900s. There is also wild and beautiful nature with inviting paths for mountain hiking.

Thue appartement ligg ved fjorden, midt i sentrum av Balestrand, nær turistinformasjonen. Se skilt: "Thue-appartement". Alle rom vart nyoppussa i 2010. Næraste nabo er eit flott akvarium som syner fisk og skalldyr frå Sognefjorden. Balestrand er kjend som kunstnerbygda og for det gamle og staselege Kvikne hotell. Her er mange fine gamle trehus i Keiser Wilhelm-stil, bygd tidleg på 1900-talet. Her er også vill og vakker natur med flotte stiar og fine høve til fotturar i heier og fjell.

Das Appartementhaus liegt in Fjordnähe, mitten im Zentrum Balestrands, in der Nähe der Touristinfo. Schauen Sie nach dem Schild "Thue-appartement". Alle Zimmer wurden 2010 neu renoviert. Gleich nebenan finden Sie ein tolles Aquarium mit Fischen und Schalentieren aus dem Sognefjord. Balestrand ist als Künstlerdorf und für das alte, prächtige Kvikne Hotel bekannt. Hier gibt es viele reizvolle Holzhäuser, die zu Beginn des 20. Jh. im Wilhelminischen Stil erbaut wurden. Die wilde, schöne Natur lädt zu Wanderungen in den Bergen ein.

Sognefjord Gjestehotell

Your host:
Kirsten & Odd E. Vangsnes

Address:
N - 6894 Vangsnes
Phone: 57 69 67 22
Mobile: 91 51 43 12
E-mail: vangpens@online.no
Web:
www.sognefjordgjestehotell.com
Best time to call: 08.00 - 22.00
GPS: 61°10'29"N 6°38'16"E

Double-/twin room:	**990,-**	Dobbelt-/tosengsrom:	**990,-**	Doppel-/Zweibettzi.:	**990,-**
Single room:	**790,-**	Enkeltrom:	**790,-**	Einzelzimmer:	**790,-**
Family room:	**1290,-**	Familierom:	**1290,-**	Familienzi.:	**1290,-**
Extra bed:	**200,-**	Ekstraseng:	**200,-**	Extrabett:	**200,-**
No. of rooms: 9		Antall rom: 9		Anzahl Zimmer: 9	
Discount for children		Rabatt for barn		Ermäßigung für Kinder	
Breakfast buffet		Frokostbuffét		Frühstücksbüfett	
Dinner:	**100,- to 200,-**	Middag:	**100,- til 200,-**	Abendessen:	**100,- bis 200,-**
Prices valid for 2011		Priser gyldig for 2011		Preise gültig für 2011	
TV available		TV tilgjengelig		TV vorhanden	
Boat for rent		Båtutleie		Boot zu mieten	
VISA, MC, AmEx accepted		Vi tar VISA, MC, AmEx		Wir akzept. VISA, MC, AmEx	
Open year round		Åpent hele året		Ganzjährig geöffnet	
Some English spoken				Sprechen etwas Deutsch	

Sognefjord Guesthotel is situated near the ferry dock at Vangsnes with views out towards Sognefjord and Kvinnefossen waterfall on the opposite side. Sognefjord Guesthotel is a good base for visiting the many attractions along the Sognefjord. Among others, you can enjoy stave churches, glacier tours and day-trips by express boat from Bergen to Flåm and by ferry to Fjærland (the Jostedalsbreen glacier).
The Guesthouse is fully licensed.

Sognefjord Gjestehotell ligger ved Vangsnes fergekai med utsikt mot Sognefjorden og Kvinnefossen på andre siden av fjorden.
Sognefjord gjestehus er et godt utgangspunkt for å besøke de mange attraksjonene langs Sognefjorden. Her kan det nevnes blant annet stavkirker, brevandring og dagsturer med ekspressbåt fra Bergen til Flåm og ferje til Fjærland (Jostedalsbreen).
Gjestehotellet har alle serveringsrettigheter.

Das Sognefjord Gjestehotell liegt am Kai in Vangsnes und bietet eine schöne Aussicht auf den Sognefjord und den Wasserfall Kvinnefossen am anderen Fjordufer. Das Haus ist ein guter Ausgangspunkt, um die vielen Sehenswürdigkeiten entlang des Sognefjords zu entdecken; hierunter zählen Stabkirchen, Gletscherwanderungen oder Tagestouren mit dem Schnellboot von Bergen nach Flåm oder mit der Fähre nach Fjærland (Abstecher zum Gletscher Jostedalsbreen).
Das kleine Hotel verfügt über alle Schankrechte.

Eri Gardshus

Your host:
Anlaug Eri & Rolf Jakobsen

Address:
N - 6887 Lærdal
Phone: 57 66 65 14
Mobile: 91 34 44 18 / 98 59 04 98
E-mail: rolja@online.no
Web:
www.mamut.net/erigardshus

Best time to call:
08.00 - 21.00
GPS: 61°5'8"N 7°30'42"E

A: 'Jesastova'
Guesthouse for 2-9 persons
3 bedrooms, bath, kitchen, LR
Whole unit for 2 pers.: **400,-**
Whole unit for 3-7 pers.: **700,-**

B: 'Kvitastova'
Guesthouse for 2-13 persons
5 bedrooms, kitchen and two baths
Whole unit for 2 pers.: **500,-**
Whole unit for 3-7 pers.: **1000,-**

Bed linen fee: **60,-**
Discount for children
Prices valid for 2011/12/13
TV available
Yard/terrace/patio
Boat for rent
Open year round
English spoken

A: 'Jesastova'
Gjestehus for 2-9 personar
3 soverom, bad, kjøken, stove
Heile eininga for 2 pers.: **400,-**
Heile eininga for 3-7 pers.: **700,-**

B: 'Kvitastova'
Gjestehus for 2-13 personar
5 soverom, kjøken og to bad
Heile eininga for 2 pers.: **500,-**
Heile eininga for 3-7 pers.: **1000,-**

Tillegg for sengeklede: **60,-**
Rabatt for born
Priser gjeld for 2011/12/13
TV tilgjengeleg
Hage/Terrasse/uteplass
Båtutleige
Ope heile året

A: 'Jesastova'
Gästehaus für 2-9 Personen
3 Schlafzi., Bad, Küche, Stube
Ganze Einheit für 2 Pers.: **400,-**
Ganze Einheit für 3-7 Pers.: **700,-**

B: 'Kvitastova'
Gästehaus für 2-13 Personen
5 Schlafzi., Küche und zwei Bäder
Ganze Einheit für 2 Pers.: **500,-**
Ganze Einheit für 3-7 Pers.: **1000,-**

Mieten von Bettwäsche: **60,-**
Ermässigung für Kinder
Preise gültig für 2011/12/13
TV vorhanden
Garten/Terrasse/Außenbereich
Boot zu mieten
Ganzjährig geöffnet
Sprechen etwas Deutsch

The hosts of Eri Gardshus are involved in pork and milk production. The Eri farm is located 3.5 km from Lærdal city center. The rental cottage is situated 1 km from the main farm and has its own courtyard.

Vertskapet på Eri Gardshus driv med svin- og mjølkeproduksjon. Garden Eri ligg 3,5 km frå Lærdal sentrum. Utleigehusa ligg i eit eige tun 1 km frå garden.

Die Gastgeber betreiben Schweine- und Milchproduktion. Der Hof liegt 3,5 km vom Ort Lærdal entfernt. Das Ferienhaus liegt ca. 1 km entfernt auf einem eigenen Hofgrundstück.

Do not follow where the path may lead.
Go instead where there is no path and leave a trail.
~Ralph Waldo Emerson~

Urnes Gard

Your host:
Randi Kristin &
Marianne Bugge

Address:
N - 6870 Ornes
Mobile: 90 76 82 84 / 91 53 27 84
E-mail: urnesgard@urnes.no
Web: www.urnes.no

Best time to call:
17.00 - 22.00
GPS: 61°17'54"N 7°19'23"E

Double room:	**800,-**	Dobbeltrom:	**800,-**	Doppelzimmer:	**800,-**
1 pers. in double room:	**400,-**	1 pers. i dobbeltrom:	**400,-**	1 Pers. im Doppelzi.:	**400,-**
No. of rooms: 2		Antal rom: 2		Anzahl Zimmer: 2	

Breakfast tray; or buffet w/ 4 p. min. | Frukostbrett, fra 4 pers.: frk.buffét | Frühstückstablett, ab 4 Pers.: Büfett
Prices valid for 2011/12 | Prisar gjeld for 2011/12 | Preise gültig für 2011/12
Terrace/patio | Terrasse/uteplass | Terrasse/Außenbereich
Boat for rent | Båtutleige | Boot zu mieten
Open 1 June - 1 Sept. | Ope 1. juni - 1. sept. | Geöffnet 1. Juni - 1. Sept.
English spoken | | Sprechen etwas Deutsch

Urnes gard lies on the south side of the beautiful Lusterfjord and is the nearest neighbor to Urnes stave church, the oldest in Norway and is on the Unesco world heritage list. The farm has a long history and at the end of the 1400s was one of the biggest manor farms in Norway. Since the 1600s the farm has belonged to the Bugge family. The hosts operate a fruit and berry farm, growing apples, raspberries, strawberry, cherries and blueberries, along with juice and jam production. On the farm's cafe one may enjoy a cup of coffee with new-baked waffles, homemade cakes and other snacks. Farm produce and home-craft items are for sale. Deer stable on the farm with possibility of tours. Walking trails and scenic mountains. In summers: the ferry to Solvorn in operating.

Urnes Gard ligg fint til på sørsida av den vakre Lusterfjorden og er næraste nabo til Urnes stavkyrkje, som er den eldste i Noreg og ligg på verdsarvlista til UNESCO. Garden har lang historie og var mot slutten av 1400-talet den største adelsgarden i Noreg. Sidan slutten av 1600-talet har garden vore i slekta Bugge. Vertsfolket driv frukt- og bærproduksjon av eple, bringebær, jordbær, moreller og blåbær med videreforedling til saft og syltetøy.
På gardskaféen kan ein nyta ein kaffikopp med nysteikte vafler til, heimelaga kaker eller andre småretter. Eige utsal med gardsprodukt og husflid. Hjortefarm på garden med høve til omvisning. Turterreng og flotte fjell. Om sommaren går ferge over til Solvorn.

Der Urnes Hof ist schön gelegen auf der Südseite des Lusterfjords und befindet sich gleich neben der Stabkirche von Urnes - der ältesten Norwegens u. ein UNESCO Weltkulturerbe. Der Hof hat eine lange Geschichte und war zu Ende des 15. Jh. der größte Adelshof Norwegens. Seit Ende des 17. Jh. ist der Hof in Besitz der Fam. Bugge. Die heutigen Gastgeber bauen Obst u. Beeren an - Äpfel, Himbeeren, Erdbeeren, Kirschen, Blaubeeren - und verarbeiten diese zu Sirup u. Marmelade. Im Hofcafé kann man eine Tasse Kaffee mit frischen Waffeln, selbstgebackenen Kuchen u. anderen Kleinigkeiten genießen. Verkauf von Hof- und traditionellen Handwerksprodukten. Führungen über die eigene Hirschfarm möglich. Im Sommer geht eine Fähre auf die andere Seite des Fjords.

A: Apartment for 2-4(6) persons
2 bedrooms, bath, kitchen, LR, terr.
Price for whole unit: **850,-**
One night stay only; add: **100,-**

B: "Eldhuset" for 2-4(5) persons
1 bedroom, bath, kitchen, sofa corner, family-style bunk beds, terrace
Price for whole unit: **650,-**
One night stay only; add: **100,-**

C: Twin room in guesthouse
Shared bath/kitchen/LR, yard
Price per pers.: **250,-**

Bed linen fee: **80,-**
Breakfast service available
up to 3 p.: brkfast tray: **70,-**/pers.
4 pers. or more: buffet: **95,-**/pers.
Prices valid for 2011/12
Boat for rent
Open 1 June - 1 Sept.
English spoken

A: Husvære for 2-4(6) personer
2 soverom, bad, kjk, stove, terrasse
Pris for heile eininga: **850,-**
Enkelnattstillegg: **100,-**

B: "Eldhuset" for 2-4(5) personer
1 soverom, bad, kjk, sofakrok,
familiekøyeseng og terrasse
Pris for heile eininga: **650,-**
Enkelnattstillegg: **100,-**

C: Tosengsrom i gjestehus
Delt kjk/bad/stove, uteplass
Pris pr. pers.: **250,-**

Tillegg for sengeklede: **80,-**
Frukost kan bestillast
t.o.m. 3 p.: frukostbrett: **70,-**/pers.
f.o.m. 4 p.: frukostbuffet: **95,-**/pers.
Prisar gjeld for 2011/12
Båtutleige
Ope 1. juni - 1. sept.

A: Wohnung für 2-4(6) Personen
2 Schlafzi., Bad, Küche, Stube, Terr.
Ganze Einheit: **850,-**
Zuschlag für nur 1 ÜN: **100,-**

B: "Eldhuset" für 2-4(5) Personen
1 Schlafzi., Bad, Küche, Sofaecke,
Dobbelstockbett für 3 u. Terrasse
Ganze Einheit: **650,-**
Zuschlag für nur 1 ÜN: **100,-**

C: Zweibettzimmer im Gästehaus
Gemeins. Bad/Küche/Stube
Preis pro Person: **250,-**

Mieten von Bettwäsche: **80,-**
Frühstück auf Bestellung
bis zu 3 P.: Frühst.tablett: **70,-**/P.
ab 4 P.: Frühstücksbüffet: **95,-**/P.
Preise gültig für 2011/12
Boot zu mieten
Geöffnet 1. Juni - 1. Sept.
Sprechen etwas Deutsch

Directions:
From the village of Sogndal: take
RV 55 towards Sognefjellet. Exit
towards the ferry stop at Solvorn
after 17 km, where you can take a
ferry every hour during daytime. If
you drive over Sognefjellet on RV
55: take a left in Skjolden and
follow signs to Ornes, driving 30
km out along the fjord.

Vegforklaring:
Frå tettstaden Sogndal køyrer ein
RV 55 mot Sognefjellet. Etter 17
km tek ein av til fergestaden Solvorn der det går ferge kvar time på
dagtid.
Hvis ein kjem over Sognefjellet,
langs RV 55, tek ein til venstre i
Skjolden, skilta til Ornes, og køyrer 30 km utover langs fjorden.

Wegbeschreibung:
Von der Ortschaft Sogndal auf der
Str. 55 Richtung Sognefjell fahren.
Nach 17 km abbiegen zum Fähran-
leger Solvorn, von wo tagsüber
stündlich eine Fähre abfährt.
Aus Richtung Sognefjell: Auf der
Str. 55 bis Skjolden; dort links ab-
biegen beim Schild "Ornes" und
dann 30 km am Fjord entlang.

To my mind, the greatest reward and luxury of travel is
to be able to experience everyday things as if for the first time,
to be in a position in which almost nothing
is so familiar it is taken for granted.
~Bill Bryson~

I'm less interested in why we're here.
I'm wholly devoted to while we're here.
~Erika Harris~

Eplet Bed & Apple

Your host:
Trond Henrik Eplet

Address:
Eplet
N - 6879 Solvorn
Mobile: 41 64 94 69
E-mail: trondhenrik@eplet.net
Web: www.eplet.net

Best time to call:
17.00 - 23.00
(e-mail booking preferrred)
GPS: 61°18'6"N 7°14'37"E

Double room:	**550,-**	Dobbeltrom:	**550,-**	Doppelzimmer:	**550,-**
Single room:	**450,-**	Enkeltrom:	**450,-**	Einzelzimmer:	**450,-**
Tripple room:	**750,-**	Trippelrom:	**750,-**	Dreibettzimmer:	**750,-**
One night stay only; add:	**50,-**	Ettdøgnstillegg:	**50,-**	Zuschlag für nur 1 ÜN:	**50,-**
Extra matress:	**100,-**	Ekstra madrass:	**100,-**	Extra Matratze:	**100,-**
Dorm (7 beds), per pers.:	**180,-**	Sovesal (7 senger) pr. pers.:	**180,-**	Schlafsaal (7 Betten) pro P.:	**180,-**

Bed linen included
No. of rooms: 8
Internet available
Terrace/deck/yard
Bikes available
Open 1 May - 1 October
English, some Fr., Sp. & Russian

Sengetøy er inkludert
Antall rom: 8
Internett tilgjengelig
Terrasse/uteplass/hage
Terrengsykler tilgjengelig
Åpent 1. mai - 1. oktober

Inkl. Bettwäsche
Anzahl Zimmer: 8
Internet verfügbar
Terrasse/Außenbereich/Garten
Mountainbikes zur Verfügung
Geöffnet 1. Mai - 1. Oktober
Sprechen etwas Deutsch

Eplet Bed & Apple opened in 2005. Eplet is a cozy "bed" without "breakfast", a modern hostel in the middle of spectacular fjord landscape. In the basement there's a juice factory where the smell of unsprayed freshly squeezed raspberry juice emanates on late summer evenings. Eplet Bed & Apple is in Solvorn, a small pearl lodged in Sognefjorden.
Eplet has a home-style atmospher with a hammoc in the garden, plentiful library, climbing wall, croquet. Daily shuttle bus to Breheim center in Jostedalen, glacier tours, paddling glacier rivers, rafting and horseback riding. On the fjord; kayaking, in the forest; hiking trails.

Eplet Bed & Apple åpnet i 2005. Eplet er et hjemmekoselig "bed" uten "breakfast", et moderne herberge midt i det mest spektakulære fjordlandskapet. I kjelleren har vi en liten juicefabrikk hvor lukten av usprøytede, ferskpressede bringebær siver ut sene sommerkvelder.
Eplet Bed & Apple ligger i Solvorn, en liten perle inderst i Sonefjorden. Eplet har hjemmehyggelig atmosfære, hengekøyer i hagen, velassortert bibliotek, klatrevegg og krokettgolf. Buss til breheimsenteret i Jostedalen hver dag, med breturer, padling på brevann, rafting og hesteridning. På fjorden; selsafari med kajakk, i skogen; merkede stier.

Eplet Bed & Apple öffnete 2005. Es ist ein gemütliches "Bed ohne Breakfast" und ein modernes Hostel mitten in der spektakulärsten Fjordlandschaft. Im Keller haben wir eine kleine Saftfabrik, aus der an späten Sommerabenden der Duft von ungespritzten, frischgepressten Himbeeren strömt. Eplet liegt in Solvorn, einer kleinen Perle im Innersten des Sognefjords. Hier kann man sich wie zu Hause fühlen, in der Hängematte liegen, die Kletterwand erklimmen, Krocket spielen, in der Bibliothek lesen. Täglicher Bus zum Gletscherzentrum in Jostedalen: Gletschertouren, Paddeln/ Rafting auf dem Gletscherfluss, Reiten. Robbensafaris auf dem Fjord.

Nes Gard

Your host:
Mari & Asbjørn Månum

Address:
N - 6875 Høyheimsvik
Phone: 57 68 39 43
Mobile: 95 23 26 94
E-mail: post@nesgard.no
Web: www.nesgard.no

Best time to call:
08.00 - 22.00
GPS: 61°23'13"N 7°21'55"E

Double room w/bath: **840,-/1020,-**	Dobbeltrom m/bad: **840,-/1020,-**	Doppelzi. m. Bad: **840,-/1020,-**
Double room, sh/bath: **780,-/860,-**	Dobbeltrom u/bad: **780,-/860,-**	Doppelzi. ohne Bad: **780,-/860,-**
1 pers. in dbl. room: **600,-/780,-**	1 pers. i dobbeltrom: **600,-/780,-**	1 Pers. im Doppelzi.: **600,-/780,-**
Discount for stay over 3 days	Rabatt ved 3 døgn eller mer	Rabatt ab 3 ÜN oder mehr
No. of rooms: 14	Antall rom: 14	Anzahl Zimmer: 14
Breakfast buffet	Frokostbuffét	Frühstücksbüfett
Dinner 7pm	Middag kl. 19.00	Abendessen 19.00
Prices valid for 2011	Priser gyldig for 2011	Preise gültig für 2011
TV/Internet available	TV/Internett tilgjengelig	TV/Internet verfügbar
Patio/yard	Uteplass/hagen	Außenbereich/Garten
Boat and bike for rent/rowb. free	Båt- og sykkelutleie, robåt til låns	Boot und Fahrrad zu mieten
VISA, MC, AmEx accepted	Vi tar VISA, MC, AmEx	Wir akzeptieren VISA, MC, AmEx
Open 15 May - 30 Sept.	Åpent 15. mai - 30. sept.	Geöffnet 15. Mai - 30. Sept.
English and some French spoken		Sprechen etwas Deutsch

Nes Gard is situated with a view of Lusterfjorden and Feigumfossen waterfall. The beautiful farmyard is from 1850. The farm has been in the family for 200 years. The 7th generation is now growing apples, pears, plums and cherries. The hosts offer accommodations in the main building, newly renovated and with new bathrooms.
Unique possibilities for mountain hikes, guided glacier tours and bicycling. Down by the fjord one can swim or use a rowboat or motorboat to explore the fjord.
Consider taking trips to Jostedalen, Nærøyfjorden and Fjærland.

Nes Gard ligger fint til med utsikt utover Lusterfjorden og Feigumfossen. Det vakre tunet er fra 1850. Gården har vært i familiens eie i 200 år. Det er 7. generasjon som nå dyrker epler, pærer, plommer og moreller. Vertskapet tilbyr overnatting i hovedbygningen, nyoppusset og med nye bad.
Unike muligheter for fotturer i fjellet, brevandring med guide og sykkelturer. Nede ved fjorden kan man bade og med robåt eller motorbåt kan man komme seg utpå fjorden.
La deg friste til å ta utflukter til Jostedalen, Nærøyfjorden og Fjærland.

Der Nes Hof aus dem Jahre 1850 ist schön gelegen mit Aussicht auf den Lusterfjord und den Feigumfossen Wasserfall. Seit 200 Jahren ist er in Familienbesitz und es ist heute die 7. Generation, die Äpfel, Birnen, Pflaumen und Kirschen anbaut. Die Zimmer befinden sich alle im neu renovierten Haupthaus.
Unzählige Aktivitäten: Bergtouren, geführte Gletscherwanderungen und Fahrradausflüge. Im Fjord kann man schwimmen und mit dem Ruder- o. Motorboot hinausfahren.
Lohnende Ausflugsziele sind Jostedalen, Nærøyfjord und Fjærland.

Nesøyane Gjestegard

Your host:
Jens & Marit Vøien Nes

Address:
Veitastrond
N - 6878 Veitastrond
Phone: 57 68 78 19
Mobile: 91 19 31 57 / 97 58 85 02
E-mail: vo-ne@online.no
Web: www.nesoyane.com
Best time to call: 09.00 - 22.00 (mob.)
GPS: 61°28'42"N 7°2'5"E

Double room:	750,-	Dobbeltrom:	750,-	Doppelzimmer:	750,-
Twin room:	650,-	Tosengsrom:	650,-	Zweibettzimmer:	650,-
Single room:	450,-	Enkeltrom:	450,-	Einzelzimmer:	450,-

No. of rooms: 4	Antal rom: 4	Anzahl Zimmer: 4
Laid breakfast table or self-service	Dekka frukostbord el. sjølvbetj.	Ged. Frühstückstisch o. SB
Selfcatering possible	Høve til sjølvhushald	Selbstverpflegung möglich
Prices valid for 2011/12	Priser gjeld for 2011/12	Preise gültig für 2011/12
TV available	TV tilgjengeleg	TV vorhanden
Terrace/patio/yard	Terrasse/uteplass/hage	Terrasse/Außenbereich/Garten
Boat and bike for rent	Båt- og sykkelutleige	Boot u. Fahrrad zu mieten
Pets welcome	Kjæledyr velkomne	Haustiere willkommen
Open Easter - November	Ope påske - november	Geöffnet Ostern - November
English spoken		Sprechen Deutsch

The guest rooms are in "Knutstova", a modern picturesque little house at one end of a lake called Veitastrondvatnet. Here is a fine view of the lake and mountains. Driving here gives your soul the experienece of nature.

Your hosts, Jens and Marit plus Knut Fredrik, run a dairy farm in the village of Veitatsrond. You'll be enchanted by the inviting farm buildings. Here's a secondhand store, farm museum and a little cafe in "Gamlefjosen", the old cow barn.

Beautiful mountainous landscape and glacial hiking in the Jostedalsbreen National Park.

Utleigeromma ligg i 'Knutstova', eit moderne lite hus som ligg vakkert til ved enden av Veitastrondvatnet. Her er det flott utsyn til vatn og fjell. Å køyre vegen inn her kan i seg sjøl vera ei naturopplleving.

Vertskapet, Jens og Marit pluss Knut Fredrik, driv gard med mjølkeproduksjon med kyr i bygda Veitastrond. Du må gjerne kome innom garden som har eit triveleg gardstun. Her er bruktbutikk, gardsmuseum og ein liten café i 'Gamlefjøsen'.

Flott fjellandskap rundt og turterreng i Jostedalsbreen Nasjonalpark.

Die Zimmer befinden sich im 'Knutstova', einem modernen kleinen Haus, hübsch gelegen am Ende des Veitastrond Sees. Schöner Ausblick auf die See und die Berge. Der Weg zum Hof ist bereits ein Naturerlebnis.

Die Gastgeber Jens und Marit sowie Knut Fredrik haben Kühe und betreiben Milchwirtschaft. Sie sind hier auf dem gemütlichen Hof als Gast herzlich willkommen. Es gibt einen Secondhandladen, ein Hofmuseum und ein kleines Cafè im alten Stall.

Schöne Berglandschaft ringsherum sowie das Wandergebiet im Jostedalsbreen Nationalpark.

Directions from Sogndal:
Take the RV 55, exit to Hafslo and continue towards Veitastrond on a winding road for 20 km. along the lake. Look for B&B sign.

Veibeskrivelse frå Sogndal:
Ta RV 55, ta av mot Hafslo og videre mot Veitastrond, svingete veg 20 km langs vatnet. Sjå etter B&B-skilt.

Wegbeschreibung von Sogndal:
Str. 55, Abfahrt Ri. Hafslo und weiter Ri. Veitastrond. Folgen Sie der kurvigen Strasse entlang des Sees für 20 km, achten Sie auf das B&B Schild.

In the 'Gammelfjøsen' Marit has organized a farm shop, a second hand shop, a waffel-café and a farm museum. Guests are invited for traditional porridge (rømmegrøt) or coffee and waffels and a nice chat, and often would like nothing better than to stay longer.

I Gammelfjøsen har Marit laga til butikk, brukthandel, vaffel-kafè og gardsmuseum. Her vert gjestene invitert til rømmegraut eller kaffi og vafler og ein prat. Då vert dei ofte "gjester som ikkje vil gå".

Im "Gammelfjøsen", dem alten Stall, hat Marit einen kleinen Laden, Secondhandshop, ein Waffel-Café und Hofmuseum eingerichtet. Hierher lädt sie die Gäste zu rømmegrøt (Sauerrahmbrei), Kaffee und Waffeln, und einen Plausch ein. Viele Gäste fühlen sich hier wohl und wollen am liebsten gar nicht nehr weg.

Forget not that the earth delights to feel your bare feet and
the winds long to play with your hair.
~Kahlil Gibran~

Nigardsbreen Gjesteheim

Your host:
Tom, Jeanett & Geir Inge

Address:
Fjellheim,
N - 6871 Jostedal
Mobile: 41 77 47 47 / 41 61 61 51
E-mail: post@nigardsbreen.com
Web: www.nigardsbreen.com

Best time to call:
09.00 - 22.00
GPS: 61°39'4"N 7°16'43"E

Double-/twin room:	790,-	Dobbelt-/tosengsrom:	790,-	Doppel-/Zweibettzi.:	790,-
Single room:	600,-	Enkeltrom:	600,-	Einzelzimmer:	600,-
4-bedded room:	1190,-	4-sengsrom:	1190,-	4-Bettzimmer:	1190,-
Multibedded room, price: ask		Sovesal for 10 pers.: spør om pris		Mehrbettzi. f. 10 P.: Preis erfragen	
No. of rooms: 13		Antal rom: 13		Anzahl Zimmer: 13	
Breakfast buffet		Frokost buffét		Frühstücksbüfett	
Prices valid for 2010		Prisar gjeld for 2011		Preise gültig für 2011	
Discount for children		Rabatt for born		Ermäßigung für Kinder	
Internet available / Bike for rent		Internett tilgjengeleg / sykkelutleige		Fahrrad zu mieten / Internet verf.	
Terrace/deck access/yard		Terrasse/uteplass/hage		Terrasse/Außenbereich/Garten	
VISA, MC, DC, AmEx accepted		Vi tek VISA, MC, DC, AmEx		Akzeptieren VISA, MC, DC, AmEx	
Open 28 May - 31 Aug.		Ope 28. mai - 31. aug.		Geöffnet 28. Mai - 31. Aug.	
Open year round for weekly rent		Ope heile året for vekesutleige		Wochenmiete ganzjährig möglich	
English spoken				Sprechen etwas Deutsch	

Care to awaken to the largest glacier in Europe? Drink morning coffee barefoot in a green garden face to face with this formidable mass of ice? Nigardsbreen Gjesteheim has a great view of Nigardsbreen in Jostedalen in Sognefjorden. Nigardsbreen Gjesteheim was built in 1954 and has recently been renovated in the original 1950s-60s style. Activities with the guesthouse as a starting point include glacier exploring, kayaking, rafting, mountain hiking, skiing, small-animal hunting and climbing/bouldering. Cross-country skiing possible right up to early July!

Vil du vakne opp med utsikt til den største breen i Europa? Drikke morgenkaffien berrføtt i ein stor, grøn hage med den mektige isen rett i mot? Nigardsbreen Gjesteheim ligg med eit flott utsyn til Nigardsbreen i Jostedalen inst i Sognefjorden. Nigardsbreen Gjesteheim vart bygd i 1954 og er no renovert men har samtidig behaldt 50- og 60-tals preget. Aktivitetar med gjesteheimen som utgangspunkt er breføring, kajakk, rafting, fjellturar, skiturar, småviltjakt og klatring/buldring. Toppturar på ski er mogleg heilt fram til starten av juli.

Möchten Sie mit Aussicht auf den größten Gletscher Europas aufwachen? Ihren Morgenkaffee barfuß in einem großen grünen Garten trinken, mit der mächtigen Eiszunge gegenüber? Das Gästehaus am Sognefjord mit Ausblick auf den Nigardsbreen wurde 1954 erbaut, nun renoviert und hat dennoch seinen 50er- & 60er-Jahre-Charme behalten. Es ist der ideale Ausgangspunkt für Gletscher-, Ski-, Wander-, Kletter-, Kajak-, Raftingtouren oder um auf Jagd zu gehen. Gletscherskifahren bis Anfang Juli möglich.

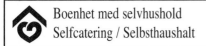

Skinlo Farm

Your host:
Celia Engstedt

Address:
Skinlo
N - 6827 Breim
Mobile: 95 20 04 96
E-mail: celia_e@live.no

Best time to call:
09.00 - 22.00
GPS: 61°44'43"N 6°26'40"E

A: Apartment for 2-6 persons 3 bedrooms, bath, kitchen, LR	**A:** Leilighet for 2-6 personer 3 soverom, bad, kjøkken, stue	**A:** Wohnung für 2-6 Personen 3 Schlafzi., Bad, Küche, Stube
Whole unit, 4-6 pers.: **850,-**	Hele enheten, 4-6 pers.: **850,-**	Ganze Einheit, 4-6 Pers.: **850,-**
Price for 2-3 pers. by agreement	Pris for 2-3 pers. etter avtale	Preis für 2-3 Pers. nach Absprache
Breakfast by agreement: **60,-**	Frokost ved avtale: **60,-**	Frühstück nach Absprache: **60,-**
B: Cabin for 2-4 persons Sleeping alcove & open sleeping loft Own shower, kitchenette, LR	**B:** Hytte for 2-4 personer Sovealkove og sovehems Egen dusj, kjøkkenkrok, stue	**B:** Hütte für 2-4 Personen Schlafnische u. Schlafboden Eig. Dusche, Küchenecke, Stube
Whole unit, price for 4 pers.: **550,-**	Hele enheten ved 4 pers.: **550,-**	Ganze Einheit bei 4 Pers.: **550,-**
Applies to both rental units:	For begge enhetene gjelder:	Für beide Einheiten gilt:
Bed linen fee: **70,-**	Tillegg for sengetøy: **70,-**	Mieten von Bettwäsche: **70,-**
Discount for children	Rabatt for barn	Ermäßigung für Kinder
Prices valid for 2011/12	Priser gyldig for 2011/12	Preise gültig für 2011/12
Internet available	Internett tilgjengelig	Internet verfügbar
Terrace/patio/yard	Terrasse/uteplass/hage	Terrasse/Außenbereich/Garten
Pets: ask host	Kjæledyr - spør	Haustiere: bitte nachfragen
Open June, July, August	Åpent juni, juli, august	Geöffnet Juni, Juli, August
English, some French/Spanish spoken		Sprechen Englisch u. etwas Franz.

Skinlo farm, 340 meters above sea level, has a beautiful view. The hostess, who formerly worked with music, has recently driven the local library. The farmer raises sheep and has a wood turning workshop on the farm. The community features three music festivals each summer: Glopperock in June, Norwegian Country in July and Gloppen classical music in August. There is much nature to experience, from glacier to fjord.

Skinlo gård ligger på 340 m.o.h. med flott utsikt. Vertinnen har tidligere hatt musikk som yrke men har de siste årene styrt lokal biblioteket. Bonden driver med sau og har eget dreieverksted på gården. Tre musikkfestivaler finner sted i kommunen hver sommer; Glopperock i juni, Norsk Country festival i juli og Gloppen Musikkfest (klassisk) i august. Mye natur å oppleve, fra bre til fjord.

Mit wunderbarer Aussicht liegt Skinlo Farm 340 m über dem Meeresspiegel. Die Gastgeberin war früher Musikerin und leitet jetzt die örtliche Bibliothek. Der Bauernhof wird u.a. mit Schafen betrieben. Im Sommer sollte man sich die Festivals im Ort nicht entgehen lassen: Glopperock im Juni, Norwegisches Country Festival im Juli und Gloppen Musikkfest (Klassik) im August. Es gibt vielfältige Natur zu erleben, von Gletscher bis Fjord.

Trollbu

Your host:
Signe Aabrekk

Address:
N - 6791 Oldedalen
Phone: 57 87 38 38
Mobile: 91 38 25 69
E-mail: sign-aab@online.no
Web: www.trollbuonline.no

Best time to call:
09.00 - 23.00
GPS: 61°40'41"N 6°48'50"E

Twin room:	**600,-**	Tosengsrom:	**600,-**	Zweibettzi.:	**600,-**
1 pers. in double room:	**400,-**	1 pers. i dobbeltrom:	**400,-**	1 Pers. im Doppelzi.:	**400,-**
No. of rooms: 2		Antal rom: 2		Anzahl Zimmer: 2	
Laid breakfast table		Dekka frukostbord		Gedeckter Frühstückstisch	
Prices valid for 2011/12/13		Priser gyldig for 2011/12/13		Preise gültig für 2011/12/13	
Terrace/patio/yard		Terrasse/uteplass/hage		Terrasse/Außenbereich/Garten	
Open year round		Ope heile året		Ganzjährig geöffnet	
Some English spoken				Sprechen etwas Deutsch	

Trollbu is on the Aabrekk farm in Oldedalen, Stryn.

The farm operation was merged with the neighbouring ones where milk and meat are corporately produced today. There are still some small livestock on the farm. The Trollbu courtyard has 3 houses, one from 1992 and 2 restored houses from the 1700's and 1800's. 2,5 km to Briksdal. There you can drive a troll car to Briksdalbreen. Possibilities for fishing and mountain hiking.

Directions:
From Olden: Drive about 20 km towards Oldedalen/ Briksdal. Look for the sign alongside the road marked "Trollbu".

Trollbutunet ligg på garden Aabrekk i Oldedalen, Stryn. Gardsdrifta er flytta til samdrift med naboene med mjølke- og kjotproduksjon. Det er fremdeles nokre smådyr på garden. Trollbutunet består av tre hus, eitt frå 1992 og to eldre hus frå 1700- og 1800-talet som er restaurerte. 2,5 km til Briksdal. Der er det høve til å kjøyre Trollbil til Briksdalsbreen. Høve til fiske i vatn og merka turstier i fjellheimen.

Vegforklaring:
Frå Olden skal du kjøyre mot Oldedalen/Briksdal, ca. 20 km. Det er skilt ved vegen som viser "Trollbu".

Trollbu liegt auf dem Aabrek-Hof im Oldetal in der Gemeinde Stryn. Die Milch- und Fleischproduktion werden heute auf dem Nachbarhof gemeinsam mit diesem betrieben. Hier auf Trollbu gibt es noch einige Kleintiere. Drei Häuser reihen sich um den Hof, ein 1992 erbautes und zwei restaurierte aus dem 18./19. Jh. 2,5km nach Briksdal, von wo aus Sie mit einem norwegischen Auto der Marke Troll zum Briksdalsbreen (Gletscher) fahren können.
Die umgebende Bergwelt bietet Möglichkeiten zum Wandern und Angeln.

Wegbeschreibung:
Von Olden fahren Sie Ri. Oldedalen/Briksdal, ca. 20 km. Achten Sie auf das Schild "Trollbu" entlang der Straße.

Loen Pensjonat

Your host:
Erik & Åsta Bødal

Address:
Lotunet
N - 6789 Loen
Phone: 57 87 76 24
Mobile: 48 29 00 22
E-mail: post@loen-pensjonat.com
Web: www.loen-pensjonat.com

Best time to call:
08.00 - 12.00 / 17.00 - 23.00
GPS: 61°52'19"N 6°51'28"E

Double-/twin room: **680,-/840,-**	Dobbelt-/tosengsrom: **680,-/840,-**	Doppel-/Zweibettzi.: **680,-/840,-**
Single room: **400,-/550,-**	Enkeltrom: **400,-/550,-**	Einzelzimmer: **400,-/550,-**
(prices for: shared bath/priv. bath)	(priser for delt bad/eget bad)	(Preise für gemeins. Bad/Eig. Bad)
Extra bed: **170,-**	Ekstraseng: **170,-**	Extrabett: **170,-**
No. of rooms: 10	Antal rom: 10	Anzahl Zimmer: 10
Discount for children	Rabatt for born	Ermäßigung für Kinder
Breakfast buffet	Frukostbufét	Frühstücksbüfett
Prices valid for 2011	Priser gjeld for 2011	Preise gültig für 2011
TV available	TV tilgjengeleg	TV vorhanden
Terrace/patio/yard	Terrasse/uteplass/hage	Terrasse/Außenbereich/Garten
Boat and bike for rent	Båt- og sykkelutleige	Boot u. Fahrrad zu mieten
Open 20 June - 25 Aug.	Ope 20. juni - 25. aug.	Geöffnet 20. Juni - 25. Aug.
English spoken		Sprechen Deutsch

Loen Pensjonat is 400 m from the centre of Loen, with a wonderful view of the fjord. The main building dates back to 1910 with several modern additions. There was an inn here from 1910-1940, and from 1956 until the present. A large garden surrounds the house. Beautiful hiking country and good fishing. There are sheep on the farm. Possibilities for glacier trekking.

Directions:
Loen is located 10 km from Stryn - towards Førde. Exit towards Lodalen in Loen and drive about 500 m. The guest house is situated just near the church in Loen.

Loen Pensjonat ligg 400 m frå sentrum, med fin utsikt over fjorden. Hovudbygninga er frå 1910 med fleire nyare tilbygg. Her har det vore dreve pensjonat i åra 1910-1940 og frå 1956 og fram til i dag. Ein stor hage ligg ikring huset. På garden driv dei sauehald. Flott turterreng og gode høve for fiske. Høve til brevandring.

Vegforklaring:
Loen ligg 10 km frå Stryn i retning Førde. I Loen ta av mot Lodalen og køyr ca. 500 m. Pensjonatet ligg like ved kyrkja i Loen.

Loen Pensjonat liegt 400 m vom Zentrum Loens. Schöne Aussicht auf den Fjord. Die Pension ist von einem großen Garten umgeben. Das Hauptgebäude stammt von 1910. Schafzucht auf dem Hof. Herrliches Wandergelände. In der Nähe gute Möglichkeiten zum Angeln und für Gletscherwanderungen.

Wegbeschreibung:
Loen liegt 10 km von Stryn entfernt in Ri. Førde. Biegen Sie in Loen in Richtung Lodalen ab und folgen Sie der Straße ca. 500 m geradeaus. Die Pension liegt gleich neben der Kirche von Loen.

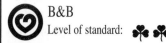

Skipenes Gard

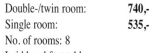

Your host:
Sigdis Skipenes
& Arild Andersen

Address:
Skipenes
N - 6770 Nordfjordeid
Phone: 57 86 08 24
Mobile: 40 20 09 26
E-mail: aria@online.no
Web: www.skipenes-gard.com

Best time to call:
17.00 - 22.00
GPS: 61°54'16"N 6°0'22"E

Double-/twin room:	**740,-**	Dobbelt-/tosengsrom:	**740,-**	Doppel-/Zweibettzi.:	**740,-**
Single room:	**535,-**	Enkeltrom:	**535,-**	Einzelzimmer:	**535,-**
No. of rooms: 8		Antal rom: 8		Anzahl Zimmer: 8	
Laid breakfast table		Dekka frukostbord		Gedeckter Frühstückstisch	

Applies to B&B and selfcatering:	Gjeld for både B&B og sjølvhushald:	Für B&B und Selbsthaushalt gilt:
Prices valid for 2011	Prisar gjeld for 2011	Preise gültig für 2011
Discount for children	Rabatt for born	Ermäßigung für Kinder
TV available	TV tilgjengeleg	TV vorhanden
Terrace/patio/yard	Terrasse/uteplass/hage	Terrasse/Außenbereich/Garten
Jacuzzi with water jets	Badestamp m/boblebad	Whirlpool
BBQ-hut	Grillhytte	Grillhütte
Boat and bike for rent	Båt- og sykkelutleige	Boot und Fahrrad zu mieten
VISA accepted	Vi tek VISA	Wir akzeptieren VISA
Open year round	Ope heile året	Ganzjährig geöffnet
English spoken		Sprechen Englisch

An old farm typical of the West Coast of Norway, with the dwelling house dating back to the 18th and 19th centuries. Breakfast is served in the formal dining room which has been restored to the old style. The farm is home to lama, goats, dwarf hens and cats. You are welcome to come along and get acquainted with the animals. Horseback riding can also be arranged. Skipenes Gard lies 800 m from Nordfjordeid city center, close to the salmon river Eidselva.

Ein gamal vestlandsgard med hus frå 1700- og 1800-talet. Frukost serverast i bestestova som er restaurert i gamal stil.
På garden har dei lama, geit, dverghøner og katt. Du kan få vere med og helse på dyra. Tur med hest kan også formidlast.
Skipenes Gard ligg 800 meter frå Nordfjordeid sentrum, like ved den lakseførande Eidselva.

Ein alter Vestlands-Hof mit Gebäuden aus dem 18. und 19. Jh. Frühstück wird in der "guten Stube" serviert, die in altem Stil restauriert ist.
Auf dem Hof gibt es Lamas, Ziegen, Zwerghühner und Katzen zu erleben. Darüber hinaus können Reittouren organisiert werden.
Skipenes Gard liegt 800 m von Nordfjordeid Zentrum entfernt, direkt am Lachsfluß Eidselva.

A: Apartment for 2-4 persons
No. of bedrooms: 2
Own bath, kitchen, LR

B: 2 Cabins for 2-5 persons
No. of bedrooms: 2
Own bath, kitchen, LR

Applies to all rental units:
Price per night; ask
Weekly rent available
Bed linen included
Discount for unused bed: **-50,-**
Breakfast service available: **75,-**

A: Husvære for 2-4 personar
Antal soverom: 2
Eige bad, kjøken, stove

B: 2 Hytter for 2-5 personar
Antal soverom: 2
Eige bad, kjøken, stove

For alle einingar gjeld:
Døgnleige: spør om pris
Høve til vekeleige
Sengeklede er inkludert
Avslag pr. seng ikkje i bruk: **-50,-**
Frukost kan serverast: **75,-**

A: Wohnung für 2-4 Pers.
Anzahl Schlafzimmer: 2
Eig. Bad, Küche, Stube

B: 2 Hütten für 2-5 Personen
Anzahl Schlafzimmer: 2
Eig. Bad, Küche, Stube

Für alle Einheiten gilt:
Preis pro Nacht: bitte erfragen
Wochenleihe möglich
Inkl. Bettwäsche
Erm. pro nicht gebrauch. Bett: **-50,-**
Frühstück auf Bestellung: **75,-**

Directions:
From Førde: The distance to Nord-fjordeid is 108 km. Take E-39 northward to the ferry dock for Anda - Lote. Continue from Lote and drive through a tunnel. After the downgrade following the tunnel, make a right turn before coming to the bridge. Skipenes Gard is 100 m from the bridge on the left side.

Vegforklaring:
Frå Førde: Køyr E-39 nordover. Avstand til Nordfjordeid er 108 km. Turen inkluderer fergestrekninga Anda - Lote. Etter Lote køyrer du gjennom ein tunell, så kjem ei nerstigning etter tunellen. Etter bakkane ser du ei bru, sving til høgre før brua. Skipenes Gard ligg 100m frå brua, på venstre side av vegen.

Wegbeschreibung:
Von Førde aus sind es 108 km bis Nordfjordeid. Fahren Sie auf der E-39 in Richtung Norden. Die Route schließt die Fährverbindung Anda - Lote mit ein. Von Lote aus führt die Strecke durch einen Tunnel. Nach dem Gefälle hinter dem Tunnel biegen Sie vor der Brücke rechts ab. Ca. 100 m weiter liegt auf der linken Seite Skipenes Gard.

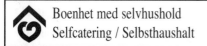
Knutegarden Norangdal

Your host:
Edith & Jon Arne Nordang
Address: Norangdal
N - 6196 Norangsfjorden
Phone: 70 06 21 02
Mobile: 99 27 94 43
E-mail: efn_4@hotmail.com
Web: www.hjorundfjord.no/
overnatting/knutegarden
Best time to call: 08.00 - 23.00
GPS: 62°11'22"N 6°39'91"E

Apartment for 2-8 pers.	Bueining for 2-8 pers.	Wohnung für 2-8 Pers.
LR, kitchen, bath and 4 bedrooms	Stove, kjk, bad og 4 soverom	Stube, Küche, Bad u. 4 Schlafzi.
Price per person: from **250,-**	Pris pr. pers.: fra **250,-**	Preis pro Pers.: ab **250,-**
Bed linen included	Sengeklede er inkludert	Inkl. Bettwäsche
Prices valid for 2011/12/13	Prisar gjeld for 2011/12/13	Preise gültig für 2011/12/13
Internet/TV available	Internett/TV tilgjengeleg	Internet/TV verfügbar
Patio/Yard	Uteplass/hage	Außenbereich/Garten
Boat for rent	Båtutleige	Boot zu mieten
Open year round	Ope heile året	Ganzjährig geöffnet
English spoken		Sprechen Englisch

Knutegard is a farm fully operational with a busy farmyard. The farm is about 250 m. from Norangsfjorden. There are many animals: fjord horses, rabbits, fox, cattle and cats.

Guest stay is the Old Farmer apt. in the main building, with separate entrance and yard. There are other farms and homes in the area.

Fishers find ocean fish in the fjord or trout and char in the lake, and salmon in the river.

Diving in Lygnstølsvatnet Lake. Knutegarden-Norangdal is a great departure point for mountain hikes. Slogen (altitude: 1,564 m.) is the best-known mountain.

"We have fantastic and wild nature in all directions, and that's no bragging."

Knutegarden-Norangdal er ein gard i full drift med aktivitet i tunet. Garden ligg ca. 250 m frå Norangsfjorden. Her er mange dyr; fjordhest, kanin, rev, storfe og katt. Bueininga er ein "kårbustad" i hovudhuset, med eigen inngang og eigen hage. Det ligg fleire gardsbruk og bustader rundt.

Høve til sjøfiske i fjorden eller aure og røyr i vatn, og laksefiske i elva. Dykking i Lygnstølsvatnet. Knutegarden-Norangdal er eit glimrande utgangspunkt for fjellturar. Slogen (1564 m.o.h.) er det mest kjende fjellet.

"Vi har ein fantastisk vill og vakker natur rundt oss på alle kantar, og det er ikkje skryt!"

Knutegarden-Norangdal ist ein voll betriebener Hof und liegt ca. 250m vom Norangs-Fjord entfernt. Hier gibt es viele Tiere: Fjordpferde, Kaninchen, Füchse, Rinder und Katzen.

Die Wohneinheit liegt im Haupthaus, mit eigenem Eingang und Garten. Landwirtschaftliche Betriebe und Häuser ringsherum. Gute Angelmöglichkeiten im Fjord, im See (u.a. Lachsforelle) und im Fluss (Lachs). Tauchen im 'Lygnstøls'-See. Knutegarden-Norangdal ist ein hervorragender Ausgangspunkt für Bergtouren. Der 'Slogen' ist der bekannteste Berg (1564 m.ü.NN).

"Ringsherum haben wir eine fantastische wilde, schöne Natur und das ist keine Übertreibung".

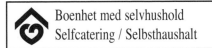
Hellesylt Ferie-Hytter

Your host:
Åse & Glenn Stadheim
Address: **Stadheim Gård**
N - 6218 Hellesylt
Phone: **70 26 18 02**
Mobile: **93 64 68 26**
E-mail:
hellesyltferiehytter@online.no
Web: **www.hellesyltferiehytter.com**
Best time to call: **09.00 - 22.00**
GPS: **62°4'21"N 6°54'25"E**

Cabin for 2-8 persons	Hytte for 2-8 personer	Hütte für 2-8 Personen
Own bath, kitchen, LR, DR	Eget bad, kjøkken, stue, spisestue	Eig. Bad, Küche, Stube, Esszi.
Price per pers.: **300,-**	Pris pr. pers.: **300,-**	Preis pro Pers.: **300,-**
No. of units: 4	Antall enheter: 4	Anzahl Einheiten: 4
Bed linen fee: **90,-**	Tillegg for sengetøy: **90,-**	Mieten von Bettwäsche: **90,-**
Towel fee: **35,-**	Tillegg for håndkle: **35,-**	Mieten von Handtüchern: **35,-**
Prices valid for 2011/12	Priser gyldig for 2011/12	Preise gültig für 2011/12
Terrace/patio/yard	Terrasse/uteplass/hage	Terrasse/Außenbereich/Garten
Boat for rent	Båtutleie	Boot zu mieten
Open year round	Åpent hele året	Ganzjährig geöffnet
English spoken		Sprechen etwas Deutsch

Cabins range in size and have 4-8 sleeping places. They're in peaceful surroundings, each with a west-facing veranda. Here you can rent a boat and try your luck at fishing with the possibility of catching salmon. And it's great for people who like to walk in the mountains. In the winter there is Sunnmørsalpane Skiarena, only 30 minutes by car. And the mountains are good for both telemark skiing and loose-snow skiing. From Hellesylt city center it's 50 min. by ferry over Geirangerfjord to Geiranger, a tour you don't want to miss.

'Hellesylt Holiday Cabins' are 2.5 km. from Hellesylt. Follow the signs.

Hyttene varierer i størrelse og har fra 4 til 8 sengeplasser. De ligger i rolige omgivelser, hver med egen vestvendt veranda. Her kan du leie båt og prøve fiskelykken, også muligheter for å prøve seg på laksefiske. Her er det fint for deg som liker å gå i fjellet. For vintersport er Sunnmørsalpane Skiarena det nærmeste, bare 30 min. med bil fra hyttene. Fjellheimen passer også godt for løssnøkjøring og telemark-kjøring. Fra Hellesylt sentrum tar det 50 min. med ferge inn Geirangerfjorden, til Geiranger, en tur du ikke bør gå glipp av.

Hellesylt feriehytter finner du 2,5 km fra Hellesylt sentrum. Følg skilting.

Die Hütten sind unterschiedlich groß mit 4 bis 8 Schlafplätzen. Sie liegen in ruhiger Umgebung, mit jeweils eigener nach Westen gerichteter Terrasse. Man kann hier Boote mieten und sein Angelglück versuchen. Schöne Umgebung für Ausflüge in die Berge. Für Wintersport inkl. Tiefschneefahren ist die Sunnmørs Alpen Skiarena in nur 30 min mit dem Auto zu erreichen. Vom Zentrum Hellesylts hinein in den Geirangerfjord bis Geiranger dauert es 50 min mit der Fähre - ein Ausflug, den Sie sich nicht entgehen lassen sollten.

Die Hellesylt Ferienhütten liegen 2,5 km vom Zentrum entfernt und sind ausgeschildert.

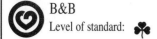
Hesthaug Gard

Your host:
Hilde & Jan Olav Hesthaug

Address:
N - 6215 Eidsdal
Mobile: **97 43 37 70**
E-mail: **j-hesth@online.no**
Web: **www.hesthaug-gard.no**

Best time to call:
09.00 - 22.00
GPS: 62°14'30"N 7°8'20"E

Double room:	**900,-**	Dobbeltrom:	**900,-**	Doppelzimmer:	**900,-**
Single room:	**500,-**	Enkeltrom:	**500,-**	Einzelzimmer:	**500,-**
No. of rooms: 4		Antall rom: 4		Anzahl Zimmer: 4	
Laid breakfast table		Dekket frokostbord		Gedeckter Frühstückstisch	
Prices valid for 2011/12/13		Priser gyldig for 2011/12/13		Preise gültig für 2011/12/13	
TV available		TV tilgjengelig		TV vorhanden	
Terrace/patio/yard		Terrasse/uteplass/hage		Terrasse/Außenbereich/Garten	
VISA, MC accepted		Vi tar VISA, MC		Wir akzeptieren VISA, MC	
Discount for children		Rabatt for barn		Ermäßigung für Kinder	
Open year round		Åpent hele året		Ganzjährig geöffnet	
English spoken				Sprechen etwas Deutsch	

Hesthaug farm is at Eidsdal, right beside Geiranger. The farm lies 450 m. above sea level with fantastic view of the fjord surrounded by mountains. Unique possibilities for mountain hikes on both challenging and easy terrain. It's also possible to take day tours to Ålesund, Briksdalsbreen or Atlanterhavsveien.
With a location between Geirangerfjord and Trollstigen one has ideal place for daylong excursions before returning to peaceful surroundings in the evening. You can buy lunch or dinner at the farm. The farm also has animals which children can play with and help manage.

Hesthaug gard ligger i Eidsdal, like ved Geiranger. Gården ligger 450 m.o.h., med fantstisk utsikt mot fjorden og mot fjellene rundt. Unike muligheter for både fjellturer i lett terreng og toppturer. Det er også mulig å reise på dagsturer til Ålesund, Briksdalsbreen eller Atlanterhavsveien.
Med beliggenhet mellom Geirangerfjorden og Trollstigen er man midt i smørøyet for fine utflukter, for så å komme tilbake til rolige omgivelser om kvelden. Det er mulig å få kjøpe lunch eller middag på gården.
Gården har dyr som barn kan leke med resp. være med å stelle.

Der Hesthaug Hof liegt in Eidsdal, gleich neben Geiranger. Auf 450 m ü. NN hat man hier eine fantastische Aussicht auf den Fjord und die umliegenden Berge. Einmalige Möglichkeiten für sowohl leichte Wanderungen als auch Gipfelturen. Tagestouren nach Ålesund, zum Briksdalsbreen und zur Atlantikstr. bieten sich an. Mit seiner Lage zwischen dem Geirangerfjord und dem Trollstigen ist der Hof der ideale Ausgangspunkt für tolle Ausflüge, um dann abends wieder in ruhige Gefilde zurückzukehren. Es ist möglich, auf dem Hof etwas zum Mittag- und Abendessen zu kaufen. Außerdem finden Sie hier verschiedene Tiere, mit denen Kinder spielen oder die sie mit versorgen können.

Cabins for 2-7 persons
1-2 bedrooms, bath and LR with
kitchen-nook and TV
For whole unit: **400,-** to **800,-**
No. of cabins: 3

Apt. for 4-6 persons
2 bedrooms, bath and LR with
kitchen-nook and TV
For whole unit: **600,-** to **900,-**
No. of cabins: 2

Bed linen fee: **75,-**
End of stay-cleaning: **200,-**

Directions:
Along RV 63, 18 km from Geiranger or 7 km from Eidsdal. Follow the signs marked 'Hesthaug.'

Hytter for 2-7 personer
1-2 soverom, bad, stue med kjk.-
krok og TV
Pris for hel enhet: **400,-** til **800,-**
Antall hytter: 3

Leiligheter for 4-6 personer
2 soverom, bad, stue med kjk.-krok
og TV
Pris for hel enhet: **600,-** til **900,-**
Antall leiligheter: 2

Tillegg for sengetøy: **75,-**
Sluttrengjøring: **200,-**

Veibeskrivelse:
Langs RV 63; 18 km fra Geiranger
eller 7 km fra Eidsdal. Følg skilt
merket 'Hesthaug'.

Hütten für 2-7 Personen
1-2 Schlafzi., Bad, Stube mit
Küchenecke und TV
Ganze Einheit: **400,-** bis **800,-**
Anzahl Hütten: 3

Wohnungen für 4-6 Personen
2 Schlafzi., Bad, Stube mit
Küchenecke und TV
Ganze Einheit: **600,-** bis **900,-**
Anzahl Wohnungen: 2

Mieten von Bettwäsche: **75,-**
Endreinigung: **200,-**

Wegbeschreibung:
Entlang der Str. 63; 18 km von
Geiranger bzw. 7 km von Eidsdal.
Folgen Sie dem Schild "Hesthaug"

I still find each day too short for all the thoughts I want to think,
all the walks I want to take, all the books I want to read
and all the friends I want to see.
~John Burroughs~

Trollstigen
Camping & Gjestegård

Your host:
Milouda & Edmund Meyer

Address:
N - 6300 Åndalsnes
Phone: 71 22 11 12
Mobile: 91 39 01 05
E-mail: ed-mey@online.no
Web: www.trollstigen.no

Best time to call:
09.00 - 22.00
GPS: 62°29'56"N 7°40'15"E

Single room:	**560,-**	Enkeltrom:	**560,-**	Einzelzimmer:	**560,-**
Double room:	**780,-**	Dobbeltrom:	**780,-**	Doppelzimmer:	**780,-**
3 bedded room:	**1040,-**	3-sengsrom:	**1040,-**	3-Bettzimmer:	**1040,-**
4 bedded room:	**1300,-**	4-sengsrom:	**1300,-**	4-Bettzimmer:	**1300,-**
No. of rooms: 15		Antall rom: 15		Anzahl Zimmer: 15	
Discount for children		Rabatt for barn		Ermäßigung für Kinder	
Breakfast buffet		Frokostbuffé		Frühstücksbüfett	

For both B&B and Selfcatering:	For både B&B og selvhushold:	Sowohl B&B als auch Selbsthaush.:
Restaurant, fully-licensed	Restaurant, alle rettigheter	Restaurant, alle Schankrechte
Prices valid for 2011	Priser gyldig for 2011	Preise gültig für 2011
TV available	TV tilgjengelig	TV vorhanden
Terrace/patio/garden	Terrasse/uteplass/hage	Terrasse/Außenbereich/Garten
BBQ in garden	Grillplass	Grillplatz
Playground	Lekeplass	Spielplatz
Canoe for rent	Kanoutleie	Kanu zu mieten
Souvenirshop (taxfree)	Souvenirbutikk	Souvenirgeschäft (Tax-free)
VISA, MC accepted	Vi tar VISA, MC	Wir akzeptieren VISA, MC
Open year round	Åpent hele året	Ganzjährig geöffnet
English, Arabic and some French		Sprechen etwas Deutsch

Trollstigen Camping & Gjestegård is at Istedalen, along Route 63 in the direction of Trollstigen.
The farm has a dairy and cattle herds along with potatoe and Christmas tree production.
River fishing: Your hosts have their own salmon/trout river including an outdoor shelter and boat. Canoe rental, fjord fishing by boat and rent of hunting rights.

Trollstigen Camping & Gjestegård ligger i Istedalen, 10 km fra Åndalsnes langs RV 63 mot Trollstigen.
På gården er det produksjon av kjøtt, melk, poteter og juletrær.
Elvefiske, utleier har egen laks- og ørretelv med gapahuk og båt.
Utleie av jaktrettigheter, og kanoutleie. Fjordfiske fra båt er også mulig.

Trollstigen Camping & Gjestegård liegt in Istedalen, 10 km von Åndalsnes entlang der Str. 63. Auf dem Hof werden Milch und Fleisch produziert, Kartoffeln angebaut, Weihnachtsbäume kultiviert. Flussangeln möglich - der Gastgeber ist Besitzer eines eigenen Lachs- und Forellenflusses mit Schutzhütte und Boot. Jagdrechtvermietung, Kanuvermietung. Ebenfalls möglich: Fjordangeln vom Boot aus.

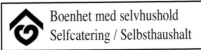

A: High standard cabin, 2-5 pers.
1 bedroom, LR w/convertible
double bed sofa, bath, kitchen
No. of cabins: 8
For whole unit: **600,-** to **790,-**

B: Lower standard cabin, 2-4 pers.
1 bedroom, kitchen nook
No. of cabind: 8
For whole unit: **400,-** to **490,-**

C: 'Isterdalshytta' for 10 pers.
5 bedrooms, kitchen, LR w/fire-
place, 3 toilets, 2 showers
For whole unit: **1600,-** to **1900,-**

D: 2 rooms in restaurant building
shared bath
Price for 1 pers.:   **400,-**
Pric for 2 pers.:   **460,-**

E: Apartment for 2-4 persons
2 bedrooms, bath, kitchen, LR
For whole unit: **750,-**

Applies to units A to E:
Bed linen fee: **60,-/85,-**
Breakfast service available: **75,-**

A: Høg Standard Hytter, 2-5 pers.
1 soverom, stue med dobbel
sovesofa, eget bad, kjøkken
Antall hytter: 8
For hele enheten: **600,-** til **790,-**

B: Lav Standard Hytter, 2-4 pers.
1 soverom,kjøkken-krok
Antall hytter: 8
For hele enheten: **400,-** til **490,-**

C: "Isterdalshytta" for 10 pers.
5 soverom, kjk., stue med peis,
3 toalett, 2 dusj
For hele enheten: **1600,-** til **1900,-**

D: 2 rom i restaurantbygget med
delt bad
Pris for 1 pers.:   **400,-**
Pris for 2 pers.:   **460,-**

E: Leilighet for 2-4 personer
2 soverom, bad, kjøkken, stue
For hele enheten: **750,-**

For enhetene A til E gjelder:
Tillegg for sengetøy: **60,-/85,-**
Frokost kan serveres: **75,-**

A: Hütte, hoher Standard, 2-5 Pers.
1 Schlafzi., Stube mit Doppel-
schlafsofa, eig. Bad, Küche
Anzahl Hütten: 8
Ganze Einheit: **600,-** bis **790,-**

B: Hütte, einfacher Standard, 2-4 P.
1 Schlafzi., Küchenecke
Anzahl Hütten: 8
Ganze Einheit: **400,-** bis **490,-**

C: "Isterdalshütte" für 10 Pers.
5 Schlafzi., Küche, Stube mit
Kamin, 3 Toiletten, 2 Duschen
Ganze EInheit: **1600,-** bis **1900,-**

D: 2 Zimmer im Restaurantgebäude
gemeinsames Bad
Preis für 1 Pers.:   **400,-**
Preis für 2 Pers.:   **460,-**

E: Wohnung für 2-4 Personen
2 Schlafzi., Bad, Küche, Stube
Ganze EInheit: **750,-**

Für die Einheiten A bis E gilt:
Mieten von Bettwäsche: **60,-/85,-**
Frühstück auf Bestellung: **75,-**

The units A to D are located in
Istedalen, 10 km from Åndalsnes,
direction Trollstigen. The name
here is "Trollstigen Camping og
Gjestegård". There is also a restaurant that serves both breakfast and
dinner, plus a sauna and canoe
rental.
Unit E, Trollstigen Gjestegård, is
where your hosts live and is located at Sogge, 6 km from Åndalsnes towards Trollstigen.

Enhetene A-D ligger i Istedalen, 10
km fra Åndalsnes, retning Trollstigen. Navnet her er Trollstigen
Camping og Gjestegård. Her er det
også restaurant med frokost og
middagservering, badstu og kanoutleie.
Enhet E på Trollstigen Gjestegård,
hvor vertskapet selv bor, ligger på
Sogge, 6 km fra Åndalsnes mot
Trollstigen.

Die Wohneinheiten A bis D befinden sich auf dem Trollstigen Campingplatz. Dieser liegt im Istedalen, 10 km von Åndalsnes entfernt in Richtung Paßstraße "Trollstigen". Im Restaurant werden
Frühstück und Abendessen angeboten, außerdem Sauna und Kanuvermietung.
Die Wohneinheit E - hier wohnen
die Gastgeber selbst - liegt in
Sogge, 6 km von Åndalsnes entfernt in Richtung Paßstraße Trollstigen.

To change one's life: Start immediately.
Do it flamboyantly. No exceptions.
~William James~

Malmestranda Romutleie

Your host:
Siv Aashild Malme

Address:
Malmestranda
N - 6445 Malmefjorden
Mobile: 93 69 48 85
E-mail: sivmalme@gmail.com

Best time to call:
12.00 - 22.00
GPS: 62°48'20"N 7°12'41"E

Closed 2011, open 2012 & 2013		Stengt 2011, åpent 2012 og 2013		2011 geschlossen, 2012/13 geöffnet	
Double room:	**550,-**	Dobbeltrom:	**550,-**	Doppelzimmer.:	**550,-**
Single room:	**350,-**	Enkeltrom:	**350,-**	Eizelzimmer:	**350,-**
One night stay only; add:	**50,-**	Ett-døgnstillegg:	**50,-**	Zuschlag für nur 1 ÜN:	**50,-**
No. of rooms: 4		Antall rom: 4		Anzahl Zimmer: 4	
Shared bath, kitchen and LR		Delt bad, kjøkken og stue		Gemeins. Bad, Küche u. Stube	
Bed linen included		Sengetøy er inkludert		Inkl. Bettwäsche	
Breakfast service on request		Frokost kan serveres v/avtale		Frühstück auf Bestellung	
Check prices for 2012/13		Sjekk priser for 2012/13		Preise für 2012/13: auf Anfrage	
Kayak available		Kajak tilgjengelig		Kajak ausleihbar	
Patio/yard		Uteplass/hage		Außenbereich/Garten	
Open year round		Åpent hele året		Ganzjährig geöffnet	
English spoken				Sprechen etwas Deutsch	

Malmestranda Romutleie is idyllically located on the inner Malmefjord in Fræna township, a 15-min. drive from Molde.
There are numerous possible day trips. One can follow footpaths up the mountain to view the fjord or further to the mouth of the fjord. A 15-min. drive takes you to the path to Trollkyrkjagrotten, a limestone cave with waterfall that leads to a pool of white lime.
A visit to Malmestranda Romutleie can be combined with a tour of Atlanterhavsveien (Atlantic Ocean Road) and /or a trip to Ona lighthouse.

Malmestranda Romutleie ligger idyllisk til innerst i Malmefjorden, i Fræna kommune, 15 min. kjøring fra Molde.
Her er utallige muligheter for dagsturer. Man kan følge tursti opp på fjellet og få utsikt over hele Malmefjorden og helt ut i havgapet. 15 min. med bil til tursti som fører til Trollkyrkjagrotten, en kalksteinshule med fossefall som styrter ned i et basseng av hvit kalkstein.
Et besøk ved Malmestranda Romutleie kan kombineres med turistruten Atlanterhavsveien og/eller en tur til Ona fyr.

Malmestranda Romutleie liegt idyllisch im Innersten des Malmefjords, in der Kommune Fræna, 15 Automin. von Molde entfernt. Unzählige Möglichkeiten für Tagesausflüge. Man kann dem Wanderweg auf den Berg folgen und erhält eine Aussicht über den ganzen Malmefjord und bis zum Atlantik. 15 Min. mit dem Auto bis zum Wanderweg, der zur 'Trollkyrkja-Grotte' führt, einer Kalksteinhöhle mit Wasserfall, welcher in ein Becken aus weissem Kalkstein mündet.
Kombinieren Sie einen Besuch bei uns mit der Atlantikstraße und dem Leuchtturm von Ona.

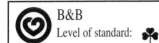
Øyastuo

Your host:
Merethe Hansen Singsdal

Address:
N - 6620 Ålvundeid
Phone: 71 69 79 50
E-mail: singsdal@hotmail.com
Web: www.oyastuo.com

Best time to call:
10.00 - 22.00
GPS: 62°44'14"N 8°42'44"E

Per person:	**300,-**	Pr. pers.:	**300,-**	Pro Pers.:	**300,-**
Discount for children: 50%		Rabatt for born: 50%		Ermäßigung für Kinder: 50%	
No. of rooms: 3		Antal rom: 3		Anzahl Zimmer: 3	
Laid breakfast table		Dekka frukostbord		Gedeckter Frühstückstisch	
Selfcatering possible Oct. - April		Høve til sjølvhushald okt. - april		Selbsthaushalt möglich Okt. - Apr.	
Prices valid for 2011		Prisar gjeld for 2011		Preise gültig für 2011	
Patio/yard		Uteplass/hage		Außenbereich/Garten	
Open year round		Ope heile året		Ganzjährig geöffnet	
English spoken				Sprechen etwas Deutsch	

Øyastuo is a cofter's log cabin from 1744. The house is a part of an active farm complex. The hosts are farmers with dairy cows, sheep and sale outlet of local art and craft.

The farm is located at the foot of Trollheimen and 2 km from the protected nature area of Innerdalen. Opportunities for easy and challenging mountain hikes summer and winter. Marked trails. Various wintersport equipped areas.

One can enjoy free trout fishing possibilities in river and lakes.

After a day in beautiful nature one can enjoy a relaxing evening in front of the fireplace.

Øyastuo er ei husmannsstove frå 1744 med tømmervegger. Stova er ein del av eit levande gardsmiljø der vertsfolket driv med kyr og sauer og sal av lokal kunst- og handverk. Garden ligg ved foten av Trollheimen og 2 km frå landskapsvernområdet i Innerdalen. Her er gode høve for både lette og krevjande fjellturar sommar og vinter. Det er merka turistløyper i fjellet. Fin bakke for telemarkkøyring på fjellet Dronninga. 10 km til skitrekk på Ålvundeid. Ein kan nytta seg av fritt fiske etter småaure i elv og vatn. Etter rekreasjon i fin natur kan ein kosa seg ved grua om kvelden.

Die Blockhütte Øyastuo ist das ehemalige Gehöft eines Kleinbauern aus dem Jahre 1744. Die Hütte ist Teil eines intakten Bauernhofs, auf dem die Gastgeber Milchwirtschaft und Schafzucht betreiben. Außerdem wird regionales Kunsthandwerk angeboten. Der Hof liegt zu Füßen des mächtigen Trollheimen-Gebirges, nur 2 km vom geschützten Innerdalen entfernt. Im Sommer/Winter sehr gute Wandermöglichkeiten für Anfänger/ Fortgeschrittene (markierte Wanderwege). Wintersportmöglichkeiten in der Nähe. Forellenangeln im Fluss und See ohne Angelschein möglich.

Nach einem ereignisreichen Tag in der Natur lässt es sich am Abend beim offenen Feuer herrlich entspannen!

Saga Trollheimen

Your host:
Morten Gåsvand

Address:
N - 6657 Rindal
Phone: 71 66 55 02
Mobile: 97 75 48 58
E-mail:
post@sagatrollheimenhotel.no
Web: sagatrollheimenhotel.no
Best time to call:
08.00 - 23.00
GPS: 63°2'57"N 9°11'48"E

Double-/twin room:	**1050,-**	Dobbelt-/tosengsrom:	**1050,-**	Doppel-/Zweibettzi.:	**1050,-**
Single room:	**750,-**	Enkeltrom:	**750,-**	Einzelzimmer:	**750,-**
No. of rooms: 30		Antall rom: 30		Anzahl Zimmer: 30	
Discount for children		Rabatt for barn		Ermässigung für Kinder	
Breakfast buffet		Frokostbuffét		Frühstücksbüfett	
Prices valid for 2011/12/13		Priser gyldig for 2011/12/13		Preise gültig für 2011/12/13	
TV/Internet available		TV/Internett tilgjengelig		Zugang zu TV/Internet	
Deck/yard		Uteplass/hage		Aussenplatz/Garten	
Bike for rent		Sykkelutleie		Fahrrad zu mieten	
Suitable for handicapped		Handikaptilgjengelig		Behindertengerecht	
Pets welcome		Kjæledyr velkommen		Haustiere willkommen	
VISA, MC, DC, AmEx accepted		Vi tar VISA, MC, DC, AmEx		VISA, MC, DC, AmEx	
Open year round		Åpent hele året		Ganzjährig geöffnet	
English spoken				Sprechen etwas Deutsch	

Saga Trollheimen Hotell has a unique historic atmosphere. Here one is transported 100 years back in time. There are old and new houses ^ in all 14 buildings around the farmstead. All houses are in old farm style but equipped with the comfortable facilities of a modern hotel. The family run hotel lies between mountainous Trollheimen and the salmon-rich Surna river. The host arranges outings and activities in nearby mountains.

Saga Trollheimen Hotell har en unik historisk atmosfære. Her blir man lett satt hundre år tilbake i tid. Anlegget består av gamle og nye hus, i alt 14 bygninger rundt et tun. Alle hus er i gammel bondestil, samtidig som det er et moderne hotell med komfortable fasiliteter. Hotellet er familiedrevet og ligger mellom fjellmassivet Trollheimen og lakseelva Surna. Vertskapet arrangerer utflukter og aktiviteter i fjellene omkring.

Das Saga Trollheimen Hotel hat eine einmalige historische Atmosphäre. Hier fühlt man sich leicht 100 Jahre zurückversetzt. Die Anlage besteht aus insgesamt 14 alten und neuen Häusern auf einem Hof. Der alte Bauernstil der Häuser wurde verbunden mit einem modern und komfortabel eingerichtetem Hotel. Das familiengefürte Hotel liegt zwischen dem Bergmassiv Trollheimen und dem Lachsfluss Surna. Die Gastgeber arrangieren Ausflüge in die Berge.

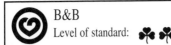
Brattset Gard

Your host:
Nancy Aalmo

Address:
Brattset Gard
N - 6693 Mjosundet
Phone: 71 64 88 50
Mobile: 98 03 62 88
E-mail: na-aalmo@online.no
Web: www.brattsetgard.no

Best time to call:
09.00 - 22.00
GPS: 63°10'18"N 8°32'28"E

Double-/twin room:	600,-	Dobbelt-/tosengsrom:	600,-	Doppel-/Zweibettzi.:	600,-
Single room:	350,-	Enkeltrom:	350,-	Einzelzimmer:	350,-
1 pers. in double room:	350,-	1 pers. i dobbeltrom:	350,-	1 Pers. in DZ:	350,-
Sleeping loft for 1 pers.:	200,-	Sovehems for 1 pers:	200,-	Schlafboden für 1 Pers.:	200,-
Extra bed:	250,-	Ekstraseng:	250,-	Extrabett:	250,-
Surcharge for 1 night stay:	100,-	En-nattstillegg:	100,-	Zuschlag für nur 1 ÜN:	100,-
No. of rooms: 4		Antall rom: 4		Anzahl Zimmer: 4	
Laid breakfast table		Dekket frokostbord		Gedeckter Frühstückstisch	
Selfcatering possible		Selvhushold er mulig		Selbstverpflegung möglich	
Other meals available		Andre måltider kan bestilles		Andere Mahlzeiten auf Anfrage	
Prices valid for 2011		Priser gyldig for 2011		Preise gültig für 2011	
TV available		TV tilgjengelig		TV vorhanden	
Yard/patio, boat for rent		Hage/uteplass, båtutleie		Garten/Sitzecke, Boot zu mieten	
Suitable for handicapped		Handikaptilgjengelig		Behindertengerecht	
Open year round		Åpent hele året		Ganzjährig geöffnet	
English, Spanish & Portuguese				Sprechen Englisch	

The farm Brattset is ecologically operated rearing sheep. There are also poultry and llama. The main house is from 1872. The location is peaceful and quiet with possibilities for hiking and fishing in the fjord and mountain lakes. The hosts also have a cabin for rent on the mountain. A place for recreation and rest in beautiful nature surroundings. The hosts can guide you on tours of the summer farm and vicinity.
On the farm they sell sheep skins and horns, meat and berries.

På garden Brattset driver de økologisk gardsdrift med sau. Det er også høner og lama på garden. Hovedhuset er fra 1872. Det er et stille og rolig sted med muligheter for fotturer og ikke minst fisking både på fjorden og i fiskevann på fjellet. Vertskapet har også ei seterbu på fjellet som man kan leie. Det er et sted for rekreasjon og hvile i naturskjønne omgivelser.
Vertskapet kan være guide på turer til setra og omegn. På garden har de salg av saueskinn, horn, kjøtt og bær.

Ökologischer Bauernhof mit Schafzucht, Hühnern und Lamas. Das Haupthaus ist von 1872. Es ist ein stiller und friedlicher Platz mit Möglichkeiten zum Wandern, Angeln im Fjord und den Gebirgsseen. Die Gastgeber vermieten auch eine kleine Almhütte in den Bergen. Der geeignete Ort zum Entspannen und Ausruhen in naturschöner Umgebung. Führungen auf dem Almhof und in der Umgebung durch die Gastgeber möglich. Verkauf von Schaffellen, -hörnern, Fleisch u. Beeren.

Drivstua Rom

Your host:
Louise Timmerman

Address:
Drivstua
N - 7340 Oppdal
Phone: 73 48 73 87
Mobile: 41 30 68 49
E-mail:
louise.timmerman@oppdal.com
Web: www.drivstua-oppdal.com

Best time to call:
09.00 - 21.00
GPS: 62°25'29"N 9°37'25"E

Apartment for 4-5 persons	Leilighet for 4-5 personer	Wohnung für 4-5 Personen
2 bedrooms, bath, kitchen, LR	2 soverom, bad, kjøkken, stue	2 Schlafräume, Bad, Küche, Stube
Room for 2 pers.: **800,-**	Pris for 2 pers.: **800,-**	Zimmer für 2 Pers.: **800,-**
Room for 4 pers.: **1000,-**	Pris for 4 pers.: **1000,-**	Zimmer für 1 Pers.: **1000,-**
Bed linen included	Sengetøy er inkludert	Inkl. Bettwäsche
Prices valid for 2011/12/13	Priser gyldig for 2011/12/13	Preise gültig für 2011/12/13
TV/Internet available	TV/Internett tilgjengelig	Zugang zu TV/Internet
Terrace/deck/yard	Terrasse/uteplass/hage	Terrasse/Aussenplatz/Garten
Pets welcome	Kjæledyr velkommen	Haustiere willkommen
VISA, MC, AmEx accepted	Vi tar VISA, MC, AmEx	Wir akzeptieren VISA, MC, AmEx
Open year round	Åpent hele året	Ganzjährig geöffnet
English, Dutch, some French spoken		Sprechen Deutsch

Drivstua Room is on E-6, 20 km south of Oppdal town center. The was built as a house for railroad officials in 1921 and is part of the Drivstua national trust area, thus offering an interesting and historic hour-long hike in grand nature.
At Drivstua Room one is nearby the mountains in the east; ski and foot trails, a slate quarry, historic Vårstigen, and Kongsvold Fjeldstue with its excellent restaurant; musk ox safari at Dovrefjell.
Oppdal is known for alpine skiing. In summer enjoy rafting, climbing and golf. Culture center with movie theater and swimming pool.

Drivstua Rom ligger langs E-6, 20 km sør for Oppdal sentrum. Huset ble bygget som funksjonærbolig i 1921 og er en del av Drivstua Stasjon Verneområdet som byr på en interessant historisk timelang vandring i storslått natur.
Fra Drivstua Rom kan man gå direkte til fjellene i øst og vest, til fots eller på ski, man kan gå til skiferbruddene i nord eller gå den historiske Vårstigen mot sør, til Kongsvold Fjeldstue med sin utmerkede restaurant. Moskussafari på Dovrefjell. Oppdal er et alpinskisted. Om sommeren; rafting klatring og golf. Kulturhus med kino, og svømmehall.

Drivstua Rom liegt entlang der E-6, 20 km südlich von Oppdal. 1921 wurde es als Beamtenwohnhaus erbaut und ist Teil des ehemaligen Bergbahnhofes Drivstua, der heute ein norwegisches Kulturgut ist. Ein einstündiger Wanderweg durch grandiose Natur bringt die interessante Geschichte des Bahnhofs näher. Mehrere Wander-, Skiwege bringen einen ab Drivstua Rom direkt in die Berge und z.B zum Kongsvold Berggasthof mit seinem ausgezeichneten Restaurant. Moschussafari im Berggebiet Dovrefjell. Oppdal ist ein großes Skigebiet. Im Sommer: Rafting, Klettern, Golfen. Kulturhaus im Ort mit Kino und Schwimmhalle.

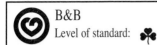
Flanderborg overnatting

Your host:
Anne Margrethe Wessel
& Tor Einar Sæther

Address:
Flanderborg 3
N - 7374 Røros
Mobile: 92 25 08 83 / 92 81 68 65
E-mail: post@linguanor.no
Best time to call: 17.00 - 23.00
GPS: 62°34'27"N 11°23'19"E

Double-/twin room:	**700,-**	Dobbelt-/tosengsrom:	**700,-**	Doppel-/Zweibettzi.:	**700,-**
1 pers. in double room:	**400,-**	1 pers. i tosengsrom:	**400,-**	1 Pers. im Zweibettlzi.:	**400,-**
Shared kitchen, LR and bath		Delt kjøkken, stue og bad		Gemeins.Küche, Stube und Bad	
Whole apt. for 4-6 pers.:	**1000,-**	Hele leil. for 4-6 pers.:	**1000,-**	Ganze Wohnung für 4-6 P.:	**1000,-**
Discount for children		Rabatt for barn		Ermäßigung für Kinder	
Breakfast; self-service		Frokost; selvbetjening		Frühstück: Selbstbedienung	
Selfcatering possible		Selvhushold er mulig		Selbstverpflegung möglich	
Prices valid for 2011		Priser gyldig for 2011		Preise gültig für 2011	
TV available		TV tilgjengelig		TV vorhanden	
Patio/yard		Uteplass/hage		Außenbereich/Garten	
Canoe for rent		Kanoutleie		Kanu zu mieten	
Pets welcome by agreement		Kjæledyr velkommen		Haustiere nach Absprache	
Open year round		Åpent hele året		Ganzjährig geöffnet	
English spoken				Sprechen etwas Deutsch	

The old mining town of Røros is on Unesco's heritage protection list. In the picturesque neighborhood Flanderborg the Sæther/Wessel family rents out the first floor of their house. The apartment features comfortably furnished living room, kitchen and modern bath. The family includes two adults, three children and a dog. It's just 2-3 minutes walk to the town center which has small shops, craftswork, galleries and the Røros Museum with its unique miniturized mobile exhibit depicting local mining operations. There is mountain hiking, fishing and swimming. Skiing in winters.

Gruvebyen Røros står på Unescos verdensarvliste. I den pittoreske bydelen Flanderborg leier familien Sæther/Wessel ut første etasjen i huset sitt. Utleieenheten har en hyggelig møblert stue, kjøkken og et moderne bad.
Familien består av to voksne, tre barn og en hund.
Det er 2-3 min. gange til byens sentrum med små butikker, kunsthåndverk, gallerier og Rørosmuseet med sin unike utstilling med bevegelige miniatyrmodeller som viser gruvedriften.
Fjellvandring, fisketurer, bademuligheter. Om vinteren spenner man på skiene rett utenfor døren.

Die Bergbaustadt Røros steht auf der Unesco Welterbeliste. In dem malerischen Stadtteil Flanderborg vermietet die Familie Sæther/Wessel die erste Etage in ihrem Haus. Die Familie besteht aus zwei Erwachsenen, drei Kindern und einem Hund. 2-3 min zu Fuss bis zum Stadtzentrum mit kleinen Geschäften, Kunsthandwerk, Galerien u. dem Rørosmuseum mit seiner einzigartigen Ausstellung von beweglichen Miniaturmodellen, die den Bergwerkbetrieb darstellen. Bergwanderungen, Angelu. Bademöglichkeiten. Im Winter kann man die Ski direkt vor der Tür anschnallen.

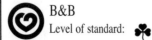
Meslo Herberge

Your host:
Ingrid Meslo

Address:
Stamnan
N - 7392 Rennebu
Phone: 72 42 66 15
Mobile: 90 96 01 90
E-mail: ingridmeslo@hotmail.com
Web: www.tilbyder.no

Best time to call:
08.00 - 20.00
GPS: 62°50'52"N 9°52'58"E

Double-/twin room:	**600,-**	Dobbelt-/tosengsrom:	**600,-**	Doppel-/Zweibettzi.:	**600,-**
Single room:	**350,-**	Enkeltrom:	**350,-**	Einzelzimmer:	**350,-**
No. of rooms: 5		Antal rom: 5		Anzahl Zimmer: 5	

Laid breakfast table or -tray
Selfcatering possible
Prices valid for 2011
TV/Internet available
Terrace/patio/yard
Pets welcome
Open year round
English spoken

Dekka frukostbord el. frukostbrett
Høve til sjølvhushald
Priser gjeld for 2011
TV/Internett tilgjengeleg
Terrasse/uteplass/hage
Kjæledyr velkomen
Ope heile året

Gedeckt. Frühstückstisch o. -tablett
Selbstverpflegung möglich
Preise gültig für 2011
TV/Internet verfügbar
Terrasse/Außenbereich/Garten
Haustiere willkommen
Ganzjährig geöffnet
Sprechen etwas Deutsch

At a traditional farm with cows and sheep you'll find Meslo Herberge where the hostess, Ingrid, welcomes guests. The houses for rent are an old storehouse and a laundry house, both of which have been restored for accommodation. The old houses have a rustic look. The farm has fishing rights for salmon and guests may try fishing in Orkla, a well known salmon-river. You may get in contact with farm animals, and at certain times guests can help with the farm work, such as hay drying and lambing.

På ein tradisjonell trøndergard med ku og sau finn du Meslo Herberge kor vertinna Ingrid ønskjer gjestar velkomne til gards. Husa som leiges ut er eit stabbur og ei mastu (bryggerhus) som begge er restaurert til føremålet. Husa er gamle og har eit rustikt preg.
Garden har laksevald og gjestene er velkomne til å prøva å fiske i Orkla, ei kjend lakse-elv. Det er høve til kontakt med dyra på garden. I enkelte periodar kan ein også delta i gardsarbeid, f.eks. hesjing, lamming o.s.b.

Meslo Herberge ist ein traditioneller Hof, betrieben mit Kühen und Schafen. Die Gastgeberin Ingrid heisst Sie dort herzlich willkommen. Sie vermietet einen ehemaligen Lebensmittelspeicher sowie ein früheres Back/Kochhaus, die beide restauriert wurden. Die Häuser sind alt und haben eine rustikale Atmosphäre.
Der Hof hat das Fischereirecht für Lachse und die Gäste sind eingeladen, ihr Angelglück im bekannten Lachsfluss Orkla zu versuchen. Auf dem Hof können Sie gern die Tiere besuchen. In manchen Perioden ist es möglich, bei der Hofarbeit zu helfen, z.B. Heu auf Heureiter aufhängen, oder bei einer Lammgeburt.

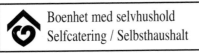
A: 'Laundry house' for 2-6 pers.
2 bedrooms and kitchen nook,
  shared bath

Price per pers.:	**250,-**
Price for whole unit:	**600,-**

B: 'Storehouse' for 2-4 pers.
1 bedroom, kitchenette,
  shared bath

Price per pers.:	**200,-**
Price for whole unit:	**500,-**

Applies to both rental units:
Bed linen included
Breakfast service available
Other meals available
Prices valid for 2011
Terrace/patio/yard
Pets welcome
Open year round. Winter; book
well ahead of time
English spoken

A: Mastu/bryggerhus for 2-6 pers.
2 soverom og kjøkenkrok,
  delt bad

Pris pr. pers.:	**250,-**
Pris for heile eininga:	**600,-**

B: Stabbur, gjestehus for 2-4 pers.
1 soverom og tekjøken,
  delt bad

Pris pr. pers.:	**200,-**
Pris for heile eininga:	**500,-**

For begge einingane gjeld:
Sengeklede er inkludert
Frukost kan serverast
Andre måltid kan bestellast
Priser gjeld for 2011
Terrasse/uteplass/hage
Kjæledyr velkomen
Ope heile året. Vinter; bestilling på
førehand i god tid

A: 'Mastu' für 2-6 Personen
2 Schlafzimmer, Küchenecke,
  gemeins. Bad

Preis pro Pers.:	**250,-**
Ganze Einheit:	**600,-**

B: 'Stabbur' für 2-4 Personen
1 Schlafzimmer, Teeküche,
  gemeins. Bad

Preis pro Pers.:	**200,-**
Ganze Einheit:	**500,-**

Für beide Einheiten gilt:
Inkl. Bettwäsche
Frühstück auf Bestellung
Andere Mahlzeiten auf Anfrage
Preise gültig für 2011
Terrasse/Außenbereich/Garten
Haustiere willkommen
Ganzjährig geöffnet; im Winter
bitte rechtzeitig vorbestellen
Sprechen etwas Deutsch

Directions:
From E-6 at Berkåk take RV 700
toward Orkanger. After 8 km
you'll find the farm on the right
side. Look for a large white house,
two old brown houses, two red
outbuildings and a barn.

Vegforklaring:
Frå E-6 på Berkåk ta RV 700 mot
Orkanger. Etter 8 km finn du gard-
en på høgre side, sjå etter ei kvit
trønderlån, 2 gamle brune hus, 2
raude uthus pluss fjøs.

Wegbeschreibung:
Von der E-6 bei Berkåk nehmen Sie
die Str. 700 Ri. Orkanger.
Nach 8 km finden Sie den Hof auf
der rechten Seite. Achten Sie auf
ein großes weißes Haus, 2 alte
braune Häuser, 2 rote Schuppen
samt Stall.

Kårøyan Fjellgard

Your host:
Magna & Ola Rønning

Address:
Kårøydalen, N - 7203 Vinjeøra
Phone: 72 45 44 60
Mobile: 98 80 24 13
Fax: 72 45 38 82
E-mail: post@karoyan.no
Web: www.karoyan.no

Best time to call:
08.00 - 22.00
GPS: 63°8'16"N 9°6'00"E

Double room:	**800,-**	Dobbeltrom:	**800,-**	Doppelzimmer:	**800,-**
Single room:	**440,-**	Enkeltrom:	**440,-**	Einzelzimmer:	**440,-**
Extra bed:	**150,-**	Ekstraseng:	**150,-**	Extrabett:	**150,-**
No. of rooms: 10		Antall rom: 10		Anzahl Zimmer: 10	
Discount for children		Rabatt for barn		Ermäßigung für Kinder	
Laid breakfast table		Dekket frokostbord		Gedeckter Frühstückstisch	
Lunch and dinner/fully licensed		Lunsj og middag/alle rettigheter		Mittag-/Abendessen/Schankrecht	
Selfcatering possible		Selvhushold er mulig		Selbstverpflegung möglich	
Prices valid for 2011/12		Priser gyldig for 2011/12		Preise gültig für 2011/12	
Internet available		Internett tilgjengelig		Internet verfügbar	
Terrace/patio/yard		Terrasse/uteplass/hage		Terrasse/Außenbereich/Garten	
Pets welcome		Kjæledyr velkommen		Haustiere willkommen	
VISA accepted		Vi tar VISA		Wir akzeptieren VISA	
Open 20 June - 20 Aug.		Åpent 20. juni - 20. aug.		Geöffnet 20. Juni - 20. Aug.	
Some English spoken				Sprechen etwas Englisch	

Kårøya Fjellgard is a fine, old farm featuring log buildings with sod roofs, interior rosemaling and carvings. The newly restored log dwelling from 1809 is available for overnight visitors. Traditional mountain fare is served from the wild. The farm has been occupied since the 12th Century and remains home to a livestock operation.

Next door the community's highest mountain offers many outdoor activities.

Hosts Magna and Ola welcome you to a worthwhile experience.

Kårøyan Fjellgard er en nydelig gammel gård i laftet tømmer og med torvtak, interiør med rosemaling og utskjæringer. Den nyrestaurerte stuelåna fra 1809 er satt i stand til overnatting og servering. Her serveres det god, tradisjonsrik fjellkost, bl.a. viltretter. På gården har vært bosetning helt siden 11-1200-tallet. Den er fremdeles i full drift med mange dyr.

Som nærmest nabo rager kommunens høyeste fjell med mange muligheter for utendørs aktiviteter.

Vertskapet Magna og Ola ønsker deg velkommen til et trivelig opphold.

Kårøyan Fjellgard ist ein reizender alter Hof aus Holz (Blockbau) mit Torfdach und mit traditioneller Rosenmalerei und Schnitzereien verziertem Interieur. Das Wohnhaus von 1809 wurde für Gäste in Stand gesetzt. Hier wird gute traditionsreiche Kost, u.a. Wildgerichte, serviert. Seit dem 12./13. Jh. ist der Hof bewohnt und noch immer wird er voll bewirtschaftet. Der höchste Berg der Kommune ist gleich nebenan und bietet viele Möglichkeiten für Aktivitäten im Freien.

Die Gastgeber Magna und Ola wünschen einen angenehmen Aufenthalt!

Kleivan vekst

Your host:
Liv Aastad

Address:
**Kleivan
N - 7350 Buvika**
Mobile: **97 69 87 15**
E-mail: **post@kleivanvekst.no**
Web: **www.kleivanvekst.no**

Best time to call:
10.00 - 20.00
GPS: 63°17'56"N 10°9'33"E

Single-/double-/twin room in pilgrims' barn:		Enkelt-/dobbelt-/tosengsrom i Pilegrimslåven:		Einzel-/Doppel-/Zweibettzimmer in der Pilgerscheune:	
1 person:	**600,-**	1 person:	**600,-**	1 Person:	**600,-**
2 persons:	**1000,-**	2 personer:	**1000,-**	2 Personen:	**1000,-**
3 or more, per pers.:	**400,-**	3 eller flere, pr. pers.	**400,-**	3 oder mehr, pro Pers.:	**400,-**
No. of rooms: 4		Antall rom: 4		Anzahl Zimmer: 4	
Laid breakfast table		Dekket frokostbord		Gedeckter Frühstückstisch	
Other meals served upon request		Andre måltider ved bestilling		Andere Mahlzeiten nach Vereinb.	
Selfcatering possible		Selvhushold er mulig		Selbsthaushalt möglich	
Prices valid for 2011		Priser gyldig for 2011		Preise gültig für 2011	
Terrace/patio/yard		Terrasse/uteplass/hage		Terrasse/Außenbereich/Garten	
Open year round		Åpent hele året		Ganzjährig geöffnet	
English & some French spoken				Sprechen etwas Deutsch	

Kleivan is 25 km southwest of Trondheim. This restored cotter's farm of 1.5 acres stems from early 1800s. The property was a botanical garden whose owner Blomster-Ola had some 750 species of plantlife from arctic to tropical climes. The old barn has been restored: pilgrims' barn with busy and cozy atmosphere (1-7 pers.); former cow-barn is restored as Ola-stu (1-3 pers.). We even built a small, intimate room for 2 under the barn-bridge (Jomfruburet). Guests should take time to appreciate the property and visit the campfire and lean-to in the forest, or just feel the silence.

Kleivan ligger 25 km sør-vest for Trondheim. Stedet er en restaurert husmannsplass på 6 mål fra begynnelsen av 1800-allet. Eiendommen har vært en liten botanisk hage. Forrige eier "Blomster-Ola" hadde ca. 750 ulike arter fra arktiske og tropiske strøk. Den gamle låven er restaurert: Pilegrimslåven med trivelig og lun atmosfære (1-7 pers.). Det som tidligere var fjøs, har blitt restaurert: "Ola-stu" (1-3 pers.). Under låvebrua har vi bygd et lite, intimt rom: "Jomfruburet" med dobbeltseng. Vi setter pris på at du tar deg tid til å bli kjent med eiendommen, besøke bålplassen og gapahuken i skogen, eller bare føle stillheten.

Die restaurierte Bauernkate Kleivan aus dem frühen 19. Jh. liegt 25 km südwestl. v. Trondheim. Das Grundstück von 0,6 ha hat sich zu einem kleinen botanischen Garten gewandelt - der Vorbesitzer "Blumen- Ola" hat ca. 750 verschiedene Blumenarten zusammengetragen, von arktisch bis tropisch. Die alte Scheune ist heute eine gemütliche und lauschige Pilgerscheune für bis zu 7 Personen. Im restaurierten alten Stall "Ola-Stube" finden heute bis zu 3 Personen Platz. Das kuschelige "Jungfrauenzimmer" bietet ein Doppelbett. Lernen Sie den Hof kennen, nutzen Sie den Feuerplatz m. überdachter Sitzmöglk. im Wald oder fühlen Sie einfach die Stille.

Fjellvær Gjestegård

Your host:
Anne Brit Berg
& Asbjørn Fjeldvær

Address:
Fjellvær
N - 7242 Knarrlagsund
Phone: **72 44 01 32**
Mobile: **92 80 12 64**
E-mail: **mail@fjellvar.no**
Web: **www.fjellvar.no**

Best time to call:
10.00 - 23.00
GPS: 63°38'3"N 9°8'30"E

Stay in the farm house:
Double-/twin room: **860,-/655,-**
Single room: **655,-**
No. of rooms: 4
Discount when using own bedding
Laid breakfast table
Prices valid for 2011
TV/Internet available
Yard
Boat and bike for rent
Pets welcome
VISA, MC, Eurocard accepted
Open year round
English and some French spoken

Overnatting i våningshus:
Dobbelt-/tosengsrom: **860,-/655,-**
Enkeltrom: **655,-**
Antall rom: 4
Rabatt v/bruk av eget sengetøy
Dekket frokostbord
Priser gyldig for 2011
TV/Internett tilgjengelig
Hage
Båt- og sykkelutleie
Kjæledyr velkommen
Vi tar VISA, MC, Eurocard
Åpent hele året

Übernachtung im Wohnhaus:
Doppel-/Zweibettzi.:   **860,-/655,-**
Einzelzimmer: **655,-**
Anzahl Zimmer: 4
Rabatt bei Nutzung eig. Bettzeugs
Gedeckter Frühstückstisch
Preise gültig für 2011
TV/Internet vorhanden
Garten
Boot und Fahrrad zu mieten
Haustiere willkommen
VISA, MC, Eurocard akzept.
Ganzjährig geöffnet
Sprechen Deutsch

Fjellvær farm has been in operation since the Bronze Age. After the Reformation this was the farm of the beiliff until becoming privately owned in 1750. The Fjeldvær family has owned it since 1802.
The farm is on Fjellvær Island with view over the Trondheim sea passage. Today the island is connected to mainland via the Hitra tunnel and a bridge from Hitra to Fjellværøya. Beautiful nature from water's edge to tallest peak, all within walking distance. Abundant plant life and wide variety of birdlife.

Gården Fjellvær har vært drevet helt tilbake i bronsealderen. Etter reformasjonen var den fogdegård til den gikk over på private hender rundt 1750. Den har vært i Fjellvær- familiens eie siden 1802.
Gården ligger på Fjellværøya med utsyn over Trondheimsleia. Idag er øya landfast gjennom Hitratunnelen og bru fra Hitra til Fjellværøya.
Flott natur, fra fjære til høyeste tinde, alt innen gangavstand. Mangfoldig flora og rikt fugleliv.

Der Hof Fjellvær wurde bereits im Bronzezeitalter betrieben. Nach der Refomation war der Hof im Besitz eines Amtsrichters bis er um 1750 privatisiert wurde. Seit 1802 ist der Hof im Besitz der Familie Fjeldvær. Er liegt auf der Fjellvær Insel mit Aussicht auf die Bootspassage nach Trondheim. Heute ist die Insel zwischen dem Hitra-Tunnel und der Brücke von Hitra bis Fjellværøya mit dem Land verbunden. Es erwartet Sie eine wunderschöne Natur; vom Watt bis zum Hochgebirge, mit vielfältiger Flora und buntem Vogeltreiben - das alles ist jeweils zu Fuss erreichbar.

Stay in cabins:	Overnatting i hytter:	Übernachtung in Hütten:
Cabins with 1-2 and 4 bedrooms	Hytter med 1-2 og 4 soverom	Hütten mit 1-2 und 4 Schlafzi.
Own bath, kitchen nook, LR	Eget bad, kjk.-krok, stue	Eig. Bad, Küchenecke, Stube
Whole unit: from **700,-** to **1900,-**	Hel enhet: fra **700,-** til **1900,-**	Ganze Einheit: ab **700,-** bis **1900,-**
Bed linen fee: **100,-**	Tillegg for sengetøy: **100,-**	Mieten von Bettwäsche: **100,-**
Breakfast service available: **105,-**	Frokost kan serveres: **105,-**	Frühstück auf Bestellung: **105,-**
Prices valid for 2011	Priser gyldig for 2011	Preise gültig für 2011
TV available	TV tilgjengelig	TV vorhanden
Terrace/patio/yard	Terrasse/hage/uteplass	Terrasse/Garten/Außenbereich
Boat and bike for rent	Båt- og sykkelutleie	Boot und Fahrrad zu mieten
Pets welcome	Kjæledyr velkommen	Haustiere willkommen
VISA, MC, Eurocard accepted	Vi tar VISA, MC, Eurocard	VISA, MC, Eurocard akzept.
Open year round	Åpent hele året	Ganzjährig geöffnet
English and some French spoken		Sprechen Deutsch

If we would only give, just once, the same amount of reflection to
what we want to get out of life that we give to the question of
what to do with a two weeks' vacation,
we would be startled at our false standards
and the aimless procession of our busy days.
~Dorothy Canfield Fisher~

Heidi Hansen

Your host:
Heidi Hansen

Address:
Pottemakerveien 25
N - 7048 Trondheim
Phone: 73 91 44 59
Mobile: 48 03 37 50
E-mail: hms@instituttet.no

Best time to call:
07.00 - 23.00 (mobile)
GPS: 63°25'15"N 10°26'21"E

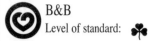

Fam.room: **600,-/650,-/750,-** bunk bed for 3, own bath	Familierom: **600,-/650,-/750,-** familiekøye, eget bad	Familienzi. **600,-/650,-/750,-** Doppelstockb. f. 3 Pers., eig. Bad
Double room: **500,-/600,-**	Dobbeltrom: **500,-/600,-**	Doppelzi.: **500,-/600,-**
Twin room: **350,-/450,-** 1 sigl. bed, 1 bed on loft	Tosengsrom: **350,-/450,-** 1 enkeltseng, 1 seng på hems	Zweibettzi.: **350,-/450,-** 1 Einzelb., 1 Bett auf Schlafboden
No. of rooms: 3	Antall rom: 3	Anzahl Zimmer: 3
Children under 12 yrs. for free	Barn under 12 år fri	Kinder unter 12 Jahren frei
Other meals available	Andre måltider på forespørsel	Andere Mahlzeiten auf Anfrage
Selfcatering possible	Selvhushold er mulig	Selbstverpflegung möglich
Prices valid for 2011	Priser gyldig for 2011	Preise gültig für 2011
TV/Internet available	TV/Internett tilgjengelig	TV/Internet vorhanden
Terrace/patio/yard	Terrasse/uteplass/hage	Terrasse/Außenbereich/Garten
Bike for rent	Sykkelutleie	Fahrrad zu mieten
Open year round	Åpent hele året	Ganzjährig geöffnet
English and French spoken		Sprechen Deutsch

At Tyhold the host, Heidi Hansen, rents out two rooms in her home where she lives with her child aged 11. The house is 300 m east of a local landmark, the TV tower at Tyholt. The restaurant at the top of the tower offers a fantastic view in all directions. It's 2,5 km walk to Nidaros Cathedral and Trondheim center.
The host can organize guided tours and mountain hikes with accommodations in tourist cabins.

På Tyholt leier vertinnen Heidi Hansen ut to rom i huset sitt, hvor hun bor sammen med ett barn på 11 år. Huset ligger 300 m øst for TV-tårnet som er et kjent landemerke. Restauranten i toppen av tårnet gir en fantastisk utsikt 360 grader. Det er 2,5 km å gå til Nidarosdomen og Trondheim sentrum. Vertinnen kan organisere guiding og fjellturer med overnatting i turisthytter på forespørsel.

In Tyholt vermietet Heidi Hansen zwei Zimmer in ihrem Haus, wo sie zusammen mit ihrem 11-jährigen Kind lebt. Das Haus liegt 300 m östlich des Tyholter Fernsehturms. Das Restaurant oben im Turm gibt eine fantastische Rundumsicht. Es sind 2,5 km zu Fuß bis zum Nidarosdom und dem Trondheimer Zentrum. Die Gastgeberin kann auf Anfrage Führungen und Bergtouren mit Übernachtung in Touristenhütten organisieren.

Rom Trondheim, Møllenberg

Your host:
Knut Nilsen Fosland

Address:
Øvre Møllenberggate 43 F
N - 7014 Trondheim
Mobile: 92 03 22 38 / 92 03 22 40
E-mail: nilfo@online.no
Web: www.sykkelguide.com

Best time to call:
07.00 - 23.00
GPS: 63°25'50"N 10°24'50"E

Double room:	600,-	Dobbeltrom:	600,-	Doppelzi.:	600,-
Single room:	350,-	Enkeltrom:	350,-	Einzelzi.:	350,-
Shared bath/TV-room w/kitchen		Delt bad/TV-rom m/kjøkkenkrok		Gem. Bad/TV-Raum m. kl. Küche	
No. of rooms: 3		Antall rom: 3		Anzahl Zimmer: 3	
Bed linen included		Sengetøy er inkludert		Inkl. Bettwäsche	
Breakfast service available:	80,-	Frokost kan serveres:	80,-	Frühstück auf Bestellung:	80,-
Prices valid for 2011/12/13		Priser gyldig for 2011/12/13		Preise gültig für 2011/12/13	
TV/Internet available		TV/Internett tilgjengelig		TV/Internet vorhanden	
Terrace/patio		Terrasse/uteplass		Terrasse/Außenbereich	
Bike for rent		Sykkelutleie		Fahrrad zu mieten	
Pets welcome		Kjæledyr velkommen		Haustiere willkommen	
Open 15 June - 25 Aug.		Åpent 15. juni - 25. aug.		Geöffnet 15. Juni - 25. Aug.	
English spoken				Sprechen etwas Deutsch	

Here are three rooms with a simple standard available in a house in the Møllenberg neighborhood near Trondheim center. Parking on the property. The owner can also offer travelers alternative apartments in Trondheim, and rental rooms in Røros and on the coast by Hitra. At Røros it's great to go mountain hiking or canoeing. Near Hitra it's ideal for fishing.

I en villa i bydelen Møllenberg, nær Trondheim sentrum, leies tre rom ut med enkel standard. Parkering på eiendommen. Verten kan også tilby reisende rom i andre leiligheter i Trondheim og utleierom på Røros og på kysten ved Hitra. På Røros er det fint å dra på fjellturer eller kanoturer. Ved Hitra er det ideelt for sjøfiske.

Im Stadtteil Møllenberg, in der Nähe vom Trondheimer Zentrum, vermietet Ihr Gastgeber Knut in seiner Villa drei Zimmer mit einfachem Standard. Parkmöglichkeiten sind auf dem Grundstück vorhanden. Knut kann Sie auch in weiteren Zimmern in Trondheim unterbringen und Ihnen Zimmer in Røros und an der Küste von Hitra vermitteln. Von Røros aus kann man in die Berge fahren oder Kanutouren unternehmen. In Hitra gibt es sehr gute Angelmöglichkeiten.

Adopt the pace of nature: her secret is patience. ~Ralph Waldo Emerson~

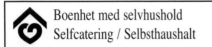
Åse's Romutleie

Your host:
Åse L. Andersen

Address:
Nedre Møllenberggaten 27
N - 7014 Trondheim
Phone: 73 51 15 40
Mobile: 41 20 86 50
E-mail: aaseander@hotmail.com

Best time to call:
08.30 - 22.00
GPS: 63°25'51"N 10°24'36"E

A: Apartment for up to 8 pers.:
No. of rooms: 4.
Shared: 2 baths, kitchen, DR, LR

Double room:	**440,-/450,-**
Twin room:	**400,-/420,-**
1 pers. in dbl. room:	**350,-**

Baby free

B: Apartment for 2-4 persons
Bath, kitchen, LR, sleeping alcove

Price per pers.:	**250,-**
Children, 7-16 years:	**50,-**

Applies to all rental units:
Bed linen fee, per night: **50,-**
Prices valid for 2011/12
TV/Internet available
Washer and dryer
Terrace
Pets welcome
2 parking spots available
Open 20 June - 25 Aug.
English spoken

In old town area and featuring renovated or newly built houses in the "Møllenberg" style. Many cozy cafés and restaurants nearby. Most of Trondheim's attractions are within walking distance.

A: Leilighet for opp til 8 pers.:
Antall rom: 4
Deles: 2 bad, spisestue, stue, kjk.

Dobbeltrom:	**440,-/450,-**
Tosengsrom:	**400,-/420,-**
1 pers. i dobbeltrom:	**350,-**

Baby gratis

B: Leilighet for 2-4 personer
Bad, kjøkken, stue, sovealkove

Pris pr. person:	**250,-**
Barn, 7-16 år:	**50,-**

For alle enhetene gjelder:
Leie av sengetøy, pr. natt: **50,-**
Priser gyldig for 2011/12
TV/Internett tilgjengelig
Vaskemaskin og tørketrommel
Terrasse
Kjæledyr velkommen
2 P-plasser på gårdsplass
Åpent 20. juni - 25. aug.

I gammel bydel med rehabiliterte eller nybygde hus i møllenbergstil. Mange hyggelige kaféer og restauranter i bydelen. De fleste av Trondheims severdigheter ligger i gangavstand.

A: Wohnung bis zu 8 Pers.:
Anzahl Zimmer: 4
Gemeins.: 2 Bäder, Küche, Stube

Doppelzimmer:	**440,-/450,-**
Zweibettzimmer:	**400,-/420,-**
1 Pers. im DZ.:	**350,-**

Baby gratis

B: Wohnung für 2-4 Personen
Bad, Küche, Stube, Bettnische

Preis pro Pers.:	**250,-**
Kinder, 7-16 Jahre:	**50,-**

Für alle Einheiten gilt:
Mieten von Bettw., pro Nacht: **50,-**
Preise gültig für 2011/12
TV/Internet verfügbar
Waschmaschine u. Trockner
Terrasse
Haustiere willkommen
2 Parkplätze auf dem Innenhof
Geöffnet 20. Juni - 25. Aug.
Sprechen etwas Deutsch

Reizvolle Lage in der Altstadt mit sanierten Gebäuden im Møllenberg-Stil. In der Nähe viele gemütliche Cafés und Restaurants. Die meisten Sehenswürdigkeiten Trondheims sind zu Fuß zu erreichen.

Klostergården

Your host:
Mona Lindsted &
Ståle Harald Anderssen

Address:
Tautra-Nordre
N - 7633 Frosta
Phone: 74 80 85 33
E-mail: staaa@online.no

Best time to call:
08.00 - 23.00
GPS: 63°35'1"N 10°37'22"E

Double room:	900,-	Dobbeltrom:	900,-	Doppelzimmer:	900,-
Single room:	550,-	Enkeltrom:	550,-	Einzelzimmer:	550,-

No. of rooms: 10
Laid breakfast table or buffet
Prices valid for 2010
Ask for updated prices
TV/Internet available
Terrace/patio/yard
Suitable for handicapped
Pets welcome by agreement
VISA, MC, DC, AmEx accepted
Open February - December
English spoken

Antall rom: 10
Dekket frokostbord el buffét
Priser gyldig for 2010
Spør om oppdatert pris
TV/Internett tilgjengelig
Terrasse/uteplass/hage
Handikaptilgjengelig
Kjæledyr velkommen etter avtale
Vi tar VISA, MC, DC, AmEx
Åpent februar - desember

Anzahl Zimmer: 10
Ged. Frühstückstisch o -büfett
Preise gültig für 2010
Aktuelle Preise: anfragen
TV/Internet vorhanden
Terrasse/Außenbereich/Garten
Behindertengerecht
Haustiere nach Absprache willk.
Wir akzept. VISA, MC, DC, AmEx
Geöffnet Februar - Dezember
Sprechen etwas Deutsch

Klostergården is situated at Tautra, next to the ruins of the old Cistercian cloister from 1207, a distinctive landmark in Trondheim fjord. Klostergården offers experiences related to nature, climate, flora and fauna--not to mention history and culture. The old main building from before 1800 was built with stones from the cloister. It's been restored and now contains a cafeteria/restaurant and boarding house. At Klostergården smithy you'll find for sale local farm-fresh foods and a big selection of craft-works.
Welcome to a satisfying visit to Klostergården.

Klostergården ligger på Tautra, like ved ruinene til det gamle cisterci-enserklosteret fra år 1207, et sær-preget landmerke i Trondheims-fjorden. Klostergården kan tilby opplevelser knyttet til natur, klima, flora, fauna og ikke minst historie og kultur. Den gamle hovedbyg-ningen fra før 1800 er bygd av stein fra klosteret. Denne er restau-rert og rommer kafeteria/restaurant og pensjonat. Her er også salg av egenproduserte gårdsmatprodukter og et stort utvalg av handverkspro-dukter i Klostergårdssmia.
Velkommen til et hyggelig besøk på Klostergården.

Klostergården liegt auf der Insel Tautra, gleich neben den Ruinen des alten Zisterzienserklosters aus dem Jahr 1207 - eine besondere Landmarke im Trondheimsfjord. Klostergården bietet vielerlei Erlebnisse verbunden mit Natur, Klima, Flora, Fauna und nicht zuletzt mit Geschichte und Kultur. Das alte Haupthaus von vor 1800 ist aus den Steinen des Klosters gebaut. Es ist restauriert und beher-bergt die Cafeteria/das Restaurant sowie die Pension. Lebensmittel vom eigenen Hof und vielerlei Handwerksprodukte aus der Kloster-hofschmiede können gekauft wer-den. Willkommen zu einem gemüt-lichen Aufenthalt im Klostergården.

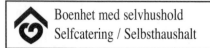
Karmhus / Trøabakken

Your host:
Sigrun & Per Storholmen

Address:
Karmhusveien 20
N - 7650 Verdal
Phone: 74 04 24 69
Mobile: 95 05 88 02 / 96 50 02 28
E-mail: per-storholmen@online.no

Best time to call:
07.00 - 09.00 / 16.00 - 23.00
GPS: 63°50'8"N 11°39'50"E

Apartment for 2-6 persons	Leilighet for 2-6 personer	Wohnung für 2-6 Personen
2 bedrooms, bath, kitchenette, LR	2 soverom, bad, tekjøkken, stue	2 Schlafzi. Bad, kl. Küche, Stube
Price for whole unit: **600,-**	Pris for hele enheten: **600,-**	Ganze Einheit: **600,-**
Min. price per pers.: **200,-**	Min. pris pr. pers.: **200,-**	Mindestpreis pro Pers.: **200,-**
Bed linen included	Sengetøy er inkludert	Inkl. Bettwäsche
Breakfast service available: **60,-**	Frokost kan serveres: **60,-**	Frühstück auf Bestellung: **60,-**
Prices valid for 2011/12/13	Priser gyldig for 2011/12/13	Preise gültig für 2011/12/13
TV available	TV tilgjengelig	TV vorhanden
Yard/garden	Hage	Garten
Boat and bike for rent	Båt- og sykkelutleie	Boot u. Fahrrad zu mieten
Open year round	Åpent hele året	Ganzjährig geöffnet
Some English spoken		Sprechen etwas Deutsch

Trøabakken is in Leksdal, in the northeastern part of Verdal, about 8 km from Stiklestad which is known for its history of kings. Summer tourist activities in Stiklestad are visits to the church, museum, cultural center, the Olsok play, historical tours, and concerts. There is commercial salmon fishing in the Verdal River, with a salmon ladder and a salmon studio. The Leksdal Lake provides good fishing both summer and winter, and a boat can be provided.

Leksdal, hvor man finner Trøabakken, ligger i nord-østre del av Verdal, ca. 8 km fra Stiklestad som er kjent for sin kongehistorie. Aktuelle turistaktiviteter på Stiklestad sommerstid er; besøk ved kirken, museet, kulturhuset, Olsokspelet, historiske turer, konserter. I Verdalselva drives det laksefiske, der er laksetrapp med laksestudio. På Leksdalsvatnet kan man fiske både sommer og vinter, båt kan skaffes til veie.

Trøabakken liegt im Ort Leksdal, im nordöstlichen Teil der Kommune Verdal, etwa 8 km vom historischen Ort Stiklestad entfernt. Stiklestad bietet im Sommer: Besuch der alten Kirche, des Museums und Kulturhauses, das Spiel vom Hl. Olav, historische Wanderungen und Konzerte. Verdalselva heisst der bekannte Lachsfluss mit Lachstreppe und Lachsstudio. Im Leksdalsee kann man Sommer wie Winter Angeln. Boot kann besorgt werden.

A vacation is what you take when you can no longer take what you've been taking. ~Earl Wilson~

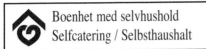
Fiskebrygga

Your host:
Marit Swensen

Address:
N - 8158 Bolga
Phone: 75 75 10 13
Mobile: 47 90 92 21
E-mail: bolgamarit@hotmail.com

Best time to call:
08.00 - 17.00
GPS: 66°80'35"N 13°23'43"E

Multibedded room for up to 7 p.:	Flersengsrom for opp til 7 pers.:	Mehrbettzi. für bis zu 7 Pers.:
1-2 persons: **600,-**	1-2 personer: **600,-**	1-2 Pers.: **600,-**
7 persons: **1200,-**	7 personer: **1200,-**	7 Pers.: **1200,-**
No. of rooms: 2	Antall rom: 2	Anzahl Zimmer: 2
Shared bath, kitchen, LR	Delt bad, kjøkken, stue	Gemeins.Bad, Küche, Stube
Disposable bed linen included	Engangssengetøy er inkludert	Einmalbettwäsche inklusive
Prices valid for 2011	Priser gyldig for 2011	Preise gültig für 2011
Outdoor furniture on the quay	Uteplass på kaia	Außenbereich am Kai
Boat and kayak for rent	Båt- og kajakutleie	Boot und Kajak zu mieten
Introduction course in kayaking	Introduksjonskurs i havpadling	Einführungskurs im Seekajakfahren
Open year round	Åpent hele året	Ganzjährig geöffnet
English, French, Spanish spoken		Sprechen etwas Deutsch

Bolga is a small island with 100 residents a couple hours by ferry south of Bodø.
Fiskebrygga (Fish harbor) lies right on the wharf at Bolga. Good for hiking, boating and kayaking. Bolga is surrounded by 300 smaller islands. In the summer a tavern is opened; fully licensed.

Directions:
From the south: From Mo i Rana take RV 12 to Fallet, continue on RV 17 to Ørnes (via 2 ferries), boat goes from Ørnes to Meløya and Bolga.
From north: RV 17 to Ørnes and continue by boat.

Bolga er et lite øysamfunn med 100 beboere, et par timer med hurtigbåt sør for Bodø.
Fiskebrygga ligger sentralt på kaia på Bolga. Her finner du flotte turmuligheter både til fots, i båt og i kajak. Bolga er omgitt av 300 mindre øyer. På sommeren er her en kro som holder åpent med alle rettigheter.

Veibeskrivelse:
Fra sør: Fra Mo i Rana RV 12 til Fallet; videre RV 17 til Ørnes (inkluderer 2 ferger); båt går fra Ørnes til Meløya og Bolga.
Fra nord: RV 17 til Ørnes og så videre med båt.

Bolga ist eine kleine Inselgemeinde mit 100 Bewohnern, mit dem Schnellboot ein paar Stunden südlich von Bodø.
Fiskebrygga liegt direkt am Kai von Bolga. Hier sind tolle Ausflüge zu Fuß, mit dem Boot oder Kajak möglich. Bolga ist umgeben von 300 kleineren Inseln. Im Sommer ist das Gasthaus der Insel geöffnet; alle Schankrechte.

Wegbeschreibung:
Von Süden: Ab Mo i Rana Str. 12 nach Fallet; weiter auf Str. 17 nach Ørnes (2 Fähren auf diesem Weg); ab Ørnes geht ein Boot auf die Inseln Meløya und Bolga.
Von Norden: Str. 17 bis Ørnes und dann weiter mit dem Boot

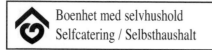

Gunnhilds overnatting

Your host:
Gunnhild Rendahl

Address:
Brekkanveien 14
N - 8150 Ørnes
Phone: 75 75 42 62
Mobile: 90 55 80 91

Best time to call:
09.00 - 22.00
GPS: 60°51'21"N 13°43'51"E

Double room:	**550,-**	Dobbeltrom:	**550,-**	Dobbelzimmer:	**550,-**
Single room:	**400,-**	Enkeltrom:	**400,-**	Einzelzimmer:	**400,-**
Bed linen included		Sengetøy er inkludert		Inkl. Bettwäsche	
Shared bath		Delt bad		Gemeins.Bad	
No breakfast, priv. kitchen available		Ikke frokost, priv.kjk. kan benyttes		Kein Frühstück; Küche zur Verfüg.	
Prices valid for 2011		Priser gyldig for 2011		Preise gültig für 2011	
Terrace/deck		Terrasse/uteplass		Terrasse/Außenbereich	
Open year round		Åpent hele året		Ganzjährig geöffnet	
Some English understood				Verstehen etwas Englisch	

Directions:
The place is called Spildra, the house is along RV 17 and 3 km from Ørsnes center.

Veibeskrivelse:
Plassen heter Spildra, huset ligger langs RV 17 og 3 km fra Ørsnes sentrum.

Wegbeschreibung:
Der Ort heißt Spildra; das Haus liegt entlang der Str. 17 und 3 km von Ørsnes Zentrum entfernt.

Ørsnes is harbour for Hurtigruten.   Ørsnes er havn for Hurtigruten.   Ørsnes ist ein Hafen d. Hurtigruten.

Nature does not hurry, yet everything is accomplished.
~Lao Tzu~

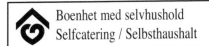

Kjerringøy prestegård

Your host:
Hans Nilsen

Address:
N - 8093 Kjerringøy
Phone: 75 51 11 14
Mobile: 99 53 69 56
prestegarden@kirken.bodo.no
www.kjerringoy.info/index.php
?id=58
Best time to call: 09.00 - 23.00
GPS: 67°52'12"N 14°77'67"E

The main house:		Hovedhuset:		Das Haupthaus:	
Dorm-style room for 4-6 persons		Flersengsrom til 4-6 personer		Mehrbettzi. für 4-6 Pers.	
Price per room:	**500,-**	Pris pr. rom:	**500,-**	Preis pro Zi.:	**500,-**
Price for 1 person.:	**290,-**	Pris for 1 pers.:	**290,-**	Preis für 1 Pers.:	**290,-**

The barn:		Fjøset:		Der Stall:	
Twin room, per room:	**500,-**	Tosengsrom, pris pr. rom:	**500,-**	Zweibettzi., Preis pro Zi.:	**500,-**

For all rooms apply:		For alle rom gjelder:		Für alle Zimmer gilt:	
Shared bath, kitchen, DR and LR		Delt bad, kjøkken, sp.stue og stue		Gemeins. Bad, Küche, Esszi.,Stube	
Bed linen fee:	**90,-**	Tillegg for sengetøy:	**90,-**	Mieten von Bettwäsche:	**90,-**
Discount for children		Rabatt for barn		Ermäßigung für Kinder	
Prices valid for 2011		Priser gyldig for 2011		Preise gültig für 2011	
TV available		TV tilgjengelig		TV vorhanden	
Terrace/deck/yard		Terrasse/uteplass/hage		Terrasse/Außenbereich/Garten	
Boat & bike for rent locally		Båt- og sykkelutleie i området		Boot u. Fahrrad zu mieten	
Suitable for handicapped		Handikapvennlig		Behindertengerecht	
Pets welcome		Kjæledyr velkommen		Haustiere willkommen	
Open year round		Åpent hele året		Ganzjährig geöffnet	
Some English spoken				Sprechen etwas Englisch	

Kjerringøy, an old priest's farm, is walking distance to the renowned old mercantile site and church at Kjerringøy. The church dates from the 1500s. Natural paradise of mountains and tidelands in close proximity.

Directions:
From Bodø: 40 km along RV 834, includes 1 ferry.

Kjerringøy gamle prestegård ligger i gangavstand til det kjente, gamle handelsstedet og kirken på Kjerringøy. Kirken har sin historie tilbake til 1500-tallet. I umiddelbar nærhet ligger også et eldorado av fjell og fjære med rike muligheter for store naturopplevelser.

Veibeskrivelse:
Fra Bodø: 40 km langs RV 834 (inkluderer 1 ferge).

Der alte Pfarrhof Kjerringøy liegt einen kurzen Fußweg von der bekannten alten Handelsstätte und der Kirche entfernt. Die Geschichte der Kirche reicht bis ins 16. Jh. zurück. Die Berge und das Watt in unmittelbarer Umgebung bieten große Naturerlebnisse.

Wegbeschreibung:
40 km entlang der Str. 834 von Bodø (1 Fähre auf der Strecke).

Norumgården
Bed & Beakfast

Your host:
Marit & Tor Mikalsen

Address:
Framnesveien 127
N - 8516 Narvik
Phone/Fax: 76 94 48 57
Mobile: 97 50 59 70
http://norumgaarden.narviknett.no

Best time to call:
08.00 - 12.00 / 17.00 - 22.00
GPS: 68°26'15"N 17°24'19"E

Double room:	600,-/700,-	Dobbeltrom:	600,-/700,-	Doppelzimmer:	600,-/700,-
Single room:	450,-	Enkeltrom:	450,-	Einzelzimmer:	450,-
1 pers. in dbl. room:	500,-	1 pers. i dobbeltrom:	500,-	1 Pers. im Doppelzi.:	500,-
No. of rooms: 4		Antall rom: 4		Anzahl Zimmer: 4	
Discount for children		Rabatt for barn		Ermäßigung für Kinder	
Laid breakfast table		Dekket frokostbord		Gedeckter Frühstückstisch	
Selfcatering possible		Selvhushold mulig		Selbstverpflegung möglich	
Prices valid for 2011/12/13		Priser gyldig for 2011/12/13		Preise gültig für 2011/12/13	
TV/radio in all rooms		TV/radio på alle rom		TV/Radio in allen Zimmern	
Terrace/patio/yard		Terasse/uteplass/hage		Terrasse/Außenbereich/Garten	
White bathrobes in all rooms		Hvite morgenkåper på alle rom		Bademäntel auf allen Zimmern	
Open year round		Åpent hele året		Ganzjährig geöffnet	
English spoken				Sprechen etwas Deutsch	

Norumgården was named after the master builder who erected it in 1925. 15 years of restoration have brought the building back to its original splendour. The restoration work has brought the owners several prizes. The house also has period furniture. Antique shop on premises.

The Norumgården is a 15 minutes walk from the town centre.
Narvik is best known for its war history, but can also offer skiing, sea fishing and hiking in the summer.

Norumgården har sitt navn etter byggmesteren som bygget huset i 1925. De siste 15 års restaurering har brakt det tilbake til sin fordums prakt. Restaureringsarbeidet har medført at eierne er tildelt flere priser. Huset er innredet med tidsriktige møbler. Egen antikvitetsbutikk.

Norumgården ligger 15 min. gange fra Narvik sentrum. Narvik, mest kjent for sin krigshistorie, tilbyr også skisport, fjordfiske og turmuligheter.

Das Haus aus 1925 ist nach dem Baumeister benannt. Nach 15 Jahren Restaurierung ersteht es nun mit zeitgerechtem Interieur in seinem ehemaligen Glanz, was den Besitzern mehrere Preise eingebracht hat. Eigener Antiquitätenladen.

15 Min. zu Fuss zum Zentrum von Narvik, bekannt für seine Kriegsgeschichte. Reiche Möglichkeiten für Angeln und Wandern im Sommer, sowie für Skisport im Winter.

Nature is my medicine. ~Sara Moss-Wolfe~

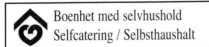
Nordbua

Your host:
Unni & Jan E. Horn

Address:
Rishaugveien 3
N - 8340 Stamsund
Phone: **76 08 91 85**
Mobil: **95 72 95 88 / 90 97 42 61**
E-mail: **uhorn@frisurf.no**

Best time to call:
18.00 - 22.00
GPS: 68°08'13"N 13°50'12"E

Guesthouse for 2-8 pers.	Gjestehus for 2-8 pers.	Gästehaus für 2-8 Pers.
No. of bedrooms: 4	Antall soverom: 4	Anzahl Schlafzimmer: 4
Own bath, LR w/kitchen	Eget bad, stue m/kjk.krok	Eig. Bad, Stube mit Küche.
Price for whole unit: **1000,-**	Pris for hele enheten: **1000,-**	Ganze Einheit: **1000,-**
Bed linen fee: **100,-**	Tillegg for sengetøy: **100,-**	Mieten von Bettw.: **100,-**
Prices valid for 2011/12/13	Priser gyldig for 2011/12/13	Preise gültig für 2011/12/13
TV available	TV tilgjengelig	TV vorhanden
Terrace	Terrasse	Terrasse
Discount off-season	Rabatt utenom sesong	Ermäßigung in der Nebensaison
Open year round	Åpent hele året	Ganzjährig geöffnet
Some English spoken		Sprechen etwas Deutsch

Stamsund has grand scenery, towering mountains, rich birdlife and good fishing. Midnight sun and dark days, too, depending on the time of year. Nordbua is centrally located in Stamsund.
Freezer space and fish-cleaning facilities are available as well, making this a good holiday for fishing enthusiasts. The best times of year are May - September, and during the traditional Lofoten fishing season from 15 February until 15 April when there are less tourists.

I Stamsund er det flott natur, høye, bratte fjell, fugleliv og fiske. Det er midnattsol og mørketid, alt etter årstiden. Nordbua ligger sentralt i Stamsund.
Gjester har tilgang til fryseboks og rom for sløying av fisk. Her ligger alt til rette for den ivrigste feriefiskeren.
Den beste sesongen er mai - september, samt fra 15. februar til 15. april under Lofotfisket, da er her mindre turister enn i sommermånedene.

Stamsund ist ein Ort mit prachtvoller Landschaft, hohen, steilen Bergen, einem reichen Vogelleben und ideal zum Angeln. Erleben Sie je nach Jahreszeit Mitternachtssonne oder Polarnacht. Nordbua liegt zentral in Stamsund. Für den eifrigen Freizeitangler liegt hier alles parat. Ein Tiefkühler u. ein Raum zum Fischeausnehmen stehen zur Verfügung.
Die beste Saison ist Mai - September, sowie vom 15. Februar bis 15. April, wo die bekannte Lofotfischerei stattfindet und weniger Touristen als im Sommer da sind.

How glorious a greeting the sun gives the mountains!
~John Muir~

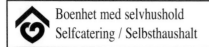
Marja-Liisas overnatting

Your host:
Marja-Liisa Martinsen

Address:
Vestpollen
N - 8316 Laupstad
Phone: 76 07 58 13
Mobile: 41 20 74 14
E-mail: marliimar@yahoo.no

Best time to call:
10.00 - 18.00
GPS: 68°19'43"N 14°41'25"E

Apartment for 2-7 persons	Leilighet for 2-7 personer	Wohnung für 2-7 Personen
1 bedroom + sleeping alcove	1 soverom + sovealkove	1 Schlafzimmer + Schlafnische
Own bath, kitchen, LR	Eget bad, kjøkken, stue	Eigenes Bad, Küche, Stube
Price for whole unit: **1000,-**	Pris for hele enheten: **1000,-**	Ganze Einheit: **1000,-**
Price per pers.: **250,-**	Pris pr. pers.: **250,-**	Preis pro Pers.: **250,-**
Bed linen included	Sengetøy er inkludert	Inkl. Bettwäsche
Breakfast service available: **60,-**	Frokost kan serveres: **60,-**	Frühstück auf Bestellung: **60,-**
Discount for children	Rabatt for barn	Ermäßigung für Kinder
Prices valid for 2011/12	Priser gyldig for 2011/12	Preise gültig für 2011/12
TV available	TV tilgjengelig	TV vorhanden
Terrace/patio	Terrasse/uteplass	Terrasse/Außenbereich
Suitable for handicapped	Handikaptilgjengelig	Behindertengerecht
Open year round	Åpent hele året	Ganzjährig geöffnet
English & Finnish spoken	Snakker finsk og norsk	Sprechen Englisch u. Finnisch

Marja-Liisa is Finnish and invites guests to her home at Austnesfjorden in the eastern part of Lofoten. The settlement is surrounded by natural beauty.
One can see the highest peaks of Lofoten. It's a short way to Svolvær and Kabelvåg with many activities to choose from.

Directions:
From Svolvær follow the E-10 north and east about 17 km. to Vestpollen. Continue on E-10, 200 m. after the sign Laukvik. Find house on the left.

Marja-Liisa er finsk og inviterer gjester til sitt hjem ved Austnesfjorden i østre del av Lofoten. Bygda ligger i naturskjønne omgivelser. Man kan se de høyeste fjelltoppene i Lofoten. Det er kort vei til Svolvær og Kabelvåg med mange tilbud og aktiviteter.

Veibeskrivelse:
Fra Svolvær følg E-10 nord- og østover i ca. 17 km til Vestpollen. Fortsett på E-10; 200 m forbi skiltet mot Laukvik finner du huset på venstre side.

Marja-Liisa ist Finnin und lädt ihre Gäste in ihr Haus am Austnes Fjord im östlichen Teil der Lofoten ein. Von dort können Sie den Blick auf die höchsten Bergspitzen der Lofoten geniessen. Das Dorf liegt inmitten schöner Natur. Kurzer Weg bis Svolvær und Kabelvåg mit vielen Angeboten und Aktivitäten.

Wegbeschreibung:
Von Svolvær der E-10 nord- und ostwärts für ca. 17 km bis Vestpollen folgen. Weiter auf der E-10; Vorbei am Schild Ri. Laukvik befindet sich das Haus nach 200 m auf der linken Seite.

Holmvik Brygge

Your host:
Ssemjon Gerlitz

Address:
**Postboks 338 Nyksund
N - 8439 Myre**
Phone: **76 13 47 96**
Mobile: **95 86 38 66**
E-mail: **post@nyksund.com**
Web: **www.nyksund.com**

Best time to call:
12.00 - 22.00
GPS: **68°59'43"N 15°00'38"E**

Double-/twin room:	**800,-**	Dobbelt-/tosengsrom:	**800,-**	Doppel-/Zweibettzi.:	**800,-**
Single room:	**520,-**	Enkeltrom:	**520,-**	Einzelzimmer:	**520,-**
No. of rooms: 9		Antall rom: 9		Anzahl Zimmer: 9	
Discount for children		Rabatt for barn		Ermäßigung für Kinder	
Laid breakfast table		Dekket frokostbord		Gedeckt. Frühstückstisch	
Selfcatering possible		Selvhushold er mulig		Selbstverpflegung möglich	
Prices valid for 2011/12/13		Priser gyldig for 2011/12/13		Preise gültig für 2011/12/13	
Terrace/patio/yard		Terrasse/uteplass/hage		Terrasse/Außenbereich/Garten	
Pets welcome		Kjæledyr velkommen		Haustiere willkommen	
VISA, MC accepted		Vi tar VISA, MC		Wir akzeptieren VISA, MC	
Open year round		Åpent hele året		Ganzjährig geöffnet	
English spoken				Sprechen Deutsch	

Holmvik Brygge, which lies in the harbor area of Nyksund, is a living museum where our guests experience how fishermen lived here more than 100 years ago. Besides the rooms we rent out there is a common room and cozy kitchen. It's possible to meet other guests in home-style surroundings. In the fall you can enjoy long mountain hikes, finding mushrooms and berries to pick. In the winter most guests enjoy crisp cold evenings under starry skies and northern lights. In spring it's time for ice fishing, spying animals and walks in snowy terrain. Get excited by the beautiful nature regardless of season!

Holmvik Brygge, som ligger i havneområdet i Nyksund, er et levende museum hvor våre gjester får en opplevelse av hvordan fiskere levde her for over 100 år siden. I tillegg til rommene vi leier ut, finnes også flere fellesrom og et koselig kjøkken. Her er det mulig å møte andre gjester i hjemmekoselige omgivelser. Om høsten kan du nyte lange fjellturer, sanke sopp eller plukke bær. Om vinteren kommer de fleste gjester hit for å oppleve klare kalde kvelder med stjernestrødd himmel og flammende nordlys. Om våren er det tid for isfiske, dyreobservasjoner og turer i snølagt terreng. La deg begeistre av den vakre naturen, uansett årstid!

Holmvik Brygge, das sich direkt im Hafen Nyksunds befindet, ist ein lebendes Museum, das Sie in das Fischerleben von vor über 100 Jahren zurückführt. Zusätzlich zu den Zimmern gibt es noch mehrere Gemeinschaftsräume sowie eine Küche. Hier können Sie in urgemütlicher Atmosphäre andere Leute treffen. Der Herbst eignet sich um lange Bergtouren zu machen und Pilze u. Beeren zu sammeln. Im Winter können Sie sternenklare kalte Nächte mit flammenden Nordlichtern erleben. Der Frühling ist die beste Zeit zum Eisfischen, für Tierbeobachtungen und Touren über schneebedecktes Gelände. Die Natur verzaubert Sie hier zu jeder Jahreszeit.

Fargeklatten Veita Gjestehus

Your host:
Grethe Kvalvik

Address:
Sjøgata 38A
N - 8480 Andenes
Mobile: 97 76 00 20
E-mail: post@fargeklatten.no
Web: www.fargeklatten.no

Best time to call:
08.00 - 23.00
GPS: 69°19'17"N 16°7'38"E

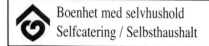

Familyroom for 4 pers.:	**1100,-**	Familierom for 4 pers.:	**1100,-**	Familienzi. für 4 Pers.:	**1100,-**
Double room:	**800,-**	Dobbeltrom:	**800,-**	Doppelzimmer:	**800,-**
Single room:	**600,-**	Enkeltrom:	**600,-**	Einzelzimmer:	**600,-**

No. of rooms: 4
Bed linen included
Breakfast in a bakery close by
Prices valid for 2011
TV/Internet available
Terrace/patio/yard
Boat and bike available for rent
Open year round
English spoken

Antall rom: 4
Sengetøy er inkludert
Frokost i bakeri like ved
Priser gyldig for 2011
TV/Internett tilgjengelig
Terrasse/uteplass/hage
Båt- og sykkelutleie er mulig
Åpent hele året

Inkl. Bettwäsche
Anzahl Zimmer: 4
Frühstück beim Bäcker nebenan
Preise gültig für 2011
TV/Internet vorhanden
Terrasse/Außenbereich/Garten
Boot u. Fahrrad zu mieten
Ganzjährig geöffnet
Sprechen etwas Deutsch

In the middle of Andenes harbor lies Fargeklatten Veita, a typical north Norway fish/agricultural farm, now renovated as a guesthouse/art studio/workplace with a barn and a lovely garden. It's all that remains of the original development of Andenes from the 1800s. The island is known for its extensive bogs, white beaches and protuding peaks. Here you can go on a whale safari, admire the "bird mountain" at Bleiksøya, or reel in your own dinner from the sea. Polar museum, Øymuseum, artists' studios, tempting eateries. Here also is bountiful fishing: trout and char in the mountain lakes, salmon in the river. Diving, bicycling and hiking.

Sentralt ved Andenes havn ligger Fargeklatten Veita som er et typisk nordnorsk fiske-/småbruk, nå renovert som gjestestue, ateliere/verksted, fjøsbygning og med en vakker hage. Dette er det eneste som er igjen av den opprinnelige bebyggelsen fra 1800-tallet i Andenes.
Øya er kjent for sine vidstrakte myrer, hvite strender og spisse fjell. Her kan du dra på hvalsafari, beundre fuglefjellene på Bleiksøya eller dra din egen middag opp av havet. Polarmuseum, Øymuseum, kunstnerverksteder, trivelige spisesteder. Her er også rikt fiske etter ørret og røye i fjellvann, laksefiske i elver. Dykking, sykkelturer og fotturer.

Fargeklatten Veita liegt zentral am Hafen Andernes. Ein typisch nordnorwegischer Fischerei-/ landwirtschaftl. Kleinbetrieb, der jetzt renoviert und zu Gaststube, Atelier/Werkstatt zusammen mit einem schönen Garten umgenutzt wurde. Es ist Andenes' einzige originale Bebauung aus dem 19. Jh. Die Insel ist bekannt für ihre ausgedehnten Moore, weißen Strände und spitzen Felsen. Auf Walsafari gehen, die Vogelfelsen auf Bleiksøya bewundern oder das eigene Abendessen aus dem Meer fangen. Polar-, Inselmuseum, Künstlerwerkstätten, gemütl. Gaststätten. Angeln (Lachs, -forelle, Saibling), Tauchen, Wander- und Fahrradtouren möglich.

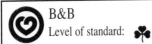
Bakkemo Gård

Your host:
Idar Hanssen

Address:
Selnes
N - 9470 Gratangen
Phone: 76 95 29 95
Mobil: 91 69 50 97 / 97 50 94 46
Fax: 76 97 79 18
E-mail: idarhans@online.no

Best time to call:
08.00 - 24.00
GPS: 77°30'90"N 36°03'91"E

Single-/double-/3- and 6-bedded r.:	Enkelt-/dobbelt-/3- og 6-sengsrom:	Einzel-/Doppel-/3- und 6-bettzi.:
Per person: **250,-**	Pr person: **250,-**	Pro Pers.: **250,-**
No. of rooms: 4	Antall rom: 4	Anzahl Zimmer: 4
Guest's common living room	Gjestestue	Aufenthaltsraum
Laid breakfast table	Dekket frokostbord	Gedeckter Frühstückstisch
Selfcatering possible	Selvhushold er mulig	Selbstverpflegung möglich
Prices valid for 2011/12/13	Priser gyldig for 2011/12/13	Preise gültig für 2011/12/13
Garden/yard	Hage	Garten
Boat and bike for rent	Båt- og sykkelutleie	Boot und Fahrrad zu mieten
Pets welcome	Kjæledyr velkommen	Haustiere willkommen
Open year round	Åpent hele året	Ganzjährig geöffnet
Some English spoken		Sprechen Deutsch

Bakkemo Farm, built in 1870 and fully restored in 1994, is in Gratangen municipality, a 30 km trip from E-6 and 90 km from Evenes Airport. Gratangen is known for its coastal culture, mountain hikes, fjord fishing, lakes, rivers and hunting.

For selfcatering also available; two cabins with 3 rooms/6 beds and outhouse, and the restored "Stone Cottage" from 1942 for two people which is located an hour's walk from the main road.

Bakkemo Gård ligger i Gratangen kommune, en avstikker på ca. 30 km fra E-6 og 90 km fra Evenes flyplass.
Bakkemo ble bygd i 1870 og restaurert i gammel stil i 1994. Gratangen er kjent for sin kystkultur. Rike muligheter til jakt og friluftsliv, fjellturer, fiske i fjorden, innsjøer og elver.

For selvhushold: Vertskapet leier også ut to hytter med 3 rom/6 soveplasser og uthus, pluss den restaurerte "Steinhytta" som ligger en drøy times krevende gangtur fra veien.

Bakkemo Gård liegt in der Kommunr Gratangen, 30 km von der E-6 und 90 km vom Flugplatz Evenes.
Das Haus wurde 1870 gebaut und 1994 im alten Stil renoviert. Gratangens herrliche Natur mit Küste und Bergen bietet Möglichkeiten für Wanderungen, Salz- und Süsswasserangeln, sowie Jagd.

Selbsthaushalt: Der Besitzer vermietet auch 2 Hütten mit je 3 Schlafzi./ 6 Schlafplätzen und Plumpsklo sowie die restaurierte "Steinhytta" für 2, die sich einen anspruchsvollen einstündigen Fußweg entfernt befindet.

Ami Hotel

Your host:
Arnt-Inge & Anette Hansen

Address:
Skolegata 24
N - 9008 Tromsø
Phone: 77 62 10 00
Fax: 77 62 10 01
E-mail: email@amihotel.no
Web: http://amihotel.no

Best time to call:
07.00 - 15.00
GPS: 69°39'2"N 18°57'1"E

Double room:	**710,-/820,-**	Dobbeltrom:	**710,-/820,-**	Doppelzimmer:	**710,-/820,-**
Single room:	**560,-/660,-**	Enkeltrom:	**560,-/660,-**	Einzelzimmer:	**560,-/660,-**
Family room for 3 p.:	**870,-/990,-**	Familierom for 3 p.:	**870,-/990,-**	Familienzi. für 3 P.:	**870,-/990,-**
Family room for 4 p.:	**1090,-/1190,-**	Familierom for 4 p.:	**1090,-/1190,-**	Familienzi. für 4 P.:	**1090,-/1190,-**
No. of rooms: 17		Antall rom: 17		Anzahl Zimmer: 17	
Guest's common living room		Gjestestue		Aufenthaltsraum	
Laid breakfast table		Dekket frokostbord		Gedeckter Frühstückstisch	
Prices valid for 2011		Priser gyldig for 2011		Preise gültig für 2011	
Discount for longer stays		Rabatt ved lengre tids opphold		Ermäßigung für Langzeitaufenthalt	
Boat and bike for rent		Båt- og sykkelutleie		Boot und Fahrrad zu mieten	
Pets welcome		Kjæledyr velkommen		Haustiere willkommen	
Open year round		Åpent hele året		Ganzjährig geöffnet	
English spoken		Sprechen Englisch		Sprechen Englisch	

Ami Hotel is a small and cozy family-run hotel in Tromsø center, next to Kongeparken. 5 min. walk to walking street.

Ami Hotel er et hjemmekoselig lite familiedrevet hotell i Tromsø sentrum, like ved Kongeparken. Det er 5 min. gange til gågaten.

Ami Hotel ist ein urgemütliches, kleines familiengeführtes Hotel im Zentrum von Tromsø, gleich neben dem Kongepark. 5 Gehminuten zur Fußgängerzone.

We live in a wonderful world that is full of
beauty, charm and adventure.
There is no end to the adventures we can have
if only we seek them with our eyes open.
~Jawaharial Nehru~

Man's heart away from nature becomes hard.
~Standing Bear~

Lauksletta overnatting

Your host:
Elin, Elisabeth & Jan Johannessen

Address:
**Lauksletta
N - 9194 Lauksletta**
Mobile: 92 08 98 24 / 92 41 20 67
E-mail: jmjohane@online.no

Best time to call:
09.00 - 22.00
GPS: 70°7'36"N 20°45'15"E

Single room:	**460,-**	Enkeltrom:	**460,-**	Einzelzi.:	**460,-**
Double room:	**920,-**	Dobbeltrom/tosengsrom:	**920,-**	Doppelzi.:	**920,-**
3-bedded room:	**1380,-**	Tresengsrom:	**1380,-**	Dreibettzi.:	**1380,-**
4-bedded room:	**1940,-**	Firsengsrom:	**1940,-**	Vierbettzi.:	**1940,-**

Shared bath, kitchen, LR / Delt bad, kjk. og stue tilgjengelig / Gemeins. Bad, ~ Küche, ~ Stube
No. of rooms: 12 / Antall rom: 12 / Anzahl Zimmer: 12

Apartment for 2-4 persons / Leilighet for 2-4 personer / Wohnung für 2-4 Personen
1-2 bedrooms, bath, kitchen, LR / 1-2 soverom, bad, kjøkken, stue / 1-2 Schlafzi., Bad, Küche, Stube

Price per pers.:	**460,-**	Pris pr. pers.:	**460,-**	Preis pro Pers.:	**460,-**

No. of apt.: 2 / Antall leiligheter: 2 / Anzahl Wohnungen: 2

Prices valid for 2011/12 / Priser gyldig for 2011/12 / Preise gültig für 2011/12
Restaurant and pub / Restaurant og pub / Restaurant und Pub
TV/Internet available / TV/Internett tilgjengelig / TV/Internet verfügbar
Terrace/deck/yard / Terrasse/uteplass/hage / Terrasse/Außenbereich/Garten
Boat, bike and snow shoes for rent / Utleie av båt, sykkel og truger / Miete: Boot, Fahrrad, Schneeschuhe
Outdoor hot tub / Utendørs badestamp / Badezuber im Garten
Suitable for handicapped / Handikapvennlig / Behindertengerecht
Pets welcome / Kjæledyr velkommen / Haustiere willkommen
VISA, MC, Maestro, AmEx acceptd. / Vi tar VISA, MC, Maestro, AmEx / VISA, MC, Maestro, AmEx akzept.
Open year round / Åpent hele året / Ganzjährig geöffnet
English spoken / Sprechen etwas Deutsch

Lauksletta has long been an active fishing village. Now there are 70 residents, and one fish processing plant still operates.
Short way to good fishing spots. Arnøya has many points of cultural interest with marked paths through the island's historic landscape.

Stedet Lauksletta har fra gammelt av vært et aktivt fiskevær. Nå bor det 70 innbyggere her og en fiske-foredlingsfabrikk er fremdeles i drift.
Kort vei til gode fiskeplasser. Arn-øya har mange kulturminner og har merkede kulturstier gjennom øyas historiske landskap.

Lauksletta ist seit jeher ein aktives Fischerdorf. Heute leben hier 70 Einwohner und eine Fischverede-lungsfabrik befindet sich noch immer in Betrieb. Nicht weit zu guten Angelplätzen. Die Insel Arn-øya hält viele Kulturschätze bereit, die durch ausgewiesene Wander-wege miteinander verbunden sind.

ANSI Turistservice
Simonsen Gårdsferie

Your host:
Nelly & Willy Simonsen

Address:
Storeng, N - 9161 Burfjord
Phone: 77 76 93 86
Mobile: 91 16 83 20
E-mail: info@ansi-turistservice.no
Web: www.ansi-turistservice.no
Best time to call: 09.00 - 22.00
GPS: 69°59'4"N 22°2'39"E

A: Naustet (61m²) for 2-4 pers.
2 bedrooms, bath, kitchen, LR
Price : 1-2 p.: **1010,-** / 3-4 p.: **1110,-**

C: Nyheim (37m²) for 2 persons
1 bedroom, bath, kitchen, LR
Price for whole unit: **765,-**

E: Hiet (26m²) Mini-cabin for 2 p.
1 room, bath, kitchen: **765,-**

Bed linen included
Breakfast service avaiable: **90,-**
Other meals served
Prices valid for 2011/12
TV/Internet available
Terrace/patio/yard, boat for rent
Grill house, hot tub, sauna
Discount after 3 days
VISA, MC accepted
Open year round
English spoken

At 70°N you'll find cozy cabins to
live in and exciting experiences
both summer and winter. The range
of possible activities is wide. There
are good fishing spots in the fjord.
The area has a fantastic nature that
entices you to wander about. Maybe
you'd like to experience winter
here, with the special daylight and
northern lights and snow?
In winter: snowmobile tours, dog-
sledding and cross country skiing.

A: Naustet (61m²) for 2-4 personer
2 soverom, bad, kjøkken, stue
Pris for 1-2 p.: **1010,-** / 3-4 p.: **1110,-**

C: Nyheim (37m²) for 2 personer
1 soverom, bad, kjøkken, stue
Pris for hele enheten: **765,-**

E: Hiet (26m²) Minihytte for 2 p.
1 rom, bad, kjøkken: **765,-**

Sengetøy inkludert
Frokost kan serveres: **90,-**
Andre måltider kan bestilles
Priser gyldig for 2011/12
TV/Internett tilgjengelig
Terrasse/uteplass/hage, båtutleie
Grillhus, badestamp, badstu
Rabatt ved leie over 2 dager
Vi tar VISA, MC
Åpent hele året

På 70 grader nord finner du flotte
hytter å bo i og spennende opplevelser både for sommer og vinter.
Aktivitetsmulighetene er mange.
Det er gode fiskeforhold i fjorden.
Området har en fantastisk natur
som lokker deg ut på vandreturer.
Kanskje du vil oppleve vinteren
her med sitt spesielle dagslys, med
nordlys og snø. Aktiviteter om
vinteren er snøscooter-turer, hunde-
sledeturer og skiturer.

A: Naustet (61m²) für 2-4 Pers.
2 Schlafzi., Eig. Bad, Küche, Stube
Preis für 1-2 P.: **1010,-** / 3-4 P.: **1110,-**

C: Nyheim (37m²) für 2 Personen
1 Schlafzi., Bad, Küche, Stube
Ganze Einheit: **765,-**

E: Hiet (26m²) Mini-Hütten für 2 P.
1 Raum, Bad, Küche, Stube **765,-**

Inkl. Bettwasche
Frühstück auf Bestellung: **90,-**
Andere Mahlzeiten auf Bestellung
Preise gültig für 2011/12
TV/Internet vorhanden
Terrasse/Garten, Boot zu mieten
Grillhütte, Badezuber, Sauna
Ermäßigung: ab 2 Übernachtungen
Wir akzeptieren VISA, MC
Ganzjährig geöffnet
Sprechen Deutsch

Auf 70°N finden Sie schöne Hütten
zum Wohnen und spannende Erlebnisse, Sommer u. Winter. Großes
Angebot an Freizeitaktivitäten:
gute Angelmöglichkeiten im Fjord,
die fantastische Natur in der Umgebung lädt zu Wanderungen ein.
Vielleicht möchten Sie auch den
Winter mit seinem speziellen Tages-
licht, mit Nordlichtern und Schnee
erleben? Schneemobiltouren, Hun-
deschlittenfahrten und Skitouren.

Repvåg Fjordhotell & Rorbusenter

Your host:
Toini & Håkon Karlsen

Address:
N - 9768 Repvåg, Nordkapp
Phone: 78 47 54 40
Fax: 78 47 27 51
E-mail: post@repvag-fjordhotell.no
Web: www.repvag-fjordhotell.no
Best time to call:
09.00 - 22.00
GPS: 70°44'48"N 25°40'18"E

Double room:	940,-	Dobbeltrom:	940,-	Doppelzimmer:	940,-
Single room:	720,-	Enkeltrom:	720,-	Einzelzimmer:	720,-
No. of rooms: 60		Antall rom: 60		Anzahl Zimmer: 60	
Breakfast buffet		Frokost buffét		Frühstücksbüffet	
Prices valid for 2011/12		Priser gyldig for 2011/12		Preise gültig für 2011/12	

Selfcatering:	Selvhushold:	Selbsthaushalt:
'Rorbu' for 2-8 persons	Rorbu for 2-8 personer	"Rorbu" for 2-8 Pers.
No. of cabins/apts.: 8	Antall rorbuer: 8	Anzahl Hütten/Wohnungen: 8
Ask for price	Spør om pris	Preis auf Anfrage

TV/Internet available	TV/Internett tilgjengelig	Zugang zu TV/Internet
Restaurant	Restaurant	Terrasse/Aussenplatz/Garten
Outdoor furniture	Uteplass	Boot zu mieten
Boat for rent	Båtutleie	Fahrrad zu mieten
Suitable for handicapped	Handikaptilgjengelig	Behindertengerecht
Pets welcome	Kjæledyr velkommen	Haustiere willkommen
VISA, MC, DC, AmEx accepted	Vi tar VISA, MC, DC, AmEx	VISA, MC, DC, AmEx
Open 1 May - 30 Aug.	Åpent 1. mai - 30. aug.	Geöffnet 1. Mai - 30. Aug.
English spoken		Sprechen Deutsch

The hotel is a real fishing settlement, rebuilt and decorated, having in mind the preservation of north Norwegian coastal culture and atmosphere.
The outstanding maritime restaurant accommodates 120 persons and is arranged with driftwood decorations and everyday fishing objects.

Hotellet er en ekte fiskebrygge, ombygd, dekorert og utsmykket med tanke på å ivareta den nordnorske kystkulturen og atmosfæren.
Den særegne maritime restauranten har plass til 120 personer og er utsmykket med dekorasjoner som er laget av drivtømmer og bruksgjenstander fra fiskeindustrien.

Der Hotelkomplex ist eine echte Fischersiedlung, die mit dem Gedanken, die nordnorwegische Küstenkultur und Atmosphäre zu bewahren, umgebaut, dekoriert und ausgeschmückt wurde.
Das besondere maritime Restaurant bietet Platz für 120 Personen und ist eingerichtet mit Treibholz Dekorationen und Gebrauchsgegenständen der Fischerei.

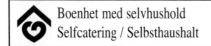
Engholm Husky design tun

Your host:
Sven Engholm

Address:
N - 9730 Karasjok
Phone: 78 46 71 66
Mobile: 91 58 66 25
E-mail: sven@engholm.no
Web: www.engholm.no
Best time to call: 08.00 - 22.00
GPS: 69°26'37"N 25°14'36"E

Cabin with own bath		Hytte med eget bad		Hütte mit eig. Bad	
Price for 3 pers.:	**1300,-**	Pris for 3 pers.:	**1300,-**	Preis für 3 Pers.:	**1300,-**
Price for 3 pers.:	**1000,-**	Pris for 2 pers.:	**1000,-**	Preis für 2 Pers.:	**1000,-**
Price for 3 pers.:	**700,-**	Pris for 1 pers.:	**700,-**	Preis für 1 Pers.:	**700,-**
Discount for children		Rabatt for barn		Ermäßigung für Kinder	
Breakfast and dinner on request		Frokost og middag kan serveres		FR, Abendessen nach Vereinbarung	
Prices valid for 2011/12		Priser gyldig for 2011/12		Preise gültig für 2011/12	
Canoe, boat and bike for rent		Kano-, båt- og sykkelutleie		Kanu, Boot, Fahrrad zu mieten	
Terrace/patio/BBQ		Terrasse/uteplass/grill		Terrasse/Außenbereich	
Sauna and hot tub		Badstu og badestamp		Sauna und Badezuber	
Pets allowed		Kjæledyr tillatt		Haustiere erlaubt	
Open year round		Åpent hele året		Ganzjährig geöffnet	
English spoken				Sprechen etwas Deutsch	

Engholm Husky is a different place with cosy log cabins around a courtyard, all built by Sven, the host. He also did all the interior design with decoration details to create a unique and personal atmosphere for each house.
Enjoy guided tours via sled dogs with your own dog team, or ski on Finnmarksvidda plateau and the coast of the Arctic Osean. Hunting for small game and fishing in the salmon river. Fishing lakes with trout and red char. There's a turf hut with open fireplace for grilling and socializing.

Engholm Husky er en annerledes plass med koselige tømmerhytter i et tun bygget av verten Sven selv. Han har også laget innredningen og alle detaljer. Egen kreativitet og fantasi har fått fritt spillerom med tanke på å skape en unik og personlig atmosfære i hvert enkelt hus.
Guidede sledehundturer med 'eget' hundespann eller med ski på Finnmarksvidda og til ishavskysten. Småviltjakt og fiske i lakseelv. Fiskevann for ørret og røye. Barta (gamme) med åpent ildsted for grilling og sosialt samvær.

Engholm Husky ist ein etwas anderer Hof mit gemütlichen Blockhüttenn, die der Gastgeber Sven alle selbst gebaut hat. Auch die Einrichtung inkl. aller Details stammen aus seiner Hand. Der eigenen Kreativität und Fantasie wurde hier Spielraum gelassen um so jeder einzelnen Hütte eine einmalige und persönliche Atmosphäre zu verleihen. Geführte Hundeschlittentouren mit eigenem Hundegespann oder Skitouren durch die Finnmark Hochebene u. bis zur Eismeerküste. Kleintierjagd, Lachs-, Forellen-, Saiblingangeln. Eine Hütte mit offenem Feuer zum Grillen steht d. Gästen zur Verfügung.

Sollia Gjestegård

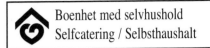

Your host:
fam. Nordhus

Address:
Storskog
N - 9900 Kirkenes
Phone: **78 99 08 20**
Fax: **78 99 07 61**
E-mail: **post@storskog.no**
Web: **www.storskog.no**

Best time to call:
08.00 - 23.00
GPS: 69°39'51"N 30°11'49"E

Twin room:	**900,-**	Tosengsrom:	**900,-**	Zweibettzi.:	**900,-**
Single room:	**750,-**	Enkeltrom:	**750,-**	Einzelzi.:	**750,-**
Bed linen incl.		Sengetøy inkl.		Inkl. Bettwäsche	
No. of rooms: 4		Antall rom: 4		Anzahl Zi.: 4	
Double room also available - ask		Dobbeltrom finnes også - spør		Doppelzi. gibt es auch - bitte fragen	

Cabin for 2-6 persons		Hytte for 2-6 personer		Hütte für 2-6 Personen	
2 bedrooms, bath, kitchen, LR		2 soverom, bad, kjøkken, stue		2 Schlafzi., Bad, Küche, Stube	
Price for whole unit:	**1050,-**	Pris for hele enheten:	**1050,-**	Ganze Einheit:	**1050,-**
Bed linen fee:	**75,-**	Tillegg for sengetøy:	**75,-**	Mieten von Bettwäsche:	**75,-**
No. of cabins: 4		Antall hytter: 4		Anzahl Hütten: 4	

Breakfast service available: **75,-**	Frokost kan bestilles: **75,-**	Frühstück auf Bestellung **75,-**
Prices valid for 2011/12	Priser gyldig for 2011/12	Preise gültig für 2011/12
TV/Internet available in cabins	TV/Internett tilgjengelig i hytter	TV/Internet in den Hütten
Deck/yard for cabins	Uteplass/hage for hytter	Terrasse/Garten an den Hütten
Boat for rent, kicksled available	Båtutleie, spark kan lånes	Boot zu mieten, Treetschlitten verf.
Pets welcome in one cabin	Kjæledyr velkommen i én hytte	Haustiere in einer der Hütten willk.
VISA accepted	Vi tar VISA	Wir akzeptieren VISA
Open year round	Åpent hele året	Ganzjährig geöffnet

Sollia Gjestegård lies right on the Russian border amid beautiful nature with forest, valleys and water. The Nordhus family has taken in guests from near and far since 1999. Besides overnight accommodations they offer spa and sauna, two restaurants and a dog farm with about 40 Alaskan husky sled dogs for winter day-tours. There are also fishing spots and hiking paths.

Sollia Gjestegård ligger helt på grensen til Russland i flott natur med skog, daler og vann. Familien Nordhus har siden 1999 tatt imot gjester fra fjern og nær. I tillegg til overnatting er her et relax-anlegg med massasjebad og sauna, to restauranter og hundegård med ca. 40 Alaska husky trekkhunder for daglige turer i vintersesongen. Her er også fiskevann og turstier.

Der Sollia Gästehof liegt direkt an der Grenze zu Russland, inmitten toller Natur mit Wäldern, Tälern und Seen. Seit 1999 begrüßt Fam. Nordhus hier Gäste. Zusätzlich zu den Zimmern finden Sie hier eine Relax-Anlage mit Whirlpool und Sauna, zwei Restaurants und ein Hundehof mit ca. 40 Alaskan Husky Schlittenhunden für Tagestouren im Winter. Angelgewässer und Wanderwege in der Umgebung.

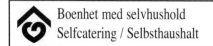
Gjestegården

Your host:
Rune Knudsen

Address:
**Strandgaten 72
N - 9950 Vardø**
Phone: 78 98 75 29

Best time to call:
08.00 - 23.00
GPS: 70°22'37"N, 31°06'54"E

Room for 2 pers.:	**350,-**	Rom for 2 pers.:	**350,-**	Zimmer für 2 Pers.:	**350,-**
Room for 1 pers.:	**300,-**	Rom for 1 pers.:	**300,-**	Zimmer für 1 Pers.:	**300,-**
No. of bedrooms: 6		Antall rom: 6		Anzahl Schlafzi.: 6	
Shared bath & kitchenette		Delt bad og kjøkkenkrok		Gemeins. Bad u. Küchenecke	
Bed linen included		Sengetøy er inkludert		Inkl. Bettwäsche	
Prices valid for 2011		Priser gyldig for 2011		Preise gültig für 2011	
TV available		TV tilgjengelig		TV vorhanden	
Terrace/yard		Uteplass		Außenbereich	
Open year round		Åpent hele året		Ganzjährig geöffnet	
Walking distance to town center		Gangavstand fra sentrum		Kurzer Fußweg ins Zentrum	
English spoken				Sprechen Englisch	

All journeys have secret destinations
of which the traveler is unaware.
~Martin Buber~

One touch of nature makes the whole world kin.
~William Shakespeare~

Nature is man's teacher. She unfolds her treasures to his search,
unseals his eye, illumes his mind, and purifies his heart;
an influence breathes from all the sights
and sounds of her existence.
~Alfred Billings Street~

I go to nature to be soothed and healed,
and to have my senses put in order.
~John Burroughs~

page 41 - Lund Gård

E: From the west on E-18 turn off toward Kallak and Trollbergtjern. Follow signs to Lund Gård from E-18. Farm lies
on the west side after the intersection, about 4 km from E18.
Along E-18 from the east pass Ørje, take off toward Kallad.
After ca. 7 km you find the farm on the right side.

N: Langs E-18 fra vest; ta av mot Kallak og Trollbergtjern.
Følg skilting til Lund Gård fra E-18. Etter veikryss ligger
gården på venstre side, ca. 4 km fra E-18. Langs E-18 fra øst;
kjør forbi Ørje, ra av mot Kallak. Etter ca. 7 km ligger går-
en på høyre side.

D: Entlang der E-18 aus Westen: abfahren Richtung Kallak
und Trollbergtjern und dann der Beschilderung zum Lund
Gård folgen. Der Hof liegt auf der linken Seite, ca. 4 km von
der E-18. Entlang der E-18 aus Osten: an Ørje vorbei fahren
und Richtung Kallak abfahren. Nach ca. 7 km liegt der Hof
auf der rechten Seite.

page 46 - Porta Fortuna

E: Take ferry from Oslo downtown (Aker Brygge) to Nesoddtangen. Take bus no. 611 to Nesodden church or bus 621
to Smia. Walk up Kirkeveien, find Bjerkerudveien to the left.
Via car from Oslo: Take E-6 south, exit toward Nesodden. In
the roundabout by Nesodden church take Kirkeveien to the
left. Bjerkrudveien is the 5th road to the left.

N: Ta båt fra Oslo sentrum, fra Aker Brygge til Nesoddtang-
en. Derfra tar du buss nr. 611 til Nesodden kirke (eller nr.
621 til Smia). Gå opp Kirkeveien og finn Bjerkerudveien til
venstre.
Med bil fra Oslo: E-6 sørover. Ta av mot Nesodden. I rundkjøring v/Nesodden kirken, ta Kirkeveien til venstre.
Bjerkerudveien er 5te vei til venstre.

D: Mit dem Boot von Oslo Zentrum (Aker Brygge) nach
Nesoddtangen. Von da mit dem Bus Nr. 611 bis Nesodden
Kirche (oder Nr. 621 bis Smia). Den Kirkeveien hochlaufen
und in den Bjerkerudveien nach links gehen.
Mit dem Auto ab Oslo die E6 Ri. Süden und Ri. Nesodden
abfahren. Im Kreisverkehr an der Kirche in Nesodden nach
links in die Kirkeveien abbiegen. Der fünfte Weg zur Linken
ist die Zielstraße, der Bjerkerudveien.

page 49 - Frogner Guestroom

E: From the Central Station you take Tram no. 12 'Majorstuen' to Lille Frogner Allé. Walk about 30 m in the same
direction, take the second street to the right which is Baldersgate. No 11 is on the opposite side. Press the doorbell named
HOLM.

N: Fra Sentralbanestasjonen tar du trikk nr.12 'Majorstuen'
til Lille Frogner Allé. Fortsett å gå ca. 30 meter i samme retning til du kommer til Baldersgate. Ta til høyre. Nr.11 ligger

på den andre siden av gaten. 'HOLM' på ringeklokken.

D: Vom Hauptbahnhof aus nehmen Sie die Straßenbahn Nr.
12 'Majorstuen' Richtung Lille Frogner Allé. Nun gehen Sie
30 Meter in die gleiche Richtung weiter und biegen dann in
die zweite Straße rechts ab. Jetzt befinden Sie sich in der
Baldersgate. Die Nr. 11., also unser Haus, liegt auf der gegenüberliegenden Straßenseite. Klingeln Sie bitte bei HOLM.

page 50 - Frogner Bed & Breakfast

E: With car: find Frogner plass along the Ring 2. The house
is right next to the round-about leading to Majorstuen. See
the sign for no. 5 on the entrance. By public transit: from
Oslo-S take the tram no. 12 towards Majorstuen, depart at
Frogner plass. House is across the street from the tram stop.
Or else take bus 31 or 32 to Frogner Church, about 5 min.
walk to Frogner plass. From other places take bus 20 along
Ring-2.

N: Med bil; finn Frogner plass langs Ring-2. Huset ligger rett
ved utkjøring av rundkjøringen i retning Majorstuen. Du ser
skilt med nr. 5 på porten.
Med offentlig kommunikasjon; fra Oslo-S ta trikk nr. 12 i retning Majorstuen, gå av på Frogner plass. Huset ligger over
veien fra holdeplassen. Eller ta buss nr. 31 eller 32 til Frogner kirke. Ca. 5 min. å gå til Frogner plass.
Fra andre steder; buss nr. 20 går langs Ring-2.

D: Mit dem Auto: Fahren Sie entlang Ring 2 bis zum
Frogner Plass. Das Haus liegt direkt am Kreisverkehr, wenn
Sie im Kreisverkehr in Richtung Majorstuen abfahren. Die
Hausnummer 5 steht am Tor.
Mit öffentlichen Verkehrsmitteln: Von Oslo-S (Hbf.) nehmen
Sie die Strassenbahn Nr. 12 in Richtung Majorstuen. Steigen
Sie am Frogner Plass aus. Das Haus befindet sich gegenüber
von der Haltestelle.
Sie können auch die Busse Nr. 31 oder 32 bis zur Haltestelle
Frogner kirke nehmen. Von dort ist es ein ca. 5 minütiger
Fußweg bis zum Frogner Plass.
Ausserdem ist es möglich den Bus Nr. 20 zu nehmen, der den
Ring-2 entlangfährt.

page 52 – Bygdøy Bed & Breakfast

E: Bus no. 30 toward Bygdøy, depart at Norsk Folkemuseem
stop. Find Museumsveien , take first rd. left.

N: Buss nr. 30 Bygdøy til Folkemuseet. Første vei til venstre
i Museumsveien.

D: Bus Nr. 30 Ri. Bygdøy bis zum Folkemuseum. Den
Museumsveien hinunter und den ersten Weg links.

page 53 - Janesplace B&B

E: Follow the E-18 highway west from Oslo. Exit at Solle-
rud/Lilleaker. Take the first right, driving up Sollerudveien to

From the garden at Residence Kristinelund, Oslo, page 51

just beyond the tram tracks. Turn immediately left and then right onto Dr. Bachesvei. House is on the right at the end of the road.

N: Følg E-18 fra Oslo vestover, ta av mot Sollerud/Lilleaker. Ta første til høyre og kjør oppover Sollerudveien, til like over trikkeskinnen. Ta umiddelbart til venstre og deretter straks til høyre. Kjør opp Dr. Bachesvei. Huset ligger på høyre side i enden av veien.

D: E-18 von Oslo westwärts, Ri. Sollerud/Lilleaker abfahren. Erste rechts und überqueren Sie den Sollerudveien. Unmittelbar nach den Strassenbahnschienen links und direkt die nächste Str. Rechts fahren. Den Dr. Bachesvei hinauf fahren. Das Haus liegt auf der rechten Seite am Ende der Strasse.

page 55 - Vinderen Bed & Breakfast

E: With car: Ring 3 to Smestad crossing, follow Sørkedalsveien toward Majorstua to the roundabout by Skeidar furniture shop. Take Diakonveien about 50 meters to Borgenveien, find number 25 A.

By metro: Take line no. 1 to Steinerud station. Follow the path along the tracks to Jacob Hansens vei, then to Borgenveien where you turn left to number 25 A.

N: Med bil: Ring 3 til Smestadkrysset, følg Sørkedalsveien i retning Majorstua til rundkjøring ved Skeidar møbelforretning. Kjør Diakonveien ca. 50 m til Borgenveien 25 A.

T-bane: Linje nr. 1 til Steinerud stasjon. Gå stien langs toglinjen til Jacob Hansens vei, så til Borgenveien. Til venstre i Borgenveien og gå til nr. 25 A.

D: Mit dem Auto: Ring 3 bis Smestadkrysset, anschließend

Sørkedalsveien in Richtung Majorstua bis zum Kreisverkehr bei Skeidar Möbelgeschäft. Biegen Sie dann in den Diakonveien ab, nach ca. 50 m erreichen Sie den Borgenveien 25 A. Mit der U-Bahn: Linie Nr. 1 bis Steinersrud Stasjon, anschließend Fußweg entlang der Bahn bis Jakob Hansens vei, dann zum Borgenveien. Dort befindet sich linkerhand das Haus Nr. 25 A.

page 56 – Villa May

E: From West, Ring 3 to Smestad, straight ahead at the crossing, first road to left (Dalsveien). Turn right on Holmenveien, find no. 22 A.

From East: Ring 3 to Vindern/Slemdal, exit to right, left on Slemdalsveien, right at Vindern. Straight up to no. 22 A.

By metro: Line no. 1 (Frognersæteren) to Vindern station. Cross tram lines, walk straight up Holmenvn. and find no. 22 A (approx. 4 minutes). Entrance to the left in yard.

N: Fra vest; kjør Ring 3 til Smestad, rett over Smestadkrysset, første vei til venstre (Dalsveien). Til høyre i Holmenvn., kjør til nr. 22 A. Fra øst; Ring 3 til Vindern/Slemdal, avkjørsel til høyre, til venstre i Slemdalsveien, til høyre ved Vindern. Rett frem til nr. 22 A.

Med T-bane: Linje 1 (Frognerseteren) til Vindern stasjon. Kryss trikkeskinnene, gå rett opp til nr. 22 A (4 minutter). Inngang til venstre i tunet.

D: Aus westlicher Richtung: Ring 3 bis Smestad fahren, über die Kreuzung und die erste Strasse nach links nehmen (Dalsveien). Biegen Sie rechts in den Holmenveien und finden Sie die Nr. 22 A.

Aus östlicher Richtung: Ring 3 bis Vindern/Slemdal, Ausfahrt rechts, dann links in den Slemdalsveien abbiegen. Bei Vinderen rechts abbiegen. Geradeaus weiterfahren bis Nr. 22 A. U-Bahn: Linie 1 (in Richtung Frognerseteren) bis zur Station Vindern. Die Straßenbahnschienen überqueren und den Holmenveien hinauflaufen bis zur Nr. 22 A (ungefähr 4 Minuten Gehzeit). Der Eingangbefindet sich auf der linken Seite.

page 57 - Solveig's Bed & Breakfast

E: Just north of Ring 3 at Tåsen in north-central Oslo. Public transportation: Take Metro Line no. 3 towards Sognsvann to Tåsen Station. Walk uphill to the left on Tåsenveien to the first corner, turn left onto Tåsen terrasse. Less than 5 min. walk.

N: Med bil følg Ring 3 til Tåsen. Tåsen Terrasse ligger like ovenfor, på nordsiden av Ring 3. Fra sentrum: Ta T-bane nr. 3 'Sognsvann' til Tåsen stasjon, gå videre oppover ca. et kvartal til Tåsenveien, ta så til venstre inn Tåsen Terrasse. Det er ca. 5 min. gange.

D: Fahren Sie auf dem "Ring 3" in Richtung Tåsen. Tåsen Terrasse liegt direkt oberhalb an der Nordseite von Ring 3. Ab Oslo Zentrum: Nehmen Sie die U-Bahn Nr. 3 (Sognsvann) bis zur Haltestelle Tåsen, folgen Sie links bergauf dem Tåsenveien bis zur ersten Kreuzung. Hier gehen Sie nach links in die Tåsen Terrasse. Der Fußweg beträgt ca. 5 Min.

page 58 - Anna's Place

E: Follow E-18 to Lysaker. Exit towards Jar. Drive 3 km and turn right at the end of the road (Vollsveien). Then take your first left onto Ringstabekkveien and turn left after the 5th speed bump onto Myrveien. Anna's Place is the 2nd house. Walking time to trolley and Metro: 7 min.

N: Følg E-18 til Lysaker. Ta av mot Jar. Kjør 3 km og i enden av veien ta til høyre (Vollsveien). Så tar du første vei til venstre som er Ringstabekkveien, og etter 5. fartsdump tar du til venstre til Myrveien. Anna's Place er 2. hus. 7 min. å gå fra hus til trikk og T-bane.

D: Folgen Sie der E-18 bis Lysaker und biegen Sie dort nach Jar ab. Nach 3 km Fahrt endet die Straße, und Sie biegen rechts ab (Vollsveien). Die nächste Straße links ist der Ringstabekkveien. Hinter der 5. Bremsschwelle biegen sie links auf den Myrveien ab. Das 2. Haus ist Anna´s Place. 7 Min. Fußweg bis zur Straßen- und U-Bahn.

pag 59 – The Blue Room

E: From Oslo: E-18 southward towards Drammen. Exit towards Billingstad and Nesøya. Turn left at the first roundabout and drive straight through the second roundabout. Drive about 1 km on a road called Billingstadsletta until you get to Nesbru. Drive under the main highway and you will see the Viking Towing Yard on the right-hand side. Opposite

the Viking station (on your left as you drive in this direction), there is a small bridge that takes you to Nesåsen. Look for no. 11 C, a brown house.

N: Fra Oslo: E-18 sørover mot Drammen, ta av mot Billingstad og Nesøya. Ved første rundkjøring, ta til venstre, og i andre rundkjøring kjør rett fram. Kjør ca 1 km på veien kalt Billingstadsletta til du kommer til Nesbru. Kjør under hovedveien, og på høyre side ser du Viking stasjon. På motsatt side, til venstre, er det en smal bru som vil føre deg til Nesåsen. Kjør denne og finn nummer 11 C, et brunt hus.

D: Ab Oslo: Die E-18 in Richtung Süden (Drammen) fahren, und Ri. Billingstad/Nesøya abfahren. Am ersten Kreisverkehr geht es links ab, am zweiten Kreisverkehr geradeaus drüber. Fahren Sie 1 km auf der Straße "Billingstadsletta" geradeaus, bis Sie nach Nesbru gelangen. Fahren Sie unter der Hauptstraße entlang. Auf der rechten Seite sehen sie einen Viking-Abschleppdienst, auf der gegenüberliegenden Seite eine schmale Brücke, die nach Nesåsen führt. Fahren Sie über die Brücke und suchen Sie die Nummer 11 C, ein braunes Haus.

page 60 - Niskinn Bed & Breakfast

E: Take E-16 from Oslo (40 km) or from Sandvika towards Hønefoss. On the long hill up towards Sollihøgda look for the abandoned gas station on the left, after 200 m turn right at Niskinnveien. When the road forks, take the right. Follow sign "cottage". From the main road it's 1 km to Niskinn. If coming from the north Niskinnveien is the 2nd road to the left after Sollihøgda Cafe.

N: Kjør E-16 fra Oslo (40km) eller fra Sandvika i retning Hønefoss. I de lange bakkene opp mot Sollihøgda se etter en nedlagt bensinstasjon på venstre side. 200m etter denne går Niskinnveien inn til høyre. Der veien deler seg, ta til høyre. Følg skiltet 'cottage'. Fra hovedveien er det 1 km inn til Niskinn. Kommer du nordfra er Niskinnveien 2dre vei til venstre etter Sollihøgda Café.

D: Fahren Sie die E-16 ab Oslo (40 km) oder Sandvika in Ri. Hønefoss. Auf der langen Anhöhe oben in Ri. Sollihøgda halten Sie bitte Ausschau nach einer stillgelegten Tankstelle auf der rechten Seite. 200 m nach der Tankstelle biegen Sie nach rechts in den Niskinnveien ab. Wo sich der Weg gabelt, biegen Sie nach rechts ab. Folgen Sie dem Schild 'Cottage'. Von der Hauptstraße sind es ca. 1 km bis Niskinn. Kommen Sie aus Ri. Norden, ist der Niskinnveien der zweite Weg nach links, hinter dem Sollihøgda Café.

page 61 - Linda's Place

E: From Oslo follow RV 4 to Nittedal. Exit at Nittedal station. Turn left on Sørliveien (before the railroad bridge). Turn left on Lysgata. Linda's Place is last house on the right.

N: Fra Oslo: Følg RV 4 til Nittedal. Ta av mot Nittedal sta-

sjon. Ta til venstre i Sørliveien (før jernbanebrua). Ta til venstre i Lysgata. Linda's Place er siste hus på høyre side.
D: Von Oslo aus folgen Sie der Str. 4 nach Nittedal. Fahren Sie Richtung Nittedal stasjon (Bhf.) ab und biegen Sie vor der Eisenbahnbrücke nach links in den Sørliveien. Biegen Sie erneut links in die Lysgata. Linda's Place ist das letzte Haus auf der rechten Seite.

page 66 - Bjerknes Gard
E: Along E-6: at Minnesund exit toward Gjøvik on RV 33. In the first roundabout you go straight ahead. After 200 m turn right, into Sætreveien toward Statsnett, after 700 m turn left into Kråkvålvegen, still toward Statsnett, and follow the road to the end.

abbiegen, nach weiteren 700 m links ab in den Kråkvålvegen (weiterhin in Ri. Statsnett) und diesem Weg bis zum Ende folgen.

page 67 - Ullershov Gård
E: Along the RV 2 in Vormsund continue 2 km east past the Vorma bridge, then turn onto Ullershovvegen road toward the Nes church ruins.
N: RV 2 i Vormsund: 2 km øst for brua over Vorma tar du av fra RV 2. Følg Ullershovvegen mot Nes kirkeruiner.
D: Str. Nr. 2 in Vormsund: 2 km östlich vor der Brücke, die über den Vorma führt, abfahren. Folgen Sie dem Ullershovvegen Ri. Nes kirkeruiner (Kirchenruinen).

Interior from Solvår's Bed & Breakfast, Elverum, page 69

N: Langs E-6: ta av ved Minnesund kjør RV 33 mot Gjøvik. I første rundkjøring kjører du rett fram. Etter 200 m sving til høyre inn Sætreveien mot Statsnett, etter 700 m ta til venstre Kråkvålvegen, fremdeles mot Statsnett, følg veien til endes.
D: Auf der E-6 bis Minnesund, dort abzweigen auf die Str. 33 in Richtung Gjøvik. Am ersten Kreisverkehr geradeaus halten. Nach 200 m rechts in den Sætreveien Ri. „Statsnett"

page 68 – Heggelund's rom og frokost
E: 45 km from Elverum and 60 km from Kongsvinger. From Flisa town center: Drive towards Elverum from the roundabout, then take your first road and your first right again. Here you will find Heggelund's Bed & Breakfast, an ochre yellow house.
N: 45 km fra Elverum og 60 km fra Kongsvinger. Fra Flisa

sentrum: Fra rundkjøringen ta mot Elverum, så første vei til høyre og første til høyre igjen. Der finner du Heggelund's rom og frokost, et okergult hus.

D: 45 km bis Elverum, 60 km bis Kongsvinger. Ab Flisa Zentrum: Im Kreisverkehr biegen Sie ab in Richtung Elverum, anschließend fahren Sie zweimal die erste Straße rechts. So erreichen Sie „Heggelund's Rom", ein ockergelbes Haus.

page 70 - Solbakken Gjestegård

E: From Oslo: Follow E-6 towards Lillehammer. Drive past the exit for Brummunddal and turn right at the sign marked "Brummunddal N./Nes 212". After 300 m, turn right at the sign marked "Brumundal 212". After another 300 m, turn left at the sign marked "Økelsrud". After 2 km, turn right at the sign marked "Veldre". After 800 m, turn right at the sign marked "Hageberg". Drive 200 m and you are here!

N: Fra Oslo, følg E-6 i retning Lillehammer. Passér avkjøring til Brumunddal og ta til høyre ved skilt til "Brumunddal N./Nes 212". Etter 300 m: ta til høyre ved skilt "Brumunddal 212". Etter 300 m: ta til venstre ved skilt "Økelsrud". Etter 2 km: ta til høyre ved skilt "Veldre". Etter 800 m: ta til høyre ved skilt "Hageberg". Etter 200 m er du framme.

D: Folgen Sie ab Oslo der E-6 in Richtung Lillehammer. Hinter der Abzweigung nach Brumundal biegen Sie am Schild "Brummunddal N./Nes 212" ab. 300 m weiter zweigen Sie am Schild „Brumunddal 212" nach rechts ab, weitere 300 m weiter am Schild „Økelsrud" nach links. Nach 2 km Fahrt geht es dann am Schild „Veldre" rechts ab und 800 m weiter am Schild „Hageberg" wieder nach rechts. Nach weiteren 200 m sind sie vor Ort.

page 71 - Kvebergsøya Gard

E: Along RV 29 turn off between Hjerkinn (E-6) and Alvdal (RV 3) at Grimsbu by the Joker grocery store. Follow sign for «Kvebergsøya» 4 km to the farm.

N: Ta av fra RV 29, mellom Hjerkinn (E-6) og Alvdal (RV 3), i Grimsbu ved Joker butikken. Herfra skiltet med "Kvebergsøya" helt frem til garden, 4 km.

D: Auf der Strase zwischen Hjerkinn (E-6) und Alvdal (Str. 3) fahrend, biegen Sie in Grimsbu beim Joker-Supermarkt ab. Von hier an folgen Sie dem Schild "Kvebergsøya" 4km direkt bis zum Hof.

page 75 - Skåden Gard

E: From E-6 take off at sign to Tingberg and Skåden Gard. You find Skåden Gard 4 km up the hillside.

N: Ta av fra E-6 ved skilt Tingberg og Skåden Gard. Gården ligger 4 km oppover dalsiden.

D: Zweigen Sie an der Beschilderung 'Tingberg'/'Skåden

Gard' von der E-6 ab. Der Hof befindet sich 4 km talaufwärts.

page 76 - Skarsmoen Gård

E: Follow E-6 north to a point about 25 km north of Lillehammer. Look for the sign marked "Skarsmoen 0,7" situated in a large woodsy area. Follow the sign.
From the north: Follow E-6 southwards past Otta and Kvitfjell look for the "Skarsmoen 0,7" sign about 6 km past.

N: Følg E-6 ca. 25 km nord for Lillehammer. Se etter skiltet "Skarsmoen 0,7" inne i en stor skog. Følg skilt videre.
Fra nord følges E-6 forbi Otta, Kvitfjell og 6 km forbi Tretten og finn skiltet "Skarsmoen 0,7".

D: Folgen Sie der E-6 bis ca. 25 km nördlich von Lillehammer. Achten Sie in einem großen Waldgebiet auf die Beschilderung "Skarsmoen 0,7". Folgen Sie der Beschilderung. Anreise aus Norden: Folgen Sie der E-6 über Otta und Kvitfjell bis 6 km nach Tretten, anschließend der Beschilderung "Skarsmoen 0,7" folgen.

page 77 - Glomstad Gård

E: Glomstad is located at Tretten, 5 km from town center on the east side of the river, 30 km north of Lillehammer. Drive through the town center and exit the main road towards Glomstad just after passing the Kiwi grocery store on the right-hand side. Remaining distance: 5 km (address: Nord Trettenveien 465).

N: Glomstad ligger på Tretten, 5 km fra sentrum på østsiden av elven, 30 km nord for Lillehammer. Kjør gjennom sentrum, og like etter at du passerer en Kiwi-butikk på høyre hånd, tar du av til Glomstad, 5 km (Adr.: Nord Trettenv. 465).

D: Glomstad befindet sich bei Tretten, 5 km von der Stadtmitte auf der Ostseite des Flusses, 30 km nördlich von Lillehammer. Fahren Sie durchs Zentrum und gleich nachdem Sie den Kiwi Lebensmittelladen zur Rechten passiert haben, biegen Sie nach Glomstad ab. Von hier sind es noch 5 km (Adresse: Nord Trettenveien 465).

page 78 - Sygard Romsås

E: Along E-6 turn off toward Fåvang center. In the main crossing turn left. After 300 m go right toward Brekkom. Follow Bygdeveien about 12 km. Turn left toward Tann, Annolseter and Saubua, a toll-road. Follow road about 5 km to Stor-Tann summer pasture. Take the forth track to the right. Follow sign to Sygard Romsås.

N: Langs E-6: Ta av mot Fåvang sentrum. I sentrumskrysset ta til venstre. Etter 300 m ta til høyre mot Brekkom. Følg Bygdeveien ca. 12 km. Ta av til venstre mot Tann, Annolseter og Saubua. Dette er en bomvei. Følg veien ca. 5 km og du kommer til Stor-Tann seter. På setra tas til høyre i førte kryss. Følg så skilt til Sygard Romsås.

D: Auf der E-6 fahrend Richtung Fåvang Zentrum abfahren. Im Kreisverkehr im Zentrum nach links ausfahren. Nach 300 m rechts Ri. Brekkom in den Bygdeveien abbiegen und diesem ca. 12 km folgen. Danach links Ri. Tann, Annolseter und Saubua abbiegen (Mautstraße!). Nach 5 km erreichen Sie den "Stor-Tann" Hof. Nehmen Sie den vierten Weg nach rechts und folgen Sie dem Schild Ri. Sygard Romsås.

page 79 - Valbjør Gard
E: From Vågåmo center take road to Øver Nordherad. It is presicely 5 km from Vågå Church.
N: Fra Vågåmo sentrum tar du veien mot Øvre Nordherad. Det er nøyaktig 5 km fra Vågå kirke.
D: Von Vågåmo Zentrum nehmen Sie die Straße nach Øver Nordherad. Es sind genau 5 km von der Vågå Kirche bis zum Hof.

page 82 - Teigen Gard
E: 3 km west of Lom center along RV 55 in the direction 'Sognefjellet'.
N: 3 km vest for Lom sentrum langs RV 55 i retning Sognefjellet.
D: 3 km westlich von Lom Zentrum entlang der Str. 55 Ri. Sognefjellet.

page 86 - Sørre Hemsing
E: From Fagernes: Take E-16 towards Lærdal and take a right turn over Hemsing bridge at Vang in Valdres. Drive approx. 1 km climbing towards Heensåsen church. (Do not exit before having driven along Vangsmjøsa lake, ca. 2 km).
N: Fra Fagernes: E-16 mot Lærdal, i Vang i Valdres ta til høyre over Hemsing bru og kjør ca. 1 km oppover mot Heensåsen kirke. (En skal ikke ta av før en har kjørt langs Vangsmjøsa, ca 2 km).
D: Von Fagernes: Auf der E-16 Richtung Lærdal, in Vang i Valdres rechts ab, über die Brücke Hemsing bru und dann ca. 1 km bergan zur Heensåsen-Kirche (biegen Sie erst ab, nachdem Sie 2 km am See Vangsmjøsa entlanggefahren sind).

page 87 - Herangtunet
E: E-16 to Fagernes. Take RV 51 toward Beitostølen, turn toward Valbu, drive over bridge and turn right where sign shows 'Herangtunet'.
N: E-16 til Fagernes. Ta RV 51 mot Beitostølen, ta av mot Valbu, kjør over broen og ta til høyre hvor skilt viser Herangtunet.
D: E-16 bis Fagernes. Nehmen Sie die Str. 51 Ri. Beitostølen. Ri. Valbu abfahren. Über die Brücke fahren und nach rechts. Dort weist ein Schild den Weg nach Herangtunet.

page 88 - Furulund Pensjonat
E: From Fagernes follow E16 till Bergen (ca. 14 km). You pass a sign called Røn and after 1 km turn right by the sign Furulund.
N: Fra Fagernes følg E16 mot Bergen (ca. 14 km). Du passerer skilt med Røn, og tar til høyre ved skilt mot Furulund etter ca. 1 km.
D: Folgen Sie von Fagernes der E16 Richtung Bergen (ca. 14 km). Sie passieren das Schild Røn, und fahren nach 1 km beim Schild Furulund rechts ab.

page 89 - Grønebakke Gard
E: From south: E-16 to Fagernes, pass the Valdres Traffiksenter (Hydro/Texaco). Turn right at the first crossing and drive towards Skrautvål. After 3 km. turn right towards Gausdal/Etnadal/Ranheim. Drive 850 m. and notice large multimailbox post on the left. Follow Øvrebygdsvegen 2.6 km to Grønebakke Gard.
N: Sørfra: E-16 til Fagernes, passér Fagernes Trafikksenter (Hydro/Texaco), ta til høyre i første veikryss og kjør mot Skrautvål. Etter 3 km ta til høyre mot Gausdal/Etnedal/Ranheim. Kjør 850 m oppover til veidele med stort postkassestativ på venstre hånd. Følg Øvrebygdsvegen 2,6 km til Grønebakke Gard.
D: Von Süden kommend E-16 bis Fagernes. Vorbei am Fagernes Trafikksenter (Hydro/Texaco), an der ersten Kreuzung nach rechts Ri. Skrautvål. Nach 3 km rechts Ri. Gausdal/Etnedal/Ranheim. 850 m bergauf fahren bis zur Weggabelung mit grossem Briefkastengestell linker Hand. Ab hier dem Øvrebygdsvegen für 2,6 km bis zum Grønebakke Hof folgen.

page 91 - Laa Gjestestugu
E: From Ål; follow the signs to Kvinnegardslia, 3.5 km. Brown wooden house with brown barn at the crossroad.
N: Fra Ål sentrum; følg skilting til Kvinnegardslia, 3.5 km. Brun låve, brun tømmerhytte ved veikryss.
D: Von Ål Zentrum; der Beschilderung bis Kvinnegardslia für 3,5 km folgen. Braune Scheune, braune Blockhütte an der Strassenkreuzung.

page 92 - Hagaled Gjestegård
E: Bergensbanen (train) or RV 7 to Nesbyen, go south on the roundabout in the sentrum with Nes Church on the right. After 600 m on Alfarvegen you see Hageled to the right. Lighted sign by entry.
N: RV 7 eller Bergensbanen til Nesbyen, ta sørover i rundkjøringen i sentrum med Nes kirke til høyre. Etter 600 m på Alfarvegen er Hagaled til høyre. Skilt med lys ved porten.
D: Str. 7 oder Oslo-Bergen-Bahn bis Nesbyen. Am Kreisverkehr im Zentrum südwärts in den Alfarvegen fahren

(Kirche auf der rechten Seite). Nach 600 Meter sehen Sie Hagaled Gjestegård auf der rechten Seite. Beleuchtetes Schild am Tor.

page 93 - Sevletunet

E: Along RV 40, 89 km north of Kongsberg; near the upper end of Norefjorden lake you slow down, to the right you will see the farm with its old wooden buildings.
From Rødberg; drive 4.5 km southwards. You get to a plain where you pass the bridge to Vrenne/Gvammen/Fjordgløtt (don't cross); look for the sign "Sevletunet" and go 500 m.

N: Langs RV 40, 89 km nord for Kongsberg; ved øvre enden av Norefjorden, sakne farten, titt inn til høyre og dere ser gården med de gamle tømmerhusene.
Fra Rødberg; kjør sørover 4,5 km, på sletta kjører du forbi broen mot Vrenne/Gvammen/Fjordgløtt, deretter ser du skilt Sevletunet 500 m.

D: Entlang der Str. 40, 89 km nördl. von Kongsberg; am oberen Ende des Norefjord Sees langsam fahren und rechts schauen - dort sehen Sie den Bauernhof mit seinen alten Blockhäusern.
Von Rødberg aus 4,5 km Ri. Süden fahren. In einer Ebene angelangt, fahren Sie an der Brücke Ri. Vrenne/Gvammen/Fjordgløtt vorbei (nicht drüber) und weiter geradeaus. Danach steht ein Schild "Sevletunet", dem Sie 500 m folgen.

page 94 - Eggedal Borgerstue

E: From Oslo: via Drammen, to Åmot (Modum) continuing from there on RV 287 to Eggedal.
Borgerstue is 100 m before the church on the right hand.
From Gol take RV 35 to Bromma, then turn right at Nor Kro, follow the sign to Haglebu/Eggedal, follow then RV 287, a scenic route over Haglebu mountain, and continue to Eggedal.

N: Fra Oslo: via Drammen, til Åmot (Modum) videre derfra RV 287 oppover helt til Eggedal Sentrum – Borgerstua ligger 100 m før kirken på høyre hånd.
Fra Gol ta RV 35 til Bromma, ta av til høyre ved Nor Kro, følg skilt mot Haglebu/Eggedal, man følger så RV 287, naturskjønn rute over fjellet Haglebu, og videre ned til Eggedal.

D: Von Oslo aus fahren Sie via Drammen bis Åmot/Modum, von dort aus weiter auf der Str. 287 bis nach Eggedal Zentrum – Borgerstua liegt 100m vor der Kirche rechter Hand.
Von Gol aus nehmen Sie die Str. 35 bis Bromma, wo Sie rechts abbiegen beim Motell 'Nor Kro'. Folgen Sie der Beschilderung nach Haglebu/Eggedal (Str. 287) - diese landschaftlich schöne Strecke bringst Sie über den Haglebu Berg bis nach Eggedal.

page 95 - Bjørke gård

E: Bjørke gård is 50 km from Oslo, 5 km south of Hønefoss, 500 m from E-16.
Along E-16 turn toward Hole Church (Jørgen Moes vei). After about 300 m turn right (Bjørkeveien). Drive up the hill, stay to the right and you're there.

N: Bjørke gård ligger 50 km fra Oslo, 5 km sør for Hønefoss, 500 m fra E-16. Langs E-16 ta mot Hole kirke (Jørgen Moes vei). Etter ca. 300 m ta mot høyre (Bjørkeveien). Kjør opp bakken, hold til høyre og du er fremme.

D: Der Bjørke Hof liegt 50 km von Oslo entfernt, 5 km südlich von Hønefoss und 500 m von der E-16. Auf der E-16 fahrend biegen Sie in Hole in Richtung Kirche ab (in den Jørgen Moes vei). Nach ca. 300 m nach rechts in den Bjørkeveien einbeiegen. Den Hügel hinauf fahren, rechts halten und Sie sind am Ziel.

page 100 - Nordbø Pensjonat

E: Easily noticeable along E-134 about 40 km from Notododden and X km from Seljord.

N: Lett synlig langs E-134. Ca. 40 km fra Notodden og Xkm fra Seljord.

D: Südlich entlang der E-134 gelegen. Ca. 40 km von Notodden und X km von Seljord.

page 101 - Huldrehaugen

E: From Notodden, take RV 134 to Flatdal. Look for Nutheim Gjestgiveri in the hills approaching Flatdal. 400 m further down look for sign: "ROM", take a left, red house at the top.

N: Fra Notodden; RV 134 til Flatdal. I bakkene ned mot Flatdal skal du se etter Nutheim Gjestgiveri. 400 m lenger nede se skilt "ROM", ta opp til venstre, helt opp, rødt hus.

D: Von Notodden: Nehmen Sie die Str. 134 bis Flatdal. Fahren Sie den Berg hinunter in Richtung Flatdal. Achten Sie auf den Gasthof "Nutheim Gjestgiveri". 400 m weiter talwärts auf der linken Seite steht ein Schild mit der Aufschrift "ROM". Fahren Sie hier nach links bis zum roten Haus ganz oben.

page 106 - Dalen Bed & Breakfast

E: The house is located along RV 45 in Dalen town center. Look for a yellow house.

N: Huset ligger like ved RV 45 i Dalen sentrum. Et gult hus.

D: Das Haus liegt direkt an der Str. 45 in Dalen Ortsmitte. Es ist ein gelbes Haus.

page 110 - Fyresdal Bed & Breakfast

E: Fyresdal is on route RV 355. In the town center look for signs to Bed & Breakfast.

N: Fyresdal ligger langs RV 355. I Fyresdal sentrum se skilt Bed & Breakfast.

D: Fyresdal liegt entlang der Str. 355. Im Zentrum von Fyresdal ist das Bed & Breakfast ausgeschildert.

page 111 - Ettestad Gård

E: From Drangedal center drive toward Dalen. After 6 km turn at the sign for Ettestad. Drive 6 km further on a gravel road to the farm.

N: Fra Drangedal sentrum kjør mot Dalen, etter 6 km ta av hvor ved skilt Ettestad, kjør videre 6 km (grusvei) til gården.

D: Von Drangedal Zentrum Ri. Dalen fahren, nach 6 km beim Schild Ri. Ettestad abbiegen. Die Fahrt 6 km weit auf dem Schotterweg bis zum Hof fortsetzen.

page 112 - Hulfjell Gård og Hytteutleie

E: Exit E-18 towards Drangedal. About 5 km before Drangedal town center, exit highway at the sign "Hulfjell Gård, hytte, gårdssalg og kanoutleie". Farm 1.5 km.

N: Ta av fra E-18 retning Drangedal. Ca. 5 km før Drangedal sentrum, ta av ved skilt merket "Hulfjell Gård, hytte, gårdssalg og kanoutleie". Det er da 1,5 km til gården. Velkommen!

D: Zweigen Sie von der E-18 in Richtung Drangedal ab. Folgen Sie ca. 5 km vor Drangedal Zentrum dem Schild "Hulfjell Gård, hytte, gårdssalg og kanoutleie". Von da an noch ca. 1,5 km zum Hof. Willkommen!

page 113 - Templen Bed & Breakfast

E: From Oslo: Exit from E-18 at the Bjorbekk/Hisøy sign, west of Arendal. Turn left in the Bjorbekkrysset (crossing) towards Hisøy. Drive 2 km on road 407 to a plumbing service on the right roadside (Egil Bringsverd). Turn left onto the side-road called Gamle Bievei. The road splits into two: you take Vestre Bievei to the left and continue on a gravel road and up a small hill. The house will be visible straight ahead.

N: Fra Oslo: ta av fra E-18 ved Bjorbekk/Hisøy-skiltet vest for Arendal. I Bjorbekkrysset sving til venstre mot Hisøy. Kjør 2 km på RV 407 til en rørleggerforretning (Egil Bringsverd) på høyre side. Sving inn på en sidevei til venstre som

heter Gamle Bievei. Denne deler seg i to; følg så Vestre Bievei. Kjør Vestre Bievei til venstre, så inn på en grusvei, opp en liten bakke, og da ser dere huset rett fremfor dere.

D: Von Oslo: Biegen Sie westlich von Arendal von der E-18 ab in Richtung Bjorbekk/Hisøy. An der Kreuzung Bjorbekk-krysset links ab nach Hisøy. Nach 2 km (Str. 407) liegt auf der rechten Seite ein Installateurbetrieb (Rørlegger Egil Bringsverd). Dort nach links auf eine kleine Straße einbiegen (Gamle Bievei). An der Gabelung dem Vestre Bievei nach links folgen, dann in einen Kiesweg einbiegen und einen kleinen Hang hinauf bis zum Haus.

page 115 - Døblane Bed & Breakfast

E: Follow the RV9 toward Setesdalen. At the round-about take the RV405 toward Vennesla. Turn off at the second exit, Centrumsveien, then watch for the sign showing Tvidøblane to the right. Follow 600 meters Tvidøblane 46, total 18 km.

N: Kjør RV9 mot Setesdalen. I rundkjøring ta RV405 mot Vennesla. Ta så av i 2dre avkjørsel inn på Sentrumsveien. Ta til høyre hvor skilt er merket Tvidøblane. Etter 600 meter er du fremme ved Tvidøblane 46. Totalt 18 km.

D: Fahren Sie die Str. 9 in Richtung Setesdalen. Im Kreisverkehr nehmen Sie die Str. 405 in Richtung Vennesla. Nehmen Sie die zweite Ausfahrt, die auf den Sentrumsveien führt. Fahren Sie am Schild "Tvidøblane" nach rechts. Nach 600 Metern sind Sie am Tvidøblane 46 angekommen. Fahrtweg insgesamt 18 km.

page 118 - Heddan Gard

E: Heddan Gard is easy to find, along E 39 Kristiansand - Stavanger turn north at Lyngdal on RV 43 toward Eiken, after 30 km see sign for Heddan Gard. On RV 42 there's a sign for Heddan Gard in Eiken.

N: Heddan Gard er lett å finne, kommer du langs E 39 Kristiansand - Stavanger, tar du nordover i Lyngdal på RV 43 mot Eiken, etter 30 km er det skiltet til Heddan Gard. På RV 42 er det skiltet til Heddan Gard i Eiken.

D: Heddan Gard ist leicht zu finden. Von der E 39 Kristansand - Stavanger kommend, fahren Sie in Lyngdal nordwärts auf die Str. 43 Richtung Eiken. Nach 30 km ist Heddan Gard ausgeschidert. Kommen Sie von der Str. 42, ist Heddan Gard in Eiken ausgeschildert.

page 119 - Magne Handeland

E: Exit E-39, 3 km north of Moi, to the right towards Hovsherad. Drive 5 km and look for Bjørnestad. It is the third house on the right-hand side.

N: Langs E-39, 3 km nord for Moi, tar du til høyre mot Hovsherad. Kjør 5 km og se etter Bjørnestad. Det er det 3dje hus på høyre hånd.

D: Entlang der E-39, 3 km nördlich von Moi biegen Sie rechts in Richtung Hovsherad ab. Fahren Sie 5 km und halten Sie nach Bjørnestad Ausschau. Es ist das dritte Haus auf der rechten Seite.

page 120 - Skjerpe Gård Hytter

E: Along the E-39, 20 km. north of Moi or 18 km. south of Helleland. Exit at the sign with the cabin & church symbols. Follow sign to Skjerpe, right next to Heskestad Church.

N: Langs E-39, 20 km nord for Moi eller 18 km sør for Helleland; ta av ved skilt med hytte- og kirkesymbol. Deretter følg skilt til Skjerpe som ligger like ved Heskestad Kirke.

D: Entlang der E-39, 20 km nördlich von Moi bzw. 18 km südlich von Helleland. Abfahren beim Schild mit Hütten- u. Kirchensymbol. Danach dem Schild bis Skjerpe folgen, Skjerpe liegt direkt bei der Heskestad Kirche.

page 121 - Bjørg's Bed & Breakfast

E: Along RV 507, Nordsjøveien, look for Vik, a little west of the towncenter of Orre.

N: Langs RV 507, Nordsjøveien, finn Vik, litt vest for tettstedet Orre.

D: Entlang der Str. 507, Nordsjøveien, nach Vik, etwas westlich der Ortschaft Orre.

page 123 - Bed, Books & Breakfast

E: From Stavanger center take Muségaten past the Stavanger Museum, continue through the round-about. You are now on Rogalandsgaten. Take first road to the right, Byfoged Christensensgate.

N: Fra Stavanger sentrum: ta Muségaten forbi Stavanger Museum, fortsett rett frem gjennom to rundkjøringer. Du er nå i Rogalandsgaten. Ta 1ste vei til høyre som er Byfoged Christensensgate.

D: Vom Stavanger Zentrum: Nehmen Sie die Muségaten, vorbei am Stavanger Museum. Geradeaus weiterfahren, durch zwei Kreisverkehre. Jetzt befinden Sie sich auf der Rogalandsgaten. Die erste Straße rechts ist die Zielstraße Byfoged Christensensgate.

page 124 - Byhaugen

E: E-39 toward Bergen through the Tjensvollkrysset intersection, also when coming from the north, and pass through the Byhaugtunnel. Exit towards Nedre Stokka. Turn left at the first road. Drive up Byhaugveien at Egenes kolonihage. The second road on the left is Bruveien. From down town; Bus no. 25 from SR-bank.

N: Følg E-39 mot Bergen gjennom Tjensvollkrysset., evt. nordfra og gjennom Byhaugtunellen. Ta av mot Nedre Stokka. Ta av neste vei til venstre. Ved Egenes kolonihage,

kjør opp Byhaugvn. Andre vei til venstre er Bruveien. Fra sentrum; Buss nr. 25 fra SR-bank.

D: Folgen Sie der E-39 durch Bergen bis zur Kreuzung "Tjensvollkrysset"; aus Norden kommend durch den Byhaugtunnel. Zweigen Sie anschließend ab in Richtung Nedre Stokka und an der nächsten Abbiegung nach links. Bei "Egenes Kolonihage" geht es die Straße "Byhaugveien" hinauf. Zweite Straße links ist dann der "Bruveien". Ab Zentrum: Der Bus Nr. 25 ab SR-Bank.

page 125 - Åmøy Fjordferie

E: Follow the E-39 from Stavanger north towards Mortavika/ Haugesund. After the tunnel turn right to cross the bridge to Åmøy. Proceed to Åmøy Fjordferie, about 2 km.

N: Følg E-39 fra Stavanger nordover mot Mortavika/Haugesund. Etter tunellen ta til høyre over broen til Åmøy. Skilt videre til Åmøy Fjordferie, ca. 2 km.

D: Der E-39 von Stavanger nordwärts Ri. Mortavika/Haugesund folgen. Nach dem Tunnel rechts über die Brücke bis Åmøy. Beschilderung Ri. Åmøy Fjordferie folgen, ca. 2 km.

page 126 - Høiland Gård

E: Høiland Gard lies 30 km from Tau in the direction of Hjelmeland, 2 km from Årdal, look for sign along RV 13.

N: Høiland Gard ligger 30 km fra Tau i retning Hjelmeland, 2 km fra Årdal, godt skiltet fra RV 13.

D: Høiland Gard liegt 30 km von Tau in Richtung Hjemeland, 2 km von Årdal, gut ausgeschildert von der Str. 13.

page 134 - Guddalstunet

E: 3 km south of Rosendal along RV 13, you come to Seimsfoss. Exit the main highway near the Fokus store and follow the sign towards Guddal. Stay to the left when the road forks after 1 km. Drive to the left over the bridge where there is a sign marked Guddal. One more kilometer and you have arrived at Guddalstunet. Drive into the courtyard with the homemade sign for "Guddalstunet".

N: Langs RV 13, 3 km sør for Rosendal, kommer du til Seimsfoss. Ta av i veikryss ved Fokusforretningen hvor skilt viser til Guddal. Etter 1 km deler veien seg i to. Ta til venstre, over brua, med skilt til Guddal. Så 1 km til, og du er framme i Guddalstunet. Kjør opp i tunet med privat skilt "Guddalstunet".

D: Auf der Str. 13 gelangen Sie ca. 3 km südlich von Rosendal nach Seimsfoss. Biegen Sie am Geschäft „Fokus" an der Kreuzung ab und folgen Sie der Beschilderung nach Guddal. Nach ca. 1 km teilt sich die Straße. Folgen Sie der linken Straße über die Brücke (Beschilderung Guddal). Nach 1 km erreichen Sie den Guddals Hof. Fahren Sie auf den Hof, an dem Sie auch ein Schild „Guddalstunet" finden.

page 135 - Heradstveit Herberge

E: RV 49 between Nordheimsund and Tørvikbygd. Find the sign for 'Heradstveit Herberge' and follow the road for about 3 km to the last farmyard.

N: RV 49 mellom Nordheimsund og Tørvikbygd: Du finn eit skilt 'Heradstveit Herberge', følg denne vegen ca. 3 km til siste tunet.

D: Entlang der Str. 49 zwischen Nordheimsund und Tørvikbygd finden Sie ein Schild "Heradstveit Herberge". Folgen Sie dieser Strasse für ca. 3 km bis zum letzten Hof.

Interior from Guddalstunet, Rosendal, page 134

page 136 - Lerkebo

E: From Bergen: take RV 553/580 towards Flesland airport. Take RV 580/582 Skjold, Fanavegen, towards Nesttun from the roundabout nearest Lagunen shopping centre and then make a right in the first lighted intersection onto Sætervegen. Look for a sign with "40-64 Sætervegen" and turn left here. Enter the driveway just past the post boxes.

N: Fra Bergen: ta RV 553/580 mot Flesland flyplass. I rundkjøringen ved Lagunen senter ta RV 580/582 Skjold, Fanavegen, mot Nesttun og ta så til høyre i første lyskryss, dette er Sætervegen. Se så etter skilt med "40-64 Sætervegen" og ta til venstre her. Kjør inn oppkjørselen rett etter poststativet.

D: Von Bergen: Auf der Straße 553/580 Richtung Flughafen Flesland. Am Kreisverkehr beim Lagunen-Center auf die Straße 580/582 Skjold (Fanavegen) Richtung Nesttun, und dann an der ersten Ampelkreuzung nach rechts in die Straße "Sætervegen". Am Schild "Sætervegen 40-64" links ab. Nehmen Sie die Einfahrt gleich hinter dem Briefkastengestell.

page 137 - EkerGarden

E: Driving RV 555 toward Sotra, over Sotrabroen bridge, after 5 km pass Straume/Sartor center, continue on the main road and turn left toward Lie before the tunnel, follow sign toward Lie. Follow to Døsjevegen and then Ekrhovdvegen. Turn right by the rainbow sign: 'EkerGarden' on a white fence. Large dark brown house with parking outside.

N: Kjør RV 555 mot Sotra, over Sotrabroen, etter ca. 5 km passeres Straume/Sartor Senter, fortsett hovedveien og ta til venstre mot Lie (før tunnell), følg skilting mot Lie. Ta Døsjevegen og videre Ekrhovdvegen. Ta til høyre ved regnbue-skiltet; 'EkerGarden' på hvitt plankegjerde. Stort mørkebrunt

hus med parkering utenfor.

D: Fahren Sie die Str. 555 Ri. Sotra, über die Sotra-Brücke drüber, nach 5 km passieren Sie Straume/Sartor Zentrum. Die Fahrt auf der Hauptstrasse fortsetzen und nach links Ri. Lie vor dem Tunnel abbiegen. Folgen Sie der Beschilderung Ri. Lie. Den Døsjevegen entlangfahren, dann auf den Ekrhovd-vegen. Beim Regenbogen-Schild 'EkerGarden' auf dem weissen Zaun nach rechts. Grosses dunkelbraunes Haus mit Park-möglichkeit davor.

page 139 - Anne's Gjestehus

E: From all entrances to Bergen follow the signs to Akvariet (aquarium), continue in direction of city center, swing to the left after the avenue. The house is the closest neighbor to the Amalie Skram statue in Klosterhaugen park.

N: Alle innkjørsler til Bergen: følg skilt til Akvariet, fortsett tilbake mot sentrum, sving til venstre etter alléen. Huset ligger som nærmeste nabo til Amalie Skram statuen i parken på Klosterhaugen.

D: Zunächst können Sie aus allen Ri. nach Bergen fahren, dann folgen Sie dem Schild zum Aquarium ('Akvariet'). Sie setzen Ihren Weg fort zurück in Ri. Zentrum. Fahren Sie hinter der Allee nach links. Das Haus liegt im Park Kloster-haugen, neben der Statur von 'Amalie Skram'.

page 140 - Skiven Gjestehus

E: By foot from the railway station: a short city block north of the station, take Kong Oscarsgate to the left towards downtown and then turn right on the second street Dankert Krohnsgate. At the end of the road (100 m) steps lead up to

Skivebakken. No. 17 is the first house to the left . By car: Take Kong Oscarsgate towards downtown and turn right at the traffic lights four city blocks past the railway station onto Heggebakken. Skivebakken is 100 m down the road on your right-hand side.

N: Til fots fra jernbanestasjonen; ett lite kvartal nord for stasjonen: ta Kong Oscarsgate til venstre mot sentrum, deretter andre gate, Dankert Krohnsgate, til høyre. Ved enden av denne (150 m) leder en trapp opp til Skivebakken. Nr. 17 er første hus til venstre. Med bil: kjør Kong Oscarsgate mot sentrum, fire kvartaler etter jernbanestasjon; sving til høyre, inn Heggebakken, etter 100 m finner du Skivebakken til høyre.

D: Zu Fuß vom Bahnhof: ein kurzer Stadtblock nördlich des HBF: Kong Oscarsgate links in Richtung Stadtzentrum gehen, danach die zweite Strasse nach rechts (Danker Krohnsgate). Am Ende der Strasse (in 150 m) führt eine Treppe hinauf zum Skivebakken. Nr. 17: erste Haus auf der linken Seite. Mit dem Auto: Kong Oscarsgate in Ri. Stadtzentrum fahren. Vier Blöcke nach dem Hauptbahnhof; nach rechts fahren in Heggebakken, nach 100 m sehen Sie Skivebakken auf der rechten Seite.

page 142 - Bøketun overnatting

E: From Bergen follow the signs toward Sotra, then to Askøy. At the end of the bridge turn right toward Kleppestø. Drive to Ask (9 km.) Drive through the crossroad where the sign for Ask is posted, then immediately, after 25 m., look for a yellow sign on your left reading "Åsebø 6". Take a U-turn and drive up the narrow, steep road behind the sign, the road is surrounded by large trees. Continue into the forest where road gets even smaller. The 3rd house.

N: Fra Bergen: Følg skilt mot Sotra. Ta av til Askøy. På slutten av broen tar du til høyre, mot Kleppestø. Kjør til Ask (9 km). Kjør rett fram i krysset der skiltet 'Ask' står, etter bare ca. 25 m se etter skiltet 'Åsebø 6'. Ta en U-sving og kjør opp en smal svinget bakke bak skiltet. Store bøketrær på sidene. Fortsett inn i skogen hvor veien blir enda smalere. Du skal til det tredje huset.

D: Ab Bergen: Folgen Sie der Ausschilderung nach Sotra, dann nach Askøy. Hinter der Brücke geht es rechts ab in Richtung Kleppestø. Nach 9 km erreicht man Ask. Die Kreuzung beim Ortseingangsschild "Ask" geradeaus überqueren, aber nur ca. 25 m weit. Halten Sie Ausschau nach einem gelben Schild "Åsebø 6" auf der linken Seite. Wenden Sie und fahren den kleinen Weg hinter dem Schild hinauf (kurvig und hügelig; sehr grosse Buchen säumen den Weg). Weiter in den Wald hinein fahren, wo die Strasse immer schmaler wird, bis zum dritten Haus.

page 143 - Fjordutleie Solheim aktivitetsgard

E: From Bergen take RV 555 toward Sotra. Take exit to Askøy on RV 562. After the bridge continue for 14 km and follow the road to "Herdla". After the forest you'll notice a sign for "Kjerrgarden", then continue down a hill and up another hill and down a hill to an intersection where you turn to the right toward Nordre Haugland and Berland. From here turn right at each crossing until you get to an open place. There take the first turn to the left. Yellow house on the farmstead.

N: Fra Bergen; ta RV 555 i retning Sotra. Ta av mot Askøy, RV 562. Etter broen; kjør ca. 14 km, og der følg veien videre mot 'Herdla'. Etter skogen ser du skilt 'Kjerrgarden', fortett ned en bakke, opp en bakke og ned en bakke til et kryss; ta til høyre mot 'Nordre Haugland' og 'Berland'. Herfra ta til høyre i alle kryss til du finner en snuplass. Her tar du første vei til venstre. Gult hus i et gårdstun.

D: Von Bergen nehmen Sie die Str. 555 in Ri. Sotra. Fahren Sie ab in Ri. Askøy, Str. 562. Nach der Brücke fahren Sie ca. 14 km und von dort folgen Sie dem Weg in Ri. 'Herdla'. Nach dem Wald sehen Sie das Schild 'Kjerrgarden', fahren Sie den Berg hinunter, den Berg hinauf und wieder hinunter, bis zu einer Kreuzung; fahren Sie nach rechts in Ri. 'Nordre Haugland' und 'Berland'. Von dort fahren Sie immer rechts an allen Kreuzungen, bis Sie an einen Wendeplatz kommen. Dort nehmen Sie die erste Str. nach links. Das gelbe Haus auf dem Hof ist Ihr Ziel.

page 144 - Fjordside Lodge

E: North of Bergen, take E-39 for about 20 km untill you pass Hylkje and get to a 70 speed limit zone. Take first right toward Steinestø/Hordvik. Follow the road untill you see the sign Fjordside on the right side, before the quay.

N: Følg E-39 ca. 20 km nord for Bergen til du passerer Hylkje og kommer til 70-sone. Ta første vei til høyre mot Steinestø/Hordvik. Følg veien helt til du ser skiltet Fjordside på høyre side, før kaien.

D: Folgen Sie der E-39 bis ca. 20 km nördlich von Bergen bis Sie Hylkje passieren und die 70-Zone erreichen. Dort biegen Sie nach rechts ab in Richtung Steinestø/Hordvik. Folgen Sie der Straße bis Sie das Schild Fjordside auf der rechten Seite sehen, vor der Anlegestelle.

page 145 - Skjerping Gård

E: Exit E-16 onto RV 566 at the sign marked "Osterøybrua". From Bergen: You will find the turn-off past the Arnanipa Tunnel. From Voss: The turn-off is past the small towns of Dale, Vaksdal and Trengereid. Drive over the bridge and follow the signs towards Lonevåg, through the tunnel. Turn right at the sign 'Gjerstad', drive about 2-3 km and look for a private road to the right with a sign marked "Skjerping", which is situated alongside a group of mailboxes with a grass-covered roof.

N: Når du kjører E-16 skal du ta av ved skilt som sier "Osterøybrua" RV 566. Fra Bergen finner du avkjørselen etter Arnanipatunnellen. Fra Voss er det etter tettstedene Dale - Vaksdal - Trengereid. Kjør så over brua og følg skilt i retning Lonevåg, gjennom tunnelen. Ta til høyre ved skilt 'Gjerstad' og kjør ca. 2-3 km og se etter en privat vei til høyre med skiltet "Skjerping" plassert sammen med et postkassestativ med gress på taket.

D: Von der E-16 beim Schild 'Osterøybrua' auf die Str. 566 abfahren. Von Bergen: Die Abfahrt befindet sich hinter dem Arnanipa Tunnel. Von Voss: Die Abfahrt liegt hinter den kleinen Ortschaften Dale, Vaksdal und Trengereid. Überqueren Sie die Brücke und folgen Sie den Schildern Ri. Lonevåg, durch den Tunnel. Beim Schild 'Gjerstad' nach rechts abbiegen, dann fahren Sie ungefähr 2-3 km und schauen rechts nach einem Privatweg - Beschilderung 'Skjerping' neben Briefkästen mit grasbewachsenem Dach.

page 148 - Bergagarden/Skomakarhuset

E: Exit E-16 towards Bolstadøyri, and follow the signs to Bergagarden Farm. From Bergen: 70 km. From Voss: 30 km.

N: Langs E-16; ta av mot Bolstadøyri, følg skilt til Bergagarden. Fra Bergen 70 km. Fra Voss 30 km.

D: Entlang E-16: Ri. Bolstadøyri abfahren, den Schildern bis Begagarden folgen. Von Bergen 70 km, von Voss 30 km.

page 149 - Haugo Utleige

E: Drive through Voss center from the west, cross the bridge by Hotel Jarl, turn to the right, take second road to the right and find sign for 'Haugo Utleige'.

N: Frå vest, (Bergen), køyr gjennom Voss sentrum over brua ved hotell Jarl. Ta til høgre, følg skilt "Haugo Utleige". Køyr eit lite stykke til neste skilt "Haugo Utleige", ta til høgre. Følg vegen og du vil sjå huset og hytta.

D: Aus Westen/Bergen kommend durch das Zentrum von Voss fahren, dann über die Brücke beim Hotel Jarl. Hier nach rechts und dem Schild "Haugo Utleige" folgen. Ein kurzes Stück weiter beim nächsten Schild "Haugo Utleige" wieder rechts abbiegen. Dem Weg folgen, bis Sie das Haus und die Hütten sehen.

page 151 - Solund Gjestegård

E: By arriving Krakhella in Solund follow the signs to Hardbakke. When you arrive Hardbakke you come to a church. Here you drive to the right until reaching the backside of the church. Here you will find a sign "Solund Gjestegaard"

Entrance to Fjordside Lodge, Hordvik, page 144

N: Når du kommer til Krakhella i Solund følger du skilting til Hardbakke. Ved ankomst Hardbakke tar du til høyre ved Kirken og kjører opp bak på oversiden av Kirken. Der ser du et stort skilt på vegg med Solund Gjestegaard.

D: Wenn Sie in Krakhella in Solund ankommen, folgen Sie der Beschilderung bis Hardbakke. In Hardbakke fahren Sie an der Kirche rechts rein und zur Rückseite der Kirche. Dort finden Sie ein grosses Schild "Solund Gjestegaard"

page 152 - Flesje Gard

E: 4.5 km from Balestrand town center. Follow RV 55 towards Høyanger.

N: 4,5 km frå Balestrand sentrum, følg RV 55 mot Høyanger.

D: 4,5 km von Balestrand Stadtmitte. Folgen Sie der Strasse 55 in Richtung Høyanger.

page 154 - Sognefjord Gjestehotell

E: From Bergen: Drive past Voss, Vinje and over Vikafjellet to Vik, then proceed to Vangsnes. From Oslo: Drive via Gol, Hol, Aurland, Vinje and proceed to Vangsnes. Express Boat from Bergen to Vangsnes (via Vik): Approx. 4 hours.

N: Fra Bergen: kjør til Voss, Vinje og over Vikafjellet til Vik og videre ut til Vangsnes. Fra Oslo: kjør via Gol, Hol, Aurland, Vinje og videre til Vangsnes. Ekspressbåt fra Bergen til Vangsnes (via Vik) Ca. 4 timer.

D: Von Bergen: Fahren Sie nach Voss, Vinje und über den

Vikafjellet nach Vik, danach weiter nach Vangsnes. Von Oslo: Fahren Sie über Gol, Hol, Aurland, Vinje und weiter nach Vangsnes. Es gibt auch ein Schnellboot von Bergen nach Vangsnes (über Vik): Fahrtzeit ca. 4 Stunden.

page 158 - Eplet Bed & Breakfast
E: From Sogndal take RV 55 toward Lom, exit toward Solvorn and drive 3 km. Well posted.
N: Fra Sogndal; ta RV 55 mot Lom, ta av mot Solvorn og kjør 3 km. Godt merket.
D: Von Sogndal kommend nehmen Sie die Str. 55 Richtung Lom. Fahren Sie Richtung Solvorn ab und noch 3km weiter. Gut ausgeschildert.

page 162 - Nigardsbreen Gjesteheim
E: From Sogndal take RV 55 toward Gaupne/Lom. After about 28 km, by Gaupne, exit toward Jostedal/Nigardsbreen, RV 604.
From Lom and Gudbrandsdalen drive along RV 55 over Sognefjellet to Fortun and continue along the fjord to Gaupne.
N: Frå Sogndal ta RV 55 mot Gaupne/Lom. Etter ca. 28 km, ved Gaupne, ta av mot Jostedal/Nigardsbreen, RV 604.
Frå Lom og Gudbrandsdalen køyrer du RV 55 over Sognefjellet til Fortun og vidare ut fjorden til Gaupne.
D: Von Sogndal der Str. 55 Ri. Gaupne/Lom folgen. Nach ca. 28 km bei Gaupne Ri. Jostedal/Nigradsbreen abbiegen und der Str. 604 folgen.
Von Lom und Gudbrandsdalen fahren Sie die Str. 55 über den Sognefjell bis Fortun und weiter entlang des Fjords bis Gaupne.

page 163 - Skinlo Farm B&B
E: From E-39 in Byrkelo take RV 60 toward Stryn. After about 5 km up the hills turn left at the sign for 'Reed'. After 500 m turn right at the bus stop shelter. Drive 600 m to the fourth farm on the left, a yellow house.
N: Fra E-39 i Byrkjelo: ta RV 60 i retning Stryn, etter ca 5 km oppover bakkene ta til venstre ved skilt til'Reed'. Etter 500 m ta veien til høyre ved busskuret, kjør 600 m til den fjerde gården på venstre side, et gult hus.
D: Von E-39 in Byrkjelo: nehmen Sie die Str. 60 Ri. Stryn. Fahren Sie ca. 5 km bergauf. Beim Schild 'Reed' nach links fahren. Nach 500 m bei der Bushaltestelle rechts abbiegen. Jetzt sind es noch 600 m bis zu dem vierten Hof auf der linken Seite, einem gelben Haus.

page 168 - Knutegarden Norangdal
E: Follow route RV 655 from Hellesylt or from Leknes Ferry launch. At Øye exit at the sign for Norang/Stenes/Knutegarden-Norangdal, cross a little bridge and see the sign on the house.

N: Du følgjer RV 655 frå Hellesylt eller frå Leknes fergeleie; like ved Øye ta av ved skilt Norang/Stenes/Knutegarden-Norangdal, over ei lita bru. Skilt på huset!
D: Von Hellesylt oder vom Leknes Fährkai der Str. 655 folgen. Bei Øye Ri. Norang/Stenes/Knutegarden-Norangdal abfahren, über eine kleine Brücke und halten Sie Ausschau nach dem Schild am Haus.

page 174 - Malmestranda Romutleie
E: From Molde take route RV 64 towards Eide, drive through Tusseltunnel. Exit towards Aureosen. After about 1 km. it will be the third farm on the right.
N: Fra Molde: Ta RV 64 mot Eide, kjør gjennom Tussentunellen. Ta av mot Aureosen. Etter ca. 1 km er du framme, den 3dje gården på høyre hånd.
D: Von Molde: Str. 64 Ri. Eide, durch die Tussen-Tunnel fahren. Ri. Aureosen abfahren. Nach ca. 1 km ist man am Ziel, dem dritten Hof auf der rechten Seite.

page 175 - Øyastuo
E: RV 70 north of Sunndalsøra; after 10 km you come to Ålvundeid. Turn right toward Innerdalen. After 10 km you see a parking sign. Up a hill you find a red house on the right side.
N: RV 70 nord for Sunndalsøra; etter 10 km finn du Ålvundeid. Ta til høgre mot Innerdalen. Etter 10 km sjå etter eit P-skilt. Opp ein bakke finn du eit raudt hus på høgre side.
D: Str. 70 nördlich von Sunndalsøra; nach 10 km erreichen Sie Ålvundeid. Fahren Sie nach rechts Ri. Innerdalen. Achten Sie nach 10 km auf ein Parkplatz-Schild. Das rote Haus befindet sich auf der rechten Seite auf einem Hügel.

page 176 - Saga Trollheimen
E: Along RV 65 take an exit toward Rindal center. Saga Trollheimen appears after 1 km or 3 km depending on which exit you take.
N: Langs RV 65 ta av mot Rindal sentrum. Saga Trollheimen ser du etter 1km eller etter 3 km avhengig av hvilken avkjøring du tar.
D: Entlang der Str. 65 Ri. Rindal Zentrum abfahren. Abghängig von welcher Abfahrt Sie nehmen, sehen Sie das Hotel nach 1 bzw. 3 km.

page 177 - Brattset Gard
E: Brattset Gard is located on Ertvågøya. Along E-39 between Orkanger and Kristiansund; at the Hennset ferrydock, take the ferry over to Arasvika. Drive toward Mjosundet. You find Brattset Gard after 6 km.
From Kristiansund; RV 680 toward Aure, at Giset follow sign to Mjosundet, 17 km.
N: Brattset Gard ligger på Ertvågøya. Langs E-39 mellom

Orkanger og Kristiansund; ved fergekaia Hennset, ta fergen over til Arasvika. Kjør mot Mjosundet. Du finner Brattset Gard etter 6 km.
Fra Kristiansund; RV 680 mot Aure, ved Giset følg skilt til Mjosundet, 17 km.
D: Brattset Gard liegt auf der Insel Ertvågøya. Entlang der E-39 zwischen Orkanger und Kristiansund bei der Anlegestelle Hennset, nimmt man die Fähre hinüber nach Arasvika. Fahren Sie nun Ri. Mjosundet und nach ca. 6km erreichen Sie Brattset Gard. Von Kristiansund: Str. 680 Ri.

Nærmeste togstasjon er Korsvoll.
D: Aus Süden kommend der E-6 über die Bergkette Dovrefjell folgen. 15 km nach dem Kongsvold Berggasthof (Fjeldstue) passieren Sie das Schild "Drivstua". 800 m hinter dem Schild nach links abfahren, über die Brücke und an der nächsten Kreuzung wieder links. Drivstua Rom ist ein rotes Haus zwischen dem Bahnhofsgebäude und der alten Schule. Von Oppdal: nach 20 km sehen Sie das Schild "Drivstua". 1 km weiter oben nach dem Schild rechts in eine Schotterstraße einbiegen und an der nächsten Kreuzung nach links.
Nähester Bahnhof in Korsvoll.

Brattset Gard, Mjosundet, page 177

Aure, bei Giset der Beschilderung nach Mjosundet folgen; nach 17 km erreichen Sie das Ziel.

page 178 - Drivstua Rom:
E: From south follow E-6 over Dovrefjell. 15 km after Kongsvold Fjellstue you pass a sign for Drivstua. After 800 m exit to left, after bridge go left at the intersection. Drivstua Room: the red house between the station and the old school.
From Oppdal: after 20 km notice sign for Drivstua, about 1 km further turn right on the gravel road. Turn left at next intersection. Nearest train station is Korsvoll.
N: Fra sør: Følg E-6 over Dovrefjell. 15 km etter Kongsvold Fjellstue passerer du skiltet Drivstua. Etter 800 m ta avkjørsel mot venstre, over brua og i krysset tar du til venstre. Drivstua Rom er et rødt hus mellom stasjonsbygningen og den gamle skolen.
Fra Oppdal: etter 20 km ser du skiltet Drivstua. Ta til høyre 1 km lenger oppe, ved en grusavkjøring. Til venstre i neste kryss.

page 179 - Flanderborg overnatting
E: From the south take RV 30 towards Røros. In the round-about turn right onto RV 31; take first road to the left, Dalsveien, which turns into Nedre Flanderborg. Take third road to the right; Flanderborg, No. 3 is a gray house on the right.
N: Sørfra: RV 30 inn mot Røros, i rundkjøringen ta til høyre (RV 31), ta så første vei til venstre inn Dalsveien som videre blir til Nedre Flanderborg. Ta tredje vei til høyre; Flanderborg. Nr. 3 er et grått hus på høyre side.
D: Aus Ri. Süden: Str. 30 bis Røros hinein fahren, im Kreisverkehr nach rechts (Str. 31), erste Str. nach links in den Dalsveien, der im weiteren Verlauf zum Nedre Flanderborg wird. Dritte nach rechts, Flanderborg Nr. 3 ist ein graues Haus auf der rechten Seite.

page 182 - Kårøyan Fjellgard
E: Along E-39 on the Vinjeøra between Trondheim and Kristiansund; exit to Kårøyan. Drive 10 km. to the road's end.
N: Langs E-39, på Vinjeøra mellom Trondheim og Kristiansund; ta av mot Kårøyan. Kjør 10 km til veien slutter.
D: Entlang der E-39, in der Ortschaft Vinjeøra zwischen Trondheim und Kristiansund. Ri. Kårøyan von der E-39 ab- und 10 km weiterfahren bis die Straße endet.

page 183 - Kleivan vekst
E: Along route E-39 take the Buvika exit. After Hydro/Texaco turn left towards Ilhaugen and continue towards Belsås. After 2.5 km, under a high-voltage wire, turn left to Kleivan.
N: Langs E-39, ta av til Buvika. Etter Hydro/Texaco ta venstre mot Ilhaugen og fortsett mot Belsås, etter ca. 2,5 km, under en høyspentlinje ta til venstre til Kleivan.
D: Entlang der E-39, Abfahrt Ri. Buvika. Hinter Hydro/

Texaco nach links Ri. Ilhaugen und dann Ri. Belsås weiterfahren. Nach ca. 2,5 km unter einer Hochspannungsleitung
nach links abbiegen bis Kleivan.

page 186 - Heidi Hansen
E: Bus no. 60 or 20 from city center. Depart at Telenorbyg-
get. Cross the road and turn right at Pottemakerveien.
N: Buss nr. 60 eller 20 fra sentrum. Gå av ved Telenorbyg-
get. Gå over gaten og ta til høyre inn Pottemakerveien.
D: Bus Nr. 60 oder 20 vom Zentrum. Steigen Sie beim
Telenor-Gebäude aus. Gehen Sie über die Straße und nach
rechts in den Pottemakerveien.

page 188 - Åse's Romutleie
E: From south: Find Bakke Bru (bridge) and cross over the
river. Turn left in the roundabout. Turn right where sign is
showing Rosenborg, the road is named Nonnegata. Cross
over Kirkegata. Turn right in next intersection, which is Nedre Møllenberg. Find crossing street Bakkegata and a yellow
house on your left.
N: Fra sør: Finn Bakke Bru og kjør over denne. Ta til venstre
i rundkjøringen. Ta til høyre hvor skilt viser Rosenborg, denne veien heter Nonnegata. Kryss over Kirkegata. Ta til høyre
i neste kryss som er Nedre Møllenberg. Kjør rett fram til
kryssende vei heter Bakkegata. Gult hus på venstre side.
D: Von Süden: Finden Sie Bakke Bru (Brücke) und fahren
Sie über den Fluss. Im Kreisverkehr nach links. Beim Schild
Rosenborg rechts in die Nonnegata fahren. Kreuzen Sie die
Kirkegata. An der nächsten Kreuzung nach rechts in die Str.

Nedre Møllenberg. Geradeaus, bis die Bakkegata kreuzt.
Gelbes Haus auf der linken Seite.

page 194 - Norumgården Bed & Breakfast
E: Drive over the bridge from the main square in Narvik.
Follow the signs towards the airport. Once you have passed
Narvik kirke (church), you will drive straight ahead for about
200 m. The house is on the right-hand side and has a large
white fence. Our nearest neighbor is the nursery school.
N: Fra torget i Narvik; kjører over broen. Følg skilt i retning
flyplassen. Når du har passert Narvik kirke, kjør ca. 200 m
rett frem. Huset ligger på høyre side, med et stort hvitt gjerde
rundt. Nærmeste nabo er en barnehage.
D: Vom Marktplatz in Narvik fahren Sie über die Brücke und
folgen anschließend der Beschilderung zum Flughafen.
Hinter der Narvik Kirche geht es noch ca. 200 m geradeaus.
Das Haus befindet sich auf der rechten Seite (großer weißer
Gartenzaun ringsum). Direkt daneben liegt ein Kindergarten.

page 195 - Nordbua
E: Drive to Stamsund, swing to the left by the ICA store,
over the bridge left of ICA and swing to the right, there is
Nordbua. Call the mobile number if the host has not arrived.
N: Kjør til Stamsund, sving til venstre v/ICA, over broen til
venstre for ICA og sving så til høyre, der er Nordbua. Ring
mobil dersom vertskap ikke har kommet.
D: Bis Stamsund fahren, beim ICA-Supermarkt links abbieg-
en, über die Brücke linkerhand vom ICA fahren und dann
nach rechts. Dort liegt Nordbua. Bitte rufen Sie an, sollten

Interior from one of the cabins at Engholm Husky design tun, Karasjok, page 204

die Gastgeber noch nicht vor Ort sein.

page 197 – Holmvik Brygge
E: From Sortland take RV 820 to Frøskeland; turn right, RV 821 to Myre; then take a right turn into Støveien, after 1.4 km follow RV 821b toward Nyksund: 11 km.
N: Fra Sortland RV 820 til Frøskeland; ta til høyre RV 821 til Myre; ta Støveien til høyre; etter 1,4 km ta RV 821b mot Nyksund; etter 11 km er du fremme.
D: Ab Sortland die Str. 820 bis Frøskeland; hier rechts abbiegen auf die Str. 821 bis Myre; rechts in den Støveien einbiegen und nach 1,4 km auf die Str. 821b nach Nyksund fahren. Nach b11 km sind Sie am Ziel.

page 202 - ANSI Turistservice, Simonsen Gårdsferie
E: From Alta follow E-6 toward Narvik. After about 90 km look for sign, 'ANSI 0.8'. If driving on E-6 from the south: 8 km after Burfjord drive past Storeng and 'ANSI 0.8'.
N: Fra Alta: følg E-6 i retning Narvik. Etter ca. 90 km se etter skiltet ANSI 0,8. E-6 sørfra: 8 km etter Burfjord kjør etter skilt Storeng og ANSI 0,8.
D: Von Alta: Folgen Sie der E-6 in Richtung Narvik. Achten Sie nach ca. 90 km auf das Schild ANSI 0,8. E-6 aus Süden: 8 km nach Burfjord dem Schild "Storeng" und "ANSI 0,8 km" folgen.

Let us permit nature to have her way.
She understands her business better than we do.
~Michel de Montaigne~

In dwelling, live close to the ground.
In thinking, keep to the simple.
In conflict, be fair and generous.
In governing, don't try to control.
In work, do what you enjoy.
In family life, be completely present.
~Lao Tzu~

Memory is a way of holding onto the things you love,
the things you are, the things you never want to lose.
~From the television show The Wonder Years~

A memory is what is left when something happens
and does not completely unhappen.
~Edward de Bono~

Every man's memory is his private literature.
~Aldous Huxley~

Evaluation / Evaluering / Beurteilung

To present even better updates of this B&B book we are interested in hearing from you. Please share of your experiences and opinions after you have been our guest.

For å kunne presentere et enda bedre B&B-tilbud i neste utgave av denne boken tar vi gjerne imot dine synspunkter og erfaringer etter at du har vært vår gjest.

Damit die nächste Ausgabe des B&B-Buches noch besser werden kann, möchten wir gerne Ihre Ansichten und Erfahrungen nach Ihrem Aufenthalt wissen.

Jeg var gjest hos: / I was a guest at: / Ich war als Gast bei: ....

1. Living standard and cleanliness / Bostandard og renhet / Wohnstandard und Sauberkeit
2. Breakfast and food / Frokost og servering / Frühstück und Servierung
3. Hospitality and service / Gjestfrihet og service / Gastlichkeit und Service
4. Price and value / Pris i forhold til standard / Preis im Verhältnis zum Standard
5. B&B book's information / B&B bokens informasjon / Information im B&B-Buch

Commentary / Kommentarer / Kommentare:

....

....

....

....

....

....

....

....

....

....

....

....

....

....

....

Start ditt eget Bed & Breakfast

Ønsker du å starte romutleie for turister? Har du et ledig soverom, eller kanskje flere? Liker du mennesker og kan tenke deg å ta imot gjester i ditt hjem? Det er ikke mer som skal til. Da kan du starte din egen romutleie - en hyggelig binæring som du lett kan kombinere med annen aktivitet. Som deltaker i The Norway Bed & Breakfast Book og på våre web-sider får du markedsført dine rom og mulighet til å møte mennesker fra fjerne himmelstrøk. For mer informasjon om å delta i neste bok; send noen ord til:

Bed & Breakfast Norway, v/ Anne Marit Bjørgen
Dalsegg, 6653 Øvre Surnadal, Tlf.: 99 23 77 99, Finn vår e-post adr. på web: www.bbnorway.com